Advance Praise for *Prying Eyes*

"At a time when many Americans are worried about losing their privacy, *Prying Eyes* provides a broad, useful survey of the issues as well as practical tips on how to protect oneself. This book is a terrific guide for every citizen, written by one of America's rising stars."

David Gergen, *Kennedy School of Government,*
Harvard University and Editor-at-Large,
U.S. News & World Report

"Eric Gertler has produced a comprehensive, eye-opening, and—above all—useful guide to protecting personal privacy against a host of modern intruders. I learned a lot from this book, and I think that readers at every level of technical sophistication will find surprising tips and insights."

James Fallows, *National Correspondent,* The Atlantic Monthly

"One of the great historical and self-evident truths about Americans is that they want control of their lives and their identities. Eric Gertler's *Prying Eyes* outlines the many ways Americans' privacy is at risk and the surprising number of strategies they have to protect themselves. This is an indispensable guide for thinking about citizenship in the 21st Century."

Lee Rainie, *Director, Pew Internet & American Life Project*

"The invasion of privacy is a 21st Century crime and it affects us all. Identity theft and financial fraud are the most serious issues I encounter every day in the credit card processing business. In *Prying Eyes*, Gertler not only reveals the real risks we all face, but also the real ways in which we can reduce our exposure."

Raf Sorrentino, *Senior Vice President of Risk and Fraud Management, First Data Corp.*

"For the first time, an author has collected in one place the legal rights, technological tools, and practical steps available to each of us to protect our own privacy. *Prying Eyes* is an indispensable guide to life in the information age."

Fred H. Cate, *Distinguished Professor of Law and Director of*
the Indiana University Center for Applied Cybersecurity Research
and author of Privacy in the Information Age

PryingEyes

PROTECT YOUR PRIVACY

FROM PEOPLE WHO SELL TO YOU, SNOOP ON YOU, AND STEAL FROM YOU

Eric J. Gertler

RANDOM HOUSE
REFERENCE

New York

Prying Eyes: Protect your privacy from people who sell to you, snoop on you, and steal from you

RANDOM HOUSE is a registered trademark of Random House, Inc.
Please address inquiries about electronic licensing of reference products for use on a network, in software or on CD-ROM to the Subsidiary Rights Department, Random House Reference, fax 212-572-6003.

This book is available for special discounts for bulk purchases for sales promotions or premiums. Special editions, including personalized covers, excerpts of existing books, and corporate imprints, can be created in large quantities for special needs. For more information, write to Random House, Inc., Special Markets/ Premium Sales, 1745 Broadway, MD 6-2, New York, NY, 10019 or e-mail specialmarkets@randomhouse.com.

Cover design by Tigist Getachew
Book design by Tina R. Malaney

This book is not intended to provide legal advice, nor does it endorse any of the products referenced.

Visit the Random House website: www.randomhouse.com
Library of Congress Cataloging-in-Publication Data is available.
First Edition

0 9 8 7 6 5 4 3 2 1

ISBN: 0-375-72093-6

Contents

Acknowledgments

YOU LIVE IN A WORLD WHERE EXCITING NEW TECHNOLOGIES AND DEVELOPMENTS are introduced every day. In so many unprecedented ways, these emerging technologies make your life more productive and more fulfilling and permit you to protect and keep connected to your loved ones, friends, and colleagues. At the same time, whether you realize it or not, these conveniences often compromise your privacy and result in your sensitive personal information being used against you in unlimited ways. You cannot possibly keep abreast of the adverse effects that these new technologies have on your life, nor can legislation keep pace with these changes.

Through my experience as CEO at Privista, an identity theft and credit protection company, I became exposed to the horrors caused by identity theft and the world of personalized information and data marketing. In time, it became clear that most people have little understanding of how their personal information is used, both positively and negatively. Privista was widely recognized as a premier company that helped to educate and protect consumers. *Prying Eyes* is intended to further help you understand how your personal information may be accessed and by whom, and provide you with the tools necessary to gain as much control as possible in these changing times. It seeks to educate you and empower you as a consumer and as a citizen. In this way, I hope that this book enriches your life.

Prying Eyes may be a book about privacy, but it is not a book about anonymity. Many colleagues, friends, family, and loved ones deserve recognition and credit for their invaluable input and support of this book. *Prying Eyes* is very much a product of their collective efforts, and I am deeply indebted to them.

First and foremost, I would like to thank the Random House Information Group for taking a chance with a first time book author. From the beginning, they grasped the changing nature of privacy in our country and fully supported this project. Indeed, their enthusiasm and recognition of the seriousness of the subject matter were such that they wanted to publish the book within months of their offer. For me, it was indeed a daunting challenge that never would have been realized without the guidance, encouragement, and talent of my editor Jena Pincott. From the initial outline to the first page and in chapter after chapter, Jena kept me focused and motivated and shaped my words and thoughts into a level of quality that I would never have reached on my own. I deeply appreciate her contribution to this effort. In addition, Laura Neilson conducted first-rate research and work that helped to strengthen key topics of the book. I also want to thank David Naggar, the president of the Random Information Group, and Sheryl Stebbins, the publisher, who ensured that this book received the necessary resources to achieve its goal. I would also be remiss if I failed to recognize Bonnie Ammer, Jeanne Kramer, Ellen Browne, and Erica Kestenbaum.

I was also truly blessed to have enjoyed the assistance of a strong group of researchers. Ginger Thoerner, a long time friend and associate who worked with me years ago at *U.S. News & World Report*, focused on the chapters about home, work, and everyday life. I knew her work would be exceptional and of the highest quality. But her friendship, support, and sharp intellect combined with her wonderful sense of humor energized me in times of great need during this project. Raya Kuzyk provided important and detailed research, and helped to uncover many of the interesting anecdotes in the book. I could not have been more fortunate to have her involved, as her devotion to this book was invaluable. Jardine Libaire provided extraordinary work on the chapters about health, spying, and shopping. Molly Townsend contributed superb research on the computer chapter.

Others helped to inspire me, took the time to review certain chapters in the book, or offered guidance on certain parts of the book. Harry Evans' initial support reassured me that this book deserved to be published and provided invaluable guidance to start me on my way. Bob Brody, my former business partner and someone of the highest integrity and intellect, introduced me to important parts of the information business years ago and then provided great feedback on the credit chapter. Raf Sorrentino has provided unique insights into the world of identity theft and financial scams and Matt Breitfelder helped shape my views on this subject years ago and gave me important feedback throughout the writing process. Fred Cate thoroughly reviewed the entire manuscript and provided valuable feedback. Dr. James Underberg, Gerry Goldstein, Bruce Menin, Julie Menin, Marc Kramer, Jerry Lefcourt, Nathan Hochman, Jeff Bandman, Jay Rosensweig, F. Josiah Leicht, Leslie Stern, and Barnet L. Liberman all reviewed different parts of the book and provided much needed feedback and encouragement.

Much of this book was written in my office. I need to thank Ken Landis and Eva Jeanbart-Lorenzotti; I am privileged to have them as friends. Julie Subotky, Carly Sacher, and Sarah Swanson also supported this project in numerous ways.

Writing this book in such a concentrated period of time meant that I was less responsive to important people in my life. Thankfully, I have been blessed with an immediate and extended family that has always provided a strong support system through both the good and more challenging times. My parents, Pauline and David, and my brothers, Andrew and Jamie, have been always been loving and encouraging. I also want to recognize my uncle Mort for his support on this project and over the years, and my dear aunts Carmen, Nettie, and Sylvia, who have always been there for me. Countless friends and others patiently understood when I did not return phone calls or emails, continuously rescheduled plans, and regrettably missed important events in their lives.

Most importantly, I would like to acknowledge Jessica Gerstle, whose love, unwavering support, and constructive criticism were my bedrock throughout this demanding project. Her inspiration was invaluable to me throughout this process. Words alone cannot express my love and gratitude.

I sincerely hope that this book meets the expectations of all those who contributed to it. To you, the reader, please continue turning the pages. Enjoy, learn, and, above all, take control of your personal information.

I welcome your feedback at pryingeyesbook@yahoo.com.

Introduction: Your Life

TONIGHT, LIKE ON EVERY OTHER NIGHT OF THE WEEK, you can sit down in front of your television set to watch a reality show based on someone else's personal life. Featuring real people instead of actors, the latest sweep of reality-based shows runs the gamut from *The Simple Life,* in which two rich kids are planted at a farm in Arkansas, to *The Bachelor,* in which you can watch a bevy of women vie to marry the contestant, to *The Apprentice,* in which ambitious job seekers compete to win a job with Donald Trump's real estate corporation. As you might expect, these shows are immensely popular. For *The Apprentice* alone, more than 15 million Americans have tuned in weekly to witness Trump fire some poor soul.

But there is a reality show that is even more popular, although you may not be aware that it's broadcast. This show is called *Your Life,* and it's on every day of the week. In fact, the show is on twenty-four hours a day for every day of your life, and *you* are the star. As in other reality shows, you expose your entire life to people you have never met, and these strangers get to see every intimate detail of your existence. But *Your Life* features some twists that are different from the reality shows on television: you don't know what information you reveal, you don't know how your audience obtains it, and you don't know what they do with it. Your audience may watch *Your Life* out of simple curiosity. They may also watch it to sell something to you, or, worse, to steal something from you. Unlike other reality shows, *Your Life* isn't edited and no one can pull the plug.

In *Your Life,* you don't compete for money, or a job, or for love. There are no prizes. You may discover that *Your Life* is being watched only when you suffer from identity theft or when someone uses your information to impersonate you; when you discover that your image is being filmed by a hidden camera operated by a total stranger; when someone uses your credit card to spend your money on items you never purchased; or when an intimate or embarrassing piece of information about you is revealed to your friends and others. Sounds like a fun show, right?

Of course, in reality, *Your Life* does not exist as a show. But in your everyday life, you are, in different ways, constantly tracked and monitored. Whether you like it or not, and whether you believe it or not, you (and everybody else around you) are likely to be exposed to millions of prying eyes, including snoops, spies, and thieves, over a lifetime. This is the reality of living in the twenty-first century.

Don't believe it? Perhaps statistics on the increasing number of identity thefts might convince you. Identity theft happens when a thief uses your personal information such as your name, social security number, or credit card number to commit fraud or other crimes. The more your personal information is exposed, the more likely you are to become a victim of identity theft. In the past five years, more than 27 million Americans had their identities stolen. Almost 10 million Americans had their identities stolen in 2003 alone. Identity theft is so rampant that it is the leading consumer fraud complaint to the Federal Trade Commission. As discussed in chapter 3, "Your Identity," the issue you face is no longer *if* you will have your identity stolen, but *when* you will have your identity stolen and how to deal with it.

Not only are you likely to have your identity stolen, but given the staggering number of surveillance cameras, camcorders, and other video devices, chances are good that people will also steal glimpses of you wherever you go. Most of the memorable images you see on television were never intended for public consumption. Do you remember the camcorder footage of the Los Angeles policemen beating Rodney King? Riots erupted around the country when that footage was broadcast. Were you appalled when you saw the tape of the Indiana woman beating her daughter in a public parking lot? Do you recall the heartbreaking images of an unknown man approaching eleven-year-old Carlie Brucia outside of a car wash in Sarasota, Florida? The girl's corpse was later discovered a few miles from the car wash. None of these images came from television crews stationed at these sites; instead, these pictures came from one of the myriad cameras that unblinkingly record the world.

It is nearly impossible to travel anywhere without a video camera filming you. Planning to go to New York City to see a Broadway show? Walk through Times Square, for example, and within a six-block radius almost three hundred surveillance cameras, many on private property, will capture you and your date rushing to get to the theater on time. Want to visit the Smithsonian in Washington, DC? Authorities there are building a network that will link the hundreds of existing surveillance cameras with new cameras that will feed hundreds of images into a single command center that oversees the entire city. Eventually, cameras in the nation's capitol will be omnipresent. But Washington, DC, is just beginning to scratch the surface of surveillance. By comparison, London is years ahead, with 1.5 million video cameras in public places. The typical Londoner is photographed three hundred times per day on average.

Getting the picture yet? Layer on top of that today's sophisticated satellite technology, which can cover and focus in with high quality and resolution on almost any location in the world. Did you know that the Federal National Imagery and Mapping Agency used spy satellite technology to assist the Secret Service and FBI with security during the Winter Olympics in Salt Lake City? Given the increasing number of cameras and the limited resources of law enforcement, one entrepreneur has even proposed the establishment of a citizen task force to help monitor all these cameras and thereby assist with the country's national security protection.

If you believe that the increased numbers of surveillance cameras are the byproduct of antiterrorist initiatives in big cities or at big events, think again. The government, law enforcement agencies, private businesses, and individuals are setting up cameras all over America, including in small towns. Some record your selection of soft drinks at your local convenience store. Others monitor whether you stop at red lights or gauge your speed to determine if you violate speed limits. Others may record your comings and goings in public places and at work. Perhaps your ex-husband has planted a camera in your bedroom ceiling. Some cameras, in the hands of cell phone camera owners, may catch you bending down to pick up a quarter. Yet others tape you as you cross the street and go about the everyday business of *Your Life*.

But remember that your reality show reveals much more about you than your face. Identity thieves and marketers can't get much information about you from surveillance cameras and satellite monitoring alone. Instead, they rely on numerous sources. For example, the public record. From the moment you are born, information about you gets recorded in public documents that others can examine and copy. Every major transition in your life, no matter how sensitive or sentimental, including your marriage or divorce, home purchase or home sale, is recorded and may be accessed. Your achievements, sorrows, and life-changing events are public records for your neighbors, friends, and strangers to discover. Chapter 2, "Your Personal Information and the Public Record," examines these issues in greater detail.

Wherever you go and whatever you do, you dispense vital information about yourself. Chapter 4, "Your Credit," reveals how when you apply for credit cards, loans, and mortgages, your information gets compiled in credit reports that credit bureaus provide to banks and other financial institutions. Chapter 5, "Your Money," reveals what your bank knows about you and what it can disclose to other businesses. Chapter 6, "Your Shopping," discusses the ways retailers and stores collect information about you. When you complete surveys and return warranty cards, or enroll in a loyalty card program, a retailer gathers and retains information about you so the retailer can market to you more efficiently in the future. Chapter 10, "Your Health," describes how your health history is circulated among doctors, insurance companies, and billing facilities that can view your entire record.

When you enter the online world, every action you take is tracked. When you send an e-mail, buy a gift online, or surf the Internet, information about you and your activities is captured and stored by websites, Internet Service Providers (ISPs) and others, including users of spyware. As chapter 7, "Your Computer and the Internet," discusses, your information and data can be compiled and compared with certain patterns to develop a detailed profile of you that predicts what kind of person you are, your spending habits, and the advertising you might like to see. The sensitive information that you unknowingly reveal as you surf the Web, participate in chat rooms, and go to bulletin boards can be combined with information that you personally provide to websites when you visit or shop.

In the workplace, your employer has the almost-complete right to watch over you and your daily job activities. For example, your boss may monitor your activities in some obvious ways, perhaps with the use of a video camera as you enter and exit your building. Your employer may also require you to wear a badge that lets you into the building, and provides or denies access to certain areas of it, thereby tracking your daily whereabouts. Your employer also watches over you in less-obvious ways. It may be reading your e-mails, listening to your voice mail, eavesdropping on some of your conversations, or installing software on your computer to track every website you visit.

Although your employer's actions may appear to be a little ominous, they fall within its legal rights, as chapter 9, "Your Workplace," points out.

You cannot even enjoy the comfort of being in the privacy of your own home. Your home is a ripe target for telemarketers who constantly bombard you during dinnertime. Direct marketers also deluge you with offers for every imaginable credit card and insurance product. Even actions within your home can be monitored, as chapter 8, "Your Home" describes. For example, if you subscribe to TiVo, your television habits are monitored and a viewer profile of you is developed. The profile is so detailed that TiVo is able to suggest upcoming shows that you might enjoy watching.

The technologies and inventions that you rely on to improve your life also infringe on your privacy in unforeseen ways. As chapter 11, "Your Everyday Life," reveals, your cell phone or car may include a global positioning system (GPS) that can pinpoint your location at all times. When you fly, new systems may link your airline reservation to various commercial databases revealing certain personal and consumer information about you. The airline may not view your medical information or see your bank account information, but it may learn about your consumer habits, your magazine subscriptions, or your family life.

The reality of *Your Life* is that everything you do, say, type, work on, or get examined can now be tracked and monitored. Is there *anything* you can do to protect yourself? The answer is that you have more control than you might think. The crucial first step is to be aware of all the ways in which you expose yourself when you're at home, at work, at the mall, and on your computer or phone. In many situations you *can* control how much you reveal. For example, to keep a low profile in marketing databases, you can opt out of information sharing programs and avoid loyalty and warranty cards. To keep your sensitive conversations private, you can use landline phones and avoid making calls at work. To reduce the number of entities that see your medical file, you can exercise certain new privacy rights. To limit your chances of identity theft, you can shred your junk mail and watch out for scams. This book discusses these steps and dozens of others to protect what's left of your privacy.

The synopsis: In *Your Life* you still have choices. Remember, you're the star of the show. You can decide if you want your character's complete life history revealed at first glance, or if you would prefer that prying eyes turn their gaze elsewhere.

What Privacy Means to You

So, IT'S AGREED—WE GO AHEAD WITH THE INFORMATION-MATCHING.

CIA

DIRECT MARKETING

CHRIS

© Chris Slane/Slane Cartoons Limited

SCOTT MCNEALY, CEO OF SUN MICROSYSTEMS, shocked the nation in 1999 when he said "You have zero privacy. Get over it." Some people interpreted his statement as a foreshadowing of an Orwellian state in which citizens would suffer from an oppressive government or uncontrollable business interests. Others have come to see the loss of privacy as a harsh reality of living in the information age, and not an altogether bad thing if it means reducing the chances of terrorist attacks. Still others view the diminishment of privacy as a necessary evil for the conveniences you enjoy with the emergence of the Internet, wireless devices, and other new technologies.

What does privacy mean to you? Ask your friends and family the same question. No doubt, you almost certainly will have a different view from anyone you ask. You may view privacy as freedom from annoying everyday disruptions such as telemarketers and junk mail. Your friends may define privacy as the ability to write personal e-mails from work without someone else reading them, get a blood test without others knowing the results, cross the street without being caught on video, or pay for a meal with a credit card without the fear of identity theft. Your spouse may define privacy as security for your family, such as protection from cyberstalkers who may approach your children with sexual advances. Ironically, your children may define privacy as the freedom to do what they want without your oversight as a parent.

If everyone had the same definition, there would be little discussion on this subject. But privacy means different things to different people, and everyone takes a different approach to protecting it. Lawyers, philosophers, architects, doctors, historians, soldiers, politicians, political scientists, and teachers all have different views on privacy. Political scientist Alan Westin has articulated four separate definitions of privacy:

1. Privacy is equated with solitude. According to this definition, you seek to distance yourself so other people cannot observe you, whether by actual observation or indirect observation through various forms of audio or video devices, or other technology.

2. Privacy may be defined in the context of your intimate relationships with certain individuals or between certain groups of people. This definition certainly encompasses your activities as a lover, as a spouse, and within your family. But it also applies to certain encounters in society where you expect privacy, such as with your lawyer, where you are protected by attorney-client privileges, or with your psychiatrist or psychologist, or with your priest or rabbi, or even in business negotiations you conduct with other companies.

3. Privacy may be "reserve," meaning that you have no desire or obligation to reveal certain aspects of yourself to others.

4. Privacy may be akin to anonymity, or the concept of not being identified in a public setting. If you are aware you are being watched in public, you will become self-conscious and that will ultimately disrupt your enjoyment of being in public.

Today, the debate about privacy is largely a question of the nature and extent of personal information about you that may be collected, stored, and used. It concerns the balance between the needs of government and businesses to track and store your personal information versus your right to protect it. The debate rages about what information can be collected, in what context, and in what ways you can control or access any information that is collected. If information is collected for one purpose, may that information be disclosed for another purpose? If your personal information is collected, will it be stored or kept in a secure manner, preventing others from exploiting it?

> You probably assume that privacy is your legal right as a U.S. citizen. In fact, the Constitution does not provide an explicit right to privacy.

Do You Have a Constitutional Right to Privacy?

You probably assume that privacy is your legal right as a U.S. citizen. In fact, the Constitution does not provide an explicit right to privacy. Indeed, for a country developed on the notion of "life, liberty, and the pursuit of happiness" and the individualistic associations related to this concept, it is surprising that the Constitution does not provide for a right to privacy.

Does this mean that there is no right to privacy? Of course not. The Constitution does not convey the right to do many things you take for granted—including, for example, the right to marriage, which has become a divisive issue of late for gay couples who demand the same legal privileges of marriage that heterosexual couples enjoy. Rather, the Constitution was written as a framework for what government *can* do, or more precisely, it articulates the limited rights and powers given to the federal government. The Bill of Rights sought to protect certain individual liberties, and thereby outlines what government *may not* do. For example, the First Amendment restricts the government from passing laws to abridge your freedom of speech or religion; the government may not search or seize your property without due process of law by virtue of the Fifth Amendment; and the Sixth Amendment provides that the government may not jail you indefinitely without a trial. Therein lies the balance of our governing documents: the Constitution limiting what government may do and the Bill of Rights identifying what government may not do. In this way, the Founding Fathers created the Constitution to reflect that a government needed flexibility, and the Constitution needed to be able to stand for generations.

It is in this context that you can understand your legal right to privacy in the United States. The push to define privacy and establish laws to protect it in the wake of new technologies began more than one hundred years ago. In his 2000 book *Ben Franklin's Web Site: Privacy and Curiosity from Plymouth Rock to the Internet,* Robert Ellis Smith shows a direct link between the privacy concerns voiced in the 1890s when the camera, telephone, and the tabloid newspaper were invented through to the 1990s, when the Internet and cell phones and other wireless devices became widely used.

Scholars gave little thought to privacy until 1890, when Samuel Warren and Louis Brandeis penned their law review article entitled "The Right to Privacy." As legend has it, they were upset that the *Saturday Evening Gazette* had invaded the privacy of Warren's family when it published a gossip column about a breakfast party that Warren had hosted for his daughter's wedding. In many ways, the article provided an initial definition of privacy that was just as relevant then as it is now. In the words of Warren and Brandeis:

> Recent inventions and business methods all call attention to the next step which must be taken for the protection of the public and for securing to the individual what Judge Cooley calls *the right to be let alone.* Instantaneous photographs and newspaper enterprise have invaded the sacred precincts of private and domestic life; and numerous mechanical devices threaten to make good the prediction that "what is whispered in the closet shall be proclaimed from the housetops." The intensity and complexity of life attended upon advanced civilization have rendered necessary some retreat from the world. And man under the refining influence of culture has become more sensitive to publicity so that solitude and privacy have become more essential to the individual; but modern enterprise and invention have through invasions upon his privacy subjected him to mental pain and distress far greater than what can be inflicted by mere bodily injury.

Warren and Brandeis foresaw that invasions of privacy affect people in both tangible and intangible ways, and their article broadened the legal concept of privacy. Brandeis continued to influence the debate on privacy even

4

after he became a Supreme Court justice. Almost forty years after he and War-ren wrote their famous law review article, the Supreme Court ruled in the 1928 case of *Olmstead* v. *United States.* Roy Olmstead, the defendant, was a suspected bootlegger, and federal agents installed wiretaps in the basement of Olmstead's office building and in the streets near his home without judicial approval. Olmstead was later convicted with evidence obtained from the wire-taps. In his dissent in this case, Justice Brandeis wrote:

> The makers of our Constitution . . . sought to protect Americans in their beliefs, their thoughts, their emotions and their sensations. They conferred as against the Government, *the right to be let alone*—the most comprehensive of the rights of man and the right most valued by civilized men.

In 1965, Justice William Douglas picked up where Brandeis and Warren left off. In *Griswold* v. *Connecticut,* a landmark case concerning the privacy of a married couple's decision to use contraceptives, Douglas concluded that the state could not interfere with family planning services, laying the groundwork for the right to a safe and legal abortion. While acknowledging that there is no explicit right to privacy in the Constitution, Douglas asserted that the First Amendment's right of association, the Third Amendment's prohibition against quartering soldiers in citizens' homes, the Fourth Amendment's pro-tection against illegal searches of homes, the Fifth Amendment's protection against self-incrimination, and the Ninth Amendment's statement that indi-viduals may enjoy rights not specifically defined in the Constitution create in combination what he called the penumbra, or shadows, of a right to privacy. Striking down state laws that made the use of contraceptives by married cou-ples illegal, Justice William Douglas wrote in the majority opinion, "Specific guarantees in the Bill of Rights have penumbras, formed by emanations from those guarantees that help give them life and substance. . . . Various guaran-tees that create zones of privacy."

Then, on January 22, 1973, the U.S. Supreme Court announced its decision in *Roe* v. *Wade,* a challenge to a Texas statute that made it a crime to perform an abortion unless a woman's life was at stake. The case involved an unmarried woman called Jane Roe who wanted safely and legally to end her pregnancy. Siding with Roe, the Court struck down the Texas law. In its ruling, the Court recognized for the first time that the constitutional right to privacy "is broad enough to encompass a woman's decision whether or not to terminate her pregnancy."

Despite the Supreme Court's decisions in *Griswold* and *Roe,* the Supreme Court has not applied the right to privacy in a consistent manner and to all areas of life. One example is the Supreme Court's treatment of one's right to sexual privacy, particularly with respect to consensual sex between adults of the same sex. In 1986, the Supreme Court ruled in the case of *Bowers* v. *Hardwick,* which involved the arrest of Michael Hardwick for violating the Georgia criminal antisodomy statute. The arrest took place after the police walked into Hardwick's bedroom and witnessed Hardwick having sex with another man. Here, the Court refused to hold that Georgia's antisodomy laws were unconstitutional, even if the prohibited sexual activity involved two mutually consenting adults in their own home. In 2003, however, the Supreme Court came to the opposite conclusion in a case that involved almost identical facts. In this case, *Lawrence and Garner* v. *State of Texas,* the Supreme Court overruled *Bowers* by extending the right to privacy and declaring state antisodomy laws unconstitutional. (See chapter 8, "Your Home," for specific details.)

New Challenges to Your Privacy

The privacy rights established in the family planning cases and the reversal of antisodomy laws exemplify the struggle for privacy rights. Today's most pressing concerns involve new challenges to individual privacy resulting from technology—the same issue that Brandeis and Warren wrote about in 1890, following the invention of instant photographs and tabloids, that "what is whispered in the closet shall be proclaimed from the housetops." The same desire to preserve "the sacred precincts of private and domestic life" applies today.

The Internet and other new technologies, such as camera cell phones and other wireless devices are exciting and important developments but are still in their early stages, so the full scope of their threat and risks has not been fully explored. Many of these technologies have already led to an increase in crime, including the creation of computer viruses, the destruction and theft of sensitive personal information, Internet cyberstalkers, credit card theft, identity theft, and much more.

If you're like some people, you may not really care about privacy until you lose it. For example, you probably don't think about unwanted privacy invasions until that telemarketing call wakes you up or interrupts your dinner, or until identity theft or credit card fraud depletes your bank account, demolishes your credit, and creates havoc in your life.

What you may not realize is that the ways in which your sensitive personal information may be used against you are unlimited. For example, you may innocently share personal information in an online user group whose members are HIV-positive, or you might buy illicit items and later discover that information about your purchases has been entered in a database and combined with other personal information about you. When the database is purchased or shared, it is possible that you could be hurt if, say, an employer, insurance company, spouse, or others see the sensitive information that you don't want disclosed.

> **What you may not realize is that the ways in which your sensitive personal information may be used against you are unlimited.**

Notwithstanding these risks to you, governments and businesses gather and rely on your personal information for a variety of important reasons. The government may use it to test the effectiveness of new medical drugs, for example. Courts use personal information to track down deadbeat dads who fail to pay their child obligations. Law enforcement agencies use it to track down criminals. People in need of organ and blood donations or bone marrow transfers depend on accurate and up-to-date databanks on donors.

Businesses use personal information to better understand their markets so they may develop new products, improve customer service, or even develop personalized services that consumers demand. Over the long term, the collection of such data may lead to more effective marketing and theoretically helps reduce the consumer price for goods.

Nevertheless, networked commercial databases that maintain personal information about you are a growing threat to your privacy. Today, nearly every company that markets consumer products is compiling databases to track and monitor its customer base. In addition, although estimates vary, privacy experts believe hundreds if not thousands of data aggregators are in the business of maintaining comprehensive information about you. Companies use these lists to solicit consumers with special promotions or offers. For example, Acxiom, a database company based in Arkansas, has developed and maintains a real-time database that collects and processes information on nearly every American household. The company's clients can use the comprehensive information stored in its database to develop and deepen relationships with customers based on all sorts of criteria, including zip code, income, lifestyle, or even a profile of "timeless elders" or "Single City Struggles." Companies will often buy lists from data aggregators and combine these lists with their own customer databases.

> Each individual electronic transaction you make—from the use of a credit, debit, or ATM card to "loyalty" cards, online bill payment, and check payment—provides clues to parts of your life. When these individual pieces of information are integrated, they create a vivid picture of you and your personal life.

The information that many companies track and maintain goes far beyond simple demographic data, such as your name, how much you make, and where you live. Indeed, the extent of available information is limited only by technology itself. Each individual electronic transaction you make—from the use of a credit, debit, or ATM card to "loyalty" cards, online bill payment, and check payment— provides clues to parts of your life. When these individual pieces of information are integrated, they create a vivid picture of you and your personal life. For example, when a supermarket clerk swipes your loyalty card through a scanner, a database links your identity with the bar code on every item you have purchased. Although you may not consider your taste for frozen pizza dinners an especially tantalizing piece of information, when combined with your age, credit standing, ethnicity, religion, and marital status, such information becomes quite interesting to marketers.

The number of companies that offer personalized marketing is growing. The technology these companies use is increasingly efficient, enabling businesses to sort and categorize data to target specific people for specialized marketing purposes. For example, a class-action lawsuit against Metromail Corporation revealed the types of information contained in its database. The computer file on one individual, Beverly Dennis, included nine hundred personal details printed out on twenty-five pages and dating back an entire decade. Among other things, Metromail knew Dennis's income, hobbies, and ailments, her preferred brand of antacid tablets, whether she had dentures, and how often she used room deodorizers, sleeping aids, and hemorrhoid remedies. Another company, the New York–based firm American Student Lists, sells the personal information it gathers on millions of high school students from such diverse sources as driver's licenses, student directories, magazine subscriptions, yearbook publishers, class ring vendors, formal wear companies, fast food companies, and book clubs. There are also companies that sell lists of people with particular medical conditions, ranging from patients who are clinically depressed, women who have yeast infections, and diabetics, to people who suffer from Alzheimer's disease, birth defects, Parkinson's disease, or physical handicaps. The extent to which businesses engage in the trade of personal information is astounding.

September 11 and Your Privacy

Any discussion of privacy rights must be put into the context of the devastating effects of the September 11 terrorist attacks and the consequences associated with the attacks. Without question, September 11 was a watershed in terms of its effect on the American public's views of privacy. Principles and laws established by Brandeis and Douglas and others had set a precedent toward more privacy rights, but September 11 had the opposite effect. As a result of the terrorist attacks, national security became Americans' primary concern and invariably trumped concern for individual privacy.

Prior to September 11, privacy was a key issue in the minds of Americans. One survey conducted in 1999 by the *Wall Street Journal* and NBC indicated that privacy was the issue of *greatest* concern facing Americans at the turn of the 21st century—more important, ironically, than terrorist attacks on American soil, overpopulation, or global warming. In early 2001, Chief Justice William Rehnquist stated, "Technology now permits millions of important and confidential conversations to occur through a vast system of electronic networks. These advances however raise significant privacy concerns. We are placed in the uncomfortable position of not knowing who might have access to our personal and business e-mails, our medical and financial records, or our cordless and cellular telephone conversations."

In the months before September 11, Americans viewed a company's commitment to an individual's privacy as essential for doing business. In a national survey conducted in September 2000 by the Privacy Council and Privista, survey respondents stated that a company's commitment to privacy was as important as maintaining product satisfaction, offering customer dis-counts, or having an 800 number for consumer feed-back. Moreover, companies that failed—whether intentionally or not—to respect or manage privacy concerns had to deal with the serious consequences of real or perceived privacy violations. For example, after a hostile public reaction, DoubleClick, a suc-cessful Internet and technology company, aban-doned its plans to integrate its online database of customer profiles with the offline database it had secured when it acquired the company Abacus. Another company, Geocities, now part of Yahoo, was the subject of a privacy violation complaint by the Fed-eral Trade Commission for sharing customer information in a manner incon-sistent with its privacy policy. As a result, the company experienced a serious drop in its stock price, though the stock later regained much of its value. The bottom line was clear: companies had to take a serious look at their privacy commitment to their customers.

> After September 11, privacy and the individual rights associated with it were outweighed by an interest in enhanced national security.

At the same time, numerous privacy laws were being considered in Con-gress and in the statehouses. The emphasis on the protection of privacy was moving in the direction of creating new legal rights to privacy, and legislators in both the Democratic and Republican parties were working in tandem to pass legislation. In 2000, for example, fifty privacy bills were pending in Con-gress, dealing with both online and offline privacy concerns. Such initiatives reflected consumer reactions and polls, and thus both the states and Congress wanted to enhance individual privacy rights.

In the aftermath of September 11, consumer, legislative, and public senti-ment changed. The overwhelming desire to achieve greater national security trumped all other concerns. From all perspectives, the world had changed overnight, and the Bush administration sought and achieved a new means of dealing with the foreign threat of terrorism. In the world's greatest democracy, privacy and the individual rights associated with it were outweighed by an interest in enhanced national security. What followed stoked unwelcome memories of steps the country had taken in earlier times of great national anxiety, such as the quarantine of the Japanese during World War II and the outing of Communist Party members during the 1950s.

Forty-five days after the terrorist attacks of September 11, with little debate or scrutiny in Congress, the government passed the Uniting and Strengthening America by Providing Appropriate Tools Required to Intercept and Obstruct Terrorism Act, more commonly known as the USA Patriot Act or the Patriot Act. The name of the act itself seems to characterize even mild criticism of the act's provisions as unpatriotic—implying that if you're against the Patriot Act, you're unpatriotic. The act considerably expanded the investigative powers of the government and turned two hundred years of jurisprudence on its head. Under the act, the government no longer needs to abide by the standards of "probable cause" required for a search warrant. Rather, law enforcement agents only need to certify that the information they are seeking is relevant to an ongoing criminal investigation. Accordingly, law enforcement agents can broadly access any information relevant to their investigation, including information regarding your personal financial information, your medical records, and your school and library records. You name it, and they can obtain it. More importantly, you may never even know you are being investigated, because law enforcement officials are no longer required to tell you.

In addition to the Patriot Act, the government also sought to develop what it called a Total Information Awareness program. This program would have empowered the government to create a massive database to track all your personal information. With this centralized database, the government would have had the ability to comb through your bank records, tax filings, driver's license information, your credit card purchases, your magazine subscriptions, your online activities, your medical prescriptions, your educational records, and much more. Public outcry ultimately shut down this program in 2003. Despite the demise of the Total Information Awareness program, the government continues to use Carnivore, a computer system developed by the FBI that, when connected to the network of an Internet Service Provider (ISP), can intercept millions of e-mail messages per second. The system monitors the e-mails of both its target and innocent people who use the same ISP. The genie is out of the bottle now that the technology and database capabilities are able to track electronic correspondence.

When the Patriot Act was passed, citizens did not seem upset about the act's provisions, and Congress, the state legislatures, and the courts seemed to agree. Throughout the country, previous legislative initiatives in support of privacy rights were put on the back burner. In keeping with this spirit, in 2002, the United States Foreign Intelligence Surveillance Court of Review issued its first-ever ruling in twenty-five years of existence in which it expanded the government's right to use wiretap surveillance in criminal investigations.

> As time has passed and the country has moved further from the horrible events of September 11, the public again has demanded legislation that will protect the privacy of citizens from intrusions of both government and business.

As time has passed and the country has moved further from the horrible events of September 11, the public again has demanded legislation that will protect the privacy of citizens from intrusions of both government and business. Beginning in 2003, a number of important legislative actions have taken place in addition to the shutdown of the Total Information Awareness program. For example, on January 1, 2004, the Fair and Accurate Credit Transaction Act of 2003 went into effect helping to protect you against identity theft. The act requires credit bureaus to provide you with one free credit report per year, requires merchants and lenders to provide you with early notification of missed payments, and requires merchants to truncate your credit card number on receipts to the last five digits, among other things (see chapter 3, "Your Identity," for additional details). In 2003, the Do Not Call Registry, a federal program that restricts commercial telemarketers from calling you after you register, went into effect. The registry was designed to reduce unwanted phone calls to consumers, especially during the dinner hour. As expected, the response was overwhelmingly positive: more than 7 million telephone numbers were registered on the program's first day; more than 56 million numbers were registered by January 2004 (refer to chapter 8, "Your Home," for more information). In addition, on January 1, 2004, a federal Internet anti-spamming bill called the Can-Spam Act went into effect, restricting commercial e-mail companies or spammers from using false identities and misleading subject lines. (Chapter 7, "Your Computer and the Internet," provides more details.) In addition, about 250 municipalities around the country have passed legislation supporting individual rights in direct contravention of the Patriot Act. In December 2003, two federal appeals courts rejected the Bush administration's policy with respect to captives suspected of being terrorists. A New York federal appeals court ruled that the Bush administration lacked authority to detain indefinitely a U.S. citizen arrested in the United States simply by declaring the citizen "an enemy combatant"; and a San Francisco appeals court ruled that it was unconstitutional to imprison noncitizens captured in the Afghan War in Guantanamo Bay, Cuba, without access to an attorney.

Privacy and the Rest of the World

If you compare an individual's right to privacy in the United States with the rights enjoyed by citizens of other countries, you are faced with a paradox. You might be surprised to learn that as a United States citizen you enjoy far fewer privacy rights, at least in a commercial context, than your counterparts in other parts of the world, including other democracies. Indeed, the country that most respects individualism does the least to protect an individual's privacy, at least in the private sector. Some legal scholars argue that, even with the passage of the Patriot Act, federal and state laws in the U.S. do more than other countries to protect individual privacy in the public sector.

Nevertheless, take a look at the privacy laws in Europe. There, strict and comprehensive rules govern how governments and companies may collect or use almost any type of information, including such personal data as your age, marital status, buying patterns, and even the information on a standard business card. European retailers are required to seek permission to collect data, use information for their own marketing purposes, share data with marketing partners, or sell it—practices that data collectors in the United States can do without asking permission. European companies must allow consumers access to any personal information that is stored and the ability to correct any erroneous information. The privacy laws also broadly restrict how European companies collect and maintain information on employees—ranging from files and statistics to video surveillance tapes—and how long they can keep it. European privacy laws even regulate the manner in which European companies may transmit personal information to other countries, including the United States. The United States regulates privacy in far more limited ways.

Current U.S. antiterrorism measures conflict with European views on privacy as well as privacy laws. For example, U.S. carriers are required to collect passenger names and other information so that customs officials can assess security threats prior to a flight's arrival in the United States, while European privacy laws generally prevent European airlines flying from Europe to disclose such information. To date, a number of flights to the United States, especially during the 2003 Christmas holidays, have been cancelled because of American security concerns. For the moment, officials from the European Union and American authorities are seeking a compromise and European airlines are cooperating with United States requirements. It remains to be seen if this cooperation is the result of joint security goals or a concern that noncompliance could lead to fines or the loss of U.S. landing rights.

> Today, Canada, South America, Australia, New Zealand, and Japan, among others, have adopted privacy standards or values similar to those in the European Union. As the European Union increases the number of its member countries, the jurisdiction of these privacy laws will expand.

European privacy laws, which started to take shape in the mid-1990s, are being used to model privacy laws around the world. They restrict companies and governments much more than do the laws in the United States. As a result, some multinational corporations have been forced to change some of their business conduct. In one example, General Motors was reprimanded for compiling a directory of home phone numbers of European executives without first obtaining their permission, a standard practice for many American businesses. Today, Canada, South America, Australia, New Zealand, and Japan, among others, have adopted privacy standards or values similar to those in the European Union. As the European Union increases the number of its member countries, the jurisdiction of these privacy laws will expand.

In the United States, you do not own your privacy, at least in terms of the personal information that defines you. In simple terms, in the United States, everything is permissible except what is prohibited. In Europe, the opposite is the case, and everything is prohibited except what is permissible. But even in Europe, citizens don't have perfect privacy. While data is regulated in the EU, surveillance images, for example, are not. Video surveillance cameras are even more widespread in certain parts of Europe than they are in the United States.

Where Do You Go From Here?

In a world of widespread monitoring, is avoiding new computer technologies, cell phone cameras, credit cards, and any newfangled gadget the final answer to the privacy problem? Of course not.

In the past, any improvements in technology have been double-edged, giving people more privacy on the one hand and endangering their privacy on the other. Consumer cameras allow people to take private and informal pictures to record their lives, but the photos themselves could end up in the wrong hands and candid photos of unsuspecting subjects could be seen as a violation of privacy. The invention of envelopes with adhesive flaps boosted expectations of private letter writing between people, but also boosted an unrealistic expectation of privacy. The invention of the telephone brought direct and private communications over long distances, but subjects people to the dangers of wiretapping.

The same is true of today's new technologies. Cell phones allow you to make calls in a private place but make you vulnerable to tapping; the Internet brings the world's largest library (and mall) to the privacy of your home but subjects you to the dangers of spyware, spam, and viruses; the video camera makes it possible for you to film home videos, but anyone who gets their hands on your videos could make unlimited copies of them or post them over the Web for millions to see.

Can you imagine living your life without the technologies that make it easier? Would you really stop using a credit card even though your credit card company records all your purchases? Would you stop using an E-Z Pass if it meant an increase in waiting time at tollbooths? Or stop using the Internet because of spammers?

The reality is that you must embrace progress and new technologies. The Luddites, the notorious workers who destroyed new technologies during the Industrial Revolution, failed to stop technological progress, and modern Luddites will also fail. Just as power looms eventually led the way to a better standard of living, so, too, have today's technologies made possible the many benefits that you enjoy and probably could not forego. Understanding the privacy risks associated with them is just a part of enjoying the freedoms they offer.

Your Personal Information and the Public Record

PSSST– WANNA BUY SOME PERSONAL INFORMATION?

Your only brush with the law took place when you were in high school and you were charged with a misdemeanor for drinking and getting too rowdy at your high school graduation. You've gone on to complete your master's degree in education at an Ivy League university. You assume that your high school misdemeanor is sealed in the court records and forgotten for good. But it isn't—and you discover this fact during your sixth interview with a prospective employer.

You look into your purse and notice your wallet is not there. A few days earlier you had misplaced the same purse and gone through the hassle of replacing IDs and canceling checks, only to find the purse later with all the contents intact. Should you repeat the process or should you assume the wallet will turn up, like the last time? Unfortunately, this time the wallet had really been stolen, along with your driver's license, credit cards, checkbook, and social security number. Within days, thieves use the information to drain your personal bank account of thousands of dollars.

You go to the Department of Motor Vehicles to replace your license. The clerk behind the desk types your name into her computer, looks you in the eye, and tells you that the picture she has on file doesn't look at all like you. She swivels the monitor in your direction. You see your name, address, birth date, and driver's license number. But you have to agree with the clerk—the woman smiling widely in the photo, the one who recently renewed your license, doesn't look even remotely like you.

One of life's little ironies is that your most private information is in fact quite public. Almost every major event in your life, no matter how sensitive or sentimental, gets recorded in a public record that you and many others can easily access. From your birth to your death, marriage to divorce, home purchase to home sale, income and taxes to bankruptcy, the public record reflects your life's achievements and sorrows. Needless to say, given the existence of such public records, it is very difficult for you to protect your most personal information and your privacy.

By way of background, a public record is any record, file, or information that any unit of federal, state, or local government maintains about a particular individual. A plethora of personal information about you exists in government files—far beyond the standard fare of name, address, and social security number. The public record includes birth, marriage, divorce, and death certificates, court records, voter data, and much more, as you'll see below.

You should protect your personal information in the same way you protect your material and tangible possessions such as your home and jewelry. Quite a bit of sensitive information is in the public record, but some of this information isn't always readily available, such as your social security number. It is prudent to keep information such as your social security number as private as possible, so identity thieves cannot access it through public records and use it to create a detailed profile of you. If this happens, you may suffer from the loss of something even more valuable than your pearls or your great-grandfather's gold watch: your identity.

This chapter focuses on the general nature of the information contained in public records and how accessible it is, as well as an overview of the *most important* personal documents that you must monitor and protect. When it comes to your personal documents and the public record, the best way to protect yourself is to make sure your information is accurate and limited to the extent possible.

Information Contained in Public Records

Public records not only record the important transitions in your life, such as your birth, marriage, and death, they may also identify your occupation, your political beliefs, and even your hobbies. What might be learned about you from the public record? Almost anything, including:

- ▶ what you look like (your sex, age, height, weight, eye color)
- ▶ your marital status
- ▶ where you were born
- ▶ your occupation
- ▶ how you spend some of your leisure time (such as certain hobbies)
- ▶ any physical property you own
- ▶ whether you have certain medical conditions
- ▶ details of your stock ownership in public companies
- ▶ details of your home ownership (including the price you paid for your home, home loans that you have incurred, and the assessed value of your home)
- ▶ your car(s)
- ▶ whether you own a boat or airplane
- ▶ your political views (likelihood of voting and political contributions)
- ▶ and much, much more

Where does this information come from? It comes from federal, state, and local public files, including driver's licenses and driving records; motor vehicle registration and titles from the Department of Motor Vehicles; boat, aircraft, and other vehicle titles; land titles and property tax records; voting registration and political contribution records; occupational licenses; firearms permits and hunting and fishing licenses; certain communications use licenses; filings with the Securities and Exchange Commission; and address records from the U.S. Postal Service. In addition, there are public files about any interaction you may have had with either civil courts or criminal courts. These files may include court records related to bankruptcy, civil actions, divorces, juror information, and general court docket information. In criminal matters, public files may include criminal court records, law enforcement records, police blotters, jail lists, and compiled criminal history records.

The amount of information about you that is included in public records depends upon the state in which you live, because different states maintain different records or may have different laws that regulate their state public records. For example, New Jersey and South Dakota are among the most restrictive states; Florida and Indiana are among the most open.

Access to Public Records

Liam Youens contacted Docusearch, an Internet-based investigation and information service that relies heavily on public records, and requested information about Amy Lynn Boyer, a twenty-year-old woman who had spurned his romantic advances back in high school. For about $150, Youens secured Boyer's employment information and social security number (which Docusearch secured from a credit reporting agency). On October 15, 1999, Youens went to the dentist's office where Boyer worked and fatally shot her as she was leaving. Then Youens committed suicide. Youens maintained a website that detailed his obsession with Boyer. The site included his comment that "It's actually obsene [sic] what you can find out about people on the Internet." Boyer's family lobbied for Amy Boyer's Law, which would have prohibited the display and certain uses of social security numbers without the holder's permission, with certain exceptions. Consumer and privacy groups opposed the proposal, not-

ing the statute's significant exceptions for commercial use of social
security numbers and public records.

> Today, anyone can sit
> on a favorite lounge chair,
> place his or her feet on
> the accompanying
> ottoman, and access
> almost any public record
> with a few keystrokes.

Are you hiding a dirty little secret? Let's hope that if it is dirty, it is little, because it is not likely to be secret. Today, in the eyes of the government, or anyone with access to public record files, you cannot expect to be anonymous.

In the past, anyone who wanted to access a public record had to research the appropriate agency that might possess the particular record, travel to the agency, enter during appropriate hours of inspection, hope that the desired file was complete, and then copy the document. Before the advent of the Internet, your entire public record consisted of paper documents physically located in different locations, many of which were spread throughout the country. Today, anyone can sit on a favorite lounge chair, place his or her feet on the accompanying ottoman, and access almost any public record with a few keystrokes.

How? Some public records are available online at government offices and public records sites. Sources of public record information on the Internet are data aggregators such as ChoicePoint, West Group, Accurint (Seisint, Inc.), and Lexis-Nexis. These aggregators cull public records including (subject to individual state laws): indexes of civil and criminal court cases; bankruptcies, judgments, and liens; property records; professional license information; Department of Motor Vehicles data; voter registration data; and certain stock ownership in public companies. They may also collect information from sources that aren't in the public record, including surveys, sweepstakes questionnaires, loyalty-card programs, and monitoring of Internet shopping (see chapter 6, "Your Shopping," and chapter 7, "Your Computer and the Internet").

Data aggregators sell their information to individuals and various businesses. Marketing companies buy certain information to target their products to the best customers. The various credit bureaus use public records to monitor name changes (as a result of marriage or divorce) or address changes so their consumer credit files are up-to-date. Private investigators and attorneys

The following public records are *generally confidential:*

- ▶ tax records
- ▶ wage and personal property tax records
- ▶ health/medical records
- ▶ school records (except directory information)
- ▶ military records
- ▶ juvenile criminal proceedings
- ▶ welfare and other benefit records (such as food stamps)
- ▶ social security number

Notwithstanding the sensitive and confidential nature of these records, even this personal information can be accessed and made available in certain circumstances. For example, your tax information can be revealed if you are involved in a court action where tax issues are relevant; in the event you owe child support payments; if you are seeking financial aid under a state program; when your tax information is needed for government statistical or administrative purposes; or if law enforcement agencies require the information. Your social security number may be released to insurance companies, banks, courts, employers, and others.

Do you wonder when confidential really means confidential? It helps to keep in mind the motto of the *Aspen Daily News* "If you don't want it printed, don't let it happen." Since you cannot prevent your personal information from being filed in various public records, expect it to be made public at some point.

The Privacy Act of 1974 and the Freedom of Information Act

George Culpepper, a junior at the Metropolitan State College of Denver, claimed that his professor violated the Family Educational and Privacy Act of 1974 when she published information about Culpepper's grades in a December 2003 article in the Denver Post. *The act requires schools to have written permission from the student to release any information in a student's education record.*

For almost twenty years, reporter Seth Rosenfeld fought to obtain FBI records about the bureau's illegal and covert activities at the University of California in the 1950s. Rosenfeld sued the bureau three times for withholding information that he thought should have been revealed under the Freedom of Information Act. He finally got his story when the FBI was forced in court to release two hundred thousand pages of information that revealed the agency's incriminating activities. One censored item was FBI Director J. Edgar Hoover's infuriated response when he was informed of an optional test question on the university's 1959 English aptitude test, "What are the dangers to a democracy of a national police organization like the FBI which operates secretly and is unresponsive to public criticism?"

> Since you cannot prevent your personal information from being filed in various public records, expect it to be made public at some point.

Much of your personal information might be public, but that doesn't mean you don't have any rights or that all your information is available carte blanche to whoever orders it.

Given the public policy considerations and the sensitive nature of the information contained in your public records, many different laws at the federal, state, and local levels govern the specific categories of information available for public access, or the nature of such access, as the case may be. Two principal federal privacy laws govern access to personal information within federal government agencies. These laws are the Privacy Act of 1974 and the Freedom of Information Act. As their respective names suggest, the Privacy Act ensures that individuals can maintain confidentiality with respect to their government records, and the Freedom of Information Act assists those who seek to open government records. Combined, these two laws seek to balance public policy considerations with respect to access to public records. Every state has similar laws that incorporate many of the principles of the federal laws to govern both the privacy and access to information at a state or local level.

The Privacy Act of 1974. The Privacy Act gives you certain rights to protect your personal information contained in public records. These rights include:

- to see and copy those records that the federal government keeps on you
- to discover who has had access to your personal information
- to change any inaccurate or irrelevant information contained in your public record

Moreover, the Privacy Act imposes certain requirements on government agencies that maintain public records. For instance, the agency may only use the information for the purpose for which it was initially gathered. If you make a request to see your information, the responsible agency must respond to your request within ten days. To initiate the process, write the government agency that maintains your public file. (Use the website of the United States Government Printing Office at www.gpoaccess.gov, which contains descriptions of the records maintained on individuals and the rules agencies follow to assist individuals who request information about their records.) The agency that maintains the information has the right to deny your request, particularly if your circumstances involve law enforcement activities, the Central Intelligence Agency (CIA), litigation, or confidential government sources, among others. If you are denied access to your records, or if you believe your records have been improperly disclosed, you have the right to appeal to or sue the government agency.

> Under the Freedom of Information Act you may even order a copy of your FBI file—for a fee.

The Freedom of Information Act (FOIA). Enacted in 1966, the FOIA was the first law that gave Americans the right to access the records of federal agencies. It allows U.S. citizens to keep an eye on their government's activities by accessing and obtaining information contained in government files. In this case, the responsible agency must respond within twenty days to your request for access. Under the Freedom of Information Act you may even order a copy of your FBI file—for a fee. As with the Privacy Act, your access to information will be restricted if it involves certain parties such as the CIA and law enforcement, or if it involves certain circumstances such as litigation, sensitive government information (internal agency memos, personnel matters, classified documents, confidential government sources), and violations of an individual's privacy interests. The press uses this act to initiate requests for information it seeks to include in stories compiled for public consumption. If you are denied, you may appeal to the agency itself or sue the agency in court.

Your Personal Documents

Among your most essential personal documents are your social security card, your driver's license, and your passport. Your social security information and your driver's license information are contained in public records and are available to varying degrees depending upon your state, but your passport information is private. Whether part of the public record or not, your essential documents need to be carefully guarded against identity theft and checked for accuracy.

Social Security Information

Fraud with respect to social security numbers is so widespread that even the social security numbers of top government officials, including Central Intelligence Agency Director George Tenet, Attorney General John Ashcroft, and chief political adviser Karl Rove, are available for purchase on the Internet. The California-based Foundation for Taxpayer and Consumer Rights said it purchased the social security numbers and home addresses of these top political appointees for $26 each.

Social security numbers came into being after the passage of the Social Security Act in 1935. The act was the result of President Franklin Roosevelt's desire to provide citizens with the monetary benefits they needed to offset the effects of the Great Depression. To distribute the benefits, the government implemented a system that assigned each citizen a social security number. The system first provided only retirement benefits; now social security also pays survivor and disability benefits.

Although it was never intended to be so, your social security number is the key to accessing much of your private and essential personal information. It is part of your public record, although it is considered a confidential piece of information. Nevertheless, many entities are able to access your number.

The government uses your social security number to access all the information available about you in its various databases and the various public records about you. Your number can also be released to insurance companies, banks, attorneys, and process servers. Your social security number is used as your main record-keeping number in a variety of other contexts, including employee files, medical records, health insurance accounts, credit and banking accounts, and university ID cards, among others. Your social security number is used to connect multiple records about you, tracking you through every move, making data compilation easy for government and business alike.

> **Your social security number is used to connect multiple records about you, tracking you through every move, making data compilation easy for government and business alike.**

Because your social security number is used for so many purposes, and is the key to unlocking so much information about you, you must use extra precaution to prevent someone from stealing or otherwise fraudulently using it. Given how accessible it is to so many people, it is relatively easy for someone to use it to assume your identity and gain access to your bank account, credit accounts, utilities records, and other sources of personal information. An identity thief will use your social security card to set up credit lines, drain your savings accounts, and even obtain a credit card.

Your social security information consists of two documents: your social security card or number and your annual social security statement. It's important for you to understand these pieces of information and know how to protect them.

Your Social Security Number or Card. Your social security card has your name and social security number printed on it. If you have never been issued a social security card, if you need a replacement card, or if you have changed your name, you can apply for a new card without charge. To apply for a social security card, you must complete Form SS-5. To obtain this form, the instructions for completing the form, and the location of the nearest Social Security office, call 800/772-1213 or log on to www.ssa.gov/ssnumber. This URL also provides information about how to obtain a number for your child, an adopted child, or a foreign-born adopted child, and how to obtain a new number if you are the victim of domestic abuse. You can submit your application by mail or in person, but you must supply certain supporting documentation to prove your identity. The above link provides details on the documents needed.

> An identity thief will use your social security card to set up credit lines, drain your savings accounts, and even obtain a credit card.

Your Social Security Statement. Your social security statement is a personal record of your past earnings that represent the amounts upon which your social security taxes have been based. It also provides a summary of the estimated benefits you and your family may receive in the future. Typically, you will receive a statement annually about three months before your birthday. You can also request your statement at any time free of charge by submitting Form SSA-7004 by mail or contacting the Social Security Administration through their website. Retain your annual statements and check your statement each year for accuracy.

Mistakes on your social security statement may prevent you from receiving all the social security benefits you have earned; it may also mean that someone has assumed your identity and is diverting income from your statement or receiving benefits in your name. If the information about your past earnings is incorrect, call the Social Security Administration at 800/772-1213 (and have in hand your W-2 or tax returns for those years) or access www.ssa.gov/mystatement. The sooner you identify those mistakes, the easier it will be to correct them.

In the event that your social security number is lost or stolen, carefully read the information about identity theft in chapter 3, "Your Identity," as well as chapter 4, "Your Credit." Follow the practical tips identified in those chapters and here:

✳ **Don't disclose your social security number unless it is absolutely necessary.**
Disclose your social security number only when you are required to do so. For example, some government agencies may require your social security number for their purposes, and you must reveal it. Private businesses, on the other hand, may request your number, and unless you *must* give it to them, you should not do so. Be extra cautious when merchants ask you to

write your social security number on your checks or payment slips. Be equally wary when a company wants your social security number for added protection. Be careful about disclosing your social security number regardless of whether it is requested in person, on the phone, in an application, or online, especially when you have not previously had any transactions with the organization. Use your best judgment and always err on the side of caution.

✳ **Limit access to your social security number.** There are a number of steps you can take to limit the chances of someone gaining access to your social security number. First, avoid using your social security number as your personal identifier by not including it on your checks or other personal forms. Do not use your social security number as a password or personal identification number. Do not carry your social security card (or any other card containing your social security number) in your purse or wallet in case your purse or wallet is lost or stolen. Do not write the number on a piece of paper that you carry around with you.

✳ **Prevent others from using your social security number to identify you.** In many cases, other people or companies will use your social security number as the primary means of identifying you. Try to prevent this. For example, if your employer displays your social security number on your employee file or other company files, insist that it use a different number instead. If your bank, credit union or other financial service provider uses your social security number as a personal identification number or as the identifier for banking by phone or the Internet, request that the bank assign you a different identification number. If your state's Department of Motor Vehicles uses your social security number as your driver's license number, or if your university uses your social security number for your student number, ask for an alternate number.

✳ **Review your credit report regularly.** Order a copy of your credit report from all three credit bureaus at least annually. If you are a victim of identity theft, the credit report will contain evidence of credit or banking fraud committed by a thief using your name and social security number. It will also show other social security numbers associated with your name. Find more information on this subject in chapter 3, "Your Identity," and chapter 4, "Your Credit."

✳ **Review your social security personal earnings and benefits estimate statement.** The Social Security Administration (SSA) mails a copy of your social security statement to you each year about three months before your birthday. Be certain the information in the file is correct. You can contact the administration at 800/772-1213 to obtain this free report if you haven't received it. If the statement contains incorrect information, contact the Social Security Administration immediately. Someone may be fraudulently using your social security number for employment purposes. You can reach the Social Security Administration's fraud department at 800/269-0271.

To access your social security information or find further information on social security benefits, contact:

> **Social Security Administration**
> Office of Public Inquiries
> Windsor Park Building
> 6401 Security Blvd.
> Baltimore, MD 21235
> Phone: 800/772-1213
> www.ssa.gov/ssnumber/
> www.ssa.gov/mystatement/

Your Driver's License and Record

Rebecca Schaeffer was an actress who starred in the show My Sister Sam, *a 1980s sitcom. Robert Bardo, a deranged fan, hired a private investigator to locate Schaeffer's home address from a branch of the California Department of Motor Vehicles (DMV). With the address in hand, Bardo disguised himself as a flower deliveryman. He easily gained entry into Schaeffer's home and murdered her. As with John Lennon's killer, Mark David Chapman, before him, Bardo had a copy of J.D. Salinger's* Catcher in the Rye *in his possession at the time of his arrest. Bardo had been able to discover enough personal informa-*

*tion to devise a plan to murder Schaeffer, so laws were later estab-
lished to protect private information contained in driver's licenses.*

Sensitive information is contained on your driver's license and in your driving record. Although the specific information may vary by state, your state likely keeps records on you as a driver (such as driver's license and driver history information), and about your vehicle (such as ownership information). The information stored about you in your public record is a direct product of the requirements you must complete to get a driver's license. This information may include your:

- name
- address
- social security number
- physical description (height, weight, eye color)
- date of birth
- driver's license status
- need for corrective lenses while driving
- record of any moving violations for which you have been convicted, including drunk driving
- medical conditions that may affect your ability to drive
- enrollment in organ donation programs

Given the sensitivity of driver's license information, and as a response to Rebecca Schaeffer's murder, Congress passed a federal law known as the Driver's Privacy Protection Act of 1994 (DPPA), which regulates how personal information from records in state motor vehicle departments may be released and shared. Before the DPPA, many states sold drivers' personal information to the highest bidder—usually direct marketing data aggregators.

The DPPA restricts states from releasing your personal information to direct marketers or the public at large. The restricted personal information includes your:

- photograph
- social security number
- driver identification number

- ▶ address (but not your five-digit zip code)
- ▶ telephone number
- ▶ medical information or disability information

Information concerning traffic accidents, traffic violations, and the status of your license is *not* considered personal information by the DPPA. This information may be available with certain restrictions to anyone, including your employer, your parents, and your neighbor.

The DPPA shields your personal information by requiring states to pass measures that require your express consent in order to share your information with others. Access to your personal information is restricted unless you explicitly consent (by checking a box on your application for your driver's license or vehicle registration) or federal law authorizes such access. For example, only if you check the box on your driver's license application is your state permitted to use, rent, or sell your personal information to businesses for surveys and marketing purposes, or to solicit you for a variety of products and services. If you do not check the opt-out box, then only those entities authorized by federal law may access your record.

Because the DPPA requires each state to establish guidelines, access to your personal information and driving record depends on the laws in the state in which you live. For example, in some states, your driver's license photograph, social security number, and medical or disability information receive special protection. In New York State, the Department of Motor Vehicles will not release your photograph, your social security number, medical or disability information, or your telephone number, even to those persons who request the information and have a permissible use for it.

Nevertheless, the DPPA does provide for certain exceptions under which the personal information contained in your driving record can be released without your consent. Such cases require a permissible purpose, and what constitutes a permissible purpose is expressly outlined in the DPPA. Permissible purposes include government agencies needing to carry out their responsibilities, for automobile safety purposes (such as recalling a motor vehicle) or for use by a licensed private investigator. To review the entire list of permissible purposes, go to http://www.accessreports.com/statutes/DPPA1.htm.

Finally, the DPPA restricts access to your driving record to those who have a permissible use under the act. Of particular concern to you should be the information contained in your driving record that is available to your prospective employer when you apply for a job, such as your driving activity. Entries for moving violations usually remain on your record for three years; serious offenses or alcohol-related convictions can remain for as long as ten years. Depending on the state, your driving record may include the class of driver's license you hold, endorsements and restrictions, current status, expiration date, accidents, moving traffic violation convictions (including alcohol or drug-related convictions), license suspensions, and revocations. In principle, your prospective employer should access your driving record only to verify information you submit; in the event that he or she needs to prevent fraud, such as in an insurance case; or if driving is integral to the job for which you are applying (delivery person, bus driver). In addition, an employer may obtain any other personal information that he or she specifies in a waiver with your written consent.

> Of particular concern to you should be the information that is available to your prospective employer when you apply for a job, such as your driving activity.

Use the following practical tips to protect your driver's license information:

* **Don't opt in.** Do not check the box on your driver's license application or registration form that gives your consent to release your personal information. Remember, your information may still be accessed without your consent by government agencies and others.

* **Demand that your social security number not be printed on your license.** Some states use the driver's social security number as a default driver's license number. This practice exposes drivers to identify theft. Make sure to request that your driver's license number not be your social security number.

* **Order your driving record.** For employment, insurance, and personal reasons, you should confirm that the information on your DMV record is correct and current before you apply for a job or auto insurance. If you want to review your driving record, go to www.dmv.org/newindex2.php?linkid=149.

✳ **Understand the information that is included in your driver's license and record.** Your driver's license and driving record contain a great deal of information about you, including your name, date of birth, mailing address, sex, height, weight, eye color, vision correction, and any medical conditions that may affect your ability to drive. Your driving record may show the class of driver's license you hold, in addition to specifics about your driving history, including endorsements and restrictions, current status, expiration date, accidents, tickets and moving violation convictions, suspensions and revocations, and alcohol and drug-related convictions for the past five or more years.

✳ **Make sure the information is correct and current.** Because this information is sensitive and accessible to others in many situations, you should verify that all information on your license is correct and up-to-date. For example, has the Department of Motor Vehicles indicated the proper driving classification? Should you have any driving restrictions?

✳ **Be responsible if you lose your driver's license.** If you lose, misplace, or need to renew your driver's license, act promptly. Report a loss immediately. Don't risk identity theft. You can get a new license at your local office of the state department of motor vehicles. Many states and localities also offer license renewals and replacement through their website. To obtain the address of your local office, and to learn what you need to do in case of loss or reapplying, use the helpful links at www.dmv.org.

✳ **Think twice before you get a personalized license plate for your car.** Personalized plates are much more memorable, so don't get one if you are concerned about being easily identified.

Passport

When Abdulaziz Alomari was studying electrical engineering at the University of Colorado in 1995, a briefcase containing his passport was stolen from his apartment. Six years later, the FBI discovered that a man using Alomari's identity was one of the terrorists on the flight that hit the North Tower of the World Trade Center on Sep-

tember 11. Alomari had reported the theft, but no single worldwide agency keeps track of stolen passports. Although the Colorado police department may have informed the Saudi Embassy, the embassy wouldn't necessarily inform the U.S. State Department or the Immigration and Naturalization Service.

Your passport is not part of the public record, but you must take steps to guard this document. Your passport contains sensitive personal information such as your full name, passport number, date of birth, photograph, and signature. If you lose your passport, you will increase your chances of being victimized by identity fraud.

Follow these tips to protect the privacy of your passport:

✳ **Report lost or stolen passports.** If your passport is lost or stolen, report it immediately. By so doing, you protect yourself from identity fraud and reduce the risk that others, including possible terrorists, are using your passport to pass themselves off as U.S. citizens. To report a lost or stolen passport, you must provide detailed answers to all questions on Form DS-64, Statement Regarding A Lost or Stolen Passport. Contact:

U.S. Department of State
Passport Services
Consular Lost/Stolen Passport Section
1111 19th Street, NW, Suite 500
Washington, DC 20036
202/955-0430
www.travel.state.gov/report_ppt.html

Remember that if you report your passport lost or stolen, the document is invalidated and cannot be used for travel if you happen to find it later. If you need to obtain a first-time passport, renew or replace a passport, or get copies of your passport records, go to www.travel.state.gov/passport_services.htm.

✳ **Keep copies of your passport.** Make two copies of your passport identification page before you travel. The copies facilitate replacement if your passport is lost or stolen. Leave one copy at home with friends or relatives, and carry the other with you in a separate place from your passport.

✳ **Guard your passport.** You should protect your passport at all times. At home, keep your passport in a secure place, such as a locked file cabinet. When you travel, you may find that many hotels require guests to leave their passports at the front desk. It may not be possible, but you should avoid leaving your passport with the front desk.

Official Certificates

The most important official certificates about your life are on file in the public record. For example, you (and others) can generally access your birth certificate, marriage certificate, and divorce certificate. Unless you have superhuman qualities, you will not be able to access your death certificate, but others can.

Birth Certificate

> To steal auto body shop owner Dave Feakes's identity, Allan Ray Rick simply called the relevant agency within the state of North Dakota and bought a copy of Feakes's birth certificate, a feat easily carried out in some states. One day Feakes got a call from a bank demanding payment for $9,000 in returned checks. Soon thereafter, he was humiliated in department stores when the clerks refused to accept his checks. When he went to the DMV to renew his driver's license, the clerk typed his name into the computer and an image of Feakes's driver's license came up with Allan Ray Rick's picture on it. With a birth certificate, an identity thief can get a driver's license, a duplicate social security number, and much more.

Birth certificates are contained in the public records. An official certificate of every birth is on file in the locality where the birth occurred. Birth records usually contain the name of the child, date and time of birth, the city and the hospital in which the child was born, the parents' names, and the attending physician's name. Depending upon state and county laws, a requester may obtain a certified copy of any birth certificate by writing or going to the vital statistics office in the state or area where the birth occurred. With the exception of some states, the records are released only to the individual, if of legal age, or to parents or legal guardians. Anyone requesting a birth certificate on the behalf of someone else may need to notarize the application. To learn the address and procedure for obtaining a copy of a birth certificate in your state, log on to www.cdc.gov/nchs/howto/w2w/w2welcom.htm.

Marriage Certificate

Imagine one Parisian woman's surprise when she discovered she had been married and divorced, both without her knowledge! A foreign national she had never met stole her personal identity card, "married" her for four years (and got a marriage certificate to prove it), and divorced her once he obtained French citizenship.

An official certificate of every marriage is on file in the locality where the marriage occurred. The certificate generally includes the names of the bride and groom, the date of the marriage, and the country in which the certificate was filed. Policies regarding access vary by state. A certified copy of any marriage certificate can be requested by writing or going to the vital statistics office in the state or area where the event occurred. To learn the addresses and procedures for obtaining a copy of a marriage certificate in your state, log on to www.cdc.gov/nchs/howto/w2w/w2welcom.htm.

If you execute a public record search (see chapter 12, "I Spy, You Spy"), you can check if anyone has married you without your knowledge.

Divorce Certificate

Since 1994, in Hamilton County, Ohio, court documents have been available on the county's website, www.courtclerk.org. In 2002, a search feature was added to the site that allowed visitors to search for cases by typing in a single name. If you search divorce cases, you can dig up anything from tax returns to love letters.

Imagine that you have just undergone a difficult divorce and are looking for a job so you can earn the income you lost as a result. The details of your divorce could be damaging if anyone were to uncover them. How nervous would you be if your prospective employer ran an extensive background search on you?

Anyone can request an official certificate of any divorce in the public file in the locality where the divorce occurred but access varies by state. In New York, for example, if you are not a party to the divorce, you must have a court order or show legal cause to obtain the record. By contrast, in Florida anyone can generally acquire anyone else's divorce certificate. To obtain a certified copy of the divorce information, write or go to the vital statistics office in the state or area where the event occurred. For the address and procedure for obtaining a copy of a divorce decree in your state log on to www.cdc.gov/nchs/howto/w2w/w2welcom.htm.

Death Certificate

A television station discovered the names of fifteen thousand deceased people on the active voting lists in Georgia just days before an upcoming election. In one case, a deceased person had voted a total of three times since his death.

Jose Sison Fernandez, a World War II veteran, suddenly stopped receiving his monthly pension after five years. When he spoke with a Philippine Veterans Affairs Office supervisor about the problem, he was informed that a woman named Aurora had submitted a death certificate on his behalf, and that his checks were now being forwarded to a different address. "I never requested the PVAO to change my mailing address," he says, adding, "I am very much alive."

As with the other official certificates, an official certificate of every death is a public record in the locality where the death occurred. Access to death certificates varies by state. Those states that do consider death certificates as public information (Florida and North Dakota, for example) do not provide cause of death unless the requester is a family member. A certified copy of any death certificate is available through the vital statistics office in the state or area where the death occurred. To learn the addresses and procedures for obtaining a copy of a death certificate in your state, log on to www.cdc.gov/nchs/howto/w2w/w2welcom.htm.

A thief who steals a death certificate has the deceased's legal name and social security number—all the thief needs to apply for new credit and rack up thousands of dollars in fraudulent purchases. Protect the memory of your loved ones by filing copies of their death certificates with the three credit reporting agencies (see Resources). Filing allows agencies to be aware of fraudulent activity if anyone tries to open a credit account.

A public record search (see chapter 12, "I Spy, You Spy") will reveal if anyone has filed a death certificate in your name.

Government-Related Documents

In 2000, two New Jersey men obtained the names and social security numbers of several hundred high-ranking active-duty and retired U.S. military officers. They accessed the information from a public website that copied it from the Congressional Record. They used the information to apply for credit cards and bank and corporate credit in the officers' names.

Your government-related documents consist of your military records, citizenship/immigration records, civilian records, jury records, and voting records. Categories that are generally accessible include jury records, arrest records, and court records.

Citizenship/Immigration Documents

Citizenship and immigration papers are part of the public record. The Freedom of Information Act stipulates that any person has a right to request access to immigration records and makes exceptions only for those records exempted by the Privacy Act (e.g., classified national security, business proprietary, personal privacy, and investigative). Anyone searching for a citizenship/immigration document can go to uscis.gov./graphics/aboutus/foia/request.htm.

The Bureau of Citizenship and Immigration Services (BCIS) within the Department of Homeland Security (DHS) handles citizenship and immigration matters. To order immigration forms, call 800/870-3676 or go to the Web link: uscis.gov.

Jury Records

Jury records are public records and, with limited exceptions, are accessible to the public. A potential juror must reveal his or her name, address, and other personal information during the juror selection process known as the voir dire. In most states (with the exception of New York and Minnesota, among others), the voir dire becomes part of the public court records. In criminal cases, this information is part of the court record, but is generally sealed to the public for the jurors' protection.

Some courts have adopted the practice of referring to jurors by numbers rather than names during both voir dire and trial. This is a common practice in the Los Angeles Superior Court, and was first used for criminal trials in which retaliation from defendants or jury tampering were major concerns. Later it became a popular use during high profile trials, like the O.J. Simpson and Oklahoma City bombing trials, to prevent media contact with jurors.

You should retain any records from the county clerk or records indicating your completion of jury service for several reasons: (1) in case the court inadvertently thinks you failed to show up for jury service and finds you in contempt of court; (2) to serve as proof of your service in the event that you missed work to serve and your employer may request proof of your service; and (3) in case your state summons you prematurely to serve again.

Military Records

> A Navy retiree discovered his identity had been stolen when he received a call from American Express. It turned out that a lawyer stole the retiree's social security number from a database of veterans who had filed their DD 214s with their county courthouses.

Under the provisions of the Privacy Act of 1974, requests for military records are considered only if the individual whose records are involved has provided written consent. The Privacy Act does not apply to deceased military personnel, although the Department of Defense requires the written consent of the next of kin.

Veterans or next of kin of a deceased veteran use one type of form to request military records; all others use a different form. Instructions on how to obtain your military records are available from www.archives.gov/facilities/mo/st_louis/military_personnel_records/standard_form_180.html.

Here are some tips for former military personnel:

✳ **Safeguard your DD 214 form.** Soldiers who leave active duty receive a report of separation from the military or a Form DD 214, which contains the veteran's social security number and birth date. As a result, guard your certificate as you do your social security card and birth certificate.

✳ **Do not file your DD 214 with your local courthouse.** In the past, veterans were advised to file the form with their local courthouses to ensure that they would always be able to get a certified copy. Once the DD 214 is filed at a local county courthouse, however, it may become a public record. Privacy advocates now advise former military personnel not to file this document in the local courthouse.

Civilian Records

Civilian records are the personnel records of former federal civilian employees. As with military records, written authorization by the person of record, or proof of that person's death, is needed to access a civilian record. Requests for information from personnel or any other type of records must be made in writing; requests cannot be made by telephone or e-mail.

To obtain information on how to obtain civilian personnel records, log on to www.archives.gov/facilities/mo/st_louis/civilian_personnel_records.html.

Voting Records

By comparing voter rolls with social security data, the Indianapolis Star *discovered the names of more than three hundred deceased individuals who were currently registered to vote in the 2000 presi-*

41

dential election, most of them in Lake County, an area notorious for voter fraud.

Political candidates and organizations seeking to use voter registration information for academic, journalistic, political, or governmental purposes can often buy voter registration information that may also include your home address and telephone number.

Where your voting records are stored depends on the state in which you live, but this information is generally kept with the county clerk's office. The voter information that is in the public record is generally limited to your name, city, zip code, and party affiliation. Political candidates and organizations seeking to use voter registration information for academic, journalistic, political, or governmental purposes can often buy voter registration information that may also include your home address and telephone number.

Log on to the website of the Federal Election Commission (www.fec.gov) for details about voter registration in your state and a list of polling locations in your district.

Arrest Records

North Carolina sold basic criminal and civil-case information to data aggregators, which in turn sold the records to potential employers, landlords, and others running background checks. It seemed like a sensible thing to do: fewer people were packing the courthouses, and the data-harvesting companies contributed to the state's tax base. The courts were supposed to update their information daily, but at least one missed a day. The result? Five North Carolina residents with expunged criminal records were listed in the databases as having criminal records.

Rush fans sent angry letters to the Naples Daily News when it reported the arrest of guitarist Alex Lifeson for assault. One writer accused the editor of being a "scumsucking pig," and another reader asserted that the paper violated Lifeson's privacy by publishing his address. The editor responded that the newspaper rou-

tinely published the ages and local addresses of people who have been arrested, and that this information is a matter of public record.

Arrest records are public records. Arrest records for federal crimes are generally available to the public. State records, however, are more restricted and vary by state. The public record may include details about your arrest, the incident leading to your arrest, and the victim involved. In certain cases, arrest records are not accessible, particularly if accessing the information would impair an ongoing investigation or endanger individual citizens. Further, if you are arrested and later found innocent, you may request that the record be sealed and therefore generally not accessible to the public. Not all states make arrest records available online.

> Given that information about an arrest is stored electronically, data aggregators can now access various databases to compile "rap sheets" by searching arrest records and court files that are public records.

A record of criminal history (which is different from an arrest record) is accessible to the public depending on the state, and is generally accessible to law enforcement agencies, attorneys working on a case involving the individual, probation or parole officers, state agencies that need the information to license an individual, and employers, under limited circumstances. However, given that information about an arrest is stored electronically, data aggregators can now access various databases to compile "rap sheets" by searching arrest records and court files that are public records. Employers can use this information to run background checks on prospective employees.

Court Records and Inmate Records

Edward Socorro, a sales manager with Hilton Hotels Corp., committed a minor infraction in Illinois. He later had his record expunged. Hilton hired IMI Data Search, Inc., to run background checks on new employees, and the search wrongly determined that Socorro had spent six months in jail. Socorro was fired, and it took him seven months to find a new job.

Court records generally are considered public records. Unless a judge has sealed part of the court record, or if the record involves a juvenile, you (and anyone else) can generally access information contained in court records, which includes names, dates, and details of cases and their outcomes.

SEX OFFENDERS BY ZIP CODE

Sex offenders have had little privacy since Megan's Law went into effect in October 1996. The law was named after seven-year-old Megan Kanka, a New Jersey girl who was raped and killed by a twice-convicted child molester who had moved across the street from the family. In response to Megan's murder, the Kankas sought to have a law that would require local communities to warn the public about sex offenders in the area. Megan's Law provides the public with information about dangerous sex offenders so families can protect themselves and their children. Megan's Law also authorizes local law enforcement to notify the public about high-risk and serious sex offenders who reside in, are employed in, or frequent the community. The law is not intended to punish the offender and specifically prohibits using the information to harass or commit any crime against the offender.

Convicted sex offenders are required to register their current addresses with local law enforcement agencies, and it is a crime to fail to do so. Nevertheless, a high number of sex offenders fail to comply by either not registering after they leave jail or failing to provide an updated address. For example, over the years, the State of California has lost track of more than one-fifth of its approximately one hundred thousand registered sex offenders.

The information available on registered sex offenders includes:

- name and known aliases
- age and sex
- physical description, including scars, marks, and tattoos
- photograph, if available
- crimes resulting in registration (including rape and other sexual assault and the age of the victim[s])

> ▶ county of residence
> ▶ zip code (based on last registration)

Your local police department has a listing of the sex offenders in your area. Most states also maintain online databases of these offenders, including pictures. A listing of sex offender registries by state can be found at www.klaaskids.org/pg-legmeg2.htm. Most databases allow users to search by name or zip code.

Privacy advocates challenge the practice of making sex offender information available—especially online. They have cited problems such as the harassment of sex offenders, the harassment of innocent people who happen to have bought a sex offender's home, and the fact that such exposure may publicly identify victims of sexual abuse (such as when the offender is a parent).

Information about inmates is also available on public record. Information about inmates can include name, sex, date of birth, race/ethnicity, custody status, housing/releasing facility, date received, date released, county of commitment, and a description of the crime(s).

Depending upon the case, anyone can request a court record in the court clerk's office. The office of the court clerk maintains a file of all civil and criminal cases, including the various filings in the case and the parties involved. Like arrest records, not all states provide court records online and not all court records, particularly criminal court records, are accessible to the public in any form. Some states post lists of criminals online, to the chagrin of privacy rights groups that argue that easy access to this information makes it more difficult for convicted felons to reenter society.

Property Holdings

Real estate records are also accessible to the general public. When you purchase a home or other real estate, a record of the transaction is made by the county assessor and the county recorder. The files about your property include information about:

- ▸ the location of the property
- ▸ your name and address
- ▸ the name(s) of the previous owner(s)
- ▸ date of sale
- ▸ description of the property
- ▸ approximate value of the real estate holding

Like many other public records, these files are increasingly made available on the Internet by county government agencies and by information brokers.

To protect the privacy of your real estate records:

✳ **Set up a trust.** If it is important to you that your name is not associated with the purchase of a property, you might consider asking your attorney to open a trust. A trust designates another representative, such as a bank or trust company, as the name on the deed and other real estate documents, although you still own the property.

See chapter 8, "Your Home," for further details on privacy and your property.

Foreclosures

If a bank forecloses on your home, a notice of action and foreclosure sale dates become a part of the public record. You have little privacy if your lender forecloses on your property. The foreclosure announcement is listed at the county courthouse, in your local newspaper, and, increasingly, online. Information brokers commonly sell listings of foreclosures and even properties that may become foreclosures. The foreclosure announcement may include information about foreclosure numbers, owner and/or grantor names, attorney names, and legal addresses of the properties to be foreclosed.

Bankruptcies

If you have filed for bankruptcy, you have little privacy. Bankruptcy information usually stays on your court records for ten years as public record. (See chapter 3, "Your Credit," for information on bankruptcy and your credit report.) The bankruptcy information in the record may include:

- Name, address, social security number
- Answers to official questions and intentions regarding the disposition of assets and liabilities
- Lists of all assets owned; liens, if any, including real estate; personal property, contingency claims; potential causes of action; rights owned; ownership interests in partnerships and corporations; and contingency claims to property
- Docket information, hearing schedules, deadlines, motions filed against debtors, answers filed by debtors, and reaffirmation agreements
- Common court orders appearing in files, including dismissals, conversions, reaffirmations, motions to lift stay, modifications, confirmations, and discharge

Privacy advocates have argued that the personal information contained in public records on bankruptcy is the most vulnerable to identity theft. More than other public records, information about bankruptcy contains sensitive data such as social security numbers, financial information, credit information, income, and other details that may be a treasure trove for thieves. Moreover, privacy advocates argue that the commercial sale of such information by the government may constitute violations of the Fair Credit Reporting Act (see chapter 4, "Your Credit").

Protecting Your Most Personal Documents

Whether you like it or not, many different entities, including marketers, credit agencies, prospective employers, government agencies, the press, private investigators, and others may access your information in the public record. If these groups are accessing your personal information and possibly judging you on it, it's a good idea to review your documents yourself to ensure their accuracy. Remember that the data that becomes part of a record is often subject to human error. The best protection is to be sure you understand what is contained in your files and that the information is accurate. Follow these easy and practical tips as a first and crucial step toward guarding your privacy:

✳ **Locate your important documents.** If you are like most people, you'll need to retrieve your documents from their hiding places throughout your home. Use the list below to identify these essential personal documents. If you cannot locate certain documents, or you need to replace some documents, you can use the helpful hints, tips, and Web links provided above in this chapter to access the public records to get your own information.

✳ **Read your documents.** Are the dates correct? Is your address correct? Crucially, are the details correct? Take immediate steps to correct any inaccurate information in your public record. If information is wrong in your files, it will be wrong in the public files, and the repercussions of any errors may be very serious, even rejection for a mortgage or a job.

✳ **File your documents.** If you do not already have your own system to file and store your documents, follow these suggestions:

Find or purchase a legal-size file folder at any office supply store. Within the file folder, label individual files with the titles indicated below. Use the list below as a guide for the types of documents that should go in each file. Your filing system will be beneficial in your day-to-day life and essential in the event of an emergency.

Essential Documents
- ▸ Social security card and statement
- ▸ Driver's license and record
- ▸ Passport

Official Certificates
- ▸ Birth certificate(s)
- ▸ Death certificate(s) of family members
- ▸ Marriage certificate(s)
- ▸ Divorce certificate(s)

Government-Related Documents
- ▸ Military records
- ▸ Civilian records
- ▸ Citizenship/Immigration records

- ▶ Jury records
- ▶ Voting records

Real Estate Records
- ▶ Closing documents
- ▶ Foreclosure records

Miscellaneous Records
- ▶ Arrest records
- ▶ Court records

> Marketers, credit agencies, prospective employers, government agencies, the press, private investigators, and others may access your information in the public record.

This list is not exhaustive. Your personal documents may contain other documents that are important to you, such as any contracts you have signed, banking information, or any other record that isn't in the public record but is necessary to protect.

✳ **Store your documents.** Store the folder containing your original documents in a safe place, such as a locked fireproof file cabinet or a safety deposit box. You may want to keep a copy of the documents in at least one other safe place: (1) in your safety deposit box; (2) with your personal or family attorney; or (3) in another safe place in the house. Identify the location of the original and the copies on a separate checklist that is also kept securely.

THE BOTTOM LINE

- ▶ Even your most personal documents are public and accessible to others. The personal information about you that is contained in public records has never been easier for others to access.
- ▶ Be cautious about revealing personal information without being sure how it will be used and whether it will be shared. Be extra cautious about disclosing your social security number.
- ▶ You may not be able to escape your past. Accept it and be prepared to explain it if necessary, for example, in a job interview. Assume your prospective employer, landlord, or creditor has done a background check on you in the public record.

▶ Get organized. Develop a system to organize, manage, and protect your most important personal documents and information. Do not delay in gathering your most important personal documents and keeping them in a safe place. You will immediately see the benefits and enjoy the peace of mind.

Your Identity

You open your credit card bill and discover thousands of dollars in charges for diamonds and Rolex watches that you never purchased.

A collection agency repeatedly calls and sends you letters to collect on an account for tens of thousands of dollars of new furniture. The problem? You didn't buy any Louis XIV chairs or antique canopy beds. In fact, your house contains the same furniture you had when you moved into it ten years ago.

You paid off the mortgage on the house you've lived in for a decade. With a little spare cash, you take off for a long vacation in the Bahamas. When you return in the spring you are horrified to dis-

cover that your house has been sold. Worse, as you try to sort out the problem, you are forced to live out of a hotel room.

You receive a congratulatory letter informing you that you have been approved for a $10,000 line of credit. The credit is being offered to you by a bank that you have never heard of and in a city you have never visited.

Did you know there are thousands of people who want to be you? Don't be too flattered. To be more accurate, there are thousands of people who want to steal everything you have to your name: your house, your credit cards, your bank account, and your good reputation.

Identity theft is among the worst invasions of privacy possible. An identity thief steals various pieces of your personal information, such as your social security number, your driver's license, or your credit card, and then uses this personal information to commit fraud and theft in your name. By impersonating you, identity thieves can use your name to request credit, take out loans, withdraw funds from your bank account, purchase a car, sell your house and pocket the proceeds, and much worse. In the worst cases of identity theft, you can be arrested for crimes you did not commit, fired from jobs for acts you had nothing to do with, rejected for educational loans you need to complete your studies, and rejected for the mortgage you need to buy the dream house for which you've been saving all your working life. If you are the victim of this crime, once you discover it, you are left to pick up the pieces—such as clearing your financial and credit troubles and sometimes restoring your personal reputation.

Take what happened to Eldrick T. Woods. Anthony Taylor of Sacramento stole Eldrick's identity by stealing Eldrick's social security number, falsely obtaining a driver's license in Eldrick's name, and then applying for and receiving credit cards in Eldrick's name. With Eldrick's credit card in hand, Taylor went on a year-long shopping spree, purchasing more than $17,000 in television sets, VCRs, furniture, and other items. He stored the purchases in a rented locker. He even rented a moving truck to transport his goods around. Taylor ultimately was caught, convicted, and sentenced to jail in California. How did the police finally put an end to Taylor's shopping exploits? Well, things got a little suspicious when Taylor attempted to buy a used luxury car.

The problem was that Eldrick T. Woods is really Tiger Woods, the world's most famous golfer. It was a little difficult for the car dealer to believe that Tiger Woods wanted to buy a used car, especially given that the Buick car company was among the golfer's many multimillion-dollar endorsements.

Other celebrities, and wealthy people on the Forbes 400 list, including Ted Turner, Oprah Winfrey, and Steven Spielberg, have had their identities stolen. But identity theft doesn't happen just to celebrities; the fact is, it's likely to happen to you. Identity theft is so rampant today that the question is no longer *if* you will become a victim, but *when* you will become a victim.

> **Identity theft is so rampant today that it is no longer *if* you will become a victim, but *when* you will become a victim.**

Identity theft is not only the fastest growing crime in the United States, but also the leading consumer fraud complaint in the country. No organization knows the exact number of identity thefts that occur each year or the total impact of the crime, in part because many people either do not understand that they have fallen victim or do not report the crime. According to the Federal Trade Commission (FTC), there were approximately 9.9 million victims of identity theft in 2003 alone, and identity theft complaints were up 53 percent in 2002 over 2001. This crime costs consumers huge amounts of time and money. In 2002 alone, consumers spent almost $5 billion and 300 million hours trying to resolve the aggravations related to identity theft. Business spent upward of $48 billion annually. In the aggregate, the Federal Trade Commission estimates that identity theft costs America approximately $53 billion each year—and the numbers are rising.

How to Reduce Your Chances of Being a Victim

One Saturday evening, Chris went out to run a few errands and get some cash to pay the babysitter. He went to his local ATM, where he discovered that his checking account was frozen and overdrawn by $750. He tried to get a cash advance on his credit card, but the ATM denied the transaction. Because it was a weekend and the bank was closed, Chris was cashless. He and his wife had to cancel their night

out. On Monday morning, Chris immediately went to the bank to re-
solve the situation. It didn't take long to discover several clearly
forged checks posted against his account. When he tried to tem-
porarily resolve the situation by moving funds from his money market
account, he discovered that the money market
account had also vanished, and with it $6,000
he been saving toward his son's college tuition.
This was just the beginning of Chris's problems.

> To inflict the most
> damage, identity thieves
> must get a hold of your
> most sensitive documents,
> such as your social
> security number, your
> driver's license, and
> your credit card.

Amos Price helped his daughter buy a house.
In the normal course of business, he shared his
financial information with his mortgage broker
who, in turn, used Price's good credit to ob-
tain a mortgage to buy a $340,000 house. After the identity thief
stopped making mortgage payments, the mortgage lender tracked
down Price to pressure him for payments. Even after the crime was
realized, Price has damaged credit and health problems due to the
aggravation. According to the financial research firm Toer Group, al-
most ten thousand identity theft victims had home loans—totaling
about $300 million—taken out in their names in 2002.

What can you do to ward off identity thieves? The bad news is that you
cannot completely prevent identity theft from happening to you, much in the
way that you cannot prevent someone from breaking into your home even if
you use an alarm and put bars on the windows. The good news is that you can
significantly reduce the likelihood of this crime happening to you by following some practical advice.

To inflict the most damage, identity thieves must get a hold of your most
sensitive documents, such as your social security number, your driver's
license, or your credit card. Consider how often your social security number is
used in your daily life. You need your social security number to access your
medical records, health insurance accounts, bank accounts, university records,
and much more. With these items in hand, an identity thief is like a kid in a
candy store. With your social security number alone, think of how an identity
thief could theoretically ruin your life the next time you're on vacation:

1. Steal a social security number from a health insurance card, credit header, social security card, or other source
2. Use the social security number to order your credit report online to find out the address of your house and whether you have a mortgage
3. Use the social security number to open a false bank account in your name
4. Use the information described above to apply for a credit card in your name and have the bills sent to a P.O. box or other address
5. Use all the information described above to remortgage your house in your name and keep any cash associated with the refinancing

Your vulnerability to identity theft depends upon how you lead your life. The focus of your efforts is to minimize a thief's access to your personal information, reduce the amount of information a thief can obtain if he or she accesses your personal information, and ensure that you will be made aware of the crime as soon as possible in the event that you are a victim of identity theft.

Because there are so many ways to reduce your exposure to identity theft, this section organizes identity theft protection tips into three categories: top-priority, very important, and important.

Top-Priority Steps

Sheila received a call from the local police department informing her that someone had made a fake driver's license in her name. She wondered how the identity thief got a hold of her personal information. Sheila later remembered that she had offered her license as identification when she applied for a job at a large drugstore chain. She learned that after the chain completed its hiring, an employee at the chain tossed all the old job applications into the trash without shredding them first. Sheila's identity thief did some old-fashioned Dumpster-diving for some valuable information, including Sheila's personal data.

No matter how little time you have, these top-priority tips are crucial. They should help protect you from identity theft or limit the damage inflicted by identity thieves.

✳ **Order your credit report and monitor it annually.** Did you know that even if you check your credit card statement every month, and even if every line item seems legitimate, you still can be a victim of credit card fraud? Thieves are tricky: they apply for credit cards in your name, but they have billing statements mailed to an address that is different than your home address, such as a post office box. Unless you check your credit report, you may never know that a thief has applied for and received a credit card in your name. Any new credit card or credit account ultimately appears on your credit report, so you can check whether new accounts are legitimate. You cannot rely on anyone else to perform this task because you are the only person who would know if a particular card or line of credit is yours. That is the reason why *you must monitor your credit report.*

Ordering your credit report and reviewing it thoroughly is your first line of defense in resolving a problem before a thief inflicts even greater financial ruin. Periodic monitoring enables you to correct a problem on your timetable. As discussed in chapter 4, "Your Credit," your credit report identifies all your accounts, including your credit cards, bank loans, mortgages, and any other lines of credit. If you are monitoring your report, you will immediately be able to identify any fraud, including any account you did not open or spending you did not authorize.

Order a copy of your credit report from all three major credit bureaus at least once per year. The three bureaus are Equifax, Experian, and TransUnion. To order your report, contact the bureaus directly or go to their respective websites. (See credit bureaus in "Resources.")

Given the sensitive information in your credit report (see chapter 4, "Your Credit"), you should use extra caution when ordering your credit report online. Refer to chapter 7, "Your Computer and the Internet," when ordering any item online.

✳ **Protect your social security number.** Your social security number is the most important piece of personal information to identity thieves. They can obtain your social security number in many mischievous ways, such as stealing your wallet or purse to get your social security card; stealing or diverting your mail; scouring the Web for unsecured database pages; masquerading as an employer, landlord, or someone else with legitimate access to your social security number; and stealing from or establishing contacts at institutions like schools, banks, and workplaces. Do whatever you can to limit an identity thief's access to your social security number. For example:

▸ Do not place your social security card in your wallet or purse.

▸ Give your social security number only when it is required, and, if possible, request to use other pieces of identifying information instead.

▸ If your driver's license number (or other identification) is the same as your social security number, request to change your driver's license number.

> **Your social security number is the most important piece of personal information to identity thieves.**

▸ Do not have your social security number printed on your personal checks.

▸ Leave your actual social security card in a secure place, as discussed in chapter 2.

✳ **Be vigilant with your wallet or purse.** The most common way for a thief to steal your identity is for the thief to steal your wallet or purse. To that end, remember to:

▸ Never leave your purse or wallet unattended in public places.

▸ Be especially careful in the workplace; keep your purse or wallet in a safe place such as a locked cabinet.

▸ Do not leave your purse or wallet in open view, even in your locked car.

▸ Limit the identification information (such as social security card, birth certificate, or passport) and the number of credit, debit, or ATM cards that you carry in your wallet or purse to what you actually need. This way, if your purse or wallet is stolen, you can limit the amount of damage and financial ruin a thief can inflict upon you.

Very Important Steps

A Los Angeles man discovered his mail had been stolen when he began receiving late notices from his utility and credit card companies. Then a collection company called him about his overdue ac-

count for $8,000 of Dell Computer equipment. An identity thief had obtained the man's social security number from a piece of mail containing his student loan payment. With this information in hand, the thief was able to wreak considerable damage by opening credit accounts with Dell, Sears, and other stores. The embarrassed victim notes, "I have been fighting this for years."

The steps to preventing identity theft aren't only for the paranoid. A significant number of identity thefts happen when victims are careless about their mail (including their junk mail), their passwords, and their personal identification numbers. Never underestimate how much information a thief can secure by old-fashioned Dumpster-diving.

✳ **Guard your mail.** Your mail is a target for identity thieves. Thieves have been known to rifle through mail to steal information they can use to commit identity theft. For example, they will take one of the many pre-approved credit offers you receive in the mail and then submit applications in your name but with the bills diverted to a different address. This diversion makes you completely unaware of the credit card that has been opened in your name. What to do to protect your mail? Consider the following:

▸ Make sure your mailbox is locked, even if you have to install a lockbox.
▸ Remove your mail from your mailbox every day.
▸ If you cannot pick up your mail for an extended period (such as vacation), call the U.S. Postal Service at 800/275-8777 to request a vacation hold. The Postal Service will hold your mail at your local post office until you can pick it up or return home to receive it.
▸ Deposit your outgoing mail in post office collection boxes or at your local post office, rather than in an unsecured mailbox.

✳ **Shred your credit card receipts and other important information.** To counteract the dangers of Dumpster-divers, you should shred or destroy any sensitive information such as credit card receipts, utility bills, copies of credit applications, insurance forms, medical forms, financial statements, checks and bank statements, expired charge cards, and any credit offers (especially those pre-approved credit card offers) you receive in the mail before tossing them into the garbage.

Identity thieves will pick through your trash or the recycling bins of companies that accept credit cards (such as restaurants and stores) in an effort to find receipts that patrons discard on their way out. Since you can't control how companies discard their trash, you need to take care of your own garbage. For example, when you pay with a credit card for your dinner or go shopping, tear your receipt into tiny pieces or store the receipt in a safe place. As discussed later in this chapter as well as in chapter 4, "Your Credit," a new identity theft law that went into effect on January 1, 2004 requires merchants to truncate your credit card number on receipts, but you shouldn't take any chances.

✳ **Protect your passwords and personal identification numbers (PINs).** If possible, memorize your most frequently used passwords and PINs so you do not have to write them down. If you have to write them down, do not carry any record or paper containing those passwords or PINs in your purse or wallet. Keep this information in a secure place. Make sure no one is watching when you enter your PIN or password at an ATM by covering the keyboard the best you can. There have been cases of thieves using binoculars or cameras to zoom in on your fingers as you enter your pin code. (See chapter 5, "Your Money," for other tips on how to protect your PIN.)

✳ **Be very cautious about the information you release.** You must be particularly cautious about giving any credit card, bank, or social security information to anyone by telephone, mail, or the Internet, unless you are sure that the recipient is trustworthy and legitimate or unless you have initiated the contact by mail or going to the particular website.

✳ **Watch out for scams.** Identity thieves often create scams to entice you to release information (see page 62). They may also pose as representatives of banks, Internet service providers (ISPs), and government agencies to get you to reveal your important personal information. If you are unsure of a caller's identity, take a proactive approach by writing down the caller's phone number and returning the call, or e-mail the company directly. Ask probing questions about how the information will be used, whether it is secure, the extent to which it will be shared with others, and how the information will be discarded.

Important Steps

A twenty-four-year-old identity thief applied for sixty-one credit cards under false names; forty-five of the applications were granted. Although some of the identities were fictitious, many of them were real people the perpetrator had known from her school days and whose credit she subsequently destroyed. She even wrongly named one of the victims as her co-offender and mentor in the frauds.

For more peace of mind, consider these additional tips to further reduce your chances of being a victim of identity theft. Most of these steps involve protection of your credit card account. Considering that more than 150 to 200 million credit cards are issued in North America every year, it's no surprise that identity thieves are so successful.

✳ **Protect your banking and credit accounts.** It may be common sense, but you are not likely alone in forgetting to take these basic steps to protect your bank accounts:

- ▸ Reconcile your checking and savings accounts as well as your monthly credit card statements in a timely fashion.
- ▸ Destroy all checks immediately after you close a checking account.
- ▸ Consider picking up any new checks at your bank, instead of having them mailed to you at your home address.
- ▸ Keep a list of all your credit accounts and bank accounts (including account numbers, expiration dates, and telephone numbers of customer service and fraud departments) in a secure place so you can quickly call the issuers to inform them about missing or stolen cards.

▶ Pay attention to billing cycles. A missing credit card bill could mean an identity thief has taken over your account and changed your billing address, rendering you unaware that you are a victim of identity theft. If you do not receive your bills at the usual time, follow up with the company immediately.

✳ **Limit the number of credit cards you have.** How many credit cards does your family have? The average American household has seven to ten credit cards. Reducing the number of credit cards you have reduces the chances that thieves can obtain one of your cards (as a bonus, it probably also makes good financial sense!). If you have an inactive account or credit card, close it. Why give a thief the ability to use an account that you don't use?

✳ **Review all utility and subscription bills.** Make sure the charges are yours.

✳ **Use passwords on your credit accounts.** Using passwords makes it more difficult for identity thieves to take over your accounts. Follow these password tips:

▶ Do not use common passwords like pet names, birthdays, or the word "password."

▶ Avoid using personally identifying information (like your mother's maiden name, your birth date, your social security number, your phone number, consecutive numbers or letters) as your password or PINs. Many forms and banks request your mother's maiden name as a security password, but they do not require that you use this word. For safety's sake, use a different password. Of course, if you do so, make sure you remember that password!

✳ **Protect your personal information at home.** Keep your documents in a secure place in your home. This is particularly important if you have roommates, employ help, or have service work done in your home. See chapter 2, "Your Personal Information and the Public Record," for tips on how to keep your documents safe and secure.

IDENTITY THEFT SCAMS

Be on the alert for scams that seek any personal information from you, especially on the Internet. Internet fraud alone cost American consumers almost $200 million in 2003, with victims losing an average of $195. The total loss to fraud was more than $437 million, about $228 per victim.

Remember, identity thieves are sneaky. They will stoop to any level, including sending announcements of fake contests that offer enticing prizes or official-looking memos that scare you into parting with your information. Many Internet scams contained misspelled words and grammatically incorrect phrases, so be on the lookout for these. In particular, look out for ploys to get you to provide your personal information on online forms. Also known as *phishing,* this is a successful tactic that scammers use to get your bank account numbers, credit card numbers, social security number, and other information. All scams have one common goal: to extract sensitive personal information from you. Some popular scams include:

The "We Need You to Update Your Account" Scam

Dear Customer: We have recently updated our system. In an attempt to keep our database current, we need you to return to our website and update your credit card information. Please click on the link below and update your information.

Be very, very careful if you get a message like the one above. Beginning in 2003, thousands of PayPal's customers received an e-mail requesting that they update their accounts. The e-mail looked like an official PayPal communiqué and had an urgent message regarding maintenance of the account. Customers were asked to enter sensitive information into an online form. Customers of eBay, Bank of America, Wells Fargo, the Internal Revenue Service (IRS), and America Online (AOL) have also been the recipients of such scams.

Different versions of this "phishing" scam include:

▶ "Account Maintenance." This e-mail tells you the company is performing basic maintenance and your account has been randomly selected for verification of contact information.

- ▶ "Account Verification." This e-mail tells you your account has been suspended temporarily since the company is unable to verify your account information. The e-mail closes with the following: "If you do not verify this information within X days, your account will be permanently closed."
- ▶ "New Terms of Service." This e-mail mentions new terms of service and asks you to click the link below to read the terms. Once you click the link, it asks you for your login and password.
- ▶ "Paypal.com Credit Card Application." This e-mail seems to come from eBay or PayPal and lists full information and rates about available credit cards. The e-mail offers you a link to a site where you can fill out an application. Of the complaints received by the FTC in 2003, auction-related scams comprised the largest number of Internet-related fraud complaints, accounting for 48 percent of the total.

The "Help Me Get My Money Out of My Country and I Will Give You Some of It" Scam

I am an accountant with CITIZEN INTERNTIONAL BANK, My name is Mr Hanny kuta a Banker . . . On 30 JAN 2000, my client, his wife, and their three children were involved in the the Kenya Airways flight with registration number 5Y-BEN which departed from Nairobi to destination Lagos and they all family died in this fatal aircrash on 30 JAN 2000 . . . I have contacted you to assist in repatriating the money and property left behind by my client before they get confiscated or declared unserviceable by the bank where these huge deposits were lodged. . . .

If you use e-mail, you likely have received a horribly misspelled and grammatically incorrect e-mail from a foreign person who is trying to get a large sum of money out of his or her country. These so-called wealthy foreigners—including Mobutu's widowed wife in the Congo, Saddam Hussein's former bodyguards in Iraq, and Nigerian businessmen—say they will give you millions of dollars for helping them. Many of these letters ask you to simply give them your bank account information so that they can "make a deposit." No matter how tragic or heartbreaking the story, you must not respond to e-mails like the ones above—and most, of all, never give your bank account information to them. Clearly, these e-mails are being sent by devious scam artists posing as known or sympathetic foreigners.

The "Patriot Act" Scam

Department of Homeland Security Director Tom Ridge has advised the FDIC to suspend all deposit insurance on your bank account because of suspected violations of the USA Patriot Act. All deposit insurance will be suspended until you can verify your identity. Click on the link below to verify your identity.

Invoking the authority of the Patriot Act, this bank account scam requires you to send all your personal information to an "official website" that will verify your identity to unlock your bank account and reinstate your deposit insurance. The bank scam has many incarnations, including one sent by post that included fake IRS forms, which you are asked to fill out and fax to an enclosed fax number.

The Law on Identity Theft

Robert Christopher Lawrence of Laurel, Maryland, fraudulently obtained and used credit cards by using the personal information, such as dates of birth and social security numbers, of patients and employees of Kaiser Permanente, where he worked as a phlebotomist. Lawrence purposely chose to use the personal information of individuals whose names were similar to his. On the applications for the credit cards Lawrence listed his home address or the address of the house next door to his, and on some of the applications he used his home or work phone number. He was sentenced to thirty-three months imprisonment, to be followed by three years of supervised release, during which he had to pay restitution of $78,672.67.

Recognizing the consequences of identity theft, Congress has passed several laws to deter potential identity thieves. The Identity Theft and Assumption Deterrence Act makes it a crime under federal law or a felony under state or local law to use someone else's personal identification—which is broadly interpreted to include name, social security number, cellular telephone, or electronic serial number. Several agencies, including the U.S. Secret Service, the FBI, the U.S. Postal Inspection Service, and the Social Security Administration's Office of the Inspector General, may investigate and bring actions under this law. If prosecuted, an identity thief can be sentenced to up to fifteen years of imprisonment and a fine, and

> If prosecuted, an identity thief can be sentenced to up to fifteen years of imprisonment and a fine, and may forfeit any personal property used to commit the crime.

may forfeit any personal property used to commit the crime. Moreover, some identity theft schemes may lead to violations of other statutes, such as those pertaining to credit card fraud, computer fraud, mail fraud, wire fraud, financial institution fraud, or social security fraud. The crime may thus encompass other felonies and can lead to even more time in jail, more fines, and criminal forfeiture.

Congress also overhauled the credit laws with the passage of the Fair and Accurate Credit Transaction Act of 2003. When fully enforced at the end of 2004, this act will ultimately protect you in the following ways:

- ▸ Provides you with one free credit report per year from each of the three credit bureaus
- ▸ Gives you notification if merchants and lenders report missed payments to credit bureaus, thereby making you aware of identity theft possibly committed against you much sooner than ever before
- ▸ Restricts credit bureaus from sharing your sensitive personal information with businesses
- ▸ Establishes a nationwide system for placing fraud alerts on your credit file, including a process for overseas military personnel to place special alerts on their files
- ▸ Requires merchants to omit all but the last five digits of your credit card number from credit card receipts.

This act sets national standards for identity theft that preempt most state laws. Some states that have already passed laws related to identity theft may now consider passing tougher laws in this area. States must also decide criminal penalties for identity thieves and limits on sharing social security numbers among companies. Further, identity theft crimes may also be actionable under other state laws. Contact your state attorney general's office or local consumer protection agency or visit the FTC website—www.ftc.gov—to learn more about other laws related to identity theft. Read chapter 4, "Your Credit," to learn more details.

What to Do if You Are a Victim

Ain Jones lost her wallet. During the months that followed her loss, she watched her car insurance double in price, had her driver's license usurped, had warrants issued for her arrest for crimes that she did not commit, and had to pay a $300 court fine. Fraud warnings and notices appeared on every digital record of her person, from credit bureaus to the motor vehicle agencies. As a result of these events, Ain carries a "golden file" with her at all times. The file contains copies of her birth certificate, court documents, letters from her lawyer, and other paperwork she needs to prove she is who she claims to be. "I am still me. But I still have to prove I am me," she says.

Even if you take all the right precautions, you still can be a victim of identity theft. All it takes is a stolen pocketbook, a credit card forgotten at the cash register, a dropped receipt. One Chicago schoolteacher and artist endured such hardships after a pickpocket stole her wallet. As soon as she realized her wallet had been stolen, she reported the loss, put a stop on her checking accounts, and notified her credit card companies. Despite these precautions, the thief was able to get a driver's license in the teacher's name, use the license to obtain a $3,200 loan from her credit union, and then use the loan as a down payment on a $24,000 Toyota. The thief also withdrew more than $36,000 from the teacher's checking and money market accounts and charged more than $8,000 on her credit cards. Ultimately, the teacher was not financially liable for the purchases made in her name, but she endured a living nightmare while she cleaned up the mess.

The most worrisome part of identity theft is that victims typically have no idea they have been victimized. In many cases, victims may not know

SHOULD YOU BUY IDENTITY THEFT INSURANCE?

Many companies offer insurance or similar products that claim to protect you against the costs associated with resolving an identity theft case. There are a number of different insurance products, so make sure you understand what you are buying beforehand. For example, some of these offerings may be freestanding policies, while others may be riders to your existing homeowner's or renter's insurance. In addition, coverage levels run the gamut from $5,000 to $30,000 and more, and the benefits vary but do not typically provide for fraudulent credit card charges. Those charges must be resolved with your credit card company.

Most plans are not formal insurance policies but offer you assistance if you are victimized—by sending you identity theft information, connecting you with an identity theft specialist who can provide advice, finding an attorney for you, if needed, and paying the attorney's legal fees up to a certain dollar amount. Some policies also include reimbursement for other costs incurred such as mailing or loan reapplication costs. Finally, because of the enormous amount of time it takes to straighten out all the problems arising from having your identity stolen (an average of six hundred hours of making phone calls, writing letters, and preparing documentation often over a period of years), some policies reimburse you up to a certain cap for lost wages from taking time off from work.

Today, almost all insurance companies offer some type of identity theft insurance. Some credit issuers such as Citibank market credit cards with identity theft protection features. Identity theft insurance certainly can offset the costly burden associated with regaining your good name and reputation. But even if you take out a policy, you still have to spend the time talking to and interacting directly with creditors, credit card companies, banks, and others if your identity is stolen. Unfortunately, there is no insurance policy that will take over that task for you.

about the crime for a year or longer. A thief may change the mailing address on a particular credit account so you will not see or receive the bills or statements. As you lead your normal day-to-day life, trying to make an honest living and keeping your head above water, an identity thief may be applying for credit cards, buying thousands of dollars of merchandise, taking out loans, and applying for a cellular service in your name. The thief may also be committing crimes for which the police want you and, should you get pulled over for a minor traffic infraction, may arrest you.

> The most worrisome part of identity theft is that victims typically have no idea they have been victimized. In many cases, victims may not know about the crime for a year or longer.

If you are a victim of identity theft, you need to work as quickly and as methodically as possible to resolve the situation. The longer you delay in resolving your situation, the longer the identity theft perpetuates itself, and the more disastrous the situation may be for you. Unfortunately, the burden of proof is on you. Until you can prove that you are a victim, credit institutions will think you are just another deadbeat trying to avoid paying your bills. The consequences of identity theft may linger for years, primarily because solving each case takes a long time. And each one is so complicated, depending upon the type of theft, whether the thief sold or passed your information on to other thieves, whether the thief is caught, and how many problems you face correcting your credit report. Moreover, many victims have to wait for legal proceedings to conclude (*if* the thief was caught). Beyond the financial and credit implications, you should be prepared for a time-consuming and expensive ordeal.

As mentioned above, the Fair and Accurate Credit Transactions Act of 2003 provides protections for consumers, but it does not require full compliance until the end of 2004. If you are a victim of identity theft, the act gives you more assistance to resolve your situation. Nevertheless, given its recent enactment, you still should follow these steps to remedy the situation:

✳ **Place a fraud alert on your account.** A fraud alert is a notice that a credit bureau attaches to your credit report. When anyone, including you, seeks to establish a credit account by getting a new credit card, car loan, cell phone, and so on, the lender will contact you by phone to confirm you want to open the new account. If you cannot be reached, the new account will not be opened. As soon as one credit bureau confirms your fraud alert, the other two credit bureaus will receive the request and automatically place fraud alerts on your credit report. Unfortunately, this step does not completely solve the problem. Even if you place a fraud alert on your account, you still should monitor your credit report for any new credit accounts or inquiries you have not authorized. Moreover, fraud alerts monitor only new credit accounts and do not affect your current credit cards, mortgages, or checking accounts. If you are a resident of California, you can also apply to freeze your credit under a new law called California SB 168, which enables you to freeze all access to your credit file.

Placing a fraud alert on your account is a routine process for a credit bureau. Within a day of your telephone call to any of three credit bureaus to request a fraud alert, an alert will be placed on your credit file at all three major credit bureaus because the request for a fraud alert is automatically sent to the other bureaus. Contact Equifax, Experian, or TransUnion to place a fraud alert on your credit file (see "Resources").

Before you decide to place a fraud alert on your account, be prepared to be inconvenienced. If you want to open a new credit account, you must be available at either your work phone or home phone to approve the credit account, or the opening of any new account will be delayed. Moreover, if you are not reachable by phone, the lender will likely refuse to open the credit account. Creditors are not legally required to call you, so opening a particular account may be more difficult than you like. You also will not receive any pre-approved credit offers in the mail for up to two years, but that may not necessarily be a bad thing

✳ **Review your credit report.** Once you place a fraud alert on your account, each of the three bureaus will send a credit report. Make sure you review each of the credit reports from the three major credit bureaus as soon as you receive them. As explained in chapter 4, "Your Credit," your credit report will show any new accounts that have been opened in your name, any new credit inquiries that might have been made by someone trying to open accounts in your name, or any debts that are not yours. Bring any inaccuracies, whether due to fraud or error, to the attention of the credit bureaus as soon as possible. Even after you correct your reports, continue to monitor them to ensure that new fraudulent activity does not occur.

> In 2002 alone, consumers spent 297 million hours resolving problems related to identity theft, and the average consumer spent up to 600 hours making numerous phone calls and mailing tons of letters in connection with that effort.

✳ **File a police report.** A police report is helpful for two reasons: as an important document to send to creditors to prove that you are a victim of identity theft, and as further proof to dispute fraudulent charges. The police report should be sent to each of the three bureaus so they may block the information you are disputing in your credit reports. By law, the credit bureaus may remove the block if they believe it was wrongly placed. To file a report, go to your local police precinct and report what happened to you as an identity theft crime. It is important to report the crime in person, because the police sometimes mark a different crime on the report, in which case you won't have the proof to show that you have been a victim of identity theft. After the report is completed, make sure to get a copy of it for your files, or record the report number if you cannot get a copy of the report. To facilitate the process of filing the police report, you should show the police as much supporting documentation as possible, including collection letters, credit reports, an ID theft affidavit, and any other evidence of the identity theft. The new identity theft law forces businesses to give you any records related to fraudulent charges when you give them your police report.

✳ **Report the theft to the Federal Trade Commission and file an ID theft affidavit.** You should report the theft to the FTC by filing a complaint using the information below. The FTC serves as a federal clearinghouse for complaints of identity theft. Your complaint is entered into a searchable database that is accessible to law enforcement agencies. Law enforcement agencies use complaints filed with the FTC to aggregate cases, spot patterns, and track growth in identity theft. This information improves investigations: If there is a pattern of cases in a certain area, local authorities may give your case more attention. The FTC will provide you with an identity theft affidavit, which you can send to the credit bureaus and credit institutions to close any fraudulent accounts and debts that have been opened in your name.

THE VIRTUES OF BEING ORGANIZED

Victims of identity theft know that it takes hundreds of hours and thousands of dollars to resolve the problems associated with the theft. In 2002 alone, consumers spent 297 million hours resolving problems related to identity theft, and the average consumer spent up to 600 hours making numerous phone calls and mailing tons of letters in connection with that effort. It can take many months, if not years, before you have restored your credit and financial health and fully regained your good name. To keep track of the myriad details involved in the process, you must be extra organized and keep detailed records of everything you do. Being organized and documenting your efforts will contribute to the successful resolution of your case. As you work to resolve your case, keep in mind the following tips:

- ▶ Keep detailed notes of every conversation you have, including the name of the person to whom you spoke, his or her title and company, and the date of the conversation.
- ▶ Follow up in writing (using certified mail and return receipt requested) with all people with whom you speak and maintain a copy of all letters and documents that you send.
- ▶ Maintain the originals of all documents, including police reports, company fraud forms, and notarized letters to and from creditors. If an institution requests a document, send only copies.
- ▶ Consider using the FTC sample chart to document your efforts at www.ftc.gov/bcp/conline/pubs/credit/idtheft.htm#intro
- ▶ Document the time and money you devote to resolving your identity theft case (in some cases, you may be reimbursed for these efforts, especially if you have identity theft insurance).

To file a complaint, contact the FTC:

By phone:
Toll-free 877/438-4338; TDD: 202/326-2502

By mail:
Identity Theft Clearinghouse
Federal Trade Commission
600 Pennsylvania Ave., NW
Washington, DC 20580

Online:
www.ftc.gov to print out the Online ID Theft Complaint Form

✳ **Contact credit institutions and close unauthorized credit accounts and/or resolve fraudulent charges.** You must close any accounts that have been opened without your authorization and dispute any charges that you did not personally undertake. Such accounts may include bank accounts, credit cards, mortgages, phone and other utility services, and other credit accounts. Unfortunately, the process for closing these accounts or disputing charges is neither routine nor consistent from company to company. As a first step, contact the fraud department at the institution that holds the credit account and ask them what they require in the way of proof or evidence to resolve the situation. The frustrating part of this step is that each institution may require slightly different supporting documentation. For example, it may require a completed ID theft affidavit, a police report, or its own fraud dispute form. After you resolve the problem, make sure you get a letter from the institution stating that they have closed the disputed accounts and have discharged you of any fraudulent debt. This letter should be kept with your other records.

In addition, if your credit, debit, or ATM card has been used without your permission, you should cancel the card immediately and then request a new card. You should also change your PIN or password before you use your new credit, debit, or ATM card. In the case of missing or stolen personal checks, you should simultaneously and immediately close your checking account and inform your bank that your checks have been stolen. In these cases, if you don't act quickly enough, you may not be able to recover some of your assets.

✳ **Contact other government agencies.** Depending on your individual case, you may need to contact other government agencies:

▶ Post Office: If you think an identity thief either has submitted a change-of-address form with the post office to redirect your mail, or has used the mail to commit frauds involving your identity, contact the local office of the Postal Inspection Service.

▶ Social Security Administration: If you suspect that your social security number is being fraudulently used, call the Social Security Administration at 800/269-0271 to report the fraud.

▶ Internal Revenue Service: If you suspect the improper use of identification information in connection with tax violations, call the Internal Revenue Service at 800/829-0433 to report the violations.

▶ Police and Law Enforcement Agencies: If you believe that the identity thief has committed crimes in your name, you should get in touch with the arresting or citing law enforcement agency. The procedure to correct your criminal record varies by state and county. A good place to start is the police department that originally arrested the person who stole your identity or the court that issued the warrant for your arrest.

Long-Term Consequences

A Norfolk, Virginia, resident had her purse stolen from her SUV while she was waiting in line at a local post office. She spent forty-five minutes on the phone with police, and then visited a government website for advice on what to do next. Although she managed to shut down all her personal accounts within hours, the thief wrote forty-five bad checks in her name, a situation she has spent months trying to rectify, "Not because [the information] was not available," she says, "but because as a small business owner, wife, homemaker, and mother of two teenage boys, there [are] just not enough hours in the day. That and it takes a little while to get over the fact you have been violated in a most personal way."

When Terri McDermott moved across the country for an exciting new job, she wasn't prepared for her new employer's news on her first day. The employer told Terri that the standard background check had turned up a nine-page criminal record that included forgery and burglary. Terri knew that she had not committed those crimes, but could not start work until she cleared her name.

In most cases, you will not be responsible for paying the bills that an identity thief has racked up in your name. However, you are still left with a precarious credit situation, and you must handle the emotional stress of regaining your good name. As you try to put your credit life back in order, you may also endure years of headaches in obtaining loans, credit cards, mortgages, apartment rentals, and jobs. The faster you discover the identity theft and react to correct the situation, the less damaging the consequences will be.

What are the financial consequences of identity theft? Chapter 5, "Your Money," specifically outlines your financial exposure, but here is the overview:

Credit Cards. If you report the loss of your credit card before it is used, the card issuer cannot hold you responsible for any unauthorized charges. If a thief uses your credit card before you report it missing, the most you will owe for unauthorized charges is $50 per card.

ATM and Debit Cards. You can be responsible for ATM and debit card charges if you fail to report unauthorized charges within a timely manner. Generally, the amount for which you are liable depends on how long it takes you to report the missing ATM or debit card. For example, if you report your ATM or debit card lost or stolen within two business days of discovering the loss or theft, your liability is limited to $50. If you wait more than sixty days before you report the loss or theft of your ATM or debit card, you can lose any money taken from your account after the end of the sixty days and before you report the card missing. The benefits of promptly reporting the loss of your ATM or debit card to your bank are clear.

Personal Checks. Your liability varies, but if you take appropriate and timely action to resolve the situation and notify your bank, you will likely not be held responsible for losses from forged checks. Unfortunately, no federal law caps your losses if someone steals your checks and forges your signature, so you need to rely on the laws in your state to protect you. Most states hold the bank responsible for losses from a forged check, provided you care for your account in a reasonable way and notify the bank in a timely manner that a check was lost or stolen. Act accordingly because an explicit rule does not exist.

> **Lightning can strike twice, and so can identity theft.**

Lightning can strike twice, and so can identity theft. Unfortunately, being a victim does not immunize you from a recurrence of identity theft. Even after you have reported the identity theft crime, you should continue to monitor your credit reports and other credit and financial accounts for several months. Keep alert for other signs of identity theft.

THE BOTTOM LINE

▶ Oprah knows best. Identity theft happened to Oprah Winfrey, and it can happen to you. Identity theft is rampant today, and it is only a matter of time before it happens to you.

▶ Give yourself some credit. The most effective way to stay on top of identity theft is to monitor your credit report. Order copies of your report at least once a year. Under the new federal credit laws, it won't cost you any money to get a copy from each of the bureaus once a year.

▶ Always be on guard. Identity thieves are devious, and they are always looking for ways to entice you to reveal sensitive and personal information. Expect to encounter scams, and think twice before you release your valuable information.

▶ Tick-tock. With identity theft, the clock is always ticking. The faster you discover identity theft, and the faster you react to resolve the problem, the less severe the consequences will be.

▶ Detail the details. To properly resolve identity theft, take detailed notes about everything you do and keep your notes and documents organized. Remember that it may take years to resolve identity theft.

Your Credit

"Somebody in Boise needs my help. Run a credit check."

You and your husband decide to move from San Francisco to Boston. You have two weeks before your new job starts, and you spend the time running errands and setting up your new life. You submit an application to rent an apartment in the Back Bay of Boston, lease a new BMW that you have been coveting, purchase a new cell phone with Verizon, and open a new charge account at Filene's department store. You didn't know it at the time, but your credit report recorded and detailed each of these actions. Three weeks later, your new boss casually asks you how your new BMW is riding.

Your credit report may be the single most important piece of personal information about you. If you are like most Americans, you may not even know what is contained in your credit report and how this report and its accompanying credit score can dramatically affect your life. Your credit report contains valuable personal information about you, including your social security number, home address, employer, your housing situation, all your credit accounts, and much more.

Your credit report also includes sensitive information that you probably want to protect. Ever been arrested? Ever filed for bankruptcy? Were you late in paying your Macy's bill last spring? If so, that information will show up on your credit report. You will be able to see it and so will your prospective employer, landlord, insurer, or anyone else who has access to the report.

> Employers, insurers, and landlords rely heavily on credit reports— and so do criminals.

All of this may make you nervous, but the national credit bureaus do serve a vital purpose in our country. Indeed, the development of the bureaus as central repositories to predict one's likelihood to repay any indebtness has enabled lenders to extend credit to the middle and lower classes to buy homes, cars, and receive credit cards. The great American dream of home ownership is furthered by the developments of these bureaus.

As a result, your credit report and credit information are more important but less secure today than they were five years ago. Employers, insurers, and landlords rely heavily on credit reports—and so do criminals. Identity thieves find a treasure trove of personal information in credit reports. Enhanced access to reports through networked systems and the Internet has resulted in more people getting a hold of your credit information without appropriate authorization, giving rise to crimes and other violations of your credit privacy.

How easy is it to steal credit information? At times, quite easy. Theft and privacy violations continue unabated despite greater consumer awareness, higher security concerns by credit bureaus, and new laws passed by Congress and the states to curb such abuses. Given the sensitive information in your credit report, you must take extra efforts to learn about your report and all the details in it as well as how to safeguard and restrict access to it.

Your Credit Report Is More Important Than You Think

Ronnie Rodgers is a self-employed architect and builder whose business rests on his good name and credit. He is especially careful to make all his payments on time: "I have all kinds of credit cards, and I've never been late on a credit card payment. I mean, I'm one of the best and most reliable borrowers around," he once boasted. So when the time came for Rodgers to apply for a loan, he was shocked to discover a $500 lien he couldn't account for on his credit report.

None of the department store managers in southern California wanted to hire Bronti Kelly, and he couldn't figure out why. Even though he had ten years of sales experience, he was either rejected for a position or fired after a few days on a job. Jobless, Kelly filed for bankruptcy and lost his home. Later he discovered that an identity thief had given authorities Kelly's personal information when arrested for shoplifting and other crimes. Every time potential employers pulled up Kelly's credit report as part of their routine background checks, they discovered a fraudulent criminal record that did not bode well for Kelly's future in sales.

If you have ever applied for a loan, you know that prospective lenders always review your credit history. You learned very quickly that your credit report, your credit score, and the likelihood of obtaining the loan at the rate you want are related. This is a reality: Your ability to obtain credit entirely depends on your credit report and your credit score.

But did you know that, due to the widespread use of credit information, your credit report and score affects your day-to-day life even more dramatically? Today, more and more companies—and not just credit card issuers and mortgage and automobile lenders—take a look at your credit report to assess you as a credit risk.

For example, did you know that approximately 90 percent of auto insurers use your credit score to determine not only whether to offer you insurance but also how much to charge you? Based on a combination of historical and statistical equations, auto insurers see a direct correlation between your credit history and score and the degree to which you are able to undertake risk. In other words, your credit score plays an important part in determining whether you are a potential risk to insure.

Potential employers also value this information. They examine your credit reports to assess your stability in the workplace. In the view of some employers, you are a more reliable and trustworthy employee if you have a track record of paying your bills on time and accumulating less debt. In addi-

> **Employers might rely on your credit report to learn important details about your life.**

tion, employers might rely on your credit report to learn other important details about your life. Credit reports reveal mundane information you are likely to be comfortable in revealing, such as your current employer or current address, and more sensitive personal information that you are unlikely to want to reveal, such as whether you have been sued or arrested, or if you have ever filed for bankruptcy.

The bottom line? Even if you are not in search of a mortgage for your dream home or an auto loan to finance your new BMW convertible, you must review and understand your credit report and score and ensure that you maintain accurate information in your credit report. Make sure that the people who legitimately access your credit information are seeing an accurate version of it, and that the people who shouldn't see it are prevented from doing so.

What's In Your Credit Report?

> When Barbara applied for a credit card, she expected that the application would be approved on the spot. After all, she and her husband had a consistent record of paying their bills on time, a strong credit record, and good jobs. But the application was turned down. The reason? Their adult son had a tendency to submit late payment to the same credit card company.

Your credit report indicates how much money you spend, also whether you pay your bills on time and even some of the places where you shop. Your report shows how many credit cards you have. It can reveal whether you have a mortgage on your house or financing on your car. From the various applications you submit for credit and loans, the credit bureaus also collect sensitive personal information about you, such as your address, your social security number, your employer, and more. So the next time you complete an application for a credit card—whether an American Express card, a Citibank Visa card, a Bloomingdale's retail card, or a United Airlines mileage card—you should remember that the information you provide to get that card is sent to a credit bureau. Moreover, a record of anyone you allow to access your credit report, including car dealers and landlords, will also be recorded in your report. And there is nothing you can do about it.

Your credit report contains the following information:

- ▶ Your name
- ▶ Current and previous addresses
- ▶ Phone number
- ▶ Social security number
- ▶ Date of birth
- ▶ Current and previous employers
- ▶ Spouse's name (may appear on your version of the credit report but not on the one sent to lenders)
- ▶ Details about each of your credit accounts, such as the date opened, credit limit or loan amount, balance, monthly payment and payment history in the previous years
- ▶ Bankruptcy filings, if any, as well as state and county court records of tax liens and monetary judgments against you
- ▶ Record of those who have accessed or reviewed your credit report
- ▶ Disputed facts or statements (by both consumer and creditor) as to account status. These are included when a consumer officially disputes the status of an account, or when an investigation of the account has resulted in a disagreement between consumer and creditor

In addition, the federal law specifies what information may remain on your report indefinitely, including:

- ▶ An application for a credit transaction or life insurance information involving an amount of $150,000 or more

- Information about a job with a salary of more than $75,000
- Tax liens that are not paid
- Records of criminal convictions (these may remain on your credit report indefinitely under federal law, but some states require that records of arrest or misdemeanor complaints be removed after seven years)

On the flip side, certain other pieces of personal information *cannot* be in your credit report without your consent or must be removed after a certain time period. These include:

- Information about a lawsuit or an unpaid judgment against you (can only be reported for seven years or until the statute of limitations runs out, whichever is longer)
- Medical history and information (Note that overdue medical bills can appear on your report, and these bills contain enough information for a reader to infer details about you. Anyone looking at this information will be able to see that you had cosmetic surgery or underwent fertility treatment, that you visited a mental health provider, or that you are visiting an AIDS clinic.)
- A bankruptcy that occurred more than ten years ago
- Debts (including delinquent child support payments) that are more than seven years old
- Sensitive information such as your race, sex, marital status, national origin, religious or political preference, and personal lifestyle (although some of this may be implied by the detail that is provided, including your last name and your debts)

How Credit Bureaus Get Your Personal Information

Where does the sensitive information on a credit report come from? Some of it comes from public records (see chapter 2, "Your Personal Information and the Public Record"). Public record sources might include judgments or warnings that have been recorded with a county official or in public records. Through these sources, the credit bureaus will learn whether any liens or legal actions are pending against you or your house, including any IRS tax liens. The bureaus will also discover whether you have ever filed for bankruptcy or been arrested.

Much of the information on your credit report comes directly from you. When you complete and submit applications to lenders and merchants, they send information to the Equifax, Experian, and TransUnion credit bureaus, which maintain files on nearly 90 percent of American adults. Every time you apply for credit or a loan, a credit bureau records the information in your credit report. Your credit report will not itemize the sofa you purchased at Bloomingdale's, but it certainly will show that you owe Bloomingdale's the cost of the couch if you fail to pay the department store in time. In addition, your report will list, for example, that you have a credit card with First USA Bank or a new personal line of equity at Chase Manhattan Bank.

> When you complete and submit applications to lenders and merchants, they send information to the Equifax, Experian, and TransUnion credit bureaus, which maintain files on nearly 90 percent of American adults.

Your credit report may contain most, but not all, of your credit accounts. Major credit card issuers and large department and retail stores invariably will report your credit account to a credit bureau. Smaller and local retailers, auto dealers, gasoline card companies, or credit unions may use their own standards and practices to determine whether you are worthy of obtaining credit, and they may not report your information to a credit bureau unless you fail to pay your bills in a timely fashion. On the other hand, overdue bills from medical institutions or your cellular company may be part of your credit file. Even if your particular ailment or calls to chat lines are not listed on your credit report, the inclusion of that information may still be sensitive, if, for example, your medical bill is from a medical institution known to treat specific diseases.

Each of the three credit bureaus is likely to have a slightly different credit report about you in their databases. The reason is that some creditors maintain different relationships with each of the bureaus. For example, if you live in Atlanta and have a credit card with a local merchant, the merchant may send your information only to Equifax and not to TransUnion and Experian. A local retailer in Chicago may report only to TransUnion and not to the other bureaus. Moreover, every creditor has a different policy about when they report their accounts and negative information to a credit bureau. If you apply for a credit card in late March, your credit report for one bureau may not reflect that change until April, while another one may not register the change until early May. Finally, some creditors may wait until your account is sixty days overdue before they notify a credit bureau about an untimely payment or delinquency, while others may do so at the time they turn over your account to a collection agency.

ORDER YOUR REPORT NOW

Review your credit report at least once a year from each of the three credit bureaus. By law, you are entitled to a copy of your credit report, and it is quite simple to obtain a report. All you need to do is contact one of the three main credit bureaus:

Equifax
Box 740241
Atlanta, GA 30374
800/685-1111
www.equifax.com

Experian
Box 2002
Allen, TX 75013
888/397-3742
www.experian.com

TransUnion
Box 1000
Chester, PA 19022
800/888-4213
www.tvc.com

When you order a credit report from any of these credit bureaus, you must provide your name, address, telephone number, social security number, and credit card information, which the bureaus will use to verify your identity.

If you are not entitled to a free copy of your credit report, as explained below, you may be charged $9 to get a copy of your credit report. The FTC establishes this fee. If you live in the states of Connecticut, Maine, Minnesota, California, or Montana, you will be charged a reduced fee. If you live in Colorado, Georgia, Maryland, Massachusetts, New Jersey, or Vermont, you can request a free report.

You can obtain your credit report free of charge, regardless of which state you live in, under the following circumstances: (1) you are unemployed and plan to seek employment within sixty days; (2) you are on welfare; (3) your report is inaccurate due to fraud; or (4) a company has taken action against you as a result of information supplied by a credit bureau. In this last case, you have the legal right to know if information in your file has been used against you. Anyone who uses information from a credit report to take action against you—such as denying an application for credit, insurance, or employment—must inform you, and give you the name, address, and phone number of the credit bureau that provided your credit report.

Once the federal Fair and Accurate Credit Transactions Act of 2003 is fully effective at the end of 2004, you will be able to obtain a free credit report one time each year from each of the three bureaus. When contacting a bureau to order a report, ask whether the law is in effect before you pay for your credit report.

What Laws Protect You?

In the spring of 2002, the following e-mail made its way into the inbox of millions of Americans, who then forwarded it to others:

> *"Just wanted to let everyone know who hasn't already heard, the four major credit bureaus in the U.S. will be allowed, starting July 1, to release your credit info, mailing addresses, phone numbers . . . to anyone who requests it. If you would like to 'opt out' of this re-*

lease of information, you can call 888/567-8688. It only takes a couple of minutes to do."

The warning was completely baseless, but it terrified and confused many people and prompted a flood of calls to the toll-free number. As it turned out, the opt-out number connected callers with the division at the Credit Reporting Industry that handled opting out of unsolicited offers of credit cards or insurance products. The information in the e-mail wasn't exactly true—creditors *can't* release your information to just anyone who requests it—but the e-mail tapped into the public opinion that the companies that track personal information hold unimaginable power over all of us.

Recognizing that credit reports exert so much power over the lives of citizens, Congress passed the Fair Credit Reporting Act (FCRA) in 1970 to ensure accuracy in consumer reports and to protect the privacy of the information contained in them. The FCRA protects you by ensuring that credit bureaus do not disclose inaccurate and arbitrary personalized information about consumers. In addition, the act governs how credit bureaus may disclose your information to third parties. You also enjoy additional rights under state laws. Contact your state attorney general or local consumer protection agency for more information. To review the full text of the FCRA or learn which state agencies you should contact, log on to www.ftc.gov.

In 2003, Congress passed the Fair and Accurate Credit Transaction Act, a federal credit law that was designed to combat the steady increase in identity theft in the country, but also affects your credit rights. As a beneficiary of this law, you are entitled to one free credit report per year from each of the three credit bureaus and notification if merchants and lenders report missed payments to credit bureaus. This law also sets a national standard for identity theft with which states must comply. See chapter 3, "Your Identity," for more information about how this law protects you against identity theft. The credit bureaus have until the end of 2004 to fully comply with this new law.

Your Credit Score

The owner and director of a company opened a cellular phone ac-count for the company in his name. For business purposes he left the country and put his relative in charge of the business, including the bills. The relative neglected to pay the cell phone company, the cell phone service was turned off, and the cell phone company sent the account to a collection agency. Later, when the owner saw his credit statement he saw that his credit score was compromised due to the bad debt. He paid the debt and requested that the bad credit rating be transferred to his relative who was supposed to have paid the bills.

In addition to your credit report, you have a credit score. Just like a credit report, a credit score can affect you in important ways and can be accessed by the same people who access your credit report.

A credit score is created through a statistical model developed by the company Fair Isaac and derives a number that ranges between 300 and 850. This number, or FICO score, represents a summary of your credit history. It also compares you and other consumers with similar profiles with regard to your credit performance. The model awards points for each factor that helps predict who is most likely to repay a debt. The score is used as a predictor of your creditworthiness or your likelihood to repay a loan and make the payments on time. Many lenders and companies have also developed their own scoring models to predict the likelihood of an individual defaulting on a given loan.

The scoring model is a complex algorithm that takes into account a number of different factors. These factors are assigned different proportions, so it is difficult to know the precise ways or time it will take for you to improve your score. These scoring models generally evaluate the following five factors and information in your credit report to determine your score (in order of importance):

1. **Payment history.** Do you pay your bills on time? Your score is reduced or negatively impacted if you have a history of paying bills late, have had an account sent to collection, or have filed for bankruptcy. Timing

is also important. A recent late payment is worse than one that occurred years ago.

2. **Outstanding debt.** What is your outstanding debt? The amount of debt you have compared to your credit limits affects your score. If the amount you owe is close to your credit limit, the debt will negatively affect your score.

3. **Length of credit history.** How long is your credit history? The longer you have had accounts open, the better it is for you.

4. **Recent requests or inquiries for credit.** Have you recently applied for new credit? Recent applications for credit, or the inquiries that appear on your credit report, can affect your score. If you have recently applied for too many new accounts, it will negatively affect your score. Practically speaking, if one lender turns you down, the next lender from whom you are seeking credit will also probably turn you down. Multiple applications within a six-month period will undoubtedly hurt your score. Promotional (the prescreened or pre-approved) credit card and insurance product offers you get in the mail do not have an effect on your score since, in these cases, you are not actively seeking credit. Rather, a lender is approaching you with a credit solicitation.

5. **Type of credit.** What types of credit accounts do you have? Your score takes into consideration the type of credit accounts you have. Generally, loans from finance companies have a greater negative effect on your credit score.

In simple terms, a low score means either that you may be denied credit, or that you may be offered credit at a high interest rate. Conversely, a high score means that you are likely to be offered credit at a low interest rate. Your credit report is also used in this determination. You might think that if you always pay on time and you pay your entire balance due at that time, you would have an excellent credit score. That certainly seems logical. But you never know unless you check.

Who Accesses Your Credit Report and Score

Daniel Cohn, a Web detective, demonstrated for a Forbes *reporter how he could access the reporter's account information and other personal information using a credit header. Credit headers which are sold to informtion brokers include your name, current and previous addresses, phone number, date of birth, and social security number and are supplied by credit bureaus. Accessing data from a reseller, Cohn dug up the reporter's utility bills, two unlisted phone numbers, and a summary of his finances. With the social security number and a few more details he picked up along the way, Cohn then accessed a Federal Reserve database that revealed a $503 security deposit at Apple Bank for Savings, $7 in a forgotten savings account at Chase Manhattan Bank, and $1,000 in another Chase account. Calling Merrill Lynch and posing as licensed state investigator, Cohn used the reporter's social security number and other details to access the reporter's balance, direct deposits from work, withdrawals, ATM visits, check numbers with dates and amounts, and the name of his broker.*

Credit bureaus, or credit reporting agencies as they are referred to under the Fair Credit and Reporting Act (FCRA), are in the business of gathering information about you and how you use credit. Think about credit bureaus as data depositories of personal and sensitive information. The bureaus make money by reselling the information they collect about you back to lenders, merchants, employers, landlords, and other businesses. Fortunately, the FCRA very carefully regulates who can obtain and access your credit file.

Now it's time to put the pieces together. To whom do the bureaus sell their information? Who besides you and the agency knows that you have a Victoria's Secret Angel credit card? Here's a clue: Does the language "you have been pre-approved for this credit card" seem all too familiar? Credit card issuers mail approximately 5 billion offers for pre-approved credit cards to American households each year. How do they get your name and address? Quite simply, the FCRA allows the credit bureaus to sell this information to prospective credit card issuers and other entities as well. Here are the four entities that can generally access your credit report under the FCRA:

1. **Entities with a legitimate business reason.** The first group of people is defined under the FCRA as anyone who has a "legitimate" business reason to check your credit report. This group includes (a) any creditor to whom you have submitted an application and who is considering extending credit to you; (b) an insurer from whom you are seeking insurance; (c) a landlord from whom you are seeking to rent a unit or other property; (d) an employer or prospective employer so long as in both cases you provide your consent; and (e) any other company, provided it has a legitimate business reason and is involved in a business transaction with you that requires access to your credit report. With respect to this last category, an example may be a company with whom you have enrolled to monitor your credit on a regular basis.

> Think about credit bureaus as data depositories of personal and sensitive information. The bureaus make money by reselling the information they collect about you back to lenders, merchants, employers, landlords, and other businesses.

   The bureaus are prevented from selling your credit report information to companies that want to sell you products that are not credit-related, so don't worry that the credit bureaus will use information from your credit reports for direct marketing purposes.

2. **The government.** The government is the second group that may access your credit report, but only under certain circumstances and, in some cases, only part of it. A governmental agency may access your credit file if you have submitted an application for a government license or benefit, but only if the license or benefit is contingent upon your financial status or if the governmental or state agency is seeking to enforce child support payments. Governmental agencies can access your credit file but are limited to obtaining your name, address, former addresses, current employer, and previous employers. One exception is the new USA Patriot Act, which expands the rights of the government

to access your credit report to assist in its criminal investigations. See chapter 11, "Your Everyday Life," for details.

3. **Companies that market pre-approved credit offers.** Credit bureaus may include your name on lists they sell to companies that market pre-approved credit and insurance offers to consumers such as yourself. The FCRA considers the selling of such information to credit card issuers and insurers permissible. This is why you receive so many pre-approved offers for credit cards in the mail. It works like this:

If, for example, Capital One is introducing to the marketplace a new Gold credit card with special features such as a low APR (annual percentage rate), zero annual fee, and double frequent flyer miles for every $1 charged on the new card, it would contact one of the credit bureaus and request a list of persons who meet certain criteria and would, therefore, qualify for this card. Given the high-end nature of this particular card, Capital One might request a list of people who have a high personal income, live in urban areas, use a certain number of credit cards, and have a high credit score. The credit bureau would execute a search through its records to deliver to Capital One a specific list of those who meet Capital One's criteria. Capital One would then mail a pre-approved offer for its new credit card to the people on the list.

If you respond to an offer that arrives in the mail, the credit card company issuing the offer has the right to access your entire credit report. You should know that *pre-approved* is very different from *approved.* The fact that you received a pre-approved credit card offer does not guarantee that you will actually receive the card. If, for example, you respond to the above offer for the pre-approved card, Capital One may access your report before it grants you any credit. In the event that you do not meet its criteria because of a change in your file since the time the offer was mailed to you, Capital One will reject your application for the credit card.

4. **Brokers who buy "credit headers."** Credit bureaus are allowed to sell what are called credit headers from your credit report. A credit header includes your name, current and previous addresses, phone number, date of birth, and social security number. This information is sold to many information brokers, including data aggregators, who in turn sell

it for a variety of investigative purposes detailed in chapter 1, "What Privacy Means to You." Unfortunately, you have little control here.

Credit header information is sensitive because it includes your social security number, which businesses and the government use in many ways to access information about you. Credit headers are used for locating individuals, such as missing persons, and for target marketing. But because credit headers contain your social security number, thieves can use them to commit identity theft.

> Credit header information, which includes social security numbers, can be used to commit identity theft.

The sale of credit headers is controversial. Several bills have been passed in Congress to prohibit the sale of headers or at the very least to restrict the sale of social security numbers, which are contained in credit headers. Even then, the Gramm-Leach-Bliley Act (GLB) requires users to have a permissible purpose before accessing creditor header information.

How to Reduce Access to Your Credit Report

There is little you can do to prevent people and businesses with a legitimate reason and the government from gaining access to your credit report. If you lead a relatively normal life, creditors, insurance companies, landlords, and prospective employers will likely see your credit report. And you have little choice in the matter unless you want to rent the Unabomber's former shack in the hills of Montana and live off the land—avoiding all contact with society.

You do have some control over when other people can access your information, to what extent others have the right to share it, and the number of marketing-related inquiries you receive. Given the sensitive information in your credit report, you must be prepared not only to safeguard the data included in the report, but also to manage how the entities that have access to the information use it to market products to you. You also have some control over *how* your credit information is used as a basis for marketing. Be proactive and take the following steps:

❋ **Always ask why.** Whenever you submit an application for credit or a company requests permission to review your credit report (or asks for your social security number), ask why the information or particular information request is required and the ways in which the company protects customers' personal information. If you are not comfortable with the answers you receive with respect to the company's information practices, do not submit the application or do not permit the company to access your credit report. Do not give consent unless it is necessary. In some cases, your affirmative written consent is required before a credit bureau may release your credit report. For example, your consent is required before reports that contain medical information about you are sent to creditors, insurers, or employers. In addition, a bureau may not release your report to your employer, or prospective employer, without your written consent.

> **You do have some control over when other people can access your information, to what extent others have the right to share it, and the number of marketing-related inquiries you receive.**

❋ **Opt out.** Remove your name from the credit bureau lists that are used for pre-approved credit offers or direct marketing. To remove your name from these lists, call the following toll-free number: 888/567-8688. By calling this number, you can opt out of both the pre-approved and direct marketing lists of the three main credit bureaus. The bureaus are required by law to maintain this number for that express purpose. You may also opt out of these lists by writing to the bureaus. (See "Resources")

If you call the 800 number, your phone call removes your name and address from these lists for a two-year period. If you write a letter requesting to opt out, the credit bureaus will send you a form, which when completed removes your name from these lists permanently. Unfortunately, you are not able to opt out of the sale of your credit header information.

❋ **Respond to the annual opt-out notice.** You have the right, in most cases, to prevent financial institutions from sharing your personal information with unaffiliated third parties. Each year, financial institutions must send a notice to their customers telling them how they use customers' information and what opt-out rights the customer has. This is not a credit issue under the

FCRA but rather a means of restricting the distribution of your personal information under the GLB Act. See chapter 5, "Your Money," for more details on how to manage your financial privacy.

❋ **Complain to the appropriate government agency or file a lawsuit against anyone who inappropriately accesses your credit file.** You have this right under the FCRA.

CREDIT SCAMS

Beware of credit repair companies that claim they can resolve all of your credit woes. Many of these offers are scams to cheat you or steal your identity.

The "Credit Repair" Scam

Look out for the following lines:

Credit problems? No problem!
We can erase your bad credit—100% guaranteed.
We can remove bankruptcies, judgments, liens, and bad loans from your credit file forever!!!

Companies that make these claims are in the business of helping you improve, repair, or restructure your credit situation. Some of these businesses may be legitimate, but many are not. Keep this in mind whenever you encounter a credit repair offer: If a credit repair company requests a fee and guarantees to clean up your credit report so you can get a job, mortgage, or car loan, you should be thinking "This is a *scam!*"

As the FTC points out, these companies cannot improve your credit report overnight because credit repair usually requires a long-term personal debt repayment plan. If a company wants to be paid up front, before it provides any services, or if it instructs you not to contact any of the credit bureaus directly, it is probably not a legitimate business. The same goes for companies that offer you a Visa or MasterCard even if you have been turned down by banks. The same is true of companies that provide a 900

---

number, which could cost you $25 to $50 to call. A credit repair company lacks the power to remove accurate information—no matter how bad or embarrassing it is—from a credit report. Additionally, certain negative information, such as bankruptcy, can be removed from a credit report only after the requisite period of time passes. As stated above, federal law dictates the type of information that is contained in your report as well as how long that information can remain in your report.

If you decide to use the services of one of these companies, conduct an investigation of the company and learn as much as possible beforehand. If you need assistance, get the FTC's brochure that explains how to improve your credit and lists legitimate resources to help you.

The "We'll Erase Your Bad Credit and Give You a New Social Security Number" Scam

ERASE BAD CREDIT

A NEW CLEAN CREDIT FILE IN JUST 30 DAYS!

ANYONE CAN HAVE A NEW CREDIT FILE INSTANTLY OVERNIGHT

START ALL OVER AGAIN WITH BRAND NEW CREDIT

That's right! You see there's a program that the government just put out a couple of months ago which is giving consumers, such as yourself, who have poor credit, a second chance. With this program you can get a new number that acts as your SSN number strictly for credit purposes only.

Advertised on the Internet, radio, and television, this scam involves paying a service to apply for an Employer Identification Number (EIN), essentially a business taxpayer number, from the IRS. Once you receive the number, the company instructs you to use this number instead of your social security number on credit applications. The company will tell you that if you use this new number on your credit report, none of your creditors will see your previous file. In essence, you're buying a false identity. The problem? If you sign up for the service, you will not only lose a few hundred dollars to the scammer, but you will also have committed fraud. It is illegal to make false statements on a loan or credit application or to obtain an EIN under false premises.

Credit Tips to Protect Your Privacy

From the summer of 2000 until the fall of 2003, Philip Cummings, a thirty-three-year-old help desk worker at a small software company, stole the confidential passwords and subscriber codes from Ford Motor Company, one of his company's clients. Once Cummings had Ford's passwords and codes, he used a third-party service provider called Teledata Communications, which has easy-to-use credit-check terminals at more than 25,000 companies, to download the credit reports of 30,000 unsuspecting people. Cummings received $30 for each stolen credit report from another thief, who in turn sold each credit report for $60 to a ring of identity thieves, who then stole thousands of dollars from the unsuspecting victims. With access to the victims' social security and credit card numbers, the thieves stole more than $2.5 million. In the words of Manhattan U.S. attorney James Comey, "With a few keystrokes, these men [Cummings and his ring of identity thieves] essentially picked the pockets of tens of thousands of Americans and, in the process, took their identities, stole their money and swiped their security."

It is bad enough that legitimate lenders and merchants access your credit information and send you tons of junk mail. It's much worse, however, when an identity thief accesses your information, either through illegal access to your credit report or through any of the ways detailed in chapter 3, "Your Identity." How do you know if you're the victim of identity theft? Your credit report is one of the best indicators.

You are the only one who can look at your credit report and tell if you're a victim of identity theft. A credit bureau or bank has no way of knowing if the information about you is correct or merely represents updated information. For example, if an identity thief applies for a credit card in your name but diverts the card to a different address, your credit report will indicate a change of address. A bank would have no idea whether an identity thief has diverted your mail or you have moved residences. Accordingly, you should adhere to the following tips to protect your privacy and your credit:

✳ **Periodically review your credit.** You should review your credit report on a regular basis and at least once per year. A periodic review will allow you to catch fraudulent activity in your report.

   You should pay particular attention to the sections of the report that list accounts, inquiries, and addresses to determine if fraudulent activity is taking place. In particular, you should review:

   ▶ **Accounts:** Check the "Open Accounts" section to see if any account has been opened without your consent. If so, this may indicate fraud and that a criminal has been granted a line of credit in your name.

   ▶ **Inquiries:** Inquiries within the section "Requests Viewed by Others" represent those creditors who accessed your credit report. If this section contains any creditors with whom you are not familiar, fraud may be present or a criminal may have made an inquiry about your report.

   ▶ **Addresses:** If the addresses on your credit report are incorrect, this may be an indication that a criminal has applied for credit in your name but at a different address.

✳ **Thoroughly review your credit.** For the most thorough review, you should check your credit report at all three credit bureaus, because each bureau's report may contain slightly different information.

✳ **Review your report before others do.** Consider reviewing your credit report several months before you believe your report will be used—if, for example, you intend to apply for a mortgage, an apartment rental, an auto loan, or a job—to ensure that your report is accurate.

✳ **Pay your bills on time.** The overdue bill to the plastic surgeon wouldn't have shown up on your credit report if you paid the bill.

✳ **Be on the alert for scams.** Phony companies use all sorts of scams to obtain your personal information (see page 93). Be careful about divulging sensitive information, such as your driver's license number, mother's maiden name, social security number, and credit and bank account numbers, especially over the phone or online, unless you are familiar with the business that is asking for the information.

✳ **Keep careful records.** These records include billing statements, mortgage payments, and canceled checks. If you think something on your report is not accurate, challenge it.

> **More than half of all credit reports contain errors.**

✳ **Correct errors and inaccuracies in your report.** If you notice that your report contains errors, correct them immediately. Errors may be the result of the incorrect information being reported by lenders or merchants to the particular credit bureau or an indication of identity theft.

How to Correct Errors on Your Report

Credit reports contain errors and inaccuracies more often than you think. According to one study that appeared in the July 2000 issue of *Consumer Reports* magazine, more than half of all credit reports contain errors. An error on your credit report can happen for three reasons: First, you may have inadvertently made an error on an application you completed for a lender or merchant, and the lender or merchant submitted your information to the credit bureau with the error in place. Second, you may have been confused with or mistaken for another person with a similar name, and that person's information has been placed in your file. The third reason is the most disturbing cause of errors on your credit report: fraud. Someone may have intentionally gained access to your personal information and obtained credit in your name.

The FCRA gives you the right to correct mistakes on your credit report. In fact, under the FCRA, both the credit bureau and the company that provided the information to the credit bureau (the information provider), such as the lender or merchant, must correct any inaccurate or incomplete information in your report. It is in your best interest to immediately correct errors and inaccurate information on your credit report.

The FCRA outlines the process and procedures for correcting inaccurate information. If you believe you are a victim of fraud or identity theft, you

97

should follow the steps outlined in chapter 3, "Your Identity," to correct the problem. To protect yourself fully, you should dispute the error with both the credit bureau and the information provider. In brief, here are the three steps you should undertake to correct your credit report:

1. **Call the credit bureau and identify the information you believe is inaccurate.** Follow up on your phone call in writing and include copies of documents or information that support your position. (Make sure to retain a copy of the letter and documents you send.) Your letter should clearly identify each item in your report that you dispute, give the facts, explain why you dispute the information, and request the specific action you desire such as removal or correction (see "Resources" for credit bureau contact details).

   Upon receipt of your letter, the credit bureau generally has thirty days to complete an investigation of your request. First, it will forward the information about your dispute to the information provider. The information provider will then conduct an investigation and report the results back to the credit bureau. If the information provider finds the disputed information to be inaccurate, or the error cannot be verified, or if the information is incomplete, it must notify all the credit bureaus, which are required to correct this information in your file. For example, if you dispute your report's claim that you have been late making payments, and the investigation shows that you are not delinquent, the credit bureau must then correct the report to indicate you are current in your payments.

   Upon completion of the investigation, the credit bureau must give you the written results of the investigation. If an item is changed or removed, the credit bureau cannot put the disputed information back in your file unless the information provider verifies its accuracy and completeness, and the credit bureau gives you a written notice that includes the name, address, and phone number of the information provider. You may ask the credit bureau to send a corrected report to anyone who has requested your file in the past six months, as well as to anyone who has requested it in the past two years in relation to employment.

2. **Write to the creditor, lender, merchant, or other entity that reports information to a credit bureau to tell them that you**

dispute an item. Again, include copies of documents that support your position. Many information providers specify an address for disputes.

3. **If the credit bureau or the information provider does not correct the disputed information after completing its investigation, ask the credit bureau or information provider to include a one-hundred-word statement of the dispute in your file and in future reports.** In this way, the notice of your dispute and explanation of the item in question will be included for anyone who reviews your report in the future.

> The most disturbing cause of errors on your credit report: fraud. Someone may have intentionally gained access to your personal information and obtained credit in your name.

For more detailed information on how to dispute and correct errors in your credit report, you can access the Federal Trade Commission's website at www.ftc.gov.

THE BOTTOM LINE

▸ How do you score? Landlords, creditors, insurers, and prospective employers make decisions based on your credit report and its related score. Your credit information is not private and it dramatically affects your life.

▸ Do you know what's in your credit report? Your report contains all sorts of personal information, including your name, address, social security number, employer and past employer, and much, much more.

▸ Manage your credit report to protect yourself from identity theft and protect your privacy. Order your report from all three credit bureaus at least annually, and correct and update any mistakes. Opt out of lists for pre-approved credit cards and other marketing material.

▸ Watch out for credit scams. No one but you can improve your credit, but someone can use your personal information to steal your identity.

Your Money

GLASBERGEN

"IT LOOKS LIKE EVERYONE WILL BE GETTING WHAT THEY
WANT THIS YEAR...SOMEBODY POSTED MY CREDIT CARD
NUMBER ON THE INTERNET!"

Your stockbroker sold her PalmPilot in an online auction. She didn't realize it, but she had not completely deleted sensitive company and client information, including the financial and personal details about your account. The buyer on eBay deliberately bids on old PalmPilots and other PDAs, knowing that these used devices might be a treasure trove.

You withdraw money from an ATM at a local deli. Later you learn that you are one of three hundred people to be scammed by thieves who had rigged the ATM to collect account and personal identification numbers to create fake cards. After the thieves trans-

*ferred the information onto plastic cards, they withdrew more than
$200,000 from the accounts of their three hundred victims.*

*A computer hacker steals your credit card number, along with thou-
sands of other credit card numbers, from a store you recently visited. The hacker then publishes all the numbers on the Internet
after the store's parent company refused to pay a ransom for this
information. Suddenly, people in Romania, Venezuela, and Oregon
are using your card.*

Perhaps Mr. McGuire was on to something when, in the 1967 film *The
Graduate,* he told young Benjamin Braddock (played by Dustin Hoffman) that
the future of business would be in plastics. But to what kind of plastics did he
refer? If he meant the material that creates the credit, debit, and ATM cards
that fuel our modern monetary system, then Mr. McGuire was truly a man
ahead of his time. Today, American consumers have about 1 billion credit,
debit, and ATM cards, and they use their cards in transactions worth nearly $2
trillion a year. Americans spend more on goods with cards than with cash.

Welcome to the age of plastic money. According to economist David
Evans, author of *Paying with Plastic,* there have been only four changes to the
world's payment system in the history of humankind: barter to coins; coins to
paper; paper to checks; and checks to cards. The idea of living without ATM
cards, debit cards, and credit cards is inconceivable to most Americans. Can
you imagine going to dinner or to a store and not using a credit card to pay for
the meal or the stuff you buy? Think about it another way: how would you
feel if you had to pay cash for everything?

But credit cards do have a drawback. They create a trail for every credit
card transaction you make. Think about what your credit card purchases can
tell someone about your life, from where you shop to how much you spend, to
how often you pay your bills. Think about how many times a day you hand
your credit card or debit card to a cashier or use it at an ATM. Think about
how many opportunities an ambitious thief might have to steal your card
number or your PIN code.

Most consumers use credit, ATM, and debit cards and bank at financial
institutions even if they know they risk the theft of their sensitive financial

information and the sharing of it without their knowledge. Most of us prefer the convenience and are willing to take the risks. Have you ever stopped to assess some of these risks as well as the advantages? Consider these:

▸ By carrying credit cards instead of cash you lessen your chances of pickpocketers or muggers taking your cash. However, identity thieves can fraudulently open cards in your name or steal your credit card number from credit card receipts to bill items in your name (see chapter 3, "Your Identity").

▸ Banking at an ATM allows you to avoid long bank lines, but you risk someone stealing your Personal Identification Number (or PIN) and accessing your bank account.

▸ Paying bills online eliminates the bother of writing checks, addressing the envelope, and going to the mailbox, even if a hacker or a user of snoopware may record your passwords and access your account surreptitiously (see chapter 7, "Your Computer and the Internet").

▸ Banking at the same financial conglomerate that holds your mortgage, issued your credit cards, and perhaps serves as your travel agency is convenient, at the risk that your sensitive personal information could be mishandled or shared with other entities in the regular course of business.

Is it time to return to the old barter system? Don't plan on it, especially when the future points to a more digital payment system involving finger scanners, remote payment by cellular phones, or wireless chips. In the meantime, monitor your sensitive financial information and follow the many practical tips described in this chapter.

What Financial Institutions Know About You

The Minnesota Attorney General's Office sued Fleet Mortgage, Inc., a former unit of FleetBoston that was purchased by Washington Mutual, for sharing customer's home mortgage account numbers and other information with telemarketing companies that sold

*club memberships for everything from dental work to home protec-
tion to auto repair. Fleet and its telemarketers led consumers to believe that they were agreeing to a free trial in the club, when in fact
charges were tacked to their monthly mortgage bills when consumers failed to cancel the club. Fleet settled the charges in 2001.*

Suppose your bank, insurance company, and stockbroker shared indis-
criminately all the information each institution has collected. Consider what
would happen: Your bank could tip off stockbrokers every time there is an
increase in your account balance, so you would receive calls from your broker
or perhaps an increase in telemarketing calls. Your life insurance company
could review records of your checking account and then increase your insurance rates based on that information. Your bank could turn you down for a
loan after learning of a health problem documented on your life insurance
physical. Fortunately, this does not happen, but the reality is that your financial insitutions know more about you now than ever before and may share
this information in ways you don't know.

The result of the many mergers and acquisitions that have occurred in the
financial services industry is that theoretically you now enjoy one-stop shopping for your financial services. The bank where you maintain your principal
checking account and banking services is likely to be affiliated with other companies, such as an insurance company, a mortgage company, an investment
firm, or even a travel agency. For example, Citibank offers their customers
checking and saving accounts, credit cards, individual retirement accounts
(IRAs), insurance products, and mortgages, among other financial products
and services. In addition to offering many of the same services, American
Express also offers a full-service, diversified travel agency.

No doubt, the growth of financial services companies has changed the
way you handle your money. A decade ago, you likely had one financial institution that maintained your checking and savings accounts; a different financial institution that issued you your credit card; an insurance company, or
more likely a personal broker, who handled your insurance needs for your car,
life, and home; a stockbroker who worked at yet another company (and likely
was a family friend) who handled your investment account; and, finally, a
financial adviser who dispensed financial advice.

These new financial conglomerates do offer certain benefits, such as integrated services, lower costs, and new products. But they also gain great knowledge about you—more than any financial institution that you dealt with a decade ago (with the possible exception of the family friend who acted as your stockbroker). To become a customer of any financial institution, you are required to provide certain basic information that might include your name, address, phone number, social security number, and more. As you have learned in previous chapters, even such basic information is sensitive and private, and potentially damaging if misappropriated or misused. Depending on the nature of the application, however, you might also be required to provide your former addresses, debt level, mortgage payments, income other than salary such as child support payments, and much more. Ultimately, these financial conglomerates will be in a position to gather detailed information concerning all aspects of your personal and financial life. Such information includes the specifics of the financial accounts and information you include on an application to obtain a loan, a credit card, or other financial product or services that you hold with the institution, as well as the additional information that the conglomerate can gather from other companies.

> If you maintain your credit card, insurance policy, mortgage, and checking and savings accounts with one institution, that institution knows or can discover almost every aspect of your life.

If you maintain your credit card, insurance policy, mortgage, and checking and savings accounts with one institution, that institution knows or can discover almost every aspect of your life. Your bank maintains a record of your account balance information, payment history, and overdraft history; investments purchased or owned; credit or debit card purchase information; information used to analyze your investments; information from a credit report; and information gathered through their website (see chapter 7, "Your Computer and the Internet," to learn how websites gather information about you as you surf the site or input certain information). Included in this information are intimate and sensitive details of your life. For example, your credit card statement indicates how you spend your money; your mortgage statement provides details about your home; automatic wage deposits to your savings account may indicate your income; and checks that you write from your checking account may disclose aspects of your medical condition, political affiliations, and more.

Your financial institution may also collect information from nonaffiliated third parties, consumer reporting agencies, or pub-lic records. Some financial institutions gather infor-mation collected from consumer surveys, product registration cards, public records, and census records, and then use this information to market products and services to you that you are more likely to buy.

> Some financial institutions gather information collected from consumer surveys, product registration cards, public records, and census records, and then use this information to market products and services to you that you are more likely to buy.

Federal Protection for Your Financial Privacy

NationsBank, which later merged into Bank of America, settled with the SEC in 1998 for $7 million after the SEC accused the bank of sharing with NationsSecurities, one of its sub-sidiary affiliates, lists of customers with expiring certificates of deposit. NationsSecurities allegedly used this information to sell uninsured, risky products in a misleading manner to the CD holders.

California's Charter Pacific bank sold the credit card numbers of 3.7 million of its customers to a convicted felon. The felon then ran up $45.7 million in fraudulent charges subscribing to X-rated Internet porn sites and calling 900-number sex chat lines.

Recognizing that financial institutions gather sensitive information about you, Congress passed the Gramm-Leach-Bliley Act (GLB) in 1999. On the one hand, the act addresses the emergence of large financial conglomerates within the financial services industry. On the other hand, and important to you, this law outlines certain standards that protect your financial privacy. In general, as outlined by GLB, financial institutions must mail to you a privacy notice that explains the following:

▶ the type of information that they gather

▶ the ways in which your information might be shared with, sold to, or otherwise disclosed to other companies

▶ the means by which you can prevent or limit your information from being disclosed to other companies (known as *opting out*)

> The GLB Act will not prevent your financial institution from sharing and selling your information to other companies, although there are exceptions to this if you exercise your right to opt out

The GLB Act broadly defines financial institutions. For example, your bank, credit union, mortgage company, investment firm, or insurance company is considered a financial institution under GLB, and each of these firms must provide you with its privacy policy. In addition, financial institutions include collection agencies, credit bureaus, loan service companies, agents for leasing real or personal property, real estate appraisers, credit counselors, and businesses that sell money orders, savings bonds, or travelers' checks. For a full list of financial institutions, see www.ftc.gov/privacy/glbact/glbsub1.htm#6805.

As protective as the GLB Act is, it does not prevent your financial institution from collecting and maintaining detailed personal information about you. Moreover, the GLB Act will not prevent your financial institution from sharing and selling your information to other companies, although there are exceptions to this if you exercise your right to opt out (discussed in detail below). Under the GLB Act, your financial institution is required only to disclose to you the general categories of companies to or with which it is selling or sharing your personal information. As a result, you will never know the specific companies to or with which your financial institution is selling or sharing your personal information.

Your ability to restrict the selling or sharing of your personal information to other companies (or your right to opt out) depends on the relationship between that company and your financial institution. To understand how your information can be shared, sold, or otherwise accessed, you need to answer the following three questions: (1) Is the company in question affiliated with your financial institution? (2) Is the company in question a nonaffiliated third party (or an outside company)? (3) Is the company in question a joint marketer or service provider to your financial institution?

An Affiliated Company. An affiliated company is a company that is owned or controlled by your financial institution or its parent company. Put another way, an affiliate is considered part of the same corporate structure. Your bank's affiliates might include, as in the case of Citibank, other financial companies (such as a credit card company, a brokerage firm, or an insurance company, among others), or, as with the case of American Express, even non-financial companies (such as a travel agency). Unfortunately, you cannot prevent your financial institution from sharing your personal information with an affiliated company, regardless of whether or not the affiliate is a financial company. In fact, your financial institution may disclose your account number to an affiliate to market its own products and services. This explains why Citibank credit card holders, for example, may expect to receive marketing material for other CitiGroup products and services such as home equity lines. By sharing customer data among affiliates, and then merging the information into one database, a financial conglomerate may acquire extensive information about you. Bottom line: You *cannot* prevent information sharing among affiliates.

> You will never know the specific companies to or with which your financial institution is selling or sharing your personal information.

A Nonaffiliated Third Party. A nonaffiliated third party is a company that is not owned or controlled by your financial institution or its parent company. Nonaffiliated third parties may include other financial service providers, such as insurance companies, or nonfinancial service providers, such as retailers or nonprofit organizations, but none of these companies can be under the common control of your financial institution or its parent company. Your financial institution must give you the right to prevent your personal information from being shared with nonaffiliated third parties. As further described below, you are given the right to opt out. Bottom line: You *can* prevent your financial institution from sharing your personal information with a nonaffiliated third party.

Joint Marketers or Service Providers. Financial service companies often enter into marketing arrangements with other companies such as telemarketers or direct-mail marketers. Under such agreements, your financial institution may freely disclose your personal information to a joint marketer or service provider as long as the information is used solely for marketing the financial products or services of your financial institution. You cannot prevent such information sharing. The marketer or service provider that receives your information may not sell or share your personal information and must use such information only for the purpose of marketing the financial product. Bottom line: You *cannot* prevent your financial institution from sharing your personal information with a joint marketer or service provider.

> Your financial institution may freely disclose your personal information to a joint marketer or service provider as long as the information is used solely for marketing the financial products or services of your financial institution. You cannot prevent such information sharing.

How to Use the Law to Protect Your Financial Privacy

How would you feel if your bank sold your sensitive customer data, including your credit card numbers and account balances, to a direct marketer with whom you have had no previous relationship? What if the bank had previously assured you that it would never share, much less sell, your sensitive financial data to anyone?

US Bank sold customers' personal data, including credit limits, birth dates, marital status, occupation, account balances, and social security numbers, to MemberWorks telemarketers. The telemarketers then charged customers for memberships in outdoor, sewing, and sports clubs that customers had neither purchased nor agreed to purchase. In return, MemberWorks paid the bank $4 million plus commissions of 22 percent of net revenue on sales of club memberships.

As explained above, you can't prevent a financial institution from sharing your personal information with an affiliated company, joint marketer, or service provider, but you can limit the disclosure of your sensitive financial information to nonaffiliated third parties such as telemarketers and direct mail marketers. Pay attention to these steps to fully protect your financial privacy.

✳ **Look for your privacy notice.** Don't be surprised if you receive multiple privacy notices in the mail. According to the American Bankers' Association, the average household receives between fifteen and twenty privacy notices annually. Make sure that you actually receive a privacy notice from your financial institution(s). Your bank is required to send you the notice annually and

WARNING: YOUR FINANCIAL RECORDS MAY REVEAL INFORMATION ABOUT YOUR HEALTH

Your records and files at your financial institution may include sensitive medical information. The GLB itself does not specifically address medical information. As a result, any medical information that is contained in your bank's files or records (such as a credit card payment to your gynecologist or a check to your plastic surgeon) may be disclosed to an affiliated company. Moreover, unless you exercise your right to opt out, your personal medical information can be disclosed to nonaffiliated third parties. In some cases, financial institutions may provide an enhanced sense of privacy for your medical information. If you are particularly concerned about sensitive medical information, you should carefully read your bank's privacy notice or ask a customer representative. In addition, other laws, such as the Health Insurance Portability and Accountability Act (HIPAA) and certain state laws provide additional protection and standards for your medical information within the health community but do not generally pertain to financial institutions. See chapter 10, "Your Health," for more information on your medical privacy. Bottom Line: Assume your medical information will be shared with nonaffiliated third parties—yet another reason to exercise your right to opt out.

may do so at any time of the year. It is required to send the notice at the same time each year. In addition, you will receive a privacy notice when you open a new account with a financial institution. If you maintain accounts with a number of different financial institutions (for example, bank, credit card issuer, and so forth) that are not affiliated, you will receive a privacy notice from each of these institutions. If you have different accounts with one financial conglomerate, you will receive a single privacy notice that covers all your accounts.

> According to the American Bankers' Association, the average household receives between fifteen and twenty privacy notices annually.

You are likely to receive your privacy notice in the mail. In all likelihood, the privacy notice will be included with other information you receive from your financial institution (such as your account statement or mutual fund prospectus). In addition, every financial institution can use its own format for its privacy notice, so you may notice that the privacy notices you receive vary in design. Privacy notices are required to be "clear and conspicuous" and in writing to you personally. A general posting or verbal notice does not meet the requirements. If you conduct business online with the institution, you may receive an e-mail if you agree to receive the notice in this manner instead of by mail.

For these reasons, go through the mail you receive from your financial institution and review the e-mails or Internet messages you receive from the institution and its website. Pay special attention for the following headlines: Privacy Notice, Privacy Policy, and Opt-Out Notice.

✳ **Review your privacy notice.** Once you receive your privacy notice, review it thoroughly. Look for:

▸ Details about the types of information collected by the institution and whether the institution might share your information
▸ The categories of businesses with which the information might be shared. Any information that the institution may share with companies outside the corporate family must be described in the privacy notice you receive. Look for the broad categories that are outlined in the privacy

policy. Understand that many privacy policies are not written in language that is easy to understand, so you may find it is difficult to know whether your financial institution is exceeding the requirements of GLB.

If you don't understand how or with whom your information will be shared, call a customer service representative. After all, it's your information, and you have a right to know how your information will be used.

> **If you do not opt out, you are giving permission to your bank to share your personal information.**

❋ **Opt out.** Your privacy notice typically includes a form that allows you to opt out of information sharing. Check or mark the form as required and return it to your financial institution. You must affirmatively opt out to prevent your personal financial information from being shared with companies that are not affiliated with your financial institution. Opting out is the principal means that you have to control how your personal information is used. Although your information can still be shared in other ways—for example, with affiliates or under joint marketing agreements—opting out limits the extent to which your personal information will be shared with other companies, including many different marketing companies. You must act affirmatively by opting out to ensure that personal financial information is not shared with nonaffiliated third parties.

The good thing is that opting out is easy to do. Not only can you opt out by filling out the form that is mailed to you, but some banks also enable you to opt out online, via e-mail, or through their websites. If you do not act affirmatively by opting out or you fail to respond, you are giving permission to your bank to share your personal information.

❋ **Respond to your privacy notice in a timely manner.** After you receive the privacy notice, return the opt-out notice within thirty days to prevent your personal information from being disclosed. This period is applicable whether you receive your privacy notice by mail or e-mail. In some cases, you must respond immediately. For example, if you withdraw money from an ATM, the ATM screen might post a privacy policy that includes an opt-out notice, and you must decide at that moment whether you want to opt out.

If you decide you do not want to opt out, your bank is free to share or sell your personal information after that time. Of course, you can later decide to opt out; however, doing so at a later date affects only the future sharing of information. Information that has been previously disclosed may already have been shared with and used by other companies. Conversely, if you opt out, you can later reverse your decision.

✳ **Be proactive about your privacy notice.** Be proactive about opting out. Opting out is your primary means of preventing the disclosure of your information to nonaffiliated third parties. Be on the lookout for your privacy notice, return it on time, and opt out.

If you cannot locate the privacy notice or believe that you never received it, call your bank or financial institution and have another notice sent to you. Also be sure to follow the specified procedure to opt out as stated in its privacy notice. If the notice wants you to respond by mail, mail the form back to the issuing organization. If your bank gives you a toll-free number, you should use that method to opt out. Of course, nothing prevents you from the "belt and suspenders" method of being even more proactive by responding both by mail and by using the toll-free number. Remember: opting out is your responsibility; do not expect anyone else to do it for you.

✳ **Compare privacy policies of your financial institutions.** Before opening an account with a bank, ask to review the financial institution's privacy policy. Of course, you will consider other factors, such as financial products available, interest rate, and so on, before you open your account. In many cases, however, the way a bank deals with its privacy policy may reflect its commitment to customer service. Accordingly, if your bank goes beyond what it is required to do legally, then this might reflect a heightened sense of customer service. Your financial institution is giving you more protection than the law requires if it does some of the following:

▸ Has a blanket policy of not selling your personal financial information to outside companies

▶ Provides a simple opting-out process by providing a check-off form and a postage-paid envelope

▶ Extends your opt-out choices beyond the GLB Act by offering the option to prevent your information from being shared among affiliates and joint marketers

▶ Provides you with the opportunity to review and correct your records

▶ Provides additional information about other steps you can take to protect your privacy

✳ **Know your rights.** The GLB Act does not provide you with a right to sue your financial institution if it violates your privacy rights. If, however, you exercise your right to opt out but your financial institution continues to share your financial information with nonaffiliated third parties, you may still have cause for an action. Even if you cannot directly sue your financial institution under the GLB Act, you can still pursue three different courses of action.

First, you can complain to one of the eight federal agencies with authority to enforce GLB in the financial services area it regulates. These agencies are identified in the "Resources" section at the end of this book. Accordingly, if you complain to one of the eight agencies, that agency has the authority to investigate your complaint, and make a determination whether to bring an action against the financial institution.

Second, you may be able to bring a claim that your bank's violation of GLB violated other rights you have under state law. Check with your state's attorney general's office, because each state has different laws that may pertain to your situation. In general, California law is the most protective in terms of financial privacy.

Third, if you remain concerned about your personal information, you can simply ask your bank not to share your personal information in any manner. Although your bank has no obligation under GLB to comply with your request, it may nonetheless do so. You can obtain a form letter to send to your bank at either of the following websites: www.consumer-action.org or www.privacyrights.org (www.privacyrights.org/fs/fs24a-formletter.htm).

✳ **Use other means to protect your financial privacy.** In addition to exercising your rights under GLB, you should consider other methods of protecting your privacy. Many of these methods have been described in other chapters. For example, to more fully limit the sharing of your personal information, you should consider the following:

▸ Opt out of prescreened offers. See chapter 4, "Your Credit"
▸ Opt out of telemarketing phone calls. See chapter 8, "Your Home"
▸ Opt out of direct-mail lists. See chapter 8, "Your Home"
▸ Reduce your chances of identity theft. See chapter 3, "Your Identity"
▸ Limit the spam e-mail you receive. See chapter 7, "Your Computer and the Internet"

In addition, as described in chapter 4, "Your Credit," the FCRA allows you to limit certain types of information from being shared among corporate affiliates. In particular, the FCRA gives you the right to prevent a company from sharing information about your creditworthiness with affiliates. However, both the FCRA and GLB do not prevent your transaction and experience information (such as information about the checks you write; the credit card charges you make; your deposits, withdrawals, and wire transfers; and so on) from being shared with affiliates without your consent.

When Stolen Information Becomes Stolen Money

After enjoying a relaxing dinner at a local restaurant, you pay your tab with your credit card. A recently hired cashier makes an extra imprint of your credit card and uses your card to buy thousands of dollars in goods from various catalogs.

The loss, theft, and fraud of credit cards, debit cards, and ATM cards costs cardholders and credit card issuers billions of dollars annually. Theft and loss of your card occurs in many different and sometimes unknown ways. For example, your account number and personal identification number can be stolen without your knowledge and then transferred to a plastic card, which can be used to withdraw money from an ATM or to charge goods on your credit card. Unfortunately, you cannot prevent credit or charge card fraud from happening to you, but you can more fully protect your financial privacy by following the steps below. You can also limit your financial exposure and liability in certain situations.

Credit Cards

Before John Jacobus left for an overseas vacation, he bought a gift at an airport kiosk operated at the international gate. To pay for the gift, John handed the vendor his credit card and watched the vendor swipe his credit card through a legitimate machine. What John did not notice was that the vendor actually swiped the card a second time through an illegal device slightly smaller than a pager. John got his card back, completely unaware that his credit card number had been recorded. In fact, that same vendor managed to double-swipe more than 600 credit cards over a six-week period. When John returned from vacation and received his credit card statement, he discovered $1,000 in charges for goods he never bought.

Jill's purse was stolen while she was having lunch with her boyfriend. The purse was later dropped off at a local police station, and eventually returned to her. All the money in her wallet was gone, but Jill was relieved to find all her credit cards in place. It was not until she began receiving bills for purchases she never made that she realized the thief needed only the account number on her credit cards, and not the cards themselves, to defraud her.

Credit cards were a hit in America from the very beginning. When the Diners Club first introduced the credit card in 1950, two hundred people signed up for it and fourteen restaurants accepted it. By the end of that same year, twenty thousand people were using the Diners Club credit card. Today, if you include store and gas credit cards, the total number of credit cards in the United States is 1.3 billion. The average cardholder has 2.7 bank credit cards, 3.8 retail credit cards, and 1.1 debit cards, for a total of 7.6 cards per cardholder.

Sooner or later, chances are pretty good that you will either lose your credit card or discover that purchases have been fraudulently charged to it. Much to the chagrin of credit card issuers, credit card fraud is becoming a fact of life. The good news for you is that federal law limits the maximum exposure you can face for unauthorized use of your credit card to $50. Such exposure occurs when a thief racks up charges on your credit card before you have reported the loss or theft. If you report the loss before your credit card is used, your card issuer will not hold you responsible for any unauthorized charges. If fraud involves your credit card number, but not the card itself, as in Jill's case above, you have no liability for unauthorized use.

> **Federal law limits the maximum exposure you can face for unauthorized use of your credit card to $50.**

FRAUD PROTECTION FOR THE LAZY

A number of companies, including your credit card issuer, provide a service commonly referred to as a *credit card registration service.* For an annual fee, these companies will notify all the issuers of your credit card and ATM or debit card accounts in the event that your card is lost or stolen. This service allows you to make only one phone call to report all card losses rather than calling each individual issuer. Most services also will request replacement cards on your behalf.

Your decision to enroll in one of these services should be based on convenience or added security. If you manage your cards properly and report losses or theft promptly, these services should not be necessary. However, if you feel inclined to use such a service, make sure you are working with a credible company and one that you trust. Understand the company's policy about indemnifying you if it fails to notify card issuers promptly. Once you've called in the loss to your service, you should not be liable for unauthorized charges or transfers. One final point: You cannot be completely lazy—you still need to make that one phone call to report the loss or theft of your card.

ATM or Debit Cards

Two men set up an elaborate debit card fraud operation at a gas station. They installed a skimming device in the station's telephone line to record the information contained on the black magnetic strip of customers' ATM cards. A hidden video camera mounted in the ceiling recorded the customers' personal identification numbers. The end result? More than one thousand forged debit cards were created to access customers' accounts and steal from these unsuspecting people.

> **Your financial exposure in the event your ATM or debit card is used fraudulently can be limitless.**

A thief used a pair of binoculars to watch people who stopped at an ATM in the middle of a high-traffic area. If customers did not adequately cover the ATM monitor as they conducted their business, he was able to learn their personal identification numbers and other account information.

One weekend in July 1999, about two hundred residents in Montreal reported the mysterious disappearance from their bank accounts of amounts averaging $1,000. An eastern European organized crime ring had set up rigged debit card machines in grocery stores and gas stations. The machines contained two sets of wires: one sending a signal to the bank, and the other communicating with the criminals' computer to transfer account information to the magnetic stripe of counterfeit cards. When unsuspecting ATM users swiped their cards, all their card information and passwords were sent to the criminals to use at will.

These stories probably send chills down your spine. They should, and not just because of the surreptitious nature of these crimes. The reason is that the loss, theft, or fraudulent use of your ATM or debit card can lead to devastating consequences. Your financial exposure in the event your ATM or debit card is used fraudulently can be limitless. In this case, your financial liability depends on how quickly you report the loss or fraudulent use of your ATM or debit card. In addition to your reaction time, your liability may depend on whether your card has been stolen or lost or fraudulently used. In 2002, according to the American Bankers Association (ABA), fraud involving debit cards cost banks nearly $51 million.

In the case of loss or theft of your ATM or debit card, your liability under federal law depends on how quickly you report the loss. Here is how your liability varies:

Before fraudulent use: If you report an ATM or debit card missing before it is used without your permission, your card issuer cannot hold you responsible for any unauthorized transfers.

Within two business days: If you report the loss of your card within two business days after you realize your card is missing, you can be held be responsible for up to $50 in unauthorized charges or withdrawals.

Within sixty days: If you do not report the loss within two business days after you discover the loss, you could lose up to $500 as a result of unauthorized or fraudulent use of your card.

After sixty days: If you fail to report an unauthorized transfer within sixty days after your bank mails to you the statement that includes the unauthorized transaction, you can face unlimited losses. Think of it this way: You can lose all the money in your bank account, plus be responsible for paying off any money that has been put aside or is remaining in your line of credit.

If the fraudulent use of your debit or ATM card involves only your debit card number (and not the loss of your actual card), you are liable only for money transfers or withdrawals that occur after sixty days from the date the bank mails to you the statement that details the unauthorized use of your debit or ATM card. Once you report the fraud, you are no longer responsible for any ongoing fraudulent charges.

Follow these practical tips to avoid fraud of your credit card and ATM or debit cards and to limit your financial liability in the event of loss or theft of your cards:

✳ **Be responsible with your cards.** The best way to protect yourself against card fraud is to know where your cards are at all times and to keep them

118

secure. Carry only those cards that you think you will need. Sign your cards as soon as they arrive. Think twice before you lend your card to anyone, and do not leave cards lying around.

* **Follow up quickly.** Report the loss or theft of your credit cards and your ATM or debit cards to your card issuers as quickly as possible. Many companies maintain toll-free numbers and twenty-four-hour services to handle emergencies. After you call, follow up with a letter that includes your account number, when you noticed your card was missing, and the date you called to report the loss or fraudulent use.

> **Cover the screen or keypad of an ATM or public phone so thieves cannot watch you enter your PIN.**

* **Reconcile monthly statements carefully and promptly.** Open your monthly statements promptly and reconcile your account with your receipts in the same way you balance your checking account. If you notice discrepancies or mistakes, report them immediately.

* **Disclose your personal information carefully.** Do not provide personal or financial card information over the phone unless you know the person who is receiving the information, you are dealing with a reputable company, or you initiated the phone call. The same applies when responding to account verification requests for financial information sent over the Internet.

* **Protect your personal identification number.** To protect your ATM and debit card, guard your PIN. Do not use obvious passwords, such as your address, birth date, phone or social security number as your PIN, and consider changing your password regularly. Memorize your PIN and do not carry it in your wallet or purse. Never write your PIN on your ATM or debit card, and avoid writing your PIN on the outside of a deposit slip, an envelope, or other papers that could be easily lost or seen. Finally, before you input your PIN into an ATM machine, carefully check that you are not being monitored. Cover the screen or keypad of an ATM or public phone so thieves cannot watch you enter your PIN.

❋ **Avoid non-bank ATMs.** Although most non-bank ATMs are legitimate, the chances of someone tampering with these machines is much greater. Phony ATMs may be owned by thieves who will steal your bank card information. (See page 121.)

❋ **Be cautious with your credit and debit card receipts.** Credit card receipts contain important information. For example, write a line through blank spaces on charge or debit slips above the total to ensure that the amount cannot be changed. Void incorrect receipts. Do not sign a blank charge or debit slip. Destroy carbons and save your receipts to check against your monthly statements. Do not leave receipts lying around.

❋ **Be alert when you use your credit card.** When you use your card, keep an eye on it during the transaction. Get it back as quickly as possible. Make sure your card does not get swiped twice through a credit card machine.

❋ **Destroy old credit, debit, and ATM cards.** Destroy all old cards by cutting through the account number before discarding the cards.

❋ **Be prepared for loss or fraud.** Keep a record—in a safe place, such as a fire-proof cabinet, separate from your cards—of the important information related to your credit card. This record should include the following for each credit, debit, or ATM card you maintain: the card issuer, your account/card number, expiration dates, and the customer service or emergency telephone number of each card issuer so you can report a loss quickly. You may even create your own worksheet to keep track of this information.

❋ **Check your insurance policy.** Your homeowner's insurance policy may cover your liability for loss or theft of your credit card. If it does not, determine whether your insurance company will allow you to change your policy to include this protection.

❋ **Be persistent with your financial institution.** If you report loss, theft, or fraudulent use of your card to your bank, follow up to make sure your bank recognizes your situation. Check your monthly statement to ensure that your account has been reimbursed for any fraudulent charges. If your bank is not responding, be persistent and continue to follow up until your situation is resolved.

✳ **Remember the basics of identity theft protection.** These tips should not replace the actions you should undertake to protect yourself against identity theft. For example, continue to monitor your credit report regularly and be cautious about the personal information you disclose.

ATM AND CREDIT CARD SCAMS

Stealing your ATM and credit card PINs is one of the ways that identity thieves can easily steal your money. In many cases, they don't even need to have your card; the PIN alone will suffice because identity thieves can create their own cards with magnetic strips. Here are some common scams:

The Phony Bank Machine Scam

Some delis or gas stations are equipped with a gray box that looks like your average non-bank ATM. But these machines are not legitimate ATMs. Some rigged ATM boxes steal information via a thin, transparent-plastic overlay on the keypad that captures a user's identification code as it is entered. If you notice the overlay, you might think it is a cover to protect the keys. In fact, microchips in the device record every keystroke. Another transparent device is designed to fit inside the card slot to capture card data. As the cardholder completes the transaction, a computer attached to the overlay records all the data necessary to clone the card.

Yet another phony ATM scam involves two wires, one of which sends signals to the legitimate bank and allows you to take out cash. The other wire sends signals to a computer where the thieves collect your bank information and PIN and later use the information in conjunction with a phony card.

The "ATM Is Out of Order" Scam

ATM Out of Order. Working Machine Around the Corner.
Some scammers do their dirty work right out in the open. This successful scam involves posting a hand-lettered sign that directs ATM customers

---

away from a bank machine. The sign might explain that the legitimate machine is out of order, so customers should use another terminal. The new terminal turns out to be a card reader (as in the previous case) set up by the scammers to obtain your card data. With the card data, the scammers create bogus cards to spend your money.

The "Law Has Changed" Telemarketing Scam

Hi. This is Linda from the Credit Card Loss Protection Service. I'm calling to inform you that the law has changed, so your liability for unauthorized credit card use is now unlimited. Give me your credit card information and we will protect it.

This telemarketing scam comes in the form of an offer for credit card loss protection insurance. Once the scammers obtain your credit card information, the scammers either charge you for worthless credit card loss protection insurance, or they do exactly what they warned you about: they run up fraudulent charges on your credit card. (The good news? You are liable for only $50 if you call your credit card company.)

The "Free Peek or Free Product for Your Credit Card Number" Scam

To access fifty unforgettable love slave websites, all you need to do is give us your credit card number. We won't charge you, but we need your credit card information to prove you are eighteen or over.

In this credit card scam, you are offered a free product if you provide your credit card number. You are told that your credit card will not be charged but is needed to permit you to register for the free product. For example, many adult sites permit users to view adult images online for free if they share their credit card information to prove they are over eighteen. Another method is to offer a free custom-designed website for a thirty-day trial period, with no obligation to continue. Don't believe it. Scammers will use your credit card number to run up charges on your card.

Checks

Before leaving for a business trip, Bill Reilly completed a number of personal matters. He was particularly relieved to have finished writing out the checks for all his bills, which he placed in his mailbox on his way out. Unfortunately, a thief got to his mailbox before the postman. The thief opened the stolen mail, erased the ink on the checks with an over-the-counter solvent, and rewrote the checks to be payable to himself, increasing the amounts by thousands of dollars.

Identity thieves find crafty ways to access your checking account. As in the example above, thieves can break into your mailbox, use a solvent to remove written information on a check, and then rewrite the check, making it payable to themselves. If they get hold of your checking account number, thieves can make counterfeit checks in your name on their computer. Finally, if an identity thief is able to obtain your sensitive personal information, including your social security number, he or she may even be so bold as to open a checking account in your name and write checks from that account. Every year, financial institutions lose more than $10 billion in check fraud, and merchants lose more than $13 billion to bad checks.

Whether you're the victim of identity theft or money mismanagement, bouncing a check may have longstanding consequences. First, you will endure a certain degree of hassle, inconvenience, and embarrassment, and you will have to pay your bank predetermined charges. Moreover, your bank may start to monitor your account more closely and, in case you have too many overdrafts, your bank may close your account, viewing your relationship as a liability.

If you bounce a check or activate an overdraft, your name may end up in the ChexSystems network, a national database that alerts banks and lenders. Approximately 80 percent of the country's financial institutions subscribe to ChexSystems. If your bank closes your account, a record of that account closure is entered into the ChexSystems database. A record of your bounced check remains in the database for five years, alerting banks, lenders, and even potential employers that you could be a credit risk. When you try to open a new checking account elsewhere, you may be turned down because of that record.

What can you do? First, remember that every financial institution establishes its own policy. If your bank closed your account because of its policies and procedures, another bank may be willing to give you a second chance. Second, you can send a letter to your bank and to ChexSystems to explain why the check bounced, but ChexSystems will not delete or alter a factual record unless the bank that closed the account instructs it to do so. Third, ChexSystems has recently started a new service called About Checking, which requires individuals with records in its database to attend a class about the basics of managing a checkbook and then earn their way back to having a checking account by paying off all outstanding debts to the financial institution where their account was closed. This program, however, is not available in every state.

> A record of your bounced check remains in the database for five years, alerting banks, lenders, and even potential employers that you could be a credit risk. When you try to open a new checking account elsewhere, you may be turned down because of that record.

If your name ends up in the ChexSystems database because of an error, ChexSystems will resolve matters with your bank and remove you from the database. The ChexSystems database includes 19 million old accounts listed as Closed for Cause. Some people who are included in the database do not even know that they have been listed until they attempt to open a new account and are rejected. To get in touch with ChexSystems, use the contact information on page 126.

Use these tips to better protect your checking account:

✴ **Protect your checking account information.** As with other sensitive personal information, safeguard your checking account information. Don't carry your checkbook with you if you don't need to write checks. Be careful about disclosing your checking account information over the telephone.

✴ **Protect your checks.** Protect your checks by storing both new and cancelled checks in a secure place. If you want to discard your old checks, shred them before disposing of them. Checks needed for tax purposes, however, should be kept for seven years. Order checks that are tamper-resistant. If your mailbox is not fully secure, mail your checks directly from the post office or leave them in a drop box.

✳ **Manage your checks.** Balance your checkbook each month and immediately report any lost or stolen checks or any fraudulent activity. If you order new checks, make sure none were stolen in transit.

✳ **Consider paying bills online.** You might consider paying bills online instead of by check. You reduce the chances of people stealing your checks by paying your bills this way, and fewer people will see your checking account information. Of course, online activities may raise other privacy concerns.

DEALING WITH COLLECTION AGENCIES

If you fail to pay your bills or if a creditor thinks you haven't as a result of an error on your account, you may hear from a debt collector or collection agency. Debt collectors and collection agents have a reputation for being heavy-handed and deceptive in their efforts to try to collect debts.

Under the Fair Debt Collection Practices Act (or FDCPA), collectors are required to treat you fairly and avoid unfair and deceptive actions against you when you owe a debt. The FDCPA outlines certain actions that debt collectors may and may not undertake. For example, debt collectors must identify themselves to you if they call you on the telephone, and they must stop calling you if you so instruct them in writing. Furthermore, debt collectors may not contact you before 8 a.m. or after 9 p.m., and they may not contact you at work if they are aware that your boss would not approve. Above all, they may not lie to you (for example, telling you that you will be arrested unless you pay promptly), harass you (such as swearing at you or calling you repeatedly), or abuse you (such as telling your friends and relatives that you owe money). Bottom line: Pay your bills on time. By doing so, you not only avoid unpleasant intrusions from debt collectors, but you also ensure that you don't jeopardize your credit report and credit score.

❋ **Order your ChexSystems report.** ChexSystems is a consumer-reporting agency, similar in many ways to the three credit bureaus. You can contact ChexSystems through its Web site (www.chexsystems.com) or order your report from ChexSystems as follows:

> By fax:
> Get form from website and fax to 602/659-2197
> By mail:
> **ChexSystems**
> 12005 Ford Road, Suite 600
> Dallas, TX 75234
> Attn: Consumer Relations

Online Banking and Online Payment

In 1998, three operators from an unchartered bank known as Net-ware International Bank, which was operating only on the Internet, were indicted by a federal grand jury on wire fraud, mail fraud, and money laundering charges. The business lured in up to $650,000 with an offer of a 20 percent return on savings and 10 percent return on checking accounts on its website.

The old jokes about limited bankers' hours no longer apply now that traditional and online-only banks and a bunch of online payment services are open 24/7 on the Web. Most of these banks are legitimate, and Web-based financial services have given thousands of customers access to expanded services and the convenience of managing a bank account and/or paying bills online. An added bonus is that using the Internet for bill paying and banking reduces the risk of identity theft significantly—up to 18 percent according to one account. Banks (and businesses that accept direct online payments) benefit when you pay your bills or manage your accounts online because they reduce their costs by approximately 80 percent. They also find that customers who manage their accounts and pay bills online tend to remain with the institution offering these services for a longer period of time.

Approximately 30 million households currently pay their bills online. Banks expect nearly 100 million households to convert to online bill payment by the end of 2006. Many customers pay all their bills directly through their banks. Banks often offer the service for free or offer incentives to sign up for the service. Other customers pay their bills through a business website. Others use services that consolidate all their bills and pay them automatically or one-by-one at the customer's request. These services typically charge $5 to $15 a month.

> An added bonus is that using the Internet for bill paying and banking reduces the risk of identity theft significantly—up to 18 percent according to one account.

Online payment options include PayPal (www.paypal.com) and other similar online payment services. PayPal has approximately 40 million users worldwide. Owned by eBay, the e-auction leader, PayPal allows any individual or business with an e-mail address to send and receive payments online in a secure environment, although PayPal itself has been the subject of numerous scams. It is not a substitute for your bank—the service depends upon bank accounts and credit cards to ensure security—but PayPal is generally safe and easy to use to pay almost any bill. Moreover, your PayPal balance is FDIC-insured for up to $100,000.

If you pay bills online, you will reduce the usual risks of thieves stealing your information from the mailbox or the Dumpster. On the other hand, you do take on other risks by paying your bills in this way. Follow the steps below to reduce your risks when you bank and pay bills online:

✳ **Make sure your online bank is legitimate.** For online-only banks, make sure your deposits are federally insured. Read the description of the institution and look for language that indicates the bank is Member FDIC or FDIC-insured, which means that the bank will guarantee the security of up to $100,000 of your assets. To be double sure, go to the FDIC website (www.fdic.gov) and click "Find My Institution" to look up your bank. The FDIC site should give you further information about your bank, including its official name (an online bank may have a different name from its parent company), headquarters, insurance certificate number, and more. Contact the FDIC immediately if your bank is not on their list. If your bank is not listed, it may be chartered overseas, and the FDIC may not insure your deposits. If the bank is not insured and it fails, you will lose your money.

✴ **Look up your financial institution's privacy policy.** All financial institutions— even online-only ones—are required to send you copies of their privacy policies with the option to opt out of information sharing with non-affiliates. In particular for online banking, look up your institution's policies on cookies (See chapter 7, "Your Computer and the Internet") to determine how it might track you while you're on their site. For example, if your bank also offers travel services and you click on the promotion for discount tickets to Florida, you might end up getting calls or mail about holiday travel promotions. If you're concerned about your browsing habits being tracked or the possibility of a flooded mailbox, e-mail inbox, or an interrupted dinner, then contact your financial institution, disable cookies (see chapter 7), or do not bank or pay bills online.

✴ **Make sure the site is secure.** If you're banking online and entering sensitive information, such as account numbers and passwords, make sure your transmission is encrypted to prevent unauthorized access. Most browsers display an icon of a lock or key in the corner of your screen whenever you're on a secure site. Another indication of a secure site is a Web URL beginning with *https://* instead of *http://*.

✴ **Be careful with your passwords.** Follow the steps detailed earlier in this chapter to protect your password.

✴ **Beware spoof sites.** PayPal, in particular, has been the target of many spoof sites which look official but are actually set up by identity thieves (see page 61). Also known as *phishing*, this scam sends e-mails to users of a service indicating a link to a fraudulent website. The fraudulent site may be an exact copy of the real site, even featuring logos that look the same as those on the legitimate site. You may be lured to the site by an urgent notice asking you to update your inactive account or the like. If you go to the spoof site, you will be asked to provide your user name and password. Again, follow the tip above to make sure the site is secure before you enter any information.

✳ **Practice good general computer security.** Make sure you protect your computer with antivirus software and antispyware software (spyware and trojan horses can pick up your passwords and other sensitive information and send it to their source). Invest in a firewall that will protect your system from hackers. See chapter 7, "Your Computer and the Internet," for additional details on protecting yourself when you are online.

✳ **Keep records of your online transactions.** Compare your PayPal or other online bill payment service transactions with your bank account and credit card bills on a regular basis.

✳ **Report problems immediately to your financial institution.** The Fair Credit Billing Act (FCBA) and Electronic Fund Transfer Act (EFTA) help you to resolve errors on credit and bank account statements, including incorrect fund transfers and computational errors. The EFTA requires your financial institution to tell you the results of its investigation within thirteen business days of your report. The act also requires the bank to correct the error within one business day of the bank's determining that an error has occurred. If the institution needs more time, it may take up to ninety days, but the bank must return money to your account within ten business days of receiving notice of the error. You must report the error within sixty days of its occurrence.

Take Control of Your Financial Documents

A Pennsylvania teenager was arrested for hacking into someone else's computer and using the individual's brokerage account to sell underpriced stock options. The teenager had distributed an e-mail to people in an online chat room for investors. The letter requested individuals to download a new stock-charting tool. Little did they know that the tool was really a computer keystroke-logging program that enabled the teenager to monitor their computers remotely and learn their user names, passwords, and brokerage account numbers.

> **How would you know if your privacy has been invaded or your identity stolen if you do not keep a record of your financial information?**

An important step in protecting your financial privacy is to take control of your financial documents. How would you know if your privacy has been invaded or your identity stolen if you do not keep a record of your financial information? Taking control means getting organized and making sure that your financial information is complete, accurate, and available for you to review.

Think about what you would do if you lost your wallet tomorrow. Would you know where to locate your bank statement to assess whether you had been the victim of ATM fraud? After facing a deadline, an expiration date, or an emergency that required you to check a document quickly, have you ever felt that you needed to be better organized? If you have ever lost your wallet, you understand the hassle of retrieving your personal records, canceling and replacing credit cards and other items, and then feeling anxious about the entire situation. Further, as discussed above, if you lose your credit card or ATM or debit card, you must report the loss or theft quickly to avoid greater financial liability.

As a first step, you must create an inventory or worksheet of your important accounts and documents. In addition, you should adopt a system so this inventory of accounts and documents remains up-to-date.

Follow these tips to protect your financial documents:

✴ **Store your inventory of records in a secure place.** Placing your documents in an unsecured drawer in your house is not adequate. Instead, use a locked filing cabinet, or even better, a fireproof safe. You should use the same rule for passwords and personal identification numbers, which you should write on a piece of paper to ensure that you do not forget them. Make copies of your records, and keep the copy in a secure place.

✴ **Keep a record.** Your list of important accounts should include:

  ▶ the accounts that you maintain at various financial institutions
  ▶ account numbers
  ▶ the contact persons at these institutions

Either make a worksheet that compiles this information about every account, or make copies of each account's monthly statement and keep those copies in the secure place you have selected. For example, with respect to your credit cards, you might make a copy of both sides of your current credit cards, including the customer service 800 numbers to call in case of loss or theft. If something happens, you have the information available to cancel the cards.

✴ **Tell a trusted person about your system.** You must ensure that a trusted person, such as your spouse, your lawyer, or your accountant, knows where the originals of your documents are stored in case of your death or incapacitation.

✴ **Do not keep documents permanently.** Learn how long to keep documents. In many cases, you need not keep documentation of sensitive financial information permanently. For example, ATM slips are only needed for a month or until you balance your account; payroll stubs can be discarded annually after you receive your W-2 and annual social security statement. On the other hand, you must keep other documents for a longer period of time, such as in the case of tax records, which must be kept for the current year and previous six years. You may want to create a worksheet for your important documents (including credit card statements and receipts, insurance policies, tax records, investments, bank statements, and so on) to serve as a checklist for managing each of these documents.

✳ **Be careful when discarding documents.** Your financial documents—even old ones—contain sensitive personal information. When you discard documents, be cautious. Do not place your documents in a garbage bag. For optimum protection, use a shredder to destroy the documents. If you do not own a shredder, you should buy one. At the very least, you should destroy documents and cards to an extent that none of the sensitive information, including account information, credit card numbers, or social security number, can be identified in any manner.

THE BOTTOM LINE

► Cash was king! Long live credit! Today, American consumers purchase more items with credit cards than with cash. Welcome to the new age of money. A paper trail may now exist for every purchase you make.

► Your financial institution knows a great deal about you. It gathers detailed information concerning all aspects of your personal and financial life from the information you include on an application to obtain a loan, credit card, or other financial product or services. It gathers additional information from other companies as well.

► Money doesn't talk? Under the federal financial privacy laws, your bank or financial institution must send you a privacy notice annually. The notice must disclose how the bank will use your personal financial information. To prevent your information from being shared with nonaffiliated third parties of your financial institution, make sure to opt out by checking the box provided in the form. Respond within thirty days of receiving the notice.

► A run for your money. Theft, loss, and fraud of financial information are on the rise. If your credit, debit, or ATM card is lost, stolen, or shows unauthorized or fraudulent use, report this information as quickly as possible to your financial institution. Otherwise, you may be liable for charges, and the more time passes, the more liability you may incur.

▸ Take control of your financial information. Keep a record of your sensitive personal and financial information and store it in a secure place. Be prepared for loss or fraud. It *can* happen to you!

Your Shopping

DIGITAL CAMERAS

"Enter the date and time and press OK.
Step 7, enter your credit card number..."

You have your prescriptions filled at a big, respected supermarket at which you are a regular customer. One day, you receive marketing literature in the mail targeted to you and your specific ailment from a company with whom you have never done any business. It turns out that your supermarket shared your sensitive prescription information without your permission.

You shop for shampoo at a chain drugstore in your town. You see a small sign that vaguely indicates the store is in some sort of experimental mode. What you don't know is that every expression that passes over your face as you examine the bottle of shampoo, be-

lieving yourself to be alone, is being scrutinized by a group of people crowded around a monitor in another state.

You receive sexually explicit letters in the mail, and somehow the letter-writer knows everything about you, from your most basic information such as your name, address, age, and birthday, to more obscure and sensitive data such as the soap you use, the kind of underwear you buy, how often you drink alcohol, and your favorite kind of candy. An investigation reveals that the letter's author is a prison inmate who processed data collected by a company that compiles consumer profiles from sources such as product warranty cards, loyalty cards, and surveys.

You buy plastic bags at a drugstore. You plan to use the bags to wrap children's sandwiches for school. Shortly after your purchase the government gains access to the purchase profiles of all the loyalty card users at your store. Because you bought a large number of bags, and these are the same bags that often are used by drug dealers, law enforcement authorities make you a target of investigation.

Do you remember the days when you walked into the local store, bought your candy or comic book with a dollar bill or a few coins, and had the shop owner ring up your purchase on a metal cash register? Unless you shopped there often, the shop owner knew nothing about you. If you were a regular customer, the store owner might know your name or your parents' names. Well, those days of shopping anonymously or enjoying a trusted and personal relationship are over.

Today, the Internet and other computer technologies have changed the entire shopping experience. Without even leaving your own home, you can now buy almost anything from anywhere, whether it is oysters shipped overnight from Seattle to New York, a Jaguar XKE, or a toy for your child's birthday. At various super-stocked auction sites, you can find practically any rare item you seek, from art deco vacuum cleaners to corkscrew dogs. At any hour, you can research products, compare prices, assess different companies, and learn about upcoming sales and specially discounted programs.

Technology transforms customers into more sophisticated buyers. It also transforms businesses into more sophisticated sellers. Many stores now offer discounts if you pledge loyalty to them by providing them with information about your personal life. They can collect, buy, and sell information about your buying history, including where you shop, what you buy, and the names of your favorite brands. The convenience may become slightly unsettling only when you receive unsolicited coupons for the cold sore cream you always buy or when the maternity store across town knows you're pregnant before your uncle does.

To retailers, almost no fact about your life is irrelevant. From your favorite brand of chocolate and how often you buy it, to your pant size, your acne cream, or your subscription to *Shape* magazine, stores are fascinated by the intimate details of your shopping habits. Here is a sampling of some of the sensitive data that certain companies and retailers may be collecting about you:

- ▶ name, address, and telephone number
- ▶ date of birth
- ▶ degree of education
- ▶ clothing sizes
- ▶ religious background
- ▶ travel destinations
- ▶ credit history
- ▶ philanthropic donations
- ▶ income
- ▶ race
- ▶ ailments, from psoriasis to cancer
- ▶ marital status
- ▶ hobbies
- ▶ favorite items or brands, including magazines, music, whiskey, cigarettes, ice cream, toilet paper, and so forth

When you provide lifestyle information to retailers, they may sell your profile to an affiliate or to profiling companies for the purposes of additional marketing. Further, even if you review a company's privacy policy, and determine you are comfortable with the way a company treats your privacy, you may still face certain situations that are less controllable. Consider these common privacy risks:

▶ Discount or loyalty cards track what you buy, and over time accumulate a record of your life that you may find objectionable;

▶ Personal and financial information entered on a shopping site could become vulnerable to hackers;

▶ Company employees could release or sell the information they have in their database;

▶ Criminals could operate a fraudulent website and make you a victim of identity theft;

▶ Your information, even if protected by a company's privacy and security policies, could be subpoenaed;

▶ Your personal and financial information could be processed overseas where its handling will not be regulated by U.S. federal and state laws; and

▶ The company from which you purchased a certain item could go bankrupt or get acquired by another company with a different privacy policy, and your information would no longer be protected in the same manner.

If you provide personal information to stores, not only do you risk revealing a lot about your personal life when you shop, you also risk having your Crest toothpaste-buying, car-owning, $50,000-earning identity stolen. Whether you shop online, by phone, or in stores, the sophisticated technologies and scams that criminals now employ increase the likelihood of your becoming a victim of identity theft. See chapter 3, "Your Identity," to reduce your chances of becoming a victim of identity theft.

There are ways to outsmart marketers and thieves by buying your food and clothes with cash, shopping exclusively in out-of-the-way stores, refusing to divulge any information about yourself under any circumstances, and otherwise leading a hermit's existence. But chances are that you don't want to take these steps. There are better ways to safeguard yourself and your family from unsolicited marketing, Big Brother–like surveillance, and identity theft.

By knowing which information a merchant is and is not permitted to demand, understanding the mechanisms of a secure transaction, recognizing the widespread use of profiling lists, and staying alert to common scams, you can prevent the worst of the risks you take.

A Trade in Personal Information

In the mid-1990s, a news reporter contacted one of the larger companies that compile and sell consumer profiles. He purchased a few thousand dossiers on children from them. To make a point about how vulnerable this information is, the reporter bought the files using the highly publicized name of a man who had just confessed to murdering a child and was on trial at that time for the crime.

Personicx, a subsidiary of Acxiom Corp., relies on a number of outside sources to compile market data, including public records, third-party research, and product-warranty cards. It updates its records monthly so the information reflects the birth of your child or your latest job promotion. The goal? To identify your "velocity component," or your ups and downs on the socioeconomic ladder. Personicx also provides a household segmentation system that places each U.S. household into one of seventy segments based on that household's specific consumer and demographic characteristics.

Whenever you buy something online or from a catalog, the company that sells you the product compiles a profile on you, beginning with your name and address and the size, make, or model of the item you ordered. If you disclose information on a survey, or answer any extraneous questions attached to an order form, you are adding information to your growing dossier. The more comprehensive the profile about you, the better it is for companies to either sell or to use in the marketing of products. For example, some companies build profiles on you that can be up to thirty pages in length, and that cover every shred of information they can find about you, from your social security number, to the kind of pet you own, to your different hobbies, to your favorite brand of coffee. You may never know that they are creating this profile about you.

Retailers and companies maintain different policies about whether and how they collect data on customers, with whom they share the information, and to what end they use the information. Some companies maintain a file on you only for their own marketing purposes, but many sell their lists, including your personal information, to other companies to generate revenue. In the aggregate, the files or personal dossiers that retailers and companies may compile about you include information from many sources, including:

> Some companies build profiles on you that can be up to thirty pages in length, and that cover every shred of information they can find about you.

- ▶ consumer surveys, often mailed to your home as sweepstakes invites
- ▶ catalog sales
- ▶ product warranty cards
- ▶ charitable, lifestyle, or political organizations
- ▶ book or music clubs
- ▶ online and off-line purchase information
- ▶ discount or loyalty cards

These profiles are supplemented with data from other sources, such as census findings, Department of Motor Vehicle information, and other public records, as detailed in chapter 2, "Your Personal Information and the Public Record."

Individual stores track your buying history and so do massive data aggregators such as Acxiom and ChoicePoint. The aggregators build profiles on you from surveys, book clubs and magazine subscriptions, charitable donations, and other sources. They sell dossiers as lists to marketers who often use the information to supplement their own data. One aggregator, Acxiom, based in Arkansas, maintains a database on 96 percent of American households, which can include real-time information on you. Each consumer is placed in a defined category, such as Timeless Elders, Wealthy Urban, Retired Middle-

Class Suburban, or Rustic Living, and then each category is sold as a list. Magazine companies, which theoretically sell only name and address information, also sell data on lifestyle or interests based on the magazines to which the consumer is subscribing. For companies that sell or buy personal information, these lists of profiles become more valuable as more information is added.

> Acxiom, based in Arkansas, maintains a database on 96 percent of American households, which can include real-time information on you.

Who gets to see your personal information? For data aggregators and some companies, the sale or sharing of your personal information is an important means of generating revenue, so they are quite willing to sell your information to other companies that want to buy marketing profiles. Basic lists vary in terms of cost, but most are priced in the range of $20 to $100 per thousand names, depending on the detail or specificity provided in the list. Your individual profile cannot be bought alone, because the lists are sold not by name but by category. This, however, might not prevent a health insurance company from buying names from a medical profiler and then screening out applicants with certain ailments. Nonprofit organizations can use these lists to seek donation requests from you based on the amount of money you make and the type of charities to which you've donated in the past. Government authorities and law enforcement can use your profile to conduct investigations of you. (See information on profiling and Uncle Sam in chapter 2, "Your Personal Information and the Public Record," and CAPPS II profiling in chapter 12, "Your Everyday Life.")

Want to guess who is *not* able to see the profile that Acxiom or Wal-Mart might have compiled about you? You. You may never know what is contained in your profile or if the information is accurate. Most companies do not allow you to review your profile (one exception is ChoicePoint, which allows you to see *certain* information if you purchase it through its KnowX subsidiary). Because these profiles are sold to or subpoenaed by different government agencies for law enforcement purposes, you may be identified as a possible threat or target of an investigation based on your profile. For example, in 1997, the Drug Enforcement Administration (DEA) subpoenaed customer information from Smith's Foods to determine whether certain individuals were purchasing an inordinate number of plastic bags. In this situation you would never see the full profile on which such an assessment was based or have the chance to correct any errors.

How Companies Track You

To make their marketing efforts more efficient, companies want as much information about you as possible. The more they know about you, the better they can predict what you'll buy and how much

> You may never know what is contained in your profile or if the information is accurate.

you'll spend. The best way to protect your privacy in an age of information gathering is to understand exactly how information about you is collected.

Point of Sale

> Sam went to his local Performance store to buy an item he'd been coveting. At the cash register, the sales clerk demanded his full name to complete the transaction. Sam was planning to pay with cash, so he didn't see why he should have to share his name. It was only after he threatened to walk out of the store that the sales clerk relented. What did the store offer as a reason for needing this information? If Sam lost the receipt and wanted to return the merchandise, they could look up the transaction. "Well, okay, that's the story being offered to the customers," he says. "[But] that doesn't preclude some marketing dweeb within Performance in the future [from] deciding that there is all this nice customer data just sitting around, and it's time to mine it for marketing purposes."

Remember the days when stores offered you the option of putting your name and address on a mailing list? By doing so, you would sign yourself up to receive notices of sales and promotions for that store, and only that store. Today, that seems so straightforward as to be quaint.

Now, when you buy something at a store, the salesperson who rings up your purchase will often ask for information, including your phone number, address, e-mail address, photo identification, whether or not you wish to receive notices of sales and promotions, or whether you wish to join a discount or loyalty club. They may even take the opportunity to ask you lifestyle questions, or give you a form with those questions to fill out and return.

In some cases, this information is requested either to confirm the credit card belongs to you, or so the store has recourse against you if your check bounces, for example. Most often, the retailer is taking advantage of this moment to collect data on one of its customers, namely you. The information can be used as research for its own marketing strategies, or for a phone or mailing list for marketing, or as a commodity to be used or sold to affiliates as well as profiling companies.

The request for your e-mail address or zip code, for example, is often made while you are completing a transaction at the register. It is usually made in such a nonchalant manner that you may not realize the information is not required as part of this transaction. In some cases, the software on a cashier's register is set up so that unless the cashier secures certain information from you, the transaction cannot be completed. However, if the information request seems excessive, do not be afraid either to ask why the information is being collected, or to decline answering. You have the right to decline a request for your e-mail address or zip code.

Product Warranty Cards

Edgar Rosen bought a Sunbeam Grillmaster. He was appalled at the level of questioning on the enclosed warranty card. Among the information demanded was his income; his marital status; the number, ages, and occupations of others in his household; the credit cards people in his household used; and whether anyone there smoked cigars or wore contact lenses. The form also instructed him to check off a long list of products he owned. But the foot-long warranty card didn't stop there: it also asked specific questions about the Rosen family's health conditions and prescriptions. At the bottom of the card was the following warning in boldfaced letters: "TO NOT RETURN THIS CARD MAY AFFECT YOUR WARRANTY."

Warranty cards enclosed in the packaging of products are one of the most effective means for retailers to gather information about you. These cards often ask you about income, marital status, interests, and other profile information. If you think that you must mail in the warranty card to secure the warranty for the product you purchased, you are wrong. Companies enter this information into a data bank to use the information for future marketing purposes, or to sell profiles and marketing lists to data aggregators.

> If you think that you must mail in the warranty card to secure the warranty for the product you purchased, you are wrong.

Before you fill out a warranty card, you should first understand that the warranty for the product you purchased is almost always secure if you keep the receipt and the warranty card. The information you supply in warranty cards will almost always be used to market products to you. The only downside of not completing the warranty cards is that companies may have trouble contacting you if your product is unsafe and they must recall it. If you're concerned about this, you may consider going halfway and filling out only your name and address. Weigh the benefits and disadvantages of completing the information required in warranty cards and decide what's best for you.

Loyalty and Supermarket Cards

You bring a lawsuit against a supermarket for damages after you fall on their wet floor. Right before you go to court, though, the store's attorney informs you that your purchase of numerous bottles of wine per week will be offered as evidence against you to prove likely intoxication. This actually happened to Bob Rivera, a Los Angeles resident, whose buying habits were used against him when he sued Von's supermarket after he slipped on a yogurt spill and shattered his kneecap. Von's attorneys implied that he was a drunk because of the quantities of alcohol he purchased, all recorded on his Von's Frequent Shopper card.

You strike up a conversation with the woman standing in the checkout line behind you and discover she's been offered a better dis-

count on the same can of peas you're purchasing. Why? Her loyalty
card records show she only buys peas when they're on sale, and
that you buy them regardless.

Whatever their names—loyalty cards, club cards, value cards, smart cards, member cards, discount cards, preferred cards, or advantage cards—programs offered by supermarkets, drugstores, and other stores gather a great deal of information about you. In particular, they build a profile of you by tracking every purchase you make at their store or chain.

A cottage industry has emerged around these card programs. Consultant companies offer businesses *penetration profiles,* which are supplemental reports on a store's customers. These profiles are built from facts retrieved from other databases, such as public records. Once these records are compiled, the store has a bigger, more detailed sense of your life as a consumer, and it can work its marketing accordingly. Not only will it know your name, address, telephone number, and (in some programs) your social security number, but through outside sources it will also know your age, whether or not you're married, if you own a home, if you have kids, and much more.

What exactly do loyalty cards do for you? That depends. Retailers say that they provide valued customers with virtual coupons that are customized to customers' preferred products and brands. If you show a history of buying orange juice all the time, and a certain brand of orange juice, you may win savings on that item in the future. Some stores have divided card users into brackets, and award the biggest savings to the consumers whom they call the most valued. Other stores claim they can customize their stock better if they know you buy certain merchandise regularly.

Critics claim that retailers use these programs to blackmail you. If you want savings, you must sacrifice privacy and disclose all your sensitive personal information. Even more vehement critics claim that the savings you get are minimal, or, in some cases, nonexistent. They claim the stores manipulate prices to make it look like you are getting savings when, over a period of time, if the prices are gauged comprehensively, the savings you garner are fictitious. Privacy activists also denounce the practice of dividing card users into groups, which they claim is discriminatory: the most valued customers are determined by data from the cards to be the most profitable to the store and really represent a fraction of the consumer base.

Critics have also accused some stores of taking advantage of their loyalty programs. For example, at some stores, consumers who demonstrate that they will buy yogurt all the time regardless of price will *not* receive savings, but customers who will only buy yogurt when it is on sale will get savings as a further incentive. In this case, if you enrolled in a card program, you may ultimately decide that sacrificing your privacy leads to other customers' gains, and not your own.

> **Few loyalty cardholders realize that federal authorities may also access their store's records.**

Besides the basic threats to privacy, a store's record of you and your purchases may be susceptible to invasions that you could never imagine. Your company may have a privacy policy, but that pledge may not always be possible or practicable. All a company has to do to share your information with another company is to partner with it. For example, the Stop & Shop supermarket chain once partnered with an Internet company called SmartMouth. com. Customers could enter their loyalty card information into the Smart-Mouth system to see a list of their most recent purchases and the nutritional value of their entire list. Customer complaints eventually forced the companies to shut down the program.

In the recent past, databases of customer profiles have been the target of government officials, academics, and prestigious research centers. To what end? For one, as a tool to discover the links between advertising, eating habits, health, and obesity, among other things. It is true that public health issues are important and should be addressed, but signing up for discounts at your local supermarket does not mean you agreed to be a subject in such a study. Few loyalty cardholders realize that federal authorities may also access their store's records. Although there haven't been many reported cases of seized records, cases such as the one about plastic bags and drug dealers have occurred, and the potential for further intrusion is possible. After the terrorist attacks of September 11, federal agents used the shopper card transactions of Mohammad Atta and the other hijackers to create a profile of "ethnic tastes and terrorist supermarket-shopping preferences" in order to track citizens' possible terrorist proclivities.

Card users who resent the system have devised ways to beat it. Some consumers make stickers of their own bar codes and apply those stickers to other customers' cards so the data of four hundred customers is being erroneously treated as a profile of one consumer. Cashiers at certain stores accept a phone number if you don't have your card with you, so shoppers sometimes use random phone numbers to avoid being tracked. Others swap cards so the store is unable to create an accurate chronicle. Still others use fake names and addresses at stores that don't ask for additional identification.

The bottom line is that if you do not want your purchasing habits tracked, do not enroll in loyalty programs.

In-Store Cameras

In 2003, Tamara Perez, a shopper in a Toys "R" Us store in Atlanta, sued for invasion of privacy when she noticed a hole in the ceiling above the toilet she was using. She moved a ceiling tile and discovered a camera pointed down at her. Perez's lawyer says that Perez was appalled that a camera had been installed in a bathroom, especially a bathroom that children might use. Toys "R" Us managers claimed they had no knowledge that a camera was there, the device wasn't supposed to be there, and they did not know who put it there.

The Virginia-based company Brickstream uses advanced image-recognition software to track customers' movements throughout stores. The software, which is in use in one hundred stores, records how long customers spend in each section, how long they wait in line, and what they buy. Brickstream's software revealed that people often buy cold medicine and orange juice in the same trip, so the company was able to recommend to its client that the OJ be positioned near the medicine.

Today, it is fairly commonplace to see cameras in stores. For the store, the camera is a security mechanism to discourage theft, and this use of technology is widely accepted. But many people are so accustomed to video surveillance in stores that they forget that various privacy issues can emerge. First, if you

146

commit a crime, or allegedly commit a crime, your picture may be broadcast to a much larger audience than the security personnel overseeing the store. For example, you probably saw the film of Winona Ryder when she was accused of stealing from a store. Second, retailers are generally not permitted to place cameras in areas that are more sensitive to your privacy, such as bathrooms or changing rooms.

Still other surveillance technologies enable retailers to follow you in stores in the same way they can track you online when you surf their websites. Brickstream is one company that creates software to track customers throughout stores to determine how long they linger over certain products, where they gravitate, and how long they stand in line. Although Brickstream claims the software isn't designed to distinguish one person from the next (the cameras track only customers' heads and shoulders), privacy advocates worry about the possibility that it could one day be used in conjunction with facial-recognition software.

Signature Capture Devices

Signature capture devices are relatively new technologies that convert a handwritten signature into a digital image and store the image in computer files. These electronic tablets are often linked to the credit or debit card system and are typically located at the counter when you pay. Retailers use these new devices to make your transaction more efficient, reduce paperwork, and reduce the potential for fraud. Be aware, however, that because your signature is stored in a digital record, a hacker may be able to obtain it and use it in conjunction with other personal information to commit a crime against you, such as forging your signature on fake checks or credit card purchases. Privacy advocates say it is too soon to tell if signature capture devices reduce or increase fraud. Many stores allow their customers to sign their signatures on paper if they refuse to sign into the store's database. Talk to the store's manager if you feel uncomfortable.

Automatic Number Identification

It's 5 p.m. on your anniversary. You call the 800 number of a florist to see if you can send an overnight delivery of flowers to your wife, who is out of town on a business trip. The representative informs you that you should have called an hour earlier and that she won't be able to process your order. You hang up the phone; you're not surprised. But this time next year you will be surprised when the florist sends you reminders to order flowers early for your anniversary.

> Whenever you call a company's 800 or 900 number to order or inquire about products, your phone number may be entered into the company's database. Using an ANI reverse-directory service, the company is able to get your name, address, and even lifestyle information.

Automatic Number Identification (ANI) is a method of data capture used by companies that have 800 or 900 numbers. When ANI was first introduced, subscriber information was transmitted only in the case of calls to 911 and law enforcement emergencies. Today, any owner of a toll-free or charge number can collect personal data through ANI.

Here's how it works: whenever you call a company's 800 or 900 number to order or inquire about products, your phone number may be entered into the company's database. Using an ANI reverse-directory service, the company is able to get your name, address, and even lifestyle information. An innocuous phone call can now lead to your profile being included in a corporate database, including the time you called and the reason for your call. The company then has all it needs to solicit and market directly to you. The best way to get around this one? Use the phone number blocking code that your local phone company provides or do not call 800 or 900 numbers from your home telephone. See chapter 8, "Your Home," for additional details on blocking your home phone number when you make outgoing calls.

Radio Frequency Identification Chips (RFIDs)

You are shopping for razors. Apparently razors are shoplifted frequently, but you have never shoplifted and never will. However, by virtue of the product's notoriety, and by the mechanism of a radio frequency ID chip that triggers a camera nearby, you are the un-

knowing and perhaps unwilling subject of a photograph. The camera snaps a picture each time the razor is moved from the shelf, chronicling any would-be thieves.

In 2003, Wal-Mart and Procter & Gamble admitted to secret RFID testing in the Broken Arrow, Oklahoma, Wal-Mart store between March and July of that year. The store had installed chips in the packaging of Lipfinity lipstick. Customers who touched the package were videotaped and monitored by marketers, some of whom were hundreds of miles away. Wal-Mart had previously announced that it was not testing RFID chips.

Radio frequency ID chips, otherwise known as RFIDs, are a technology innovation that may replace bar codes. These tiny microchips can be implanted in products. Information on the chips can be picked up by readers that are strategically placed throughout the store.

As with any new technology, there are pros and cons to these devices. For the store, RFIDs expedite the checkout process because a device-implanted product can be sensed from five feet away, allowing cashiers to ring up sales at a faster rate. The devices also make inventory easier, because a box of items can be inventoried simply by putting the box to the receiver. Further, shoplifting can be controlled, because these chips cannot be removed and cameras can be triggered each time a shopper picks up an item with a history of being attractive to thieves, such as a pack of shaving razors. These chips also give companies unprecedented capabilities, because the chips provide a lifetime of data on the items that are purchased.

For you, this technology means that stores may use RFID chips to accumulate a detailed profile on you, including your history of purchases and much more. Any store that has a receiver can read all the tiny chips that you carry around with you—including the one in the chip-embedded coat that you bought at another store last year. If that coat were made by an expensive designer, say, Versace, you could theoretically be charged more for items. You could also be photographed, without being aware of it, for picking up an item that has an RFID chip in it. Moreover, any personal information you give during the transaction—whether it is your credit card number, your e-mail address, your phone number, or your photograph—can be recorded and linked to that chip. As is true of other customer information databases, if this network of chips and receivers becomes prevalent, your detailed profile may be vulnerable to use by the government, the police, or criminals. All three groups might be interested in knowing, albeit for different purposes, that you frequently wear Versace.

> Any store that has a receiver can read all the tiny chips that you carry around with you—including the chip-embedded coat that you bought at another store last year. If that coat were made by an expensive designer, say, Versace, you could theoretically be charged more for items.

If the technology catches on, there may be RFID receivers everywhere you go (not only in stores) recording what you're wearing, what you're touching, and where you're going, and crosslinking that information with data from other sources.

The RFID technology is still too expensive to be used on a large scale, but experts predict that the costs of these chips will drop dramatically within the next few years. Stores such as Wal-Mart are already testing the chips on a small scale and for individual products like Gillette razors. Other uses of RFID technology beyond the store include everything from its use in automobile paint and tires to the European Union's plan to embed the chips into EU bank notes to catch counterfeiters. One Singapore hospital has already issued RFID cards to everyone entering the emergency department of the hospital as a public health incentive. If a patient is diagnosed with SARS at or after his or her hospital visit, the hospital will know with whom he or she had contact.

Privacy advocates have discussed ways to retaliate if the use of RFID tags becomes widespread. Ideas include crushing, puncturing, or microwaving the chips, boycotting products that include them, and devising blocker tags to jam the chips' radio signal.

Advocates of the chips say that the chips and receivers are too weak for anything but in-store convenience, but privacy advocates aver that the technology could easily be made to be more sensitive. The best advice for now is to inquire whether the stores in which you shop use RFID technology, and then decide before you purchase whether you object to a microchip existing in an item you bring into your home.

SHOPPING SCAMS

From the infamous snake oil scammers of the distant past to the techno-savvy scammers of today, people have always tried to get fools to part with their money. Here are a few of the popular scams to watch out for today.

The "Better Deal" Scam

Get your Epson cartridge cheaper and faster!!! We sell your printer's ink for only $4.99 by going to www.499epsoncartidges.com. Buy in bulk for your company! Escrow services offered.

One of the most popular Internet auction scams involves a scam artist luring a bidder off the official auction site by promising a better deal. The offer seems credible because it offers an escrow service. But it is possible, as it is possible with any kind of site, to create a false escrow service website. In this case, the con artist leads the buyer to a fabricated escrow service, where your bank account or credit card information is collected. After the money is transferred to some account to which the scammer has access, the particular escrow service disappears and so does your money. The merchandise, of course, never arrives.

The "Try Out Our Product" Scam

We know that you love golf. You were recommended to us as someone who might be willing to "play test" a new line of high-quality golf clubs. Are you interested? All you have to do is test the clubs for sixty days and fill out a questionnaire.

There's just one catch: The company asks for your credit card number for a security deposit to ensure that you return the clubs. It explains that your account will be charged $1,500 for the clubs, but that the charge will be removed as soon as they are returned. Sure. Send the clubs back and you'll see that your money's in the hole.

The "Membership Fee" Scam

Super CD/DVD combo for free to members of our exclusive electronics club! All you need to do is pay a token membership fee and find five more members to join. Then you'll receive a new high-tech gadget every month.

In this scam, you are promised high-end goods—like electronic items or long-distance phone cards—for free. All you have to do is pay a small club membership fee. To receive the offered goods, you must recruit a certain number of participants. This is commonly known as a pyramid scheme. Almost the entire payoff goes to the promoters, and little to none is paid to the consumers who pay to participate.

Shopping Online

If you've signed up for My Yahoo service, you may have been asked for your birth date and your e-mail address. The service claims it needs this information so it can offer you a prompt in case you forget your user name. But just wait until your birthday comes around—you may be swimming in promotions.

The advent of the Internet has resulted in new, exciting and highly convenient ways to shop. For some, such as disabled and handicapped people, the Internet has become a necessity. However, the rules governing online merchants are different than the rules for brick-and-mortar retailers because the nature of the transaction is different. Online transactions provide no opportunity to check a photo ID against a credit card, so from the online merchant's standpoint, security is challenging. As a result, many online retailers request that you provide your name, credit card number, the credit card's billing address, and often your phone number as evidence of a legitimate transaction. Further, you will need to provide the mailing address of the place where you intend to receive your purchase.

In addition to personal information that you must input to shop online, a website collects other information that you unknowingly provide through what are known as cookies. The site may track your online activities, such as:

- the areas within the website you visited
- the last website you visited
- files that you may have downloaded
- your other online activities within the site, such as using Internet searches or participating in chat rooms or on bulletin boards

In these situations, you may not be aware that the website has obtained other, and perhaps intimate, personal information about you. Read more about how you're tracked online in Chapter 7, "Your Computer and the Internet."

Be wary if an online shopping site asks you to provide additional information. Some sites pose questions about your lifestyle, preferences, and income, and they require an answer to these questions to complete your transaction. None of these questions is essential to the transaction, and most e-merchants mark fields and questions that are required with an asterisk. Avoid responding to any questions that are not required, and if information is required that you do not feel is vital to the transaction, consider shopping at other sites. Further, be cautious if a site asks for the smaller identifying numbers that appear on your credit card. The one exception may be sites that involve a financial transaction, such as sites where you can purchase your credit report or a mortgage. These transactions may require you to supply sensitive information such as your social security number and previous addresses.

How to Tell if a Site Is Legitimate

Becky Roberts, an account executive and regular California-based eBay auctioneer, received an e-mail that appeared to be a legitimate eBay request for updated personal information. The e-mail included what seemed to be official eBay logos. Becky complied with the request and entered her credit card number, checking account number, address, and other personal information. One week later she received a notice from eBay telling her that the request was not legitimate.

One issue associated with online shopping that rarely needs to be addressed in the brick-and-mortar marketplace is determining whether or not a site represents a true business. Anyone in the world can create a website, and cyberspace con artists profit by launching websites just to obtain credit card information or other sensitive information, which they then use elsewhere to make purchases or open accounts. The safest means of shopping online, if possible, is to restrict yourself to doing business online with companies you already know.

Some hard-to-find objects may, however, only be available on websites that you have never previously visited or seen. If you dare to try a new company online, investigate it beforehand by following the tips below.

✳ **Check with the Better Business Bureau (www.bbb.org) to see if the company exists.**

✳ **Check whether the company has a listing in the phone directory.**

✳ **Search to see whether any press articles have been written about the company.**

✳ **Check whether the website provides information about the sponsoring company, such as a telephone number or physical address.** If so, call the phone number. A site is suspicious if it includes only a post office box. If you call the company but no live voice ever answers the phone, then this may also be cause for suspicion.

✳ **Look at the site's overall design.** Is it garish or amateurish? Does the site contain spelling mistakes or bad grammar? Fraudulent sites may be riddled with errors.

✳ **Ask yourself if the pricing of the products is "almost too good to be true."** The site may be suspect if it urges you to buy a product quickly so you get the best deal, or if it requires you to send cash via overnight mail or courier.

✳ **Look for any request for irrelevant information, such as your social security number.**

✳ **Consider restricting yourself to conducting online business only with U.S. merchants.** Though an online merchant based in another country is not necessarily suspect, if a problem does arise, it will be easier for you to resolve if the merchant is located within the United States. Foreign businesses are not regulated by U.S. state and federal laws, so if you do business with foreign businesses, you may not be protected in the manner you might like to be.

How to Tell if a Website Is Secure

You shop online at a store you trust. The store maintains a privacy policy that guarantees the security of your financial and personal data. At some later date you find out that it took less than a minute for a twenty-year-old independent computer programmer to locate a flaw in the site's online security. This programmer was able to retrieve the names, addresses, and credit card numbers of a half million customers.

By hacking into the New York Times *computer system, Adrian Lamo, a twenty-two-year-old California-based hacker, accessed a database containing the home telephone numbers and social security numbers of more than three thousand contributors to the* Times *Op-Ed page. Lamo then established five fictitious user names to conduct extensive computer searches using the LexisNexis information service, including searches to see whether his exploits as a hacker were mentioned.*

Before you shop online, you must ensure that the site with which you are dealing is secure. After all, to buy something online you must provide some sensitive personal data to complete a transaction. The most secure sites use encryption technologies that effectively scramble your personal information during the transaction as your data moves from your computer to those of the online vendor. Further, secure sites will maintain your data in a scrambled and encrypted format to further protect against any hacker who seeks to ransack a company's database for hundreds of names and credit card numbers.

A site can never be fully secure against online hacking, and the situations above could happen to you even if you are careful about entering your data only on secure sites. It is best to use your judgment as to whether you trust the site in the first place. To ensure that the transmission of your information is as safe as possible, follow these steps:

✳ **Check if the website has a seal from Verisign indicating that the site is secure.** The site should also provide additional information about its security so you are confident your data will be properly handled before you submit any confidential or secure information. See chapter 7, "Your Computer and the Internet," for more information on Verisign and other seals of approval.

✳ **Look out for a security alert window that pops up and indicates "you are about to view pages over a secure connection."**

✳ **Make sure the site's address begins with "https://" instead of "http://".** The s stands for secure but, occasionally, this s appears in the address only when you reach the page in which you place your order.

✳ **Look for a lock icon on the bottom of your screen, or a closed lock icon to reflect a secure session.** Most websites display their privacy policies, and this information should include details about the site's security levels. For example, the site might indicate precisely what kind of secure layers of technology or authentication systems it uses to protect the confidentiality of your information.

Your Password

A group of hackers between the ages of sixteen and twenty-one stole the passwords and personal information of more than two hundred legitimate Internet account holders and sold them through a middleman to users on the lookout for cheap, unlimited Internet access.

A New York City teenager stole more than five hundred AOL user passwords by using Trojan horse computer programs. He sent the programs to AOL users via e-mails that carried the programs as attachments. When a recipient opened the attachments, the Trojan horse programs would install themselves onto the user's hard drive and record every single one of the AOL user's keystrokes, including passwords.

Many websites create an account for you to process your transaction and to facilitate future transactions. To create such an account, you need to choose both a user name and a password for the account. You should adopt these guidelines for establishing your password:

✳ **Be careful with your password.** Never give it to anyone, either directly or indirectly. You do not need to provide it even if a representative of the website requests your password. If you forget your password, the company will usually reset the password.

✳ **Use a password you can remember, but not one composed of or incorporating your birthday, maiden name, telephone number, license number, or social security number, birth date, or nickname.**

✳ **Use letters, numbers, and symbols, if possible, in the password.** Make it as long as the site permits and as many characters as you can reasonably remember.

✳ **Use different passwords for different accounts.**

✳ **Store your passwords in a safe place that only you can access.**

✳ **Consider changing your password on a regular basis, perhaps every few months.**

✳ **Install anti-spyware on your computer to avoid Trojan horses and other means of password detection** (see chapter 7, "Your Computer and the Internet," for details).

These same tips apply to any password, regardless of whether it is a password for your online account or for your bank account. See chapter 5, "Your Money," for creating passwords for your ATM or other accounts.

Privacy Policies

> Only 33 percent of shoppers read privacy policies, and only 7 percent complain about a policy with which they disagree.

You place your trust in the online hands of a company whose brick-and-mortar stores have always been some of your favorite reputable retailers. The site guarantees that it protects your information with every available level of security. You find out, though, after having given them your personal data to store for further transactions, that they have gone bankrupt and were forced to sell all of their assets. You never dreamed that your name, address, and credit card number would be counted among those assets, but they were.

Section 4 of eBay's privacy policy reads: "In response to a verified request by law enforcement or other government officials relating to a criminal investigation or alleged illegal activity, we can (and you authorize us to) disclose your name, city, state, telephone number, e-mail address, user ID history, fraud complaints, and bidding and listing history without a subpoena."

According to a 2003 survey by *PC World,* 88 percent of respondents worry about sites sharing or selling e-mail addresses, but only 33 percent of shoppers read privacy policies, and only 7 percent complain about a policy with which they disagree. Privacy policies outline how a website collects and uses your personal information. The policies address the following areas of concern for you as a potential consumer:

- ▶ **Data collection,** referring to the data the website seeks to collect from you while you do business on the site.
- ▶ **Use of data,** which details whether your data will be used solely by the website itself in further marketing to you by e-mail, mail, or telephone,

or whether your information will be shared with third parties to do the same.

▸ **Information sharing,** which describes the types of companies with which your information will be shared, and the specifics of what information is shared, such as if the data is connected to your name or to any other personally identifying facts, or is shared in the aggregate (see paragraphs below for data aggregation vs. individual profiling).

▸ **Security of information,** referring to the security measures that protect and encrypt your information while it is stored so hackers cannot access sensitive details. This section may also detail the length of time your information is stored after the transaction is completed.

▸ **Access to your information,** which describes whether you can view the data collected about you and check its accuracy or completeness.

▸ **Choice,** referring to whether you have the option of opting in or opting out of whether and how your personal information is collected and used for other purposes (see paragraphs below explaining opting in vs. opting out).

▸ **Notice,** which details information practices that are available to you before the site uses or shares your information. This section also covers how the site informs its users of changes in its privacy or information collection practices.

▸ **Privacy violation,** referring to the method you must follow or person to contact in the event you have a complaint.

A company's privacy policy should provide you with comfort in two ways. First, the policy should give you a sense of the company's commitment to its customers, in general, and to the privacy of its customers, in particular. If a company goes beyond the basics of privacy protection—for example, by providing you greater access to correct your personal information or stating that it will not share your information with any third parties—then you should feel more comfortable with the site. In addition, the policy should outline the company's liability if your privacy or personal information is compromised as a result of bad information practices, insecure transactions, or faulty storage of your data.

It is wise to use sites that have received approval from certain third parties that have developed oversight for privacy policies. Sites that have such approval display a seal indicating their participation in a merchant group interested in self-regulating privacy standards. Two of the most recognized seals are from TRUSTe (www.truste.org) and BBBonline (www.bbbonline.org). Seals from these organizations certify that the site in question has met basic privacy standards and fair information practices, and subjects itself to ongoing monitoring to ensure compliance with such standards. These seals indicate that the website from which you may purchase goods maintains these basic privacy standards. For more information on these seals, refer to chapter 7, "Your Computer and the Internet."

A website's link to its privacy policy and the privacy seals are usually located at the bottom of the site's home page. The policy is often listed in a section called Privacy Policy, or sometimes in the sections entitled About Us or in Frequently Asked Questions (FAQs). The privacy seals may also be posted near the privacy policy.

Unfortunately, neither the privacy policies nor these privacy seals-of-approval are ironclad. Your privacy or personal information may still be compromised in a number of ways. For example:

- ▶ Even the most secure databases can be hacked.
- ▶ Some companies post privacy policies but use arcane and vague language, often obscuring their true intentions regarding the use of your personal information.
- ▶ A company's policy may have changed, and if the company does not appropriately notify its customers, you may continue buying from the company without realizing that your personal data is no longer protected in the same way or to your satisfaction.
- ▶ An employee of the company with access to the company's database may, by design or mistake, sell your consumer profile in a manner that violates that company's privacy policy.
- ▶ Large, reputable companies can sell customers' personal information in contravention of their own policies by mistake, by corruption, or by using a legal loophole.
- ▶ A company's privacy policy, though well-intentioned, may not be well-managed, thereby proving to be ineffective; and

▶ Files theoretically protected by the company's policy can be subpoenaed in court cases.

Opt-in vs. Opt-Out

Websites make available to you the option of opting in or opting out to allow or to prevent the site from sharing your information. In either case, the website is likely to indicate the different ways that your information might be used, such as to market to you additional offers from the site you are currently visiting or to market to you offers from unaf-

> Debit cards expose you to liability up to the amount of money in your account if someone obtains and fraudulently uses your card number.

filiated third parties. Look for these options whenever you type your personal information into a site:

Opt-in. To give a site permission to use or share your information beyond the purpose for which your information was initially collected, you must explicitly give your consent. In this situation, websites offer a box for you to check to allow the site to use or share your personal information.

Opt-out. To prevent your information from being used beyond the original reason for which it was collected, you must opt out. To do so, you must uncheck a box that is checked as a default setting.

Data Aggregation vs. Individual Profiling

As mentioned above, a website may share or sell your data in different ways. A site's privacy policy explains how your data may or may not be used. For example, if a website only collects, shares, or sells aggregate data, then any data that is compiled does not identify you as an individual. For example, if you purchase product A, then your purchase or data may be included in an aggregate statement, such as "25 percent of users purchased product A." Individual profiling is the opposite. In this case, the website develops records that are as detailed as possible to market other products to you in the future. Before shopping at a site, check the privacy policy to see how your data will be used.

Paying for an Online Purchase

Once you have checked to see if a site is legitimate and secure, and you have read its privacy policy, you might be ready to make your online purchase. Paying in person with cash is the best way to avoid any kind of fraud, but different rules apply online. The security problems associated with online commerce depend on how much information you provide, the security of the website, and the fact that transactions are always remote. As a result, if you make an online transaction, it is best to use a credit card. Do not use cash or a cashier's check, which are the worst alternatives. You may not want to use a debit card to pay for items you buy online because, as outlined in chapter 5, "Your Money," debit cards can expose you to greater liability.

If you use a credit card to pay for an online purchase, you can rely on the credit card company's policy for protecting you in the event of fraud. As discussed in chapter 5, "Your Money," a credit card user can challenge unauthorized use of his or her card and withhold payment while the charge is investigated and disputed, and if the charge was indeed unauthorized, the card user's total liability will not exceed $50. In fact, many credit card companies do not even enforce that $50 liability.

Use these privacy tips to further protect yourself when buying items online:

✴ **Make sure the site is legitimate and secure, and that you are comfortable with its privacy policy.**

✴ **Use a credit card to buy items online.** A credit card offers more protection than debit cards against fraud.

✴ **Print a record of all purchases you make online.** Make sure that the record includes date of purchase, item ordered, total payment, and method of payment.

✴ **Examine your credit card bills to confirm the purchase you made, and to make certain that no unauthorized charges have been applied to your account.** To facilitate matters, use one credit card for all online payments, and restrict all online activity to that account for easier surveillance.

WHAT THE LAW SAYS

In the United States, no one law governs privacy across all retail industries. Instead, a number of state and federal laws address certain situations in various industries. Most of these laws focus on general principles with respect to data, including openness, disclosure, secondary use, correction, and security. Many of the laws that relate to data collection or privacy—such as the Fair Credit Reporting Act, the Video Privacy Act, and the Right to Financial Privacy Act—have been discussed in other chapters. At the same time, some organizations that regulate specific industries, such as the Direct Marketing Association, have developed industry standards in the name of self-regulation.

Each state has implemented laws that deal with the information that merchants are allowed to require in addition to the check or credit card you use in a transaction. These laws address whether the merchant can ask for your credit card information when you pay by check, require that you supply a photo ID in conjunction with a check or credit card, and so on. Given that the law in this area varies by state, you must consult your state's official website or your state's consumer division for additional information.

Although state laws differ, you should be cautious when a merchant requests the following:

(1) when paying by credit card, information beyond what is on the front of the credit card;

(2) when paying by check, a request for you to write your credit card number on the check; and

(3) when paying by check, a request to write your social security number on the check (although your driver's license can be legally requested).

In the event that a merchant breaks a law in requiring certain information from you, you should report the action to your state attorney general. Your complaint may result in the merchant being sued or fined. Given the rise of identity theft, you should not take such infractions lightly, as inappropriate requests for information made during a retail transaction can increase the odds that a con artist will gain the information necessary to commit fraud or identity theft against you.

✳ **Protect yourself against identity theft.** Follow the steps outlined in chapter 3, "Your Identity," including ordering your credit report at least annually and protecting your confidential personal information.

✳ **Make sure your computer system is secure and free of viruses and spyware** (see chapter 7, "Your Computer and the Internet").

Auctions

James Thompson and Susan Germek of Illinois used stolen identities in an elaborate online auction scheme to sell computer software and electronics. The pair offered various items for sale through Internet auctions, then failed to deliver the products after receiving payment from the buyers. To avoid leaving a trail, they continually changed their auction user names. Eventually, the two set up bank accounts and post office boxes in other people's names. The identity theft victims included people with whom Thompson had personal relationships, people whose information Germek took from the records of a hotel where she worked, and even a person who had died.

One of the Internet's most popular forums is the online auction. These cyber-bazaars facilitate commerce between and among businesses and individuals around the globe. Both business-to-person auction sites and person-to-person auction sites demand extreme vigilance from all participants.

In most auction sites, both buyers and sellers are required to establish site identities, with screen names and passwords, and, over time, develop a profile of feedback. Before you buy something from an auction site, do the following:

✳ **Check the vendor's feedback profile.** That feedback will give you an initial sense of how reliable that vendor is likely to be, though feedback profiles are not 100 percent reliable because scammers often establish different identities to avoid being traced.

* **Look at the seller's payment options.** Some sellers require a cashier's check or money order before they will ship an item, although most business-to-person sellers process credit card payments, especially through PayPal. A credit card used in this kind of transaction is your safest bet, since a charge can be contested if the merchandise is never received or is not what was advertised.

* **Consider an escrow service.** Because you are unlikely to know with whom you are doing business, especially in a person-to-person transaction, the best options for sending payment may be an online payment and escrow service. Many sites offer access to such an online payment service because it eliminates most fraud possibilities. The buyer provides the service with credit card or bank account information, and the seller provides information on where the payment should be deposited. Neither party, however, has access to the other's financial information. Escrow services operate differently. Money from the buyer is put into an escrow account, where it is held until the buyer receives and approves the merchandise. Escrow services are especially useful when very valuable items are being transferred, and the threat of fraud is greater than usual.

* **Beware of false online payment or escrow services.** As always, use common sense. Beware of new services or ones you have never heard of before, and check sites for red flags (see page 153 to assess whether a site is legitimate).

* **Call the customer service number to confirm that the auction and payment and escrow services are legitimate.**

* **Read the privacy and security policies of the service.** Do not use a service that cannot process your payment.

Protect Your Privacy When Shopping

Even with all these potential hazards, you are not going to stop shopping, be it online or off-line. After all, these risks did not seem to stop Carrie Bradshaw on the popular *Sex In The City* show from fulfilling her Manolo Blahnik fetch. Here's a summary of the tips to follow whether you're at the register or in front of your computer:

✳ **Never disclose your personal information unless necessary.** Even then, make certain you know who is getting your information, what they will do with it, and how dedicated to and capable they are of protecting your information.

✳ **Be on the alert for information requests that seem excessive. Be concerned about any retailer who demands too much information or details that are too sensitive.** Above all, protect your social security number.

✳ **Familiarize yourself with retailers' privacy and security policies for information collection, both in terms of your off-line and online shopping.** A company's privacy policy will give you a sense of how the company respects its customers and handles your information.

✳ **Understand how companies collect information about you—by using loyalty cards, product warranty cards, surveys, browsing habits, and so on.** Make a conscious decision about whether the benefits outweigh the disclosure of your personal information. Remember that there are important exceptions to privacy policies, and other entities such as law enforcement may subpoena your data or the store might share it with its "partners."

✳ **Prevent your information from being sold, shared, or rented to other companies to the extent possible.** Check the appropriate box on websites to opt in or opt out.

✳ **If you call a company's 800 or 900 number, block your telephone number or don't call from home.**

✳ **Know your retailers by shopping with reputable merchants or researching unfamiliar e-retailers before you shop with them so you are sure they are legitimate.**

✷ **Use a credit card, as opposed to a debit card, when shopping online.**

✷ **Examine your credit or retail card statements for potential errors or fraudulent charges as soon as you receive them.**

✷ **Create a safe password for your various online accounts, and do not tell it to anyone.** Do not use your name, address, birthday, and so on. If you use multiple accounts, create different passwords. Keep a record of your passwords and store the record in a secure place.

✷ **Ensure that your computer system is secure and free of viruses and spyware.**

✷ **Remember the basic tips to prevent identity theft.** This includes reviewing your credit report for accounts opened without your authorization.

✷ **Consider shopping online only with U.S. retailers.** Foreign retailers are not subject to the same laws or standards that govern the activities of U.S. retailers.

✷ **Print, save, and keep copies of all correspondence with retailers, as well as all order information.** In the event of fraud, a paper trail is invaluable.

✷ **Be on the alert for the red flags of online fraud.** Clues include a site that is poorly designed and executed, with no physical address or live customer service.

✷ **Be especially careful when you use online auction sites.** Check the seller's or buyer's feedback. Consider online payment or escrow services before making the transaction.

THE BOTTOM LINE

▶ It's all in the details. Retailers and merchants seek to gain as much information about you as possible to make their marketing efforts more effective. No detail is unimportant. Every detail of information they collect about you is added to the personal dossier that retailers and merchants build about you.

▶ All eyes are on you. Retailers and merchants track you in many different ways, including collecting data at the point of sale and through product warranty cards, offering loyalty cards, using in-store cameras, and installing new technologies such as signature capture devices and radio frequency identification chips.

▶ Lock and loaded. When you shop online, you must ensure that the site from which you are buying is legitimate and secure. Today, anyone can create a fake site to collect information about you. Once you are confident a site is legitimate, make sure that the site is maintaining your data in a secure way.

▶ It's in the fine print. A company's privacy policy tells you how the company collects information, how it stores data, whether you have access to your information, and the extent to which your information will be shared with others. Take the time to read and understand a company's privacy policy before you buy from the company.

Your Computer and the Internet

WHAT YOU REALLY LOOK LIKE WHEN YOU'RE SURFING THE NET.

© Chris Slane/Slane Cartoons Limited

You buy a Palm Pilot and register the device on the manufacturer's website using an e-mail address you've never used for any other purpose. Soon after, you start to receive offers for other Palm products, which was to be expected. But you also start to receive advertising for banking services, credit cards, and telephone service. Later, you start to receive dozens of e-mails each month with offers ranging from travel clubs to acne remedies. All of these offers originated from that one e-mail.

You replace your four-year-old computer with a newer model. You put the old CPU out on the curb on garbage collection day. You don't worry if someone else picks it up because you deleted your old files from the hard drive. What the Dumpster diver knows that you don't know is that if you don't wipe or squeeze those files clean with specially designed software, your supposedly erased files can be easily retrieved.

You're shocked when you get an e-mail from your professor requesting sexual favors in exchange for a grade change. To your relief, it turns out that a graduate student hacked into your university's computer system and used information from more than sixty students and professors to forge e-mails and get copies of final exams. The hacker sent the fake e-mail from your professor's account.

You wake up early on a Saturday to begin your first day of the weekend. First, you scan the newspapers, reading your favorite sections, from the hard news, to the gossip pages, to the entertainment section. Then you do a little grocery shopping and head out to buy a baby present for your dear friend who recently had a baby girl. Next, you call your friend to confirm lunch and suggest a new restaurant you recently read about. You also verify that the two of you are going to see the new Nicole Kidman movie in the afternoon. The movie has just opened, and it has received rave reviews, so you decide to buy tickets before you meet for lunch. Lastly, to spice things up, you go to your favorite cosmetics counter to compare shades of red lipstick.

Guess what? All these activities—except, of course, actually eating lunch and going to the movie theater—can be done online. If you live in New York, for example, you can read the *New York Times* online, buy your groceries at the FreshDirect site at www.freshdirect.com, choose and send a baby present at the Gap online, send an e-mail to your friend to confirm lunch, buy your movie tickets online at www.fandango.com, and even compare shades of makeup on the Estée Lauder site. And you can accomplish all these tasks while still wearing your pajamas and in the comfort of your home—and by 9 A.M.

But the convenience of life online has decided drawbacks. You are being tracked at every click of your mouse. When you send an e-mail, shop online, or surf the Internet, information travels through dozens of computer systems and ISPs (Internet Service Providers) that capture and store information about you and your activities. Your information is compiled and compared with standard patterns to develop a profile of you that predicts what kind of person you are, your spending habits, and the advertising you might like to see. In the scenario above, you could be tagged as a sophisticated college-educated female who has disposable income.

As you undertake these activities, you expose yourself to certain other dangers and annoyances that are the result of being connected to the Web. You may enjoy the many conveniences of the Internet, but you must understand that the Internet poses very real threats to your privacy. These include the nuisances of junk e-mail and pop-up ads and the very real chance that your computer and all the information stored inside it could be invaded by viruses, hackers, and snoops.

How Sites Track You

You go online to look at a website for classic cars. The next day there are three e-mails in your inbox advertising auto financing deals. How did the dealers know?

DoubleClick is a technology company that had an online advertising firm. The firm operated a network of online advertising sites and used cookies to collect information from unsuspecting Internet users who accessed the more than one thousand websites within its network. It then acquired a direct-marketing database company called Abacus that could cross reference the information in its database with an individual's online activities. What does that mean? Following the purchase, DoubleClick had the ability not only to track where you went online and what you did there but also to connect those activities directly to your name, your address, and your phone number. Ultimately, New York State used its powers to halt the program. If the state hadn't taken that step, your name and phone number would be connected to the website you visited last night. The same site would have the data it needed to be able to send you a direct mail solicitation at your home, based on visits to various websites.

171

Have you bought a book from Amazon.com? In addition to the personal information that Amazon.com maintains on you, such as your e-mail address, home address, and shipping address, Amazon.com also keeps an individual profile of which books you have looked at and which books you have purchased. They use this information to suggest other books for you to buy.

> Virtually every website uses some sort of tracking software.

Who else tracks you online? The simple answer: just about everyone who may want to sell something to you or sell your address to someone. Virtually every website uses some sort of tracking software. Everyone from Fortune 500 companies to small nonprofits recognizes that retaining and analyzing information about your visits are powerful tools for marketing and other purposes. The websites may collect and share the information in a number of different ways.

On many sites you leave a very clear and detailed trail of where you have been, what you have clicked on, what you have been downloading, and, in some cases, how long you've spent there. To understand how your online activity is tracked and recorded, you must have a basic understanding of how the Internet works.

The Internet is a decentralized global network that connects millions of computers. To access it, you typically need to subscribe to an Internet Service Provider (ISP), which connects you to the Internet and usually charges you a monthly fee for the service. Some ISPs merely connect you to the Internet, while others not only link you to the Internet but also offer additional services, such as specialized content and e-mail, that are available to you as a subscriber to their service. America Online (AOL), for example, not only connects you to the Internet, it also directs you to their proprietary areas of content and e-mail. The ISP may download a piece of software onto your computer in the course of establishing your account or maintaining it. By and large, this download is not terribly intrusive, although your ISP may collect certain information from you during the downloading process, such as information about your computer hardware, and thereafter monitor your level of usage with the ISP service.

The World Wide Web is a service riding on the Internet. To find and view content on the Web, you need to use a browser. The most commonly used browsers are Netscape Navigator and Microsoft Internet Explorer. When you visit a particular website, your browser transmits certain information about you to the site that you are visiting. In particular, your browser provides that site with your Internet Protocol (IP) address, which is a unique set of numbers that your browser assigns to your computer. Your IP address is not unlike your phone number. It distinguishes your activity from other computers and allows the server, or computer, that hosts the site you are visiting to track your activity on the site. The browser is your passport to the Web and holds your personal information in its *cache* and *cookies*.

> The existence of a cache means that a record of your Internet surfing is present on your computer, and this record can be seen by you or anyone else who uses your computer.

Cache. When you visit a website your browser stores a copy of each Web page you open in an area of your hard drive called a *cache*. By storing information (text, graphics, and so on) from the sites you visit, the cache enables you to view these pages when you are not connected to the Internet and allows you to reopen these pages faster when you reconnect to the Internet. Accordingly, the existence of a cache means that a record of your Internet surfing is present on your computer, and this record can be seen by you or anyone else who uses your computer.

Cookies. Another program that tracks your online activities is called a cookie. The cookie is akin to automatic recall because it remembers the e-mail address, login name, and password you create when you visit certain Web pages. That information is sent to your browser by a particular site when you access information on that site. Your browser stores the cookie on your hard drive. If you are a frequent online shopper, you know how tedious it can be to repeatedly input your personal data, including user names and passwords, and often payment, shipping, and other information. Cookies eliminate the need to reenter all your information and preferences because they contain your registration information, online shopping cart information, and user preferences, among other things.

Cookies also play a part in the online advertising you see when you surf the Internet. In fact, cookies are responsible for rotating the banner ads you see on

Web pages so you do not see the same banner ads every time you connect. When you log on to a site, a cookie sends data to an ad clearinghouse (or third-party site) that identifies the ads you have previously viewed. This process of banner or pop-up tracking is a common method of profiling or tracking your online activities. Although these third-party clearinghouses may not be collecting your name and telephone number, they still identify you, collect data about your Internet surfing habits, and then tailor certain advertising that you might see in the future.

> **Your cookies may send certain information to the third party that manages the rotation of ads and ad banners that pop up when you're online.**

Sites collect information about you in two ways. (Actually, there are many ways, including Web bugs and spyware, and these will be revealed in more detail later in the chapter, but there are two primary ways.) First, your browser discloses certain information about you via cookies, so a site can gain clues about you by tracking your activities within the specific areas of a website that you visit. This tracking can reveal information about your interests or hobbies. Second, the owners of sites collect additional information that you yourself provide during a financial transaction, a registration for a membership, or an application for a specific service.

Let's say you use the Internet to research inexpensive plane tickets to Hawaii at travel sites such as priceline.com, cheaptickets.com, or expedia.com. The first time you visit these sites, your cookies will likely reveal the following tidbits of information about you:

- ▸ The type of computer you are using
- ▸ The height and width of your monitor
- ▸ What browser you are using
- ▸ Your IP address
- ▸ Your ISP's name
- ▸ Where you linked from
- ▸ How many pages you have visited in this session
- ▸ Whether or not your browser is enabled to use JavaScript (a computer programming language invented by Sun Microsystems to allow Web pages to incorporate animation, sound effects, and games)

If you have ever registered or bought anything from the site, your cookie will prompt the site to recall the following information about you that the site already has on file:

- ▸ Your e-mail address
- ▸ Your user name and password
- ▸ Your mailing address
- ▸ Your telephone number
- ▸ The name and e-mail address of your preferred travel partner
- ▸ An itinerary from your most recent trip

In addition, your cookies may send certain information to the third party that manages the rotation of ads and ad banners that pop up when you're on-line. If you are surfing the Web for a getaway to a Hawaiian beach, the sites you visit may alert their affiliated ad clearinghouses. Don't be surprised if you receive advertising for travel-related services or products, such as car rental companies, hotels, or even bathing suits and suntan lotion.

Sites may compile information about you either in an aggregate with other users' information or in an individual profile of you. Aggregate information is data that is compiled without revealing your identity, and it may be used and shared in a variety of ways. For example, a website may use aggregate information to tell an advertiser that 40 percent of all its visitors live in California. Or, a website may provide aggregate information to investors to reflect an increasing number of total visits to the website.

In other cases, a website may use the information it has collected about you to adapt content to appeal to your particular interests. This type of tracking is called individual profiling because it is personally identifiable to you as an online user. Sites that use individual profiling may collect information on your online actions and habits so the site can target specialized content, advertisements, or products to you. An online store may recommend specific products like weight loss pills or self-help books based on the fact that you've bought diet cookbooks and barbells in past online shopping sprees. Your individual profile is updated and compared against standard shopping patterns to try to determine the type of person you are as well as to predict your spending habits. This is how Amazon.com and other sites are able to make personal recommendations.

By managing your browser, cache, and cookies, you can decide what information you want to leave at websites or on your personal computer. Here are some basic tips as a first defense:

✳ **Turn off cookies or enable cookie alerts.** Blocking your computer's ability to store cookies is the most effective way to protect your information from sites that want to sell to you. The drawback of the decision to turn off your cookies is that your surfing experience may be less convenient. For instance, your computer will no longer be able to recall your user name, recently viewed items, or even inputted or stored information. Be aware that some sites will not load if their cookies are refused. Instead of turning off cookies, you may want to turn on cookie alerts. These alerts prompt you every time a website is trying to place a cookie on your hard drive. It gives you the option of accepting or declining the cookie.

Both Internet Explorer and Netscape Navigator give you the option of disabling or fine-tuning your computer's ability to accept cookies. For AOL users, the process for disabling cookies depends on which Web browser—Netscape or Internet Explorer—you use along with your AOL browser. Consult your browser's help menu to turn off cookies or enable cookie alerts.

✳ **Delete your cookies.** You can also manually delete cookies from your hard drive. A number of programs are available to delete unwanted cookies and prevent certain servers from accessing them. You can find cookie control software packages with a quick Internet search, and the software typically costs less than $50. Check your browser first, however; it may already contain this capability. If you want to clear your cookies yourself, consult your browser's help menu.

✳ **Clear your cache.** You can also clear your cache and thereby clear the pages that you have previously viewed and that are stored in a special folder on your computer. If you clear your cache, your browser won't be able to automatically fill in URLs you begin to type. Consult your browser's help menu to learn how to clear your cache.

✳ **Clear your history.** Your cache maintains a local version of the websites you have downloaded and viewed, but your history contains a list of every site (or URL) you have ever visited. You can also set a limit on your browser of how long you want to retain a history of your website store pages. Again, follow your browser's instructions to clear your history.

✳ **Update your browser.** Internet Explorer and Netscape Navigator/Communicator browsers are all susceptible to potentially hazardous security bugs and viruses. When you visit a website, your browser reveals certain information about you and your computer, including your IP address. If you do not update your Web browser with the latest security fixes, someone may be able to hack into your computer (more information later in the chapter) to manipulate your browser into giving up your e-mail address and other important information. Whenever an upgrade is released, you should down-

---

Surfing with Shades

Do you want to make sure no one knows you have visited a site for marijuana users or herpes sufferers? To hide your identity when surfing the Web and to reduce spam (more on this later), consider various software tools known as anonymyzers. Most anonymizers are essentially intermediary servers that act as protective walls. As a result, you are able to conceal your identifying information—such as your IP address, the browser software you use, your surfing patterns, and so forth—from any website you visit. Anonymizers prevent sites from adding cookies or other files to your computer, thereby protecting you from being profiled by marketers and retailers.

Various companies, such as www.anonymizer.com or www.freedom. net, redirect you through their anonymous servers to view any Web page identity-free. They can also create a number of aliases for you that are assigned to cookies that cannot be linked to your real identity. Another site, IDzap's Idsecure (www.idzap.com/anonsurf.php) encrypts data going to and from your browser and replaces website names and addresses in the browser with nonsensical character strings.

---

load it from your browser's site. Browser upgrades are free and easily accessed. As a rule of thumb, you should check for upgrades every few months.

✳ **Use an anonymizer.** Consider using an anonymizer if private surfing is your priority.

Unfortunately, even these tips have their limitations. For example, clearing your cache means that you are removing from your own computer your search history, and that only prevents another user on your computer from easily looking up where you've been. Disabling your cookies will prohibit you from using certain sites that require them. Don't forget that your ISP will still keep records of your online activities.

Hackers and Virus Writers and the Programs They Create

Ehud Tenebaum was put under house arrest after the U.S. Justice Department notified Israeli police that the eighteen-year-old had broken into computers at the Pentagon and commercial and educational institutions.

In 1998, a fourteen-year-old Massachusetts boy hacked into remote computer systems that move voice and data transmissions, effectively causing the Worcester Regional Airport to shut down because of the loss of phone service for six hours. His activities also knocked out the city's fire department and security system.

In 1989, a West German hacker named Marcus Hess infiltrated several computers in the United States, including those at universities and at approximately four hundred military and government computer contractors. His aim was to locate and steal national security information and sell it to the Russian government. He was found guilty of espionage and received a short prison sentence. He now writes networking software for a computer company in Germany.

The term *hacker* originally described a person with a high level of computer expertise who, for fun, attacked computer problems and navigated through systems. Hackers were not malicious, and they broke into a system to look at data and then depart without leaving a trace. More recently, the name *hacker* has been applied to any person who gains unauthorized access to computer systems with the intent to steal information or wreak havoc. The term has come to describe anyone who poses security threats online, including virus writers.

> If you think only computers at big banks or the Pentagon are hacked, you're wrong. Anyone can download a hacking program on the Internet and these programs scan the average home computer more than ten times a day.

The FBI profiles hackers as between the ages of eighteen and thirty-five and characterizes them as bright, highly motivated, creative, and adventuresome people who love a challenge. According to an IBM study, amateur hackers, also known as script kiddies, are responsible for 90 percent of all hacking activity; potential professional hackers for hire (corporate spies), for 9.9 percent, and world-class cyber criminals for 0.1 percent.

If you think only computers at big banks or the Pentagon are hacked, you're wrong. Anyone can download a hacking program on the Internet and these programs scan the average home computer more than ten times a day, and a hacker breaks into a computer somewhere every five seconds. You are most vulnerable to hacking if your computer is always online via Wi-Fi, DSL, cable, or T-1 connections.

Different hacking programs have the potential to incur varying amounts of damage. The following list details some examples of what hackers can do:

- ▸ see everything you're doing
- ▸ access any file on your disk
- ▸ write new files, delete files, edit files
- ▸ install programs onto your system without your knowledge
- ▸ steal personal information such as passwords and credit card numbers

▸ listen in on your conversations if you are using your computer's microphone

Packet Sniffing

A hacker used packet-sniffing software to pick up one hundred thousand credit card numbers from the online credit card transactions of a dozen Web retailers. Given that the cards had limits between $2,000 and $25,000, the potential cost of the crime was approximately $1 billion. Fortunately, the identity thief made the mistake of trying to sell the card numbers to a decoy crime ring set up by the FBI.

A packet sniffer is a tool that captures packets of data as they pass through a network. Packet sniffers are legitimately used to monitor network traffic and pinpoint errors and bottlenecks, but they can also be used by hackers to intercept messages. Hackers use packet sniffers to capture user names and passwords as well as a great deal of other information from e-mail traffic, including credit card numbers and other private information.

Viruses

May 4, 2000, wasn't Valentine's Day, but 1.2 million people worldwide received an e-mail that read ILOVEYOU. The virus known as LoveBug affected almost 3 million computer files, shut down corporate e-mail servers, and cost businesses worldwide approximately $2.61 billion in damages. The virus, created by a thirty-three-year-old man in Manila, corrupted files on victims' machines and sent copies of itself to everyone in the victims' address books.

In early 2004, the Mydoom virus swept the world turning unsuspecting computers into unknowing spammers. It was considered the fastest-spreading computer virus ever, generating tons of e-mails to the point that it clogged corporate computer systems and slowed all traffic on the World Wide Web.

A virus is a piece of software that disguises itself as a legitimate program and passes from computer to computer just as a cold passes from person to person. A computer virus piggybacks on other programs and is activated when a user inadvertently opens the program. Your computer might be infected with a virus through an e-mail attachment, a bulletin board, a floppy disk, or through other channels. Once executed, a virus can spread throughout your computer system and infect your operating system, your applications, and your documents. Just as viruses that affect human systems come in degrees of lethalness, so do computer viruses. E-mail viruses such as the famous Melissa virus and the ILOVEYOU virus are perhaps the most insidious. They are activated when people receive an attachment and double-click on it.

Worms

When the MSBlast worm appeared, it quickly spread via the Web and affected home users the most. In one day, the malicious program infected more than 188,000 machines and swamped Internet connections with traffic as it searched for fresh computers to infect.

A worm is a self-replicating virus that resides in a computer's active memory and duplicates itself. Worms move through a network on their own, unlike viruses, which attach themselves to other programs. Whereas a virus received by e-mail may require you to open a file before it infects your computer, a worm can activate itself. It takes residence in the network storage of your computer and copies itself on remote drives. Worms are particularly dangerous to networked computers because they can spread so rapidly, and servers may crash because of the huge increase in activity.

As with other viruses, it is not always obvious if a worm has burrowed its way into your computer. The first sign that a worm is present within your computer may be that your computer's processing time slows dramatically. But the surest way to tell is to install an antivirus program on your computer and to periodically scan your files.

YOUR WI-FI CONNECTION

You stop at your local Starbucks first thing in the morning for a jolt of caffeine. While you are sipping your latte grande and skimming the scores from last night's baseball game, the guy next to you has already started his day. He's on his laptop, pounding out e-mails and surfing the Web. How is he able to connect to the Internet? He's using Wi-Fi (short for Wireless Fidelity), or wireless Internet access, which has become an increasingly popular tool to connect to the Internet in public places, including corporations, university campuses, airport terminals, public parks, and at cafés such as Starbucks. Wi-Fi systems in your house enable you to roam throughout your home with your computer continually connected to the Internet and to use multiple computers with the same Internet connection.

Unfortunately, the convenience of Wi-Fi is offset by the ease with which a snoop can access your computer when you use it. Sure, you and your wife and kids can all tap into the same connection, but so can anyone else within a radius of several hundred feet. When you are using a Wi-Fi connection in a public place, you are particularly vulnerable to having your password and other information stolen. According to a February 2004 Secure Computing report, business travelers face significant risks of password theft when using the Internet in hotels, cafés, airports, and trade show kiosks. This report exposed the many methods cyber-criminals use to steal passwords and corporate information. In particular, the report highlighted the vulnerability of wireless access points to sniffer software. This kind of software detects unencrypted data and makes it accessible to snoops and thieves who prey on unsuspecting users of Wi-Fi hotspots.

What can you do to protect your privacy when you are using Wi-Fi? First, if you use a Wi-Fi network at home, you should encrypt any data you transmit from or on your Wi-Fi network. As discussed in more detail on page 185, encryption scrambles data and information as it leaves your computer, making it extremely difficult for a hacker to access or read your data. Wi-Fi equipment typically provides a basic type of encryption called Wired Equivalent Privacy (WEP), but in most cases the system arrives with its encryption measures disabled as a default setting. A newer encryption system called Wi-Fi Protected Access, or WPA, is more secure. You must activate the WEP or WPA security that is packaged with your home Wi-Fi system.

If you use a Wi-Fi network in a public place, chances are good that information leaving the network is not encrypted. A test by a company called AirMagnet revealed that of eighty-three access points in the Mission District of San Francisco, only thirty-nine of the points were using encryption technology. Moreover, if you are in a hotspot in your local café, even WEP may provide little protection for your data. To combat this problem, some places, such as Starbucks, are considering offering users a type of encryption key to reduce the likelihood of sniffers and spies accessing computers in such locations. The key would only protect registered customers once they log on to the network.

In the meantime, especially at home or in your office, you can use other security features that are currently available. For example, you can use your virtual private network, or VPN, which works on both wired and wireless networks and which companies typically provide to employees who wish to access the company network from remote locations. You should still use standard security features such as firewalls. But the bottom line is that you should know that the use of Wi-Fi in public places is less secure than the use of Wi-Fi on your home network, and certainly less secure than using a wired network.

Trojan Horses

In 2001, The American National Red Cross warned supporters of a credit card–stealing Trojan horse program sent via e-mail that appeared to come from the disaster-relief organization. According to the Red Cross, the code came in the form of an executable file attached to an e-mail message, which by clicking on the file, showed a donation request form to fill out for the Red Cross, United Way of America, and the September 11th Fund. Upon completion of the form, the user's personal information was saved and uploaded to a website not connected to the organization.

A *Trojan horse* is an insidious program that is disguised as a benign one. The term comes from Homer's *Iliad,* which describes the wooden horse the Greeks offered to the Trojans as an alleged peace offering. After the Trojans accepted the horse and brought it inside the walls of their fortified city, Greek soldiers emerged from the horse's hollow belly and conquered the bewildered Trojans. In the context of privacy, the Trojan horse is one the scariest programs in existence. Instead of destroying data on your computer in the way that a virus or a worm might, a Trojan horse may, for example, allow its sender to access your computer and even control the machine remotely (see "Spyware" on page 191). Trojan horses are often found in executable content software that has been developed to enable Web browsing, file sharing, and graphic design. Examples include ActiveX, Java, and JavaScript. Unlike viruses, Trojan horses do not replicate themselves. A Trojan horse can create a back end for a hacker to continue to access your system.

Unfortunately, it is nearly impossible to avoid every incidence of packet-sniffing activity or viruses, worms, and other applications that may infect your computer when it is connected to the Internet. Nonetheless, use these techniques to reduce your chances of harm:

✳ **Use a firewall and antivirus software.** Firewalls can be either hardware or software and they keep your computer files secure by blocking unauthorized access to your computer. Think about firewalls as barriers that prevent anything intrusive or destructive on the Internet from damaging your files. A firewall functions much like a physical firewall that stops a fire from spreading from one area to another. If a firewall's filters sense that certain information is potentially hazardous, the firewall will not let that information access your computer. Firewalls are becoming more common for personal use as well as business use. If you want to install a firewall, you can buy a decent one for your computer for less than $50. Be aware, however, that you will have to constantly update the software; software companies continually find security holes in their software and release patches and updates to correct them. Another sensible step is to install antivirus software on your PC. Update your antivirus software and perform systems scans as often as you can. Antivirus updates are released frequently (even daily if there is a virus outbreak), so consider setting your program to update itself automatically. Two established companies that provide firewalls and antivirus software updates include Symantec (www.symantec.com) and McAfee (www.mcafee.com).

✳ **Use encryption software.** The use of encryption has become a staple in the world of online communications. If you encode your e-mail and personal data files, you can be more confident of their security from packet sniffers. There are two kinds of computer encryption: symmetric key and public key. Symmetric key is based on the simple concept that you create a code, for example, where a=1, b=2, c=3 and so on, then you send a message to your friend along with the decoding formula. Anyone else who intercepts this message will not be able to read the message without the key. The other type of encryption is called public key, and it uses a complex combination of symmetric keys and public keys (codes given by your computer to any public computer that wants to communicate securely) to encode e-mails, files, and other components. Whatever encryption you use, you must ensure that the person receiving the message has the ability to decode the message. If you neglect this step, your message will be protected from everyone, including the person to whom you are sending the message. Encryption requires additional time and steps. You may decide to encrypt your most sensitive e-mails and data but to use unencrypted e-mail and files for everyday messages, inquiries, and memos.

A popular public key encryption is called PGP (www.pgp.com), which stands for Pretty Good Privacy and can be downloaded and mastered in a short period of time. In addition, a common Internet security protocol is the Transport Layer Security (TLS) protocol, which is used by Web browsers and Web servers to transmit sensitive information. You can tell when your browser is using a server protocol such as TLS if the "http" in the address line is replaced with "https" and a small padlock appears in the status bar at the bottom of the browser window. Another software that encrypts messages for AOL, Yahoo!, and Hotmail is Impasse (www.impasse.com).

✳ **Be careful with e-mail attachments.** Consider deleting any e-mail you receive from strangers. Avoid reading any HTML e-mail that is sent to you by an unknown source. Never open e-mail attachments unless you are expecting them.

❋ **Turn off the Windows scripting host.** Many viruses spread through Visual Basic scripting. To avoid infection, consider disabling the Windows scripting host by following these steps:
  ▸ Open My Computer
  ▸ Go to the Tools menu and select Folder Options
  ▸ Select File Types
  ▸ Find the VBScript script file and select delete
  ▸ Click OK

❋ **Avoid or take precautions when you use file-sharing programs.** When you use file-sharing programs, such as Kazaa, BearShare, LimeWire, and Grokster, you always run the risk of irresponsible users introducing viruses. If you do use one of these programs, adopt the following measures:
  ▸ Use the latest version, which is more likely to have a built-in virus protection program
  ▸ Download only premium, high-quality content
  ▸ Turn on your virus filter

❋ **Disable ActiveX, Java, and JavaScript.** You can disable these programs yourself if you use Internet Explorer or Netscape Navigator. The vulnerabilities that affect Java, JavaScript, and ActiveX often apply to e-mail as well as Web pages. You should disable these programs before you browse through sites that you are either unfamiliar with or do not trust. If you notice that a site is not working properly, you may want to go back and enable your programs.

❋ **Look for suspicious activity.** Sometimes you can notice Trojan horses by keeping an eye on the Internet connection icon in the Tray area of your Taskbar and on the lights on your CPU. If your hard drive is continually active when you are not actually doing anything online, this could be a sign of an active Trojan horse (unless, of course, you have automatic updates installed on your computer, in which case you'll regularly notice some activity).

❋ **Scan your computer with an anti-Trojan program to see if you have any Trojans in your system.** Some anti-Trojan programs are available online.

Some sites will also give you advice on how to manually remove Trojans if you have any: PC Flank's Trojan Test (www.pcflank.com/trojans_test1. htm), Trojan Scan (www.trojanscan.com), and Trend Micro's Housecall (www.trendmicro.com).

What Else Is Out to Get You: Web Bugs, Spiders, Spyware, and More

> When you are using a Wi-Fi connection in a public place, you are particularly vulnerable to having your password and other information stolen.

An employee at a major Japanese bank inadvertently sent an e-mail virus to some of the bank's customers from his personal computer. The virus installed on the recipients' computers a program that made their monitors read "You're a big stupid jerk" on the fourteenthth of every month.

Surfing the Web is one metaphor for browsing sites online. Going on safari might be another. Whenever you use the Internet you chance an encounter with Web bugs, spiders, Trojan horses, and more—a virtual zoo of applications that threaten your privacy. Some of the tools associated with virus writers, such as Trojan horses, are available as spyware and are easily accessible to any average Joe or ABC Corp. that wants to use them. Marketers, snoops, spammers, and others cultivate these pests either to access your personal information or to cause damage to your system.

Web bugs

> *Internet security company SecuritySpace.com documents the usage of Web bugs on the Internet. It posts a table of the top one hundred sites that were found to have a Web bug on them.*

A Web bug is a marketing surveillance tag in the form of an invisible clear-colored graphic known as a GIF that is embedded in a Web page or HTML-enabled e-mail. A Web bug can be as small as a single pixel on your screen. Marketing companies use Web bugs to track the sites you visit, how long you spend in various sections of a website, and at what time you surf their sites.

Web bugs can also be used by spammers who plant them in the HTML e-mails they send you. If you open the spam, the Web bug will send a message to the spammer that says "valid address." Web bugs can be linked to cookies, which can contain personal information such as your name and e-mail address. But there is a difference between a Web bug and a cookie: whereas a cookie is typically accessed only by the server that originally places it on your computer, and you have the option to set your computer to refuse cookies, Web bugs collect your information, without your permission, and allow additional servers to copy cookies from your hard drive. Consequently, websites that share an advertising network with the site into which you legitimately entered information can also obtain your data. If marketers or snoops use cookies and Web bugs together, they can see the Web addresses of other sites you've visited or the details of your past search terms. Among the companies that use Web bugs are DoubleClick and LinkExchange as well as Web giants Yahoo! and America Online.

> Beware: Web bugs are not limited to Internet sites and HTML e-mails. Web bugs can also be embedded in Word documents, Excel spreadsheets, and PowerPoint slide show files, enabling the author of a document to monitor the document and know who's accessing or reading it.

Beware: Web bugs are not limited to Internet sites and HTML e-mails. Web bugs can also be embedded in Word documents, Excel spreadsheets, and PowerPoint slide show files, enabling the author of a document to monitor the document and know who's accessing or reading it. The bug in the document will report the IP addresses, date and time of viewing, and other information when the document links to a file located on the author's Web server. Think of the scenarios here: any document can be bugged, which means that if, say, your boss sends you a document to read, he or she could theoretically know if you've read it or not and when you read it. Web bugs can also multiply and spread. For example, Word allows users to create macros, which are programs that automate tasks, and macro viruses, when opened unwittingly, duplicate themselves into other documents and spread much as any other virus would.

To reduce your chances of being bitten by a Web bug, keep the following in mind:

✳ **Check whether your computer is storing a Web bug.** A number of Web bug detectors exist such as Privacy Foundation's Web bug detector, Bugnosis (www.bugnosis.org). Bugnosis is free and easy to download, though it only works with Internet Explorer running on a Microsoft Windows operating system. If you are a savvy computer user, you can manually find a Web bug by viewing the HTML source code of a Web page and searching for IMG tags that match up with cookies stored on your computer.

✳ **Disable cookies.** If you suspect the Word, Excel, or PowerPoint document you are viewing might have Web bugs, set your browser to disallow cookies.

✳ **Beware HTML e-mails.** HTML e-mails may contain a Web bug. Opt for plain text when you have a choice.

✳ **Protect yourself.** For ongoing protection, block Web bugs by installing one of a number of different programs, such as Guidescope (www. guidescope.com), WebWasher (www.webwasher.com), or AdSubtract (http://www.intermute.com/adsubtract/). These programs are essentially ad blockers, but since Web bugs are third-party content, most ad blockers will block Web bugs, too.

Spiders

According to the Center for Democracy and Technology (CDT), spammers use software harvesting programs such as robots or spiders to collect e-mail addresses listed on websites, including both personal Web pages and institutional (corporate or nonprofit) Web pages). A March 2003 CDT study, reported in a PC World article, found that 97 percent of the spam it received was sent to addresses harvested from the Web.

Spiders may also be referred to as search engine bots, wanderers, D2s, lookers, searchers, or crawlers. They are automated software programs that run at several search engines, read the content of websites, analyze the material, and insert that content into an index. Spiders are not designed to cause harm, but they can be used for illicit purposes.

There are two kinds of spiders. One looks at the meta tags that are located in a website's code, and contain a list of keywords that search engines use to classify that particular page. (These tags are not visible to the average user, though if you are HTML savvy, you can access a website's meta tags.) Web search engines such as Google use hundreds of spiders, as does Yahoo!, Hotbot, Internet Archive, and others. The other type of spider is known as full index and is more thorough, cataloging every word of every page in a site. Spiders are often hidden inside software packages to enable the manufacturer to access your computer and virtually all of your files. As such, spiders are most common in the following types of diagnostic software:

- ▶ Updates for your hardware and software
- ▶ Fix-it and repair programs that identify problems on your hard drive and/or eradicate viruses. Examples include Norton AntiVirus, LiveUpdate Pro, and McAffee Clinic
- ▶ Tech support accessibility software that enables server and workstation problems to be resolved by remote access. Examples include Symantec's pcAnywhere and Wind Design's SupportAbility

If you've ever posted anything online, a spider will index your identity and the content of your posting. A spider's findings end up in massive databases in computer systems around the world. Test the power of spiders by going to Google and typing in "I have cancer" to see how many pages containing peoples' names pop up as a result.

Many companies and individuals run spiders that search the Internet for computers that are sharing files. The spiders then download all of the information they can find and index it for quick retrieval. At the same time, there are a growing number of computer viruses that spread by searching for computers with shared disks.

To protect yourself against spiders, remember that spammers use harvesting programs such as spiders to gather information on you, including the e-mail address you provide on websites or information you post online in discussion groups. Accordingly, pay particular attention to tips on page 200 on the ways you can protect yourself against spam e-mail.

> Test the power of spiders by going to Google and typing in "I have cancer" to see how many pages containing peoples' names pop up as a result.

Spyware

Ever received an e-greeting from an ex-lover? One spyware package lets your ex "spy on anyone" by simply sending an e-greeting. The message from your ex-lover installs a software program on your computer and then captures and records every word you type.

For more than a year, unbeknownst to people who used Internet terminals at Kinko's stores in New York, Juju Jiang was recording what they typed, paying particular attention to their passwords. Jiang had secretly installed software that logs individual keystrokes in at least fourteen Kinko's copy shops. He captured more than 450 user names and passwords, and then he used them to access and open bank accounts online.

After Michael Stone's three daughters finished playing spelling games on Reader Rabbit, an educational software program, he put them to bed and went online himself. Minutes into his session, the California attorney's desktop security program alerted him that Reader Rabbit was attempting to secretly send data from his com-

puter. Apparently, his children's software contained heavily encrypted spyware.

Spyware is a catch-all term that refers to software installed on your computer to monitor your computer or online activities. The spyware is installed without your knowledge and uses your Internet connection to gather and transmit information about you or your activity.

> Spyware may store all the keystrokes you make, access the user names and passwords you use, log all the URLs you type, retrieve your credit card numbers, log all the windows you open, take screenshots of your system at specified intervals, scan files on your hard drive, and send all this data to the spyware's author or originator.

Spyware varies in form and type, from simply annoying to potentially devastating. Some spyware programs are Trojan horse programs, as detailed above. Spyware may store all the keystrokes you make, access the user names and passwords you use, log all the URLs you type, retrieve your credit card numbers, log all the windows you open, take screenshots of your system at specified intervals, scan files on your hard drive, and send all this data to the spyware's author or originator automatically, using your Internet connection.

Apart from the privacy concerns, spyware can also consume your system's resources, thereby slowing down your system, clash with other installed software, and crash your browser or even Windows itself.

Spyware is widely accessible and virtually anyone can get hold of it. According to SpyCops.com, more than 350 computer monitoring spyware programs are available commercially, in addition to the thousands of other hacker or spy software programs that are available on the Web. Spyware is used not only by hackers, marketing companies and employers, but also by a fast-growing market of suspicious lovers, friends, parents, and spouses (see chapter 12, "I Spy, You Spy"). According to the 2003 National Cyber Security Alliance study, 91 percent of broadband users have spyware programs on their computers, and most of these programs found their way into users' computers through P2P (music and file-sharing) programs. What does this mean? Well, it depends. Not all spyware is created equal, and the programs are available in many varieties, as detailed below. Spyware may do any or all of the following to your computer:

▶ Install other programs onto your computer without your knowledge

▶ Transmit cookies to and from other spyware programs (even if you have disabled cookies in your browser)

▶ Send Trojan horses to your system (see below)

▶ Reset your auto signature

▶ Disable or bypass your uninstall features

▶ Scan files on your drive

▶ Monitor your keystrokes

▶ Change your home page

▶ Read, write, and delete files

▶ Reformat your hard drive

▶ Reroute your personal information to marketing and advertising companies

> **91 percent of broadband users have spyware programs on their computers, and most of these programs found their way into users' computers through P2P (music and file-sharing) programs.**

Here are the basic types of spyware:

Browser Helper Objects (BHOs). Commonly installed as part of Internet Explorer, a BHO is a small program that runs every time you use your browser. Some BHOs perform useful functions, such as killing pop-up windows, as with Yahoo! Companion. In this way, BHOs extend the capabilities of the browser to enhance a user's experience on the Web. However, a BHO can also be installed on your system by another software program, and used as a type of spyware to monitor your messages and actions and report that information back to its creators. You may have a BHO running on your computer if, for example, you get pornographic pop-ups while surfing the Web. It is difficult to know how extensively BHOs are being used. But BHOs can conflict with other running programs, cause a variety of page faults and run-time errors, and generally impede browsing performance. One sign that you may have a BHO running on your

193

computer is if your browser continually crashes. BHOs are not disabled by personal firewalls, because the firewall perceives the program to be part of your browser itself. Microsoft does rely on BHOs to monitor browser functions. But the very existence of BHOs creates the possibility that the BHOs can be easily hijacked and used to replace banner advertisements with other ads, report your online actions to a third party, and even change your home page.

You may have a BHO running on your computer if you get pornographic pop-ups while surfing the Web.

Follow this tip to protect your privacy from BHOs:

✳ **Manually locate and/or remove BHOs.** Follow these steps (as outlined on www.pcflank.com/art36.htm) if you're running Windows:
 1. Click on the **Start** button and go to the **Run** menu.
 2. In the Run dialog box type: regedit. But make sure you make a copy of the registry before you edit. If you make a mistake and don't have a copy, you may not be able to restart your machine.
 3. Click on the **OK** button or hit the **Enter** key. The Windows registry editor will be displayed.
 4. Drill down to the **Browser Helper Objects** registry key using the following path: HKEY_LOCAL_MACHINE\Software\Microsoft\Windows\CurrentVersion\explorer\Browser Helper Objects.

Once you have reached the BHO registry keys, you can remove any one of them by positioning your cursor over the key in question, right clicking on it, and then selecting Delete from the drop-down menu. It is wise to familiarize yourself with what these various keys do before you delete anything from the registry.

Hijackers. A hijacker is software that resets your browser's settings to redirect you to other sites, usually porn sites full of advertising. Some hijackers may capture information about you, including any URLs you type, as you are en route to your unexpected destination and then forward this information to an unseen site that captures it. If this occurs, you won't notice it but your browser may perform at a slower pace. You will certainly notice that you have arrived at a website that you were not expecting.

One hijacker program is the home page hijacker, which captures your home page request and in its place advertises some unknown search engine's site like Cool Web Search. The hijacker also replaces your search results at www.google.com with its own results. Another hijacker is the error hijacker, which occurs when you load an expired Web page or your browser generates an error. Instead of receiving a message from Internet Explorer or Netscape, you will receive a special error page from the hijacker program that either redirects you to the Cool Web Search site or displays similar information.

> Hijackers may capture information about you, including any URL's you type, as you are en route to your unexpected destination and then forward this information to an unseen site that captures it.

Regardless of the tactic, the hijacker's goal is to control your actions and collect information about you and your activities.

Hijacking is increasingly common, and pornography sites are the most notorious users of hijacking programs to capture traffic. To protect yourself from hijackers:

✳ **Install an antihijacking program.** A number of different programs will prevent hijacking. One is StartPage Guard (www.pjwalczak.com/spguard/index.php), which claims to block hijacking while letting harmless scripts through. You can download the software for free.

Keystroke loggers. Keystroke loggers are spyware programs that run in the background of your computer and record everything you type and every key you hit. Keystrokes are logged and stored on your computer for future retrieval. Sometimes keystrokes are recorded in real time and transmitted back to the perpetrator. A sophisticated type of keylog program is a Remote Administration Tool (also known as a RAT). A RAT is a Trojan horse that allows a perpetrator to essentially control your computer and server from a remote location. The perpetrators of keystroke logging range from nosy bosses to suspicious spouses to knowledgeable hackers. You should pay attention to and immediately remove any suspect hardware from your computer.

To protect your privacy from keystroke loggers:

✳ **Look for hardware keystroke loggers.** Hardware keystroke loggers look like small cylinders. They plug into the end of your keyboard's cable and connect to your PC.

✳ **Download software to search and remove software keystroke loggers.** Keystroke logging software is difficult to spot, because the applications use cryptic names and can send periodic logs of your keystrokes to anyone, anywhere. You can download a variety of programs, such as Spycop or Spydetect, to search and remove such software from your computer.

Screenshot loggers. Screenshot loggers such as Spector periodically capture screenshots of your desktop. These programs also monitor e-mail, record chat and instant messages, and log keystrokes. Another commercially available software package, eBlaster, captures both sides of chat conversations, instant messages, keystrokes typed, applications launched, and websites visited, and sends a detailed activity report to the spying party on the hour. Some spyware packages can turn on video and audio components without your knowledge and digitally record you and whatever else is in front of the computer screen. One such package, NETObserve, advertises: "With NETObserve on your side, you will have remote, realtime access to your PC, allowing you to remotely control and monitor a PC while you are away!"

Adware

If you download freeware or shareware from the Internet, you are usually downloading adware. The difference between adware and spyware is that the adware discloses that it tracks your personal information when you download it. The software is often bundled with banner ads and pop-ups and is, on the whole, more annoying than harmful. If you do not want banner ads and pop-ups, be sure to read the contents of the software's privacy policy before you agree to download it. Some adware companies have gone so far as to create virus-like software programs known as advertising Trojan horses, which install themselves on your computer and inundate you with unwanted advertising whether or not you've installed the advertising-supporting software. The latest of these require advanced computer knowledge to detect and include the TimeSink/Conducent TSADBOT and the Aureate. One spyware module has even been known to spoof a Windows system process so it cannot be terminated and is not included in the Windows End Task (Ctrl-Alt-Del) dialog box.

> Some spyware packages can turn on video and audio components without your knowledge and digitally record you and whatever else is in front of the computer screen.

In addition to the specific tips above, use these tips to reduce the chances of your computer being invaded by Web bugs, spiders, and spyware:

✳ **Be cautious when you download shareware or freeware.** Many shareware programs and P2P programs, such as Grokster, Kazaa, and others, come with an enormous amount of bundled spyware.

✳ **Install antivirus software.** Before you install antivirus software, check that the program is able to detect spyware. New versions of such software, such as Norton AntiVirus, are capable of detecting spyware. Also remember to keep your antivirus software current with regular updates.

✳ **Scan your computer.** There are various programs that will scan your computer for spyware and adware. Some will scan your computer for free. The scan takes about fifteen minutes, depending on the number of files saved on your computer. A scan should detect the presence of spyware and adware programs and their authors or owners, and it should define the degree of harm these programs can cause. Software packages that eradicate spyware and adware programs are available for less than $50. One program, Pest Patrol, protects against the full range of non-viral malware, including Trojan horses, hacker tools, spyware, and adware. Aluria's Spyware Eliminator detects and removes spyware, adware, and keyloggers from your computer, and blocks these programs if your computer comes under assault. Both are commonly recommended by sites dispensing security tips.

✳ **Check your ISP's service features.** Your ISP may have built-in software to detect and remove spyware. For example, AOL, Earthlink, and MSN offer their subscribers some type of spyware detection and removal.

✳ **Turn off your high-speed or broadband connection if you are not using it.** Disconnect the ethernet card or remove the network interface card.

✳ **Understand the risks of using a Windows system.** Most invasive software is written to target Windows systems and Microsoft applications. Macintosh computers and other operating systems, such as Unix or Linux, are not widely targeted.

Spam or Junk E-mail

In 2003, a Miami-based company used fraudulent e-mail addresses that appeared to come from Amazon.com to distribute ads for penile enlargement pills, while another company used a fake e-mail from Amazon.com to promote tools for creating and sending spam. As a result, and after much public outcry, Amazon.com had to set up a special e-mail address, stop-spoofing@amazon.com, for users to report suspected spoofing.

This pitch is probably familiar to you: A "friend" asks if you're fed up with working long hours for little pay, and wonders if you'd prefer to be your own boss and make $10,000 a month. To discover how, the e-mail tells you that you merely need to call a toll-free number and leave a message that includes your credit card number. Of course, the e-mail ends with a legal disclaimer, adding to its legitimacy. Of course, the e-mail is spam—and it is just another trick to get you to open the e-mail.

Not only do you have to worry about protecting your privacy online, but you also need to protect your sanity. If junk mail and telemarketers drive you crazy, spam will have the same result electronically. The volume of spam has grown so much that it makes up almost 50 percent of e-mails sent today, as compared to only 7 percent in 2001. AOL customers have received as many as 2.5 billion spam e-mails, in the aggregate, in a single day. Why is there so much spam? There is one universal explanation for the surge in recent years: spam is incredibly cheap. Gone are the days when marketers needed hefty budgets to pay for print production and postage to advertise their products. Now they can send bulk e-mails for practically nothing. It costs as little as $500 to send 1 million e-mails. Even if the spam marketer only sells a handful of items, it's worth it. And spammers and direct marketers both harvest and sell e-mail addresses. Perhaps this puts into context Bill Gates's suggestion to require e-mailers to apply "postage" or "stamps" as one means to stem spam e-mail.

> If your e-mail address is listed on any public Web page, including a company or association site, you can be sure that spammers will find it.

Even more lucrative than the occasional sale of cosmetic surgery in a bottle or Viagra at an 80 percent discount is the business of selling e-mail addresses to direct marketing companies. Spammers send out Web bugs, spyware, and adware to collect information about you. Companies will pay anywhere from a few cents to $1 per e-mail address for these databases. Spammers and direct marketers sell your e-mail address to other spammers and direct marketers, and information travels from one database in one part of the world to another with little oversight.

If your e-mail address is listed on any public Web page, including a company or association site, you can be sure that spammers will find it. Even unsophisticated spammers can put specialized products to work for them. They use spiders and Web bugs to cull thousands of e-mail addresses hourly from various public pages. If you participate in chat rooms, newsgroups, or other public forums, your e-mail address becomes a public posting and is easily accessed by spammers. Public postings are almost always archived, so your activity is recorded even if you participated in a forum only one time. Spammers also access other publicly available sources such as subscriber and member directories, White Pages, alumni bulletins, and domain registries. For example, your ISP maintains information about you, and the service may list your e-mail address as part of its subscriber or member directory. Or, depending on its privacy policy, the service may sell your e-mail address to direct marketers.

Spammers use many methods to enlarge their mailing lists. They may randomly generate e-mail addresses themselves. One such method is called a Dictionary attack, in which spammers use programs that create combinations of names and numbers—such as Jane001@aol.com, Jane002@aol.com, and so on—to find you. If you reply to one of their e-mails, or sometimes if you merely open the e-mail, you confirm to the spammers that your e-mail address is live, and the spammers will add your e-mail address to their database. Further, spammers may buy your e-mail address from some websites. When you shop online or register with websites, particularly those that do not post privacy policies or have policies that do not prevent disclosure or sharing of your e-mail address and other personal information, you may be more susceptible to spammers.

To fight spam, follow these steps:

✳ **Use features offered by your ISP or e-mail account.** Almost every ISP and e-mail provider, including AOL, MSN, Earthlink, and Yahoo!, offers a spam filter that either lets you sort and inspect incoming mail before you open it, or automatically places spam in a separate folder. Spammers work to bypass these filters by using generic or personal subject lines, misspelling keywords like *V1agra* (for *Viagra*), and assuming false identities like "Bob Johnson" or another familiar name. If you see such e-mail, don't even look at it or open it up. Delete it immediately.

Some ISPs block spam by requiring new or unknown senders to respond to a system message before their e-mails can be delivered. For example, if your long-lost friend from high school sends you an e-mail in an attempt to reconnect, your ISP might respond with a pop-up message and an image of an apple. The message prompts your friend to type the word *apple* before your ISP will deliver the e-mail to you. This strategy prevents mass e-mails by verifying that a live person is sending the message to you.

✳ **Use separate e-mail accounts.** You might consider using three separate e-mail addresses: one for friends and family; one for business purposes; and one for everything else. If the latter attracts too much spam, abandon it for another e-mail address.

✳ **Minimize use of your regular e-mail account.** Don't use your regular e-mail address in chat rooms or other public areas. Use a different screen name or a third e-mail address, as described above.

✳ **Protect your regular e-mail account.** Consider using an e-mail address that is more than six characters long and hard to guess. Avoid using your regular e-mail address in public areas or forums or chat rooms, or on very public sites such as eBay. If you must use your regular e-mail address in a public area, spell it out. For example, type "john smith at yahoo dot com" as opposed to "johnsmith@yahoo.com."

✳ **Avoid contests and giveaways.** Many online sweepstakes and free promotions are designed to obtain your personal information for marketing purposes. For example, some stores request e-mail addresses to send coupons and notices about store activities. Consider refusing these requests, or treating them with suspicion. You are responding at your own peril.

✳ **Opt out.** Most legitimate sites give you the choice of opting out to prevent your personal information, including your e-mail address, from being disclosed. If you have the choice, you should take advantage of any opportunities to opt out.

✳ **Ignore spam.** Do not open spam or buy anything promoted in spam. Do not forward chain letters, petitions, virus warnings, or cartoons. (These are often sneaky ways for spammers to collect addresses.) Lastly, do not reply to a spammer's unsubscribe link, because your response confirms your e-mail address.

✳ **Use additional technology.** Consider purchasing additional spam-blocking software. Install a firewall, especially if you have a high-speed or "always-on" connection.

✳ **Read privacy policies.** Make sure you read the privacy policies of websites you visit and of your ISP. Inform your ISP that you do not want your e-mail address shared or disclosed.

✳ **Protect the e-mails you send from spam filters.** You must prevent your own e-mails from being mistaken for spam and deleted by filters. To do so, use your knowledge of how spam works to format your e-mails so they are not mistaken for spam. For instance, avoid general subject lines like "Hi, How Are You," or "About Last Night." Also avoid industry-related words, such as *credit, mortgage, discount, vacation, prescription,* and so on, in the subject line. Some filters reject subject lines in capital letters and certain types of punctuation, like exclamation points.

✳ **Follow the tips in the sections above.** Protect yourself against Web bugs, spyware, adware, and other devices that spammers use to collect personal information about you.

Public Areas on the Internet

A thirteen-year-old girl from Texas made a "friend" in a chat room who claimed to be about her age and to live in Washington State. Unbeknownst to her, he was actually a forty-year-old sexual preda-tor. He arranged for the girl to visit him in Washington, and he in-structed her to remove the hard drive from her computer and bring it with her in an effort to remove evidence of their exchange. When they met, he held her captive and sexually assaulted her. She managed to escape, and she took the hard drive with her to the police.

Certain areas of the Internet are considered public and therefore offer lit-tle to no privacy. These public areas include chat rooms, bulletin boards (also known as discussion groups or newsgroups), listservs, and Web logs, which are also called blogs. Any and all of the information you provide or type is pub-lic information and therefore accessible to anyone who is either participating

ANTISPAM LEGISLATION

On January 1, 2004, the Can-Spam Act went into effect. The act restricts commercial e-mail companies or spammers from using false identities and misleading subject lines. It also requires commercial senders to include valid postal addresses in their e-mail messages. The law gives recipients the opportunity to opt out of receiving more messages. Under the Can-Spam Act, the Federal Trade Commission, state attorneys general, and ISP companies can sue spammers, but an individual cannot sue a spammer. Any spammer who violates the law may be subject to fines up to $250 per e-mail with a cap of $2 million.

The effectiveness of this new law will, of course, largely depend on enforcement. In March 2004, America Online, Earthlink, Microsoft, and Yahoo! brought the first major lawsuit under the new Can-Spam Act against hundreds of spammers, including some of the country's biggest offenders. In addition, in December 2003, the State of Virginia indicted two individuals on spam felony charges—the first indictments of their kind since the state's new anti-spam law went into effect July 1, 2003. Irrespective of these cases, it is unclear whether or when the volume of spam will decrease. For example, Earthlink has taken legal action against more than one hundred spammers since 1997. For this reason, ideas that emanate from the private sector, such as Bill Gates's idea to require a fee or postage for all e-mail, and Stanford law professor Lawrence Lessig's idea to offer bounties for the reporting of spammers, continue to be put forth.

in any of these areas, or merely monitoring a specific area. Anything you submit may be permanently searchable and reproduced on other sites. Internet marketers often use Web bugs and spiders to troll in and among the various public forums, discreetly learning information about you and subtly marketing their products with banners, for example. Even sites that you frequent often gather personal information about you when you participate in chat rooms or discussion groups or conduct a search on their site. Following is a breakdown of each of the public areas where marketers and snoops are likely to find information about you:

Chat rooms. A chat room is a place on the Internet or page within a website or online service where you can chat, or "talk," to others by typing messages to them. In chat rooms, your communication tends to be real-time communication (as opposed to e-mail, which is delayed). When you participate in a chat room or online forum, your posting, which includes any messages you type and your e-mail address, is essentially public record. In some cases, websites archive the discussion that takes place in chat rooms and online forums, and this information can be accessed by anyone for years.

> Internet marketers often use Web bugs and spiders to troll in and among the various public forums, discreetly learning information about you and subtly marketing their products with banners, for example.

Bulletin boards. Bulletin boards are similar to chat rooms except that real-time communication typically does not occur. Instead, you can post a message for everyone to read for as long as the message stays on the bulletin board. If you post a message to a bulletin board, that message is available for anyone to view, along with your name, e-mail address, and ISP. As with chat rooms, some bulletin boards are archived.

Listservs. A listserv is a form of online newsletter that is e-mailed to a dedicated list of subscribers. Typically, a listserv is focused on a particular interest, such as gourmet cheese, teaching abroad, or local politics, and one company or individual is responsible for routing messages to you. The listserv is not always privately managed, so access to the mailing list may vary. If you participate in a listserv, be aware that even if you intend to reply solely to a particular individual on the list, you may actually be sending a message to everyone on the list.

Personal Web pages and blogs. Personal Web pages and blogs have become increasingly popular, especially among teenagers. A personal Web page typically contains information about the person who creates it or commissions it. Making personal information available is the reason why people choose to post these sites. But a personal Web page and any sensitive information included on it can be accessed by anyone. A blog is a Web journal of usually short, frequently updated posts that are arranged chronologically. The content and purposes of blogs vary, and they run the gamut from links and commentary about other websites, to news about a company/person/idea, to diaries, photographs, poetry, mini-essays, project updates, and even fiction. Blogs act like instant messages to the Web. If you participate in a blog, you may reveal sensitive personal information or intimate thoughts to strangers. Finally, if you have registered a domain name for a website—even if the site has yet to be built—your registration information is public information. Ownership of a website is akin to owning a home, and a public record is created in both cases. To discover the owner of any website or domain name, you can visit various sites, including www.register.com or www.checkdomain.com.

> **Almost 90 percent of children's sites collect personally identifiable information directly from children.**

E-mail and Instant Messaging

The co-founder of a company used the same corporate e-mail address for both his work-related and personal communications for a number of years. When he was fired after a power struggle, the new president read the e-mails that continued to be sent to the man's account. Under company policy, this was perfectly legal.

When you send an e-mail or an instant message, your message carries about as much privacy as a postcard. In fact, you may have enjoyed more privacy in the game of telephone you played as a child, because most of the kids were not paying attention to your message. Now not only do may people pay attention to your e-mails and instant messages, but a record of your communication is likely to reside permanently in various places without your knowledge.

E-mail

As a result of a dispute with her Internet Service Provider, a woman lost her Internet account. Instead of canceling her user name, how-

ever, the ISP simply changed her password. Personal mail continued to flow into her old address, but she was incapable of accessing it. The ISP, on the other hand, had full access.

> If you have an e-mail account with Yahoo! or Hotmail, or other commercial account providers, your personal information may be sold to third parties for marketing puposes.

Angel Lee of El Mirage, Arizona, was sentenced to sixty days of home detention for intercepting her husband's ex-wife's e-mail. To do so, she fraudulently obtained the user name and password to the woman's e-mail account. Comparing Lee's actions to someone breaking into the woman's home and reading her diary, the sentencing Judge said that Lee's penalty of home detention was a warning to others.

E-mail affords you little privacy for a variety of reasons. As you know from earlier in this chapter, hackers using packet sniffers can easily intercept your e-mails and read them when they are in transit. Anyone with access to your computer can break into it to read any e-mails that are stored on the machine. Hackers are also capable of obtaining your e-mails from the servers that may indefinitely store your e-mail communications.

Also, as mentioned in chapter 9, "Your Workplace," do not expect privacy in your e-mail communications when you send e-mail from work. Your employer can legally monitor and read your e-mails any time it wants and without your explicit knowledge or permission. In some cases, even if your employer promises not to read or monitor your e-mail activity, you still may not have a reasonable expectation of privacy. Accordingly, in the workplace, assume you have little to no e-mail privacy.

Further, even if you are cautious and only send personal e-mails from home, your user agreement with your ISP may reduce your expectation of privacy. Although user agreements with the various ISPs vary, the agreements are written to insulate the ISP's potential liability. Accordingly, your user agreement with your ISP likely states that it may monitor your e-mail communications and disclose any information for *any* reason that it views as reasonable, including government or legal purposes. Moreover, if you have an e-mail account with Yahoo! or Hotmail, or other commercial e-mail account providers, your personal information may be sold to third parties for marketing purposes. This information may include the details you submitted when you opened the

PROTECTING YOUR KIDS ONLINE

Chat rooms, bulletin boards, personal Web pages, and blogs offer great opportunities for people to meet. Unlike traditional meeting places, like libraries, schools, or town halls, however, you don't get to see the strangers you encounter, but you do let those strangers into your house. In the anonymous virtual world where anyone can be anybody, it's not a surprise when a fifty-year-old man poses as a fourteen-year-old kid. Your daughter's new twelve-year-old friend from Moscow could be who he says he is, or he could be a pedophile, criminal, or someone else with less than honorable intentions. According to a study by the Crimes Against Children Research Center at the University of New Hampshire, at least 20 percent of teens have received sexual advances from a stranger online.

The steps you must take to protect your privacy in cyberspace are similar to the steps you take to keep yourself and your family safe in the real world. In terms of your children's protection, privacy means keeping your kids' names, addresses, and phone numbers out of the hands of strangers, and protecting your children from anyone, including companies that want to sell or send them something.

Whether you like it or not, you must accept that Internet sites gather information from and about children. According to one FTC study, almost 90 percent of children's sites collect personally identifiable information directly from children. Moreover, only about half the sites directed to children disclose their policy governing information collection. Finally, less than 10 percent of children's Internet sites provide for some form of parental control over the information collected from kids.

To make it easier for you to protect the privacy of your children's personal information on the Internet, the FTC and Congress established the Children's Online Privacy Protection Act (COPPA). COPPA seeks to enable parents to control the type and extent of information that websites may collect or use with respect to children. In particular, COPPA requires that commercial and general-audience websites with content directed at children under the age of thirteen operate their websites in accordance with certain requirements, such as providing parents with notice about their information collection practices and obtaining parental consent before collecting personally identifiable information from children and more.

A word of caution, however: Do not rely solely on COPPA. Although many sites comply with COPPA, other less scrupulous sites do not. Therefore, you must adhere to the tips listed below:

✳ **Start together.** When your child is old enough to learn about the Internet, you should learn together. At the beginning, do not allow your child to surf alone. Explain to your children that although they may be alone when using a computer, once they are logged on to the Internet, they are no longer alone.

✳ **Set the ground rules for personal information.** Explain to your children that, just like in real life, revealing their names, addresses, e-mail addresses, telephone numbers, passwords, or any other personal information about themselves, their family, or their friends could jeopardize their safety and that of others. This rule also applies to photographs: Tell your child never to send a photograph of himself or herself via e-mail to a stranger.

✳ **Monitor your child's activities online.** Monitor what your child is doing when he or she is online and the amount of time he or she is spending online. You may even want to check the cache or cookies from the sites they've visited (see instructions in the section above on cache and cookies).

✳ **Limit your child's interactions online.** Instruct your child *never* to arrange to meet in person someone he or she has met online. (If the correspondent is insistent, a parent should be present and the meeting should take place in a public place.) Instruct your child never to open e-mail from someone whose address they don't recognize because the e-mail might be an inappropriate overture from a stranger or it might be a virus. The same rules should govern instant messaging (IM), which is like chat, except that it is usually a one-on-one experience. Instant messaging between friends is safer than any exchange in a chat room. Instant messaging with a stranger, however, may be less safe, because there is no monitor involved in IM conversations.

✳ **Check your Internet Service Provider (ISP).** Consider using an ISP that offers parental controls to block access to sites that are not explicitly marked as appropriate for children, as well as chat rooms, bulletin boards, and other highly interactive areas.

✳ **Use filtering software.** Consider using filtering software, like Net Nanny or CYBERsitter. These software packages block access to certain sites and prevent children from giving out personal information online.

✳ **Pay special attention to highly interactive or revealing sites.** Chat rooms and blogs can be highly invasive areas for children. In these rooms, your child may meet someone who befriends him or her, develops an online relationship, and tricks your child into revealing personal information or, worse, agreeing to meet in person. Similarly, monitor your child's contributions to blogs. The continuity of blogging allows small revelations to be connected, so a large amount of very precise personal information can be extrapolated in a very dangerous way.

account, including your zip code, gender, birth date, occupation, and more. Check your e-mail provider's privacy policy to see if this information might be used by marketers.

The Electronic Communications Protection Act (ECPA) of 1986 oversees the legal protection of your e-mails. Under the ECPA, the interception of e-mail while it is in transit between two destinations is a federal crime. However, the ECPA protects only the transmission of e-mail and does not provide any privacy or protection for e-mails in either your computer or in the receiver's machine. Moreover, the ECPA specifically permits your ISP to review any e-mails it stores as well as incoming or outgoing e-mails if your ISP believes you are attempting to harm the e-mail system or another user. Some ISPs temporarily store all messages that pass through the system. The ECPA also enables law enforcement agents to access your e-mails and other information that is in possession of your ISP.

Finally, law enforcement agents can seize your e-mail history if they have a warrant. The USA Patriot Act, which is discussed more fully in chapter 11,

"Your Everyday Life," makes it easier for law enforcement officials to access your e-mail without a court order or subpoena.

Instant Messaging (IM)

When Nick Groleau, a technical manager in Silicon Valley, received a friend's message on his AOL Instant Messenger buddy list telling him that Osama Bin Laden had been captured, he immediately clicked on the news link to learn more about this breaking story. Instead, he was directed to a site that offered a game to download. It is a good thing he decided not to download the game. One of Nick's friends did download the game and it triggered a virus that sent the same invitation to contacts on her buddy list and simultaneously installed adware to track user activity.

Equipped with special software from AOL and several other companies, instant messaging users can connect to one another on the Internet and have a seemingly private chat in real time. For most users, instant messaging feels like talking on the phone except with text. For the most part, if you want to have a live chat with your friend, the two of you must be operating the same software. Using these applications, you create a list of others or friends with whom you want to chat. When you log on to the Internet, the software tells you which of your friends are online.

Instant messaging is about as private as typing your personal information into an unsecure website. Your messages are accessible and can be easily intercepted. Instant messages are also subject to password hacking, virus attacks, and harvesting of personal data through spiders, Web bugs, and spyware.

The most important steps you can take to protect your e-mail and instant messaging communications are:

✳ **Encrypt your e-mail.** To fully protect your e-mail communications, you must encrypt your messages. See page 185 for instruction on how to encrypt your e-mail.

✳ **Have more than one e-mail address.** If you are a frequent user of chat rooms and bulletin boards, use an e-mail address and/or user name that is specific to these activities and different from the one that your use for personal or professional communications. Be aware that other people may be doing the same thing to disguise their identities.

INTERNET SCAMS

Many viruses come from spam or inadvertent e-mails from acquaintances. Watch out for scams that sound like these:

The "Virus Warning" Virus Scam

My mother sent this to warn me about the finaldoom virus, and I downloaded it because she works for IBM and she gets this informa-tion before the rest of the world. I know there are a lot of hoaxes about, but this virus sounds pretty scary because it will send all your Word documents to everyone in your address book. Download this patch—believe me, it's better to be safe than sorry.

This scam warns you about viruses to avoid. Typically, the sender makes it clear that there is no reason to doubt the warning. If you fall for the trick and download the patch, you will infect your computer and operating sys-tem. If you forward the e-mail, the recipients of your e-mail will get the virus, and—bam—mail servers will be bogged down. The virus could also be a Trojan horse that would allow the sender to snoop on you.

The "Fill in This Form Related to Your Account" Trojan Horse Scam

PAYPAL.COM NEW YEAR OFFER: For a limited time only PayPal is of-fering to add 10 percent of the total balance in your PayPal account to your account. All you have to do is register within the next five busi-ness days by filling in this form (attached).

In this scam, which is also known as phishing, spammers send legiti-mate-looking e-mails to users of PayPal and other popular services offering

---

211

them the chance to download a form, fill it in, and get a free offer. Unlike other scams that seek personal information directly from users, the purpose of this scam is to get the user to download a file containing a Trojan horse. Users who open the compressed Zip file attached to the spam e-mail inadvertently execute a Trojan horse program that connects to a website, which sends a worm to the user's computer. The worm reproduces itself and spreads throughout the Internet.

The "Enticing Celebrity Photo" Scam

Want to see revealing photos of Catherine Zeta-Jones? Not your type? How about other female celebrities such as Britney Spears or Shakira?

In this scam, a Trojan horse purports to contain revealing photos of Catherine Zeta-Jones and other female celebrities including Britney Spears and Shakira. Once the file is opened, a backdoor Trojan horse is downloaded onto the victim's computer and installs a backdoor program that allows someone to take over the computer.

✳ **Use a password.** A password makes it more difficult for other people to access your e-mail account. A password is particularly important if you share a computer with others, or if you often use public computers. To create an effective password, use the tips you have learned in other chapters of this book.

✳ **Log off.** If you are using a public computer, such as one in the library, at a computer center, at work, at a friend's home, and even in your own home, remember to log off. A computer that is perpetually connected to the Internet is more vulnerable to hackers.

✳ **Use Web-based e-mail.** If you share your computer or other people have access to your computer, use a Web-based e-mail application such as Yahoo! or Hotmail, both of which do not store your e-mails on your local drive.

✴ **Delete your e-mail.** In many cases, e-mail can be retrieved from servers and back-up systems. Nevertheless, if your e-mails are stored locally, you can protect yourself by deleting the local copy of the e-mail you sent or received.

✴ **Update your software.** Whether you are e-mailing or using instant messaging, be sure that your software is updated with the latest security patches and set to the highest security levels.

✴ **Watch what you write!** Know that your e-mail cannot be completely protected and keep sensitive information out of cyberspace.

Protect Your Privacy Online

Protecting both your privacy online and the valuable information in your computer requires an ongoing and active commitment. Here's a summary of the most important tips to protect your privacy online:

✴ **Install a firewall.** A firewall will protect your system from viruses, hackers, and snoops.

✴ **Run antivirus programs.**

✴ **Delete or disable cookies.** Use your browser's help menu to change the settings for your cookies.

✴ **Encrypt your communications.** Protect your transactions from packet sniffers by using encryption.

✴ **Don't post sensitive content online under your own name or e-mail address.**

✴ **Clean sweep your computer.** When you delete files on your computer, your files move to the trash or recycle bin on your computer, but they are still not gone forever. This is the case even after you empty the trash. Such file dele-tion merely frees the operating system to reuse the hard drive. If you want to dispose of sensitive files on your computer you must do a clean sweep. Windows data cannot be deleted beyond recovery without the use of spe-cial sweeping software. If you are getting rid of an old computer, or if you want to erase information on your current one, sweep the files clean. Buy a file-wiping program to clean your hard drive.

✳ **Log off and turn off your computer.** If you have a DSL line, broadband cable modem, or other connection to the Internet that is up and running twenty-four hours per day, be sure to turn your computer off when you are not using it to protect yourself from spyware. If you must leave your computer running instead of turning it on and off, you should at least password-protect your PC screen saver. In this way, you will be the only one who can deactivate the screen saver and access the computer.

✳ **Manage your personal information on your computer.** If you maintain sen-sitive personal information or financial records on your computer, be espe-cially careful. Be extra cautious if you keep the information on a laptop. Place sensitive records in files that require a password before they can be accessed, and then use a strong password that contains both letters and digits. If you use different names and passwords, do not save them on your computer. Make a chart of the user names and passwords you have assigned to your files and the names of any sites with which you have regis-tered. Store the chart in a secure place. In the same way, try not to use automatic login features on websites. Finally, delete files you no longer access and empty your trash often, in both your e-mail program and on your computer.

✳ **Be cautious when you use public computers.** Be especially careful if you are picking up your e-mail on public computers in Internet cafés, airports, libraries, and so forth. If you use a public computer terminal, you may inad-vertently leave private information behind. As such, be sure to take the fol-lowing precautions:

▶ Type your password every time. Never elect to save your password

▶ Delete any e-mail you retrieve from your inbox and, if applicable, from the Trash e-mail folder as well

▶ Before logging off, undo any changes you made to the browser or e-mail software, clear the browser's cache and history, and close the browser

▶ Make sure you've officially logged off (ask for assistance if you are unsure)

▶ Make sure that no one is looking over your shoulder as you work in public terminals

▶ Never check your bank accounts from or input any financial information into a public terminal

✳ **Don't use unencrypted Wi-Fi.** If you are worried about hackers, do not use Wi-Fi for sensitive information unless you encrypt your home system. Be aware that even if you encrypt data on a Wi-Fi system, it will not be as secure as data that is transmitted via a direct connection. Wi-Fi in public hotspots is rarely encrypted.

✳ **Be proactive.** You must be proactive to protect your privacy. Update your virus software regularly. Be on the alert for security patches and repairs that you can download. Constantly delete cookies on your computer and unload your cache. Do not open files that are sent to you by strangers. Stay informed about new computer viruses.

The Bottom Line

▶ Caught in the cookie jar? Remember that as you surf the Internet you leave very clear and detailed crumbs that create a trail of where you have been, what you have clicked on, what you have been downloading, and, in some cases, how long you've spent there.

▶ Don't catch a virus. As you surf the Internet, you can expose yourself to all sorts of viruses and spyware that can capture your information and infect your computer.

▶ Spam is not just a food product. Today, over 50 percent of all Internet traffic is spam e-mail. Follow the tips in this chapter to protect yourself against spam and you'll avoid spending half your morning deleting all the spam that you may be receiving.

▶ For kids, the Internet requires an "R" rating and not just "PG." Did you know that one in five kids is approached with sexual advances online? Make sure that you do all you can to protect your children's privacy online.

▶ Your e-mail may not be so private. E-mails have little privacy for a variety of reasons. If you want to protect your email fully, use encrypted e-mail, select a password difficult for others to access, and remember always to log off your e-mail account.

Your Home

You host your first cocktail party in your new home. On the way to the kitchen you overhear two guests gossiping about you and your house. One tells the other precise and private information about your house such as the exact price you paid for it, and the terms of your mortgage.

After a long day at work you sit down with your family to eat dinner together. During your thirty-minute meal you get up three times to answer the phone. The first call is a sales pitch for a Las Vegas time-share. The second is from a local company offering aluminum siding. The third advertises super rates with Mel's Long Distance Service. By the time you get off the phone, your dinner is cold.

You move from Chicago, Illinois, to Boise, Idaho. Just a few weeks after your move, junk mail mysteriously makes its way to Boise and fills your new mailbox.

You are a divorced woman trying to purchase a Manhattan co-op apartment. During your interview with the co-op board, you are outraged when a member of the board asks how long you expect your former spouse to live. The board member says this estimate will allow the board to calculate how long your ex will be able to continue providing your alimony payments.

You are alone in the privacy of your bedroom. From the corner of your eye, you notice what appears to be a tiny speck on the picture displayed on the wall. You move closer to investigate and discover a tiny, hidden camera. It turns out your ex-husband has been spying on you for months.

Most people think of their homes as havens from public life. Home is a place to hang your hat, kick back, and let it all hang out. It's a place where you want to feel protected from judgment, scrutiny, and unwanted distractions. In the safety and privacy of your own home, you should be in control. But are you?

Unfortunately, more and more, your private life is becoming public. It all begins when landlords or lenders pry into your personal information when you want to rent or buy a home. After you move in, there's a good chance that you will be bombarded with telemarketing calls, junk mail, and other intrusions, most of them in the form of offers to sell you something.

Some violations of privacy are less obvious, such as when your caller ID tag shows up on every call you make, when high-tech surveillance devices penetrate the walls of your house to tap your wireless phone calls or pick up images from video monitors, or when thieves rifle through your trash. Using a combination of new technologies and old-fashioned guile, corporations, criminals, and others can find out more about you than you realize.

Your Property

The first invasion of your privacy often happens even before you move into your home. Whether you are renting or buying, you are required to provide detailed information about your life and financial history. That has been a fact of life. But now your privacy is threatened more than ever because technology makes your personal information public and more easily accessible than ever before. It used to be time-consuming and difficult for landlords, lenders, and co-op boards to conduct a background check on applicants. All the pieces of the puzzle were scattered. Checking rental history, for instance, involved tracking down old landlords and physically traveling to housing courts to check records (and this strategy was effective only for the apartments the applicant disclosed). Verifying employment history meant calling the applicant's past employers. It was virtually impossible to discover criminal history; criminal records are filed in the relevant courthouse. The Internet has changed all that. Now anyone with a computer and Internet connection can discover the details of your life in just a few minutes.

When You Rent

Landlords can find out more about you than you probably want them to know. If you plan to rent your home or apartment, your prospective landlord will likely perform a screening or background check on you. Understandably, your prospective landlord wants to know whether you will pay the rent on time and be law-abiding.

You will probably be asked to complete a rental application that includes references from prior landlords and employers as well as your consent for the landlord to access your current credit report. Armed with this information, the landlord can learn quite a bit about you. As you already know from chapter 4, "Your Credit," the credit check alone will reveal your credit history over the past seven years, including whether you have been late or delinquent in paying rent, bills, or student or car loans; been slapped with a money judgment (including child support judgments) or tax lien; or been involved in another type of lawsuit, such as a personal injury claim. A credit report may also reveal whether you have filed for bankruptcy.

Many landlords also pay to use outside screening services that enable them to dredge up all sorts of even more personal information about you. Two of the largest tenant-screening services in this crowded field are Fidelity Information and ScreenNow Tenant from ChoicePoint. Fidelity Information, which is located in California but conducts nationwide background checks, claims to screen about fifty thousand prospective tenants each month. These companies provide landlords with information about your utility payment history, previous eviction proceedings, criminal reports, sex offender violations, and domestic-violence history from national databases compiled from public record information. They also check your references and verify employment history. Fidelity Information offers an additional report on your habits as a previous tenant: whether you are an abusive tenant, whether you vandalized, or whether you made chronic late payments.

The terrorist events of September 11, 2001, created demand for yet another kind of background report. Now a growing number of tenant-screening companies offer terrorist registry searches. The Office of Foreign Assets Control (OFAC) in the U.S. Department of the Treasury collects data from the FBI, CIA, and other national-security agencies and compiles a list of possible terrorists, money launderers, and international drug traffickers. The screening companies charge you to search the OFAC terrorist database, but you can check it for free by going to www.brownandcompany.net/ofac/search.asp.

Problems with Background Checks

As useful as background checks are for prospective landlords, they are not always helpful to you. Here is a list of some of the problems prospective renters have faced when their prospective landlords looked them up:

Subjective or Inaccurate Information. What if the information about you incorrectly indicates that you're a sex offender or a terrorist? This problem can occur because of *mixed files.* A mixed file is a report that combines information from one individual's file with information from a second person's file. This happens sometimes to individuals with similar names or similar social security numbers. It can also be the result of data-entry errors. In 2002, a case involving a mixed file resulted in a woman named Judy Thomas receiving $5.3 million in punitive damages from an Oregon court. TransUnion mixed up Judy Thomas with a woman named Judith Upton because the two women have similar social security numbers. As a result, Judy Thomas was considered a credit pariah for years, through no fault of her own, and despite her persistent efforts to clean up her credit report.

Incomplete Information. Another serious problem is that the databases that landlords access may not have complete information. For example, the reports that cull information from housing-court cases are based on the filings rather than the judgments. This means that regardless of who was at fault, or who filed the case against whom, as a prospective tenant, you may be flagged. What if you sued your prior landlord for failure to make required repairs and the court sided with you? Your name would still appear, suggesting that you may be a difficult or litigious tenant, and thereby affect your application.

> In 2002 alone, there were about two hundred thousand cases involving an identity thief renting a house or apartment under an assumed name.

Identity Theft. Identity theft is a serious problem. Imagine if an imposter used your identity to rent an apartment, failed to pay the rent, and the landlord filed for eviction? No doubt, you would be rejected for the next apartment you sought. In 2002 alone, there were about two hundred thousand cases involving an identity thief renting a house or apartment under an assumed name, according to the FTC's 2003 Identity Theft Survey. See chapter 3, "Your Identity," for tips on preventing identity theft.

If Your Application Is Denied

If a landlord denies you tenancy based on either a credit report or a report from a tenant-screening service, the landlord must comply with the provisions of the Fair Credit Reporting Act (FCRA) and provide you with what is known as an adverse-action notice. This notice informs you that you are entitled to a free copy of your credit report or tenant-screening report, and if you feel the information is incomplete or inaccurate, you can require the credit-reporting agency or screening service to reinvestigate and record the current status of the information. If the information is found to be inaccurate or cannot be verified within thirty days, it must be deleted from your file. In all likelihood you will have lost this apartment, but correcting your credit or screening report can prevent you from being denied tenancy in the future.

An adverse-action notice is required even if the information in the credit or tenant-screening report was not the main reason for you being denied tenancy. If the information in the report plays only a small part, or indirectly results in the landlord's overall decision, you *still* must be notified. Even if your rental application wasn't denied, you are entitled to an adverse-action notice if you are required by the landlord to: have a cosigner on the lease; pay a deposit not required for other applicants, or an unusually large deposit; or pay rent that is higher than for another applicant.

If you did not receive an adverse-action notice and feel you were entitled to one, ask the landlord or management company. You have legal remedies as well: you can sue in federal court for compensatory damages, punitive damages if the violations were deliberate, and attorney's fees.

When You Buy

What if your past credit card statements revealed that you have a propensity to drink and gamble? If your bank knew about your activities, would they jeopardize your chances of getting the best mortgage rate?

If you plan to purchase a home, condominium, or co-op apartment, be prepared to reveal a lot of personal and private information about yourself—in many cases, even more than when you're renting. If you plan on taking out a mortgage, your credit history is crucial to determine what interest rate you can secure and indeed whether you qualify for a mortgage at all.

If you have a blemished credit report but still are able to qualify for a mortgage, your lender's terms will no doubt be less favorable than the terms offered to someone with strong credit. Your down payment, interest rate, and points might be significantly higher than they would be if your credit history was perfect. The reasoning is the higher the perceived risk for the bank, the higher the reward. Over the life of a thirty-year mortgage, the difference between what you would pay and what someone with good credit would pay can be substantial.

Factors other than what is contained in your credit report can also affect your application for a mortgage or your mortgage rate. As discussed in chapter 5, "Your Money," financial institutions routinely share confidential customer information with their affiliates and often with nonaffiliated third parties as well (which, however, you can prevent). What if your lender was part of a conglomerate that also owned airline and hotel websites, a shopping site, and an online ticket provider? Isn't it possible that the lender might be privy to personal information having nothing to do with your financial situation, such as how many Fifty Cent concerts you've attended or how many trips to Colombia you've made in the past year? Even if you have a perfect credit history, you can wind up overpaying for your mortgage for undisclosed reasons. With the growth of large and diversified financial conglomerates, this becomes more likely every day.

> **Even if you have a perfect credit history, you can wind up overpaying for your mortgage for undisclosed reasons.**

Co-ops

A posh Upper East Side Manhattan co-op rejected a buyer after discovering during his interview that the buyer had a J.C. Penney credit card. The co-op board felt that the buyer didn't have the right image for its building.

Prospective purchasers in some upscale co-op buildings (assuming these buildings allow dogs in the first place) must have their dogs "interviewed" by the co-op board. They must also supply letters of reference from the dogs' trainers and breeders.

In some cities, such as New York, cooperative (the official name for a co-op) ownership is the most common form of property ownership. When you buy a co-op, you are purchasing shares of stock in a corporation that owns the entire building. The shares are part of a lease that allows you (the shareholder) to rent the apartment.

When you apply to join a co-op, you are typically subject to a detailed and

THE RIGHT TO ENTER?

After disputes over money (rent, security deposit, and so forth), the most common source of tension between landlord and tenant is the landlord's right to enter a rental unit. Put another way, what is your right as a tenant to be left alone in the privacy of your home? Your landlord does have the right to enter your apartment or house, but with restrictions. It's not permissible for your landlord simply to pop in uninvited and crash your Super Bowl party; nor is it permissible for your landlord to slip into your apartment while you are at work and play dress-up with your clothes or leave love notes on your pillow. Here are the general limits to a landlord's right to enter your property, subject to state law:

Reasonable notice. Although landlord and tenant laws vary from state to state, a landlord typically cannot enter your rental premises without giving you reasonable notice. Check the provision in your rental agreement about reasonable notice, but remember none of the provisions in your lease can abridge any rights you have under state law. To see what constitutes reasonable notice in your state, visit the "Real Estate" section of the Findlaw website at public.findlaw.com.

The landlord does *not* have to provide any kind of notice in case of emergency, such as fire or a serious water leak.

Legitimate reason. In addition to providing you with reasonable notice, your landlord also needs to have a legitimate reason to enter your premises. The following are legitimate reasons for entry:
- making repairs
- determining if repairs are needed
- showing the property to prospective new tenants or purchasers
- maintaining the property during a tenant's extended absence (in many states)
- if you have granted permission
- if the landlord has a court order

onerous level of personal and financial scrutiny. In addition to a personal interview, you will be asked to supply an enormous stack of documents, together called the *co-op package,* which includes tax returns, statement of net worth, bank statements, brokerage statements, personal and business letters of recommendation, and so forth. In effect, the co-op package contains your entire life history, and copies of the package are circulated to everyone sitting on the board of directors in the co-op. Eventually, everyone in the entire building knows everything about you.

Unfortunately, there is essentially nothing that can be done about this enormous invasion of privacy. If you want to live in a co-op building, you must supply the documentation that the building requires. Worse, even if you supply all the material, you are not guaranteed approval.

Who Can Access Your Real Estate Records?

You discover a photograph of your home posted on the Internet linked to information including its exact street address, your name, and your home's value. The problem? Your home isn't for sale!

You may not like it, but anyone can access your real estate records—and it's quite easy to do so. When you purchase a home or other real estate, a record of your transaction is filed in your county assessor's or recorder's office (or the comparable office in your state). These records become part of the public domain, and anyone has a right to access the information contained in these files (See chapter 2, "Your Personal Information and the Public Record.")

Before the emergence of the Internet, it was much more difficult for someone to access your real estate information. For instance, a person would have to determine the exact county location of your property and physically travel there to look through records, which might or might not have been computerized. That person would also face the usual bureaucratic hassles, like limited hours of operation, missing files, or missing papers.

Now, if somebody wants to find out information about your real estate, a simple search on the Internet can produce a frighteningly thorough profile. If you own a home, an Internet search might reveal your name and address, the purchase price of your home, your loan balance, the property's estimated value, and, in some cases, even the day of the week the trash gets picked up. Depending on the county in which you live, you might also see a photograph of your home, posted, in all likelihood, without your knowledge or permission.

A lien search on real property may reveal even more information, including whether you (the owner) are divorced, owe child support, or are subject to a court judgment.

> If you own a home, an Internet search might reveal your name and address, the purchase price of your home, your loan balance, the property's estimated value, and, in some cases, even the day of the week the trash gets picked up.

Don't believe it? Try it for yourself. Go to www.netronline.com/public_records.htm and start your own search for information. To get a map and driving directions to your home, log on to www.mapquest.com and type in your address.

Despite all the information that can be accessed about you in the public record, you still have some ability to protect your privacy and your good name.

Consider the following tips when renting or purchasing a home:

* **Review your credit report regularly.** As mentioned previously, you must check your credit report regularly. The time to correct credit report errors is *not* when you plan to buy or refinance property, but well in advance of that time.

* **Establish a trust or other structures to acquire property.** If you are troubled by your privacy being sacrificed when you purchase real property, you can consult an attorney who will advise you about using trusts, corporations, or other vehicles as the purchaser of record in your real estate transaction. By doing so, however, you may forfeit certain tax advantages. Given the complexities of establishing trusts and other legal vehicles, you must consult an attorney if you are considering this option.

* **Use extra caution with respect to co-ops.** Keep careful count of the number of co-op packages that are copied, and demand that all packages circulated be returned directly to you. Do not trust the managing agent of the building (who runs the co-op approval process) to destroy these packages on your behalf. Packages are often never returned to the managing agent. Ensure

that you destroy or shred the packages yourself. Request that no photo-copies be permitted.

✳ **Ask questions about document storage.** Ask the landlord or management company how your personal information will be safeguarded. Try to limit the number of copies that are made. Also make sure that the material is not discarded in trash cans. Documents as sensitive as these should be shredded, and you should be the one who makes sure that happens. If you are concerned about jeopardizing your chances of getting the apartment, you might consider waiting until *after* your rental application has been approved before asking these questions.

✳ **Follow up if you are turned down.** If your application for a rental apartment is rejected, ask the landlord why you were rejected. You have certain rights under the FCRA. As mentioned, if a landlord turns you down based on a credit or tenant-screening report, the landlord must provide you with an adverse-action notice. This notice entitles you to a free copy of your tenant report, and, if the report is incomplete or inaccurate, you can require the credit agency or screening service to investigate and record the current status of the information. If the information is inaccurate or cannot be verified, it will be deleted from your file. In all likelihood you will have missed out on the apartment, but correcting your screening report can prevent you from being denied one in the future. Make sure that report has been corrected before you resume your housing search.

✳ **Be realistic and use common sense.** You cannot avoid releasing certain information. You need to live somewhere. But use common sense to make sure that your sensitive information is being returned to you.

Privacy Issues in Your Home

Once you move into your home or apartment, you would think that your privacy would be secure. Unfortunately, this is not always the case. Technology that you use every day often has the nasty habit of causing unintended consequences. In the hands of snoops or law enforcement, some technologies such as nanny cams, video monitors, and other devices can invade your privacy. There are also low-tech ways that snoops can invade your privacy, such as good old-fashioned Dumpster diving.

Nanny Cams

> Installing a nanny cam in your home can allow high-tech peeping toms to spy on you.

A privacy expert demonstrated on national television how easily camera-generated images can be intercepted by someone sitting in a car outside on the street. The expert tapped into a camera's signal and displayed the images on his laptop, using only a makeshift antenna constructed from an empty can.

A nanny cam is a video monitor used by people who want to watch their nannies, children, elderly parents, or pets from a remote site. If you watch national news shows on television, you have probably seen disturbing nanny cam footage of caregivers abusing children. A combination of parental concern and drastically declining prices has caused a boom in the nanny cam business. Some nanny cams are so small they can be concealed in almost anything, including alarm clocks, tissue boxes, humidifiers, and even teddy bears. Almost a million wireless cameras have been sold by X10 Wireless Technology, whose ubiquitous ads pop up when you surf the Internet. Wireless versions enable you to access your nanny cam via remote computer. Simply log on from work or from your business trip to check on your family. Although some people believe that nanny cams are an essential protection tool in today's dangerous world, others reject the devices on moral grounds as an invasion of privacy.

There is another privacy concern surrounding wireless nanny cams that is not well known, but is highly disturbing. In a strangely ironic twist, installing a nanny cam in your home can allow high-tech peeping toms to spy on *you*. Strangers could be peering into your private life, spying on your home and your kids. The wireless nanny cam operates by sending a signal to a nearby receiver that is plugged into your TV, DVD player, or VCR. This signal is easily intercepted from more than a quarter-mile away by cheap, off-the-shelf electronic equipment. To add insult to injury, this type of snooping is generally not illegal because wiretap laws apply to intercepting sound, not video.

Follow this tip if you still feel the need to install a nanny cam despite the privacy risks:

❋ **Secure your nanny cam as well as possible.** Your nanny cam should be either a hard-wired device, or a wireless system with a proven encryption technology.

IS IT A CRIME TO SNOOP USING VIDEO SURVEILLANCE?

From a legal standpoint, snooping on people with a video camera in your own home is generally legal, except perhaps in bathrooms, changing rooms, or other places where an individual would have a reasonable expectation of privacy. Audio recording, however, is usually illegal under wiretap laws.

What if someone is spying on you? Remember the creepy Sharon Stone movie, *Sliver,* in which the residents of an entire apartment building in New York were watched and videotaped in their most intimate moments by their landlord? Numerous cases involving landlords spying on their tenants have filled the headlines. In certain instances, the landlords were not prosecuted; in others, they were charged only with trespassing. These stories have exposed gaping holes in current legislation. Many states do not have laws that adequately address high-tech snooping because the technology of modern peeping has evolved faster than the law. The law, however, is beginning to catch up.

In June 2003, a new law was enacted in New York, making video voyeurism a felony (highly unusual in most states). The new law, called Stephanie's Law, allows for punishment of up to seven years in jail for secretly videotaping a person in a private setting such as a bedroom, changing room, or bathroom. Stephanie Fuller lobbied for the law after her landlord—who secretly taped her through a camera hidden in the smoke detector above her bed—was convicted of a minor trespassing charge that carried no jail time.

Home Intercom Systems and Baby Monitors

Most home intercoms and baby monitors operate by emitting radio frequencies and are easily intercepted by scanners, cordless phones, or other baby monitors nearby. If you are concerned about your privacy, turn these devices off when not in use, or, as with a nanny cam, use a hard-wired unit instead of a wireless one when possible.

> Snoops who intercept nanny cam signals are not breaking the law because wiretap laws apply to intercepting sound, not video.

Cordless Telephones

Cordless phones are not secure devices. They operate like mini radio stations, sending radio signals back and forth from the base unit to the handset, and these signals are easily intercepted. As with cell phones (discussed in chapter 11, "Your Everyday Life"), the older, analog models offer no security and can be monitored by anyone with an inexpensive scanner. Newer digital cordless phones offer better security, but they are not invulnerable. Under the Electronic Comunications Privacy Act, it is generally illegal to intercept cordless phone conversations.

Follow these privacy tips when using a cordless phone:

✳ **Use a digital cordless phone.** A digital cordless phone that operates on a higher frequency is more secure.

✳ **Use a cordless phone that randomly assigns a new digital code every time the handset is returned to the base.** This design feature won't protect against eavesdropping, but it will prevent people nearby with similar handsets from attaching to your phone line and driving up *your* long distance bill.

✳ **Never use cordless phones, even a digital cordless phone, when disclosing sensitive financial or personal information.** Use a landline phone instead.

Caller ID

From a privacy standpoint, Caller ID is a double-edged sword. On the one hand, it enhances your privacy by enabling you to identify who is calling before you answer the phone. You have control because you decide whether or not to answer. Caller ID is a useful means of minimizing the intrusiveness of the telephone, and using it may result in fewer telemarketing, obscene, or crank calls.

On the other hand, your own privacy is compromised when you make outgoing telephone calls if the person or business you are calling is also using Caller ID. You lose your right to control to whom you give your phone number. There are situations where you might prefer to remain anonymous, such as if you call AIDS or mental-health hotlines, police tip lines, and so on. Furthermore, if you call a business that is using Caller ID, the business is capturing your telephone number, and can add it to their marketing databases, resulting in yet *more* telemarketing calls.

If you want to prevent your name and number from appearing on someone else's Caller ID box:

✳ **Take advantage of any blocking options that exist in your area.** In some places you can block your telephone number from appearing on someone else's phone on either a per-call basis or for all calls. Many of these services are free. Check with your local telephone company.

Biometric Scans

You return home to your apartment building, struggling to keep hold of your grocery bags, briefcase, and gym bag. Forget fumbling in your pockets for your keys; you simply press your finger next to the fingerprint-identification door lock to open the door. Is this your sci-fi fantasy or a privacy nightmare?

Biometric devices turn physical characteristics, such as fingerprints or patterns in eye retinas, into data that computers can use to identify people. Biometric-enabled security devices have gained popularity in security-sensitive locations like airports, hospitals and police stations. It is only recently, however, that biometric locks have found their way into apartment and co-op buildings. A few upscale buildings in New York City now use biometric locks to admit residents into elevator banks, gyms, and garages. (You still need keys to get into your own apartment, but biometric apartment locks cannot be far behind.) Clearly one's desire to emulate the Jetsons is a big selling point in choosing these security devices. According to the developer of one of the buildings, the feature was chosen not so much for security but to "reflect the lifestyle" of the target buyer.

The notion of key-free living may be attractive, but it does raise complex privacy issues that are only beginning to be studied. A 2003 report by the National Research Council advises caution when using biometric security systems. According to the report: "These technologies can pose serious privacy and security concerns if employed in systems that make use of servers to compare biometric samples against stored templates (as is the case in many large-scale systems)." When used on a smaller scale, such as an individual unit used as a lock to your home or laptop, they raise fewer privacy issues.

> **Do you really want your fingerprint allowing your nosy landlord or the police to monitor your comings and goings?**

Do you really want your fingerprint allowing your nosy landlord or the police to monitor your comings and goings? Or worse, do you want to risk finding your fingerprint for sale one day on the Internet? The answer is clearly no, but these are issues that you are likely to grapple with in the future.

Television Viewing Habits

You're hopelessly addicted to The Bachelor, *celebrity infomercials, and the occasional Playboy special, yet you profess to watch nothing but* Civil War Journal *on the History Channel. Luckily no one will ever know . . . or will they?*

Your television-viewing habits can reveal a frightening amount of personal information about you. Cable-viewing records are supposed to be confidential under the terms of the federal Cable Communications Policy Act. The act states that cable operators can't use the cable system to collect your personally identifiable information or disclose it without your prior written consent. The cable companies have been doing a good job of safeguarding your personal information, but as these companies grow and branch into areas that are not covered by the act, there is concern that the law is not strong enough to protect your privacy. For instance, Comcast, the largest cable provider in the United States and the acquirer of AT&T Broadband, has been challenged for its vague and possibly illegal privacy policy. The policy allows Comcast to share customer information with "potential business transition partners," "professional advisers," and "service providers" for "legitimate business activities." Bowing to pressure, Comcast agreed to rewrite its privacy policy, but skeptics have yet to see the revised policy.

> With only a company promise to keep your anonymity and no law to enforce it, privacy advocates are worried that TiVo—or other DVRs—may become a peephole into your living room.

The current law does not apply to newer technology such as satellite TV, interactive TV, cable modems, or TiVo, which is the best known of the digital video recorders (DVRs). TiVo allows television viewers to pause live shows, skip commercials, show instant replays, and record shows. TiVo's technology allows it to know that you watch *Celebrity Mole* at 3 A.M. and replayed the Janet Jackson Super Bowl 2004 halftime show a dozen times. More importantly, TiVo's technology tracks your viewing habits to develop a profile of you that permits TiVo to recommend shows you may enjoy based on a review of your previous television habits. This information is a treasure chest for advertisers and broadcasters, and they are dying to get their hands on it. Recently, TiVo announced that it *would* sell audience-viewing data, but only on an anonymous basis. (TiVo came under fire in 2001 for having the capability to link its viewer information with individual customers, though the company promised it would never do so.) With only a company promise to keep your anonymity and no law to enforce it, privacy advocates are worried that TiVo—or other DVRs—may become a peephole into your living room. Indeed, the Electronic Freedom Foundation believes that DVRs present "one of the great privacy issues of our time."

Law Enforcement and High-Tech Snooping

In Florence, Oregon, narcotics officers stopped in front of the house of Danny Kyllo in the dark hours of the early morning. The police suspected Kyllo of growing marijuana, but they did not have enough evidence to get a warrant. Sitting in their van across the street, the police aimed a thermal-imaging device at the outside of Kyllo's house and detected high levels of heat from the exterior walls. The police surmised that Kyllo was using heat lamps to grow marijuana inside his house. The thermal images enabled the police to secure a warrant and arrest Kyllo. Kyllo claimed that his Fourth Amendment rights were violated because the police failed to get a search warrant before using the technological device to "search" his house.

In the case of Danny Kyllo, it was the police—and not some business or ordinary snoop—using technology to violate his privacy. Under the Fourth Amendment, you are protected from unreasonable searches and seizures in your own home. You probably already also know—or have learned from *Law & Order* and other police dramas—that to comply with the law, the police must have a warrant to enter and search your house. But what if the police could search your house, as they did with Kyllo, without ever entering?

In 2001, the Supreme Court ruled in *Kyllo* v. *U.S.* that when the government uses cutting-edge technology that is not ordinarily used by the general public to obtain information about the interior of a home, the surveillance is unreasonable in the absence of a search warrant. The Court reasoned that technologies such as the thermal-imaging device could be used to determine very intimate details about someone's private life, such as "at what hour each night the lady of the house takes her daily sauna and bath."

The Supreme Court ruling in the *Kyllo* case is significant for many reasons. First, it affirms your right to privacy within the sanctity of your own home. Second, the case extends the original understanding of the Constitution into the technological age. Finally, the case has broader implications because it limits technology-assisted searches in a variety of places, not just the home. How the government's use of its broad and intrusive surveillance powers under the Patriot Act (see chapter 11, "Your Everyday Life") meshes with the *Kyllo* ruling remains to be seen.

Sexual Privacy

In 1998, the Houston police entered the apartment of John Lawrence after receiving a call from Lawrence's neighbor. The neighbor claimed *there was a man in Lawrence's apartment who had a gun and was "going crazy." When the police entered the apartment, they discovered Lawrence engaging in anal sex with Tyron Garner. They were immediately arrested under a Texas law that prohibited "deviate sexual behavior" between persons of the same gender. Lawrence and Garner were jailed, prosecuted, and fined more than $200 each.*

In the same way that the Supreme Court deals with the effects of technology on privacy, it confronts the effects of changing attitudes and lifestyles with respect to your sexual privacy. In *Lawrence and Garner v. Texas,* which was decided in 2003, the Supreme Court struck down a Texas statute banning sodomy between same-sex couples. The Court found that the state could not pass laws that would demean its residents' existence "by making their private sexual conduct a crime."

Beyond just striking down the Texas statute, the ruling established for the first time, in the view of many legal analysts, a broad constitutional right to sexual privacy. The ruling would most likely invalidate the laws of the thirteen other states that outlaw sodomy between same-sex or heterosexual couples, as well as virtually any other law governing private sexual conduct among consenting adults in their homes.

Garbage

The police believed that Billy Greenwood was dealing drugs from his house. They wanted to obtain a warrant to search the property, but they could not gather enough evidence to get one. To solve their problem, the police searched the garbage bags that Greenwood left at the curb for pickup. When they looked through Greenwood's garbage, the police found a number of drug-related clues, which gave them enough evidence to get a warrant to search Greenwood's house. That search uncovered illegal drugs, and Greenwood was arrested on felony charges.

Unlike the previous two cases that expand your privacy rights, the Supreme Court ruling in the case of *Greenwood* v. *California* (1988) demonstrates that there are still some areas where you might expect to have a privacy right, but in fact do not. In the *Greenwood* case, the court ruled that you have no expectation of privacy in your garbage. Therefore, the police don't need a warrant before snooping through the contents of your trash, nor is it illegal for anyone to sift through your trash.

> The police don't need a warrant before snooping through the contents of your trash, nor is it illegal for anyone to sift through your trash.

The effect of this ruling is that your privacy may be greatly compromised. Garbage routinely contains items of a deeply personal nature, such as empty prescription bottles labeled with an individual's name and drug name; credit card receipts; financial documents; cashed checks; confidential correspondence; and birth control packaging.

You might think that when you place your garbage in an opaque bag or place it in a sealed trash container on your property or at the end of your driveway, that you could reasonably expect your trash to remain private. But the Supreme Court ruling in *Greenwood* says that if you are concerned about the privacy of your personal garbage, you must use a shredder, black out prescription labels, and jump through other hoops to keep any sensitive information from prying eyes.

The *Greenwood* case does not prohibit states from providing their citizens with a higher level of privacy. To date, at least six states have ruled that garbage is private and that the police must secure a warrant before they perform a search.

When you put out your trash, remember to:

✳ **Shred sensitive documents, receipts, and junk mail.** If this information gets in the hands of an identity thief, you could be in big trouble.

✳ **Destroy the labels from prescription bottles or any other packaging that you don't want to be seen.** Do you want your neighbors knowing you take antidepressants? Do you want potential thieves knowing you just bought a diamond necklace?

Unsolicited or Junk Mail

From the moment you buy or rent your home or apartment, you will be exposed to telemarketers and direct-market solicitors—more commonly known as junk mailers—who will constantly bombard you with their increasingly prolific and aggressive tactics. Junk mail comes in the form of credit card offers, coupons for car rentals and carpet cleaners, sweepstakes applications, and flyers for sales at local stores. You might also receive solicitations from charities, sometimes with personalized mailing labels or stickers and other gifts to encourage you to give. Today, in the course of a week, you're likely to get more than *ten* times as much junk mail as regular mail. In fact, Americans as a whole receive about 4 million tons of junk mail each year. Not only is junk mail an environmental threat, it is also an annoying burden in your mailbox.

But is junk mail a threat to your privacy? It's intrusive, often unwanted, and also not completely harmless. First of all, junk mail is a sure sign that somehow your name and personal information have been entered into a marketing database. More importantly, the information contained in junk mail could get in the wrong hands. The junk mail you throw out in the trash contains your personal information that any stranger can access with a little snooping in the Dumpster. You might reject the offer for the pre-approved Platinum Visa card with bonus miles and 12.5 percent annual percentage rate, but the identity thief who rummages through your trash might not be so discriminating—especially since the thief can apply for the credit in your name! Be aware, too, that some junk mail is itself a scam to get you to reveal your personal information.

If you receive junk mail (which almost all of us do, often including children who are too young to read much less make or spend money), you should know how it finds you and how you should handle it. And if you feel that junk mail invades your privacy, is harmful to the environment, or wastes your time, there *is* something you can do about it. It is unlikely that you will ever be 100 percent free from junk mail, but there are steps you can take that will significantly reduce the amount of junk mail you receive.

How Direct Mail Marketers Get Your Name and Address

Getting hold of your name and address is big business. The Direct Marketing Association (known as the DMA) projects that direct marketing–driven sales will surpass $1.7 trillion in 2003, with projections estimating almost $2.5 trillion by 2008. As long as the motivation exists, direct marketers will continue to add or keep your name and address on their marketing lists. The information on these lists comes from countless sources, including public records. Sources you probably thought were private can be easily penetrated.

Here are some sources that direct marketers use to get your personal information:

▶ **Phone books.** Mailing-list companies compile a list of all people listed in the more than four thousand phone books in the United States.

▶ **Birth, marriage, and divorce records.** Marketing companies review public-record databases for changes in your legal status so they can market products that may interest you.

▶ **Voter registration records.**

▶ **U.S. Census information.**

▶ **Business or professional associations.** Organizations to which you belong, such as the Chamber of Commerce or the Rotary Club, might sell your name and address to third-party solicitors and marketers.

▶ **Licenses and permits.** The lists of professional organizations of people who must hold a state license to work, such as doctors and lawyers, or groups that oversee requirements for a permit, allowing the holder to drive, hunt, or own a dog, for example, may be accessed.

▶ **Legal information.** Marketers may discover if there are any judgments, bankruptcies, or real estate titles in your name.

▶ **Vehicle registrations.** Some marketers access vehicle registration lists.

And the list goes on. If you have ever:

▶ purchased an item from a catalog
▶ given money to a political campaign
▶ contributed to a charity
▶ filled out a product warranty card
▶ ordered a magazine subscription
▶ taken a mail-in survey; or

238

any number of other seemingly innocuous acts, the chances are that any personal information you have provided has been combined with information available on public record and is recorded in a computer database. As a result, you will more than likely hear from direct marketers repeatedly, given their interest in developing long-term relationships with you as a customer or contributor. At the same time, the very same companies with whom you have done business will sell or rent their lists with your information to *other* companies. This is how you wind up getting mail from organizations you know nothing about.

> Americans as a whole receive about 4 million tons of junk mail each year.

Some of the biggest players in the direct-marketing field are Acxiom, Donnelley Marketing, Equifax, Experian, and TransUnion. Three of these companies are credit reporting agencies (CRAs). As discussed in chapter 6, "Your Shopping," data conglomerators collect a great deal of information about you and sell it to various companies who then market products to you.

How to Reduce Your Junk Mail

There are many things you can do to minimize the amount of junk mail you receive and prevent new junk mail from being delivered. To reduce the amount of junk mail you get, pay attention to these privacy tips:

✳ **Sign up for the Direct Marketing Association's Mail Preference Service (MPS).** The Direct Marketing Association (DMA) is the oldest and largest trade association in the direct marketing field. About 70 percent of national direct marketers belong to the DMA. One of the easiest and most important ways you can lessen your junk-mail load is to sign up for this organization's Mail Preference Service (MPS).

The MPS is largely a do-not-mail list. By signing up with the MPS, you will largely eliminate solicitations from the major national direct marketers that belong to the DMA. This one action will significantly reduce the amount of junk mail you receive. However, the MPS will not totally eliminate your junk mail. You will still get unsolicited mail from local advertisers, charities, politicians, and commercial organizations that are not participants in MPS, as well as mail addressed to "resident" or "occupant." You will also continue to receive direct mail from companies with which you have a relationship.

When you register with MPS, your name is placed on a list that is sent to members of the DMA four times a year, in January, April, July, and October. The member marketers match their lists against the MPS list and must delete from their lists the names and addresses supplied by the MPS. Once your name is on the DMA do-not-mail list, you will receive no more junk mail from member marketers, or from other companies that may buy or rent DMA lists. After five years, you need to reregister. Within three months of registering, you should start to see an appreciable reduction in junk mail.

> Once your name is on the DMA do-not-mail list, you will receive no more junk mail from member marketers, or from other companies that may buy or rent DMA lists.

There are two ways to register. First, you can send in a postcard or letter containing your name, complete home address, and signature to the following address:

DMA Mail Preference Service
Box 643
Carmel, NY 10512

Registering by mail is free.

Second, you can register online by going to www.dmaconsumers. org/cgi/offmailinglist. At the site, complete the registration form, and print out a copy for your files. The online registration costs $5, which you will need to pay with a credit card. (The credit card payment is processed over a secure server.)

✳ **Contact the big direct marketers directly.** Even though the big direct-marketing companies belong to the DMA, you might decide you want to contact them directly:

Acxiom. To request an opt-out form, leave a message on its Consumer Advocate Hotline at 877/774-2094, or send an e-mail message to optout@acxiom.com.

Database America Compilation Department. Write to 100 Paragon Drive, Montvale, NJ 07645, or call 800/223-7777 or 201/476-2000.

Donnelley Marketing. Request an opt-out by writing to them at Database Operations, 416 S. Bell, Ames, IA 50010.

Equifax (formerly Polk), List Suppression File, 26955 Northwestern Hwy., South Field, MI 48034, 800/873-7655.

Experian Consumer Services (formerly Metromail), 901 West Bond, Lincoln, NE 68521. To opt out, call 402/458-5247.

TransUnion, List Division, Box, 97328, Jackson, MS 39288, 888/567-8688.

> Credit card direct marketers mail about 5 billion unsolicited credit card offers annually. That means that you can expect to receive twenty-five offers this year.

✳ **Opt out of offers of pre-approved credit.** An easy tip for reducing junk mail is to reduce those offers of pre-approved credit cards that flood your mailbox. Credit card direct marketers mail about 5 billion unsolicited credit card offers annually. That means that you can expect to receive twenty-five offers this year.

As outlined in chapter 4, "Your Credit," the three major credit bureaus—Experian, Equifax, and TransUnion—provide credit card issuers with lists of names of potential new customers. If you call the credit bureaus' toll-free numbers, you can prevent this from happening. The number to call is 888/5-OPT-OUT or 888/567-8688.

When you call the number, an automated voice system will answer and lead you through the opt-out process in about three minutes. You need only provide your name, phone number, and social security number (don't worry about giving it out; they have it already).

After releasing this information, the first option lets you remove your name for two years. The opt-out goes into effect after five business days. If you prefer to keep your name off these lists permanently, wait for the second option. If you choose to opt out permanently, you will receive a form in the mail within five business days. You must fill out the form and return it; otherwise, your opt-out request will be downgraded to two years. If at a later date you decide you would like to resume getting those pre-approved offers, call the same number. If you move, you must repeat the call.

❋ **Refuse and return mail.** The U.S. Postal Service is required to deliver your mail, but you are not required to *accept* it. You can use these simple tactics to easily handle two situations:

For your own junk mail: For first-class junk mail, cross out the address and bar code, circle the first-class postage, and write REFUSED: RETURN TO SENDER—REMOVE NAME FROM MAILING LIST. The U.S. Postal Service will send the junk mail back to the sender. As a rule, you will be removed from that marketer's list. Note this tactic does not work for bulk mail. The U.S. Postal Service discards bulk mail that is undeliverable. In this case, refusing the mail may feel good but the tactic does no good. To interrupt bulk-mail deliveries, you have to communicate directly with the sender.

For others' junk mail: In some cases, you receive mail addressed to people who no longer live at your address. To eliminate this junk mail, write on the outside of the envelope REFUSED: RETURN TO SENDER; RECIPIENT HAS MOVED and mail it back. You should see results with this trick. You can also fill out a Mail Forwarding Change of Address Form (Postal Form 3575) for the former residents. Write MOVED, LEFT NO FORWARDING ADDRESS as the new address. Sign your own name but write AGENT FOR THE ABOVE below your signature. If possible, give this form directly to your mail carrier so you can be sure the information is entered into the National Change of Address database. If all else fails, you may even need to follow up with a phone call to the post office to ensure that the change gets effectuated.

❋ **Remove yourself from sweepstakes, catalog, and coupon lists.** By making a phone call or filling out an e-mail form, you can remove your name from sweepstakes, catalog, and coupon lists. Use these numbers to help reduce your mail:

Sweepstakes: Call the 800 number and ask to be removed from the publisher's mailing list. Here are some important numbers:

> **Publisher Clearing House Sweepstakes**
> 800/645-9242
> **American Family Publishers**
> 800/237-2400

Catalogs: Call the catalog's 800 number and ask to be removed from its mailing list. Calling will prevent you not only from receiving the catalog in the future, but also from winding up on someone else's list. Have the mailing label handy when you make the call.

Coupons: Use these numbers to reduce coupon mailings:

ADVO (mail looks like supermarket fliers, arrives without an address and accompanied by a postcard with a picture of a missing child). Call 888/241-6760 to get off the list, or log on to www.advo.com/html/contacts/index.htm to do so online.

Val-Pak Coupons (a fat envelope full of coupons). The easiest way to get deleted from this list is to log on to www.coxtarget.com/removal_request.html. Val-Pak has regional lists, so if you want to unsubscribe by mail, send your request to whatever address is printed on the envelope you receive.

✳ **Consider NOT filling out a change of address form if you move.** When you fill out the U.S. Postal Service's Change of Address Form, the information is entered into their National Change of Address (NCOA) database, and your name and new address in effect get sold to mailing list companies nationwide. This is why junk mail finds its way into your mailbox after you move to a new address.

To avoid getting junk mail at your new address, use these two tactics:

▸ Send your own postcards announcing your change of address to those whose mail you want (or in the case of bills, *have*) to receive

▸ Fill out an address change form but indicate FOR TEMPORARY MOVE ONLY, implying that you will return to your old address in one year. The postal service only forwards first-class mail for a year anyway, and temporary address changes apparently do not find their way into the NCOA database and therefore do not get sold.

✳ **Do not fill out product registration or warranty cards.** What do your vegetable garden and the number of people living under your roof have to do with preserving the warranty on your new hair dryer? Nothing. Like many others, you have probably been fooled for years into believing that warranty cards with their questions about hobbies, income, family, and so on actually have something to do with warranties. As discussed in more detail in chapter 6, "Your Shopping," these cards are marketing tools to gather your personal information, which will wind up on mailing lists. As a result, a recently enacted California law requires companies to inform California residents and consumers that failure to fill out product registration cards will not in any way affect a consumer's warranty rights.

Instead of filling out the warranty card, keep your product receipt and discard the card. The only reason to return a warranty card is to be informed of future product recalls. If you want to receive information about recalls, return the card but include only minimal information, like name, address, product serial information, and date of purchase, and be sure to write a note stating that this information is not to be sold, traded, or shared.

If you believe that you have filled out warranty cards in the past and want to be removed from the marketing lists created from them, write a letter to the following address requesting that your information be removed from their list and not shared with any third parties:

National Demographics and Lifestyles
List Order Department
1621 18th Street, Suite 300
Denver, CO 80202

✳ **Decide whether or not you want to be listed in the phone book.** If your name is listed in the white pages of the phone book, you are easy prey for direct marketers. You may consider having an unlisted number, or listing just your name and phone number, but not your address. There are also directories that are organized by street address and phone number, rather than name. These are sometimes called reverse directories, crisscross directories, or street address directories. These directories are available as printed books and online. Go, for instance, to anywho.com, infospace.com, switchboard.com, or phonenumber.com, and select the reverse-lookup option. Using these directories, anyone can input your phone number and find your address and your name. Ask your phone company to remove your listing from its street address directory. Also contact the following directory companies to request that your name be removed from their mailing lists:

Haines & Company, Inc., publisher of Criss-Cross Directory
Send written requests to:
Attn: Director of Data Processing
8050 Freedom Ave., NW
North Canton, OH 44720
800/562-8220

Equifax (formerly R.L. Polk & Co)
Send written requests to:
Attn: List Suppression Files
26955 Northwestern Hwy.
South Field, MI 48034

AnyWho.com
Send residential removal requests to:
AnyWho Directory Service
Attn: Listing Removals
Box 944028
Maitland, FL 32794-4028

Be sure to include your exact listing as it appears on the site, including your phone number.

InfoSpace.com
Edit/remove your information via their website:
First look yourself up on the website, then click on the option to edit/remove your listing. You will be asked to check a box asserting that you

---

THE DIRTY LIST CLEANERS

The U.S. Postal Service may not admit that it sells your new address to direct marketers. It actually does, but it does so cleverly and indirectly. They use this loophole: the Postal Service charges a licensing fee to third-party companies, or "list cleaners," whose job it is to take old direct-mailing lists, revise them with new information, and then send them back to direct marketers.

are in fact the person described in the listing, and the site requires that you must be able to receive an e-mail confirmation that contains a link that you must click to confirm that the listed information can be changed or removed.

✳ **Monitor your purchases by mail.** Whenever you buy something by mail or online, indicate on your order form that you do not want your name shared, sold, or traded. Many online shopping sites also offer the option of taking yourself off future mailing lists.

✳ **Be thorough.** If you want to cover all the bases, register with the MPS multiple times using slight variations of your name (e.g., William Johnson, William E. Johnson, Bill Johnson) and address (e.g., 36 Fifth Street, 36 Fifth Street Apt. 5). If you have many iterations of your name, you will probably want to do this by free mail-in registration.

✳ **Watch the calendar.** If three months after registering with MPS you are still getting junk mail specifically addressed to you, you might want to write each company directly and request removal of your name. Make sure to reregister with the MPS every five years after your initial signup.

✳ **Shred your offers, especially the pre-approved ones.** If you do want to receive pre-approved offers, and do not opt out, do not forget to shred, rip up, or otherwise mangle this mail before you discard it. These pieces of mail provide prime opportunities for identity thieves! Review chapter 3, "Your Identity," for information about how identity thieves steal your mail and apply for credit cards in your name.

✳ **Do not enter sweepstakes.** Your odds of winning are infinitesimal, but your odds of having your name put on lists and being sold to others is likely.

Junk Faxes

Steve Kirsch, a Silicon Valley entrepreneur, has been waging a personal campaign to eliminate illegal junk faxes by suing junk-fax *senders. Mr. Kirsch has filed a $2.2 trillion class action lawsuit against Fax.com, the biggest offender of the junk-fax law. He has also set up a website, www.junkfax.org, for those wanting to learn more about stopping junk faxes.*

An attorney in Washington, DC, successfully sued Fax.com for $2.25 million after his law firm received a thousand unwanted faxes in one day alone.

Did you know that junk faxes are illegal in the United States? Even if the junk fax contains information about how to stop further junk faxes, it is still illegal. Junk faxes are illegal whether they are sent to your home or your office. The only unsolicited faxes that *are not* illegal are ones containing religious or political messages, faxes from companies with which you have an existing business relationship, or faxes from companies to whom you have expressly given written consent to fax you.

To stop illegal faxes, try the following:

✳ **Call the offender.** Call the phone number at the top of the fax (every fax is required by law to list this, though some list phony numbers). Tell the faxer that you wish to be removed from its list. Also mention that if you ever get another junk fax from the faxer, you will file a complaint with the Federal Communications Commission (FCC) and your state's attorney general's office.

✳ **File a complaint with the FCC.** Under the law, the FCC has the power to levy fines against junk faxers. If the offender is particularly egregious, the FCC has in the past levied fines in the million-dollar range. To file a complaint, you can call 888/225-5322, fill out an extensive online complaint form at www.fcc.gov/cgb/complaints.html, or mail a letter of complaint explaining that you received an illegal fax to Federal Communications Commission, Common Carrier Bureau, Consumer Information, 445 12th Street SW, Washington, DC 20554. In your letter, include the date of the offense, your name, address, phone number, and your fax number, and *be sure to attach the offending fax.*

✳ **File a complaint with your state's attorney general's office.** To contact your state's attorney general, go to the site of the National Association of Attorneys General at http://www.naag.org or see the list compiled by Yahoo! at http://dir.yahoo.com/Society_and_Culture/Crime/Law_Enforcement/Attorneys_General/U_S__States/.

> Thanks to recent federal legislation that established the National Do Not Call Registry (DNC), you can reduce the telemarketing calls you receive by up to 80 percent.

Telemarketing Calls

You are at a critical stage of kneading pie dough; you are in the throes of a life-altering fight with your spouse; you are just sitting down to dinner with your family; you've just emerged dripping wet from a relaxing shower, when the phone rings. You drop everything to answer it, but you wish you had not. The caller is neither a family member nor a friend, but a telemarketer—a stranger trying to sell you a product or service.

Today, using new technologies such as automated-dialing response systems, telemarketers are estimated to make as many as 104 million calls daily, according to statistics from the Federal Communications Commission. It is mildly annoying when you get an unsolicited telemarketing call on, say, a Monday afternoon, but it is hugely aggravating—and not coincidental—that the calls usually come at the most inopportune times. Telemarketers know when you're most likely to be home.

To be fair, telemarketers are simply trying to make a living. But the fact is that telemarketers also tried to undo the law to maintain their livelihood. The United States Court of Appeals for the Tenth Circuit ultimately rejected the telemarketers challenges to the law, instead preserving the Do Not Call rules and upholding their constitutionality.

If you're like most people, you may feel that telemarketing calls are a constant disruption and add more stress to your already busy life. You may also believe that these calls represent yet another example of a loss of privacy in your day-to-day life, and perhaps most galling of all, the calls are an intrusion that come directly into your home.

TELEMARKETING SCAMS

Scams involving junk mail and telemarketing are designed to steal your money or get you to disclose your personal information so the scammers can steal it from you. In other instances, they are designed to trick you into agreeing to receive telemarketing calls. Watch out for these scams:

The "Free Gift By Calling a Seemingly Local Number" Scam

You have just won an amazing prize. To claim the prize, you have to call a number beginning with area code 809, 284, or 876 right away.

The phone number sounds like a normal domestic number, so you make the call. What you won't know until your exorbitant phone bill arrives is that the number you are calling is in the Dominican Republic, the British Virgin Islands, or Jamaica, all unregulated places where phone companies can charge whatever they want. The so-called 809 scam is among the telemarketing scams that cost Americans $40 billion annually, according to the FTC. Next time you get a message to call a number with an unfamiliar area code, check the location of the number you're calling at www.allareacodes.com.

Also, beware of mail, e-mail, and telemarketing scams designed to trick you into giving consent to receive telemarketing calls. Consumers who register to win a sweepstakes or to receive a free gift might inadvertently be granting permission to be solicited. It is important to read all the fine print. Do not check any "opt-in" boxes unless you intend to grant consent.

The "Call from the Official with the Do Not Call Registry" Scam

Hi! My name is Delores! I am an official with the Do Not Call Registry and I need to verify that you do not want to receive telemarketing calls. I'll need some information from you to verify that I'm talking to the correct person. Can you give me your social security number or a telephone calling-card number?

Many scams use Do Not Call registration as a means of stealing your personal information. It appears that identity thieves are calling consumers and identifying themselves as officials with the Do Not Call Registry. These scammers tell the consumer that they need to verify that the consumer indeed meant to sign up with the registry, and to do so they will need some personal information (like social security number, or telephone calling-card number.) Be on the lookout for scams like this, and remember that once you register with the Do Not Call Registry *no one will call you to confirm.*

The Do Not Call Registry

If you are not brazen, do not want to be impolite, or are not devious enough to get rid of these calls without having to listen to the entire pitch, there *is* something you can do. Thanks to recent federal legislation that established the National Do Not Call Registry (DNC), you can reduce the telemarketing calls you receive by up to 80 percent.

The Do Not Call Registry is a federal program, implemented by the Federal Trade Commission (FTC) in 2003, that generally prevents commercial telemarketers from calling you once you register (exceptions are listed below). If you think this program is a good idea, you are not alone. On the first day of the list's existence, more than 7 million numbers registered. As of January 2004, the number of registered phone numbers swelled to nearly 56.3 million. Although the FTC had originally estimated that people would register 60 million numbers in the first year, that estimate now looks conservative in light of the interest that has been shown thus far.

The Do Not Call Registry requires telemarketers to check their lists every three months against the phone numbers in the registry and scrub from their lists those numbers contained in the registry. The list is set up so within three months of signing up for the program, you should notice a significant reduction in telemarketing calls to your home.

The law also requires that telemarketers transmit their phone numbers and names (or the name of the firm making the call) to your caller ID service. The display must also include a phone number that you can call to request that the particular company no longer call you. These requirements further protect your privacy, increase accountability, and help in enforcement efforts. If you do pick up a telemarketing call, the law also requires an actual sales representative to answer within two seconds of your greeting. This requirement will reduce the number of hang-up calls you get from telemarketers using automated dialing equipment.

There are several ways to sign up for the Do Not Call List, and each one is quick and easy:

✳ **Register by Phone.** Call the FTC's toll-free phone number: 888/382-1222. When you register by phone, you must call from the telephone number you want to register. You may register only one phone number at a time when you call the Do Not Call Registry.

✳ **Register Online.** Register online at the FTC's website: www.donotcall. gov. If you register online, you must provide an e-mail address. The registry will send you a confirmation e-mail. To finalize your registration, you must click on the link in the e-mail. (Your e-mail address will not be shared.) You may register up to three telephone numbers at a time if you register online. You will receive a confirmation e-mail for each number you register, and you

---

WHAT TO DO IF TELEMARKETERS STILL CALL

If your name has been on the national Do Not Call Registry for at least three months and you receive what you believe to be an illegal telemarketing call, you may file a complaint with the FTC at www.donotcall.gov/Complain/ComplainCheck.aspx. You must provide the date of the call, and *either* the phone number or the name of the company that called you. You may also file a complaint by calling the registry's toll-free number at 888/382-1222. Both the Federal Trade Commission and the Federal Communications Commission have the authority to fine telemarketers up to $11,000 per violation. This fine can be assessed for each illegal phone call made to a number included in the registry.

must click on the link in each e-mail to complete the process. If you wish to register more than three numbers, you may repeat this process online as many times as you wish.

The Do Not Call Registry is only for personal phone numbers; it does not apply to business numbers. You can also register your cell phone number.

Your number will remain on the registry for five years from the date you register unless either you choose to remove it from the registry, or your phone number is disconnected. If your phone number is disconnected for any reason (if, for example, you temporarily move, or a billing dispute results in your service being discontinued), you must reregister. If you move and get a new phone number, you must also reregister. If you are not sure when your protection will lapse, click on the Verify a Registration button at www.donotcall.gov/confirm/Conf.aspx to check your registration's expiration date. It is a good idea to print out your registration page at the time you sign up and save it as a record.

You can always take your name off the list and resume receiving telemarketing calls. To do so, call toll-free 888/382-1222. You must make the call from the phone number you want to delete from the registry. Your number will be removed from the Do Not Call Registry the next day, but it can take up to three months for the telemarketers to start calling you again.

Be aware that many states have their own registries that automatically transfer the numbers from their lists to the national Do Not Call Registry. Check www.ftc.gov/bcp/conline/edcams/donotcall/statelist.html to see if this is the case for your state. In the event your state has a registry that is more stringent than the national list, the state's laws will govern. If you have any doubt about which registry extends better protection, you should consider signing up for both your state and national programs.

Telemarketing Calls That Are Still Allowed

Signing up for the Do Not Call Registry will eliminate *most* of your telemarketing calls, but not *all* of them. Certain telemarketing groups may still continue to call you, but they are limited to calling you only between the hours of

8 A.M. and 9 P.M. If you have signed up for the Do Not Call Registry, you can still expect to receive calls from:

▸ **Political organizations.** If you do not wish to receive future calls from political organizations, ask to be placed on their internal do-not-call lists (many organizations maintain these).

▸ **Charities.** If you do not wish to receive calls from charities, ask to be placed on the charity's in-house do-not-call list (many charities maintain these).

▸ **Telephone surveyors.** If the call is truly to conduct a survey, it is permissible. If, however, the caller conducts a survey in conjunction with selling goods or services, this is impermissible.

▸ **Companies with which you have an existing business relationship.** Those companies with which you have an existing business relationship, such as your bank, utility company, or phone carrier, are permitted to continue to call you. However, you can ask these companies to put you on their internal do-not-call lists. Note that if you purchase a product or service from any company, that company is deemed to have an existing business relationship with you, but the company may only make phone solicitations for eighteen months after the date the purchase took place. In addition, an implied business relationship with a company is created if you make an inquiry to the company or submit an application, even if no purchase ever took place. In this case, the company can call you for three months after you made the inquiry or application.

▸ **Companies to which you have given written permission to call.** There still may be some telemarketing calls you want to receive, even after signing up with the Do Not Call Registry. In this case, notify the specific companies in writing, and include your signature and phone number in your letter. Your letter enables these companies to contact you legally until you tell them otherwise.

▸ **Affiliates.** People are often unaware of the loophole that allows telemarketing by affiliates of a company with which you have an existing business relationship. It is often hard to tell who is an affiliate, but the rules of thumb in this context are: the name of the affiliate should be similar to the name of the company, and the affiliate should provide a similar service.

The Do Not Call Registry is your strongest protection against the assaults of telemarketers. Bear in mind these tips when you register and whenever you receive telemarketing calls:

✴ **Register online if you do not have a private phone exchange.** If you live in a dormitory or a senior housing complex with a private branch exchange (PBX), or if you live in an extremely rural area, you may not be able to register by phone.

✴ **Keep a record.** When you sign up for the Do Not Call Registry, keep a record of your registration. If you register online, print a copy of your confirmation. If you register by phone, note the time and date of your phone call.

✴ **Reregister if your phone number changes or is disconnected.** If your phone number is disconnected for any reason (because you temporarily move, or if a billing dispute resulted in your service being discontinued), you must reregister. If you move and get a new phone number, you must also reregister.

✴ **Demand to be removed from a telemarketing list.** Whether or not you sign up for the Do Not Call Registry, you can still request that those companies from which you do not wish to receive calls put you on their internal do-not-call lists.

✴ **Employ basic technology strategies.** You can use basic technology to enhance your privacy. An answering machine and/or Caller ID will screen your calls.

✴ **Give your cell phone number as your home phone number.** As of now, it is illegal for a telemarketer to call a cell phone if the consumer would have to pay for the call.

THE BOTTOM LINE

- ▶ Open house or open book? Renting or buying a home or apartment will result in others learning a great deal of personal information about you; try to prevent or correct inaccuracies in your credit report and other records, and be vigilant about what others do with your documents.
- ▶ Going wireless in the home? Be aware of wireless devices in your home, including nanny cams and cordless phones—they can be easily intercepted.
- ▶ Mail reduction. To reduce junk mail, sign up for the DMA Mail Preference Service, opt out of pre-approved credit offers, and directly contact companies from which you do not want to receive mail.
- ▶ Don't call me, I'll call you. To reduce direct-marketing calls, sign up with the Do Not Call Registry. Reregister after five years or whenever you move.
- ▶ Junk faxes are illegal. Notify the company and the Federal Communications Commission to stop the flow of junk faxes.

Your Workplace

© Mike Baldwin / Cornered

"Meet the new head of security."

www.CartoonStock.com

You have worked for the same company for many years. One day, management enacts a new policy that requires background checks. Yours reveals a seven-year-old misdemeanor for selling a pistol, and before you know it your job is on the line. But you have never had a run-in with the law, much less touched a gun; the background check has mistaken you for someone else.

You work in a posh resort in Atlantic City. You are required to wear a badge that beeps if you fail to wash your hands long enough or use soap when you go to the rest room. Every hygiene infraction is recorded in your employee file, which is stored in your boss's computer.

You send your wife romantic e-mails from work. Two weeks later you are officially disciplined because you are exploiting company resources for personal use.

You spill personal and painful details of your life to a psychiatrist who is employed by the company at which you have worked for more than twenty years. The company required that you be evaluated by the company's psychiatrist in order to receive workers' compensation. The fifteen-page intimate psychiatric report, which you believed to be confidential, was then circulated by your boss to a colleague, and the information instantly became water-cooler gossip. You are later told that the report is not considered private.

> In almost all cases, your privacy as an employee is outweighed by your employer's business interest.

How much is your privacy worth in the workplace? About as much as your stock options in your old Internet company. Many people worry about the government's Orwellian-like intrusion into their privacy. But government is not the only Big Brother. Few people fully grasp the extent to which their own bosses keep tabs on them. As it turns out, there are two Big Brothers, and one sits in the big office upstairs.

Perhaps Lewis Maltby of the ACLU Workplace Rights Project put it best: "When most Americans go to work in the morning, they might just as well be going to a foreign country, because they are equally beyond the reach of the Constitution in both situations. And unfortunately, federal law does very, very little to fill this void."

The same actions that may be viewed as unconstitutional violations of your rights when performed by the government are perfectly permissible if performed by your boss. Your employer can:

▸ Read your e-mail—even if your message is marked "private" or even if it is deleted
▸ Listen to your voice mail, even if you have a password
▸ Monitor what is on the screen of your computer and what you have saved on your hard drive

- ▶ Monitor every website you have ever visited
- ▶ Install software that monitors every keystroke you type into your computer, even if you have deleted the text
- ▶ Require you to produce a urine sample so the company can test for drugs
- ▶ Read your credit reports and look at your medical records
- ▶ Probe your innermost thoughts with psychological tests
- ▶ Share your personal information with creditors and others

In matters governing the relationship between employer and employee, the balance of power is clearly tipped in favor of the employer. In almost all cases, your privacy as an employee is outweighed by your employer's business interest.

The degree to which your privacy rights are protected depends on whether you are a public or private employee. If you are a public-sector employee, the Fourth Amendment to the Constitution may provide some protection if you have a "reasonable expectation of privacy." What is "reasonable" depends entirely on your situation.

If you work in the private sector however, the Fourth Amendment is not applicable; instead you must rely on federal and state statutes as well as common law for protection. State laws vary and common law is both confusing and unsettled, so you have little legal support to claim that your privacy rights have been violated in the workplace. To win a case, you must demonstrate that you had a "reasonable expectation of privacy" in the matter at issue. Courts rarely find an employee has a reasonable expectation of privacy in the workplace when using company property to do anything, particularly if you have had advance notice of a company policy concerning the conduct at hand.

In addition to having legal precedents, employers can utilize new technologies to monitor your actions in the workplace as never before. From keyboard-tracking programs, which record every bit of data you enter into your computer, to badges that track your every movement within a building, employers now have a disturbingly detailed window into your daily workplace activities.

Pre-Employment

You think your experience makes you a cinch for the job. You aced the interview. Your prospective boss has even asked when you can start work. But before you start planning what to wear on your first day, think again. Just because the inquiry is over doesn't mean the scrutiny has ended.

Your privacy may be compromised before you're even hired. Your prospective employer will gather a great deal of personal information about you in the interview and background check: your driving record, your credit history, and the results of a drug or psychological test are all available to potential employers. You'll be asked to verify the details of your résumé, and you can expect your prospective employer to do its own extensive double-check.

If you claim that you have a Harvard law degree, employers will want to verify that you did in fact go to Harvard Law. They will also check whether you actually made that six-figure salary. According to a 2002 study conducted by ADP Screening and Selection Services, over 40 percent of job applicants lie on their résumés. Remember the headlines about California's poet laureate or Bausch & Lomb's CEO, both of whom included "inaccuracies" on their résumés? Or the stories about the president of an evangelical Christian college in Georgia who lied about having a master's degree, and a former president of the U.S. Olympic Committee who lied about having earned a doctorate? Their lies were unveiled, and it's likely that yours will be, too.

According to one survey of eighty-seven Fortune 500 companies with a combined 3.2 million employees, 75 percent of the companies said they collect information about employees beyond what workers voluntarily provide (and almost half do so without informing the employees). Much of this information about you, such as criminal-background and credit checks, comes from data collection companies such as ChoicePoint. Other information comes from personal interviews and perhaps even medical and drug testing. Some employers use even more extreme methods such as handwriting analysis, psychological testing, genetic testing, and more.

Why do employers feel compelled to spend so much time and money screening job applicants? The most important reason is that employers want to find the most reliable and qualified people to hire. On average in U.S. businesses, at least half of new hires do not work out. It costs approximately $7,000 to replace a salaried employee, $10,000 to replace a mid-level employee, and $40,000 to replace a senior executive.

Your employer also may have legitimate concerns about employee theft, disclosure of trade secrets and other confidential information, and being subjected to lawsuits involving workplace violence and sexual harassment. Lack of due diligence on a job applicant can wreak havoc with a company's reputation and cost millions. For example, under state statutes that regulate negligent hiring practices—and more than half the states have enacted such statutes—your employer may be held criminally and financially liable for illegal actions taken by employees who were not subjected to reasonable pre-employment screening, even if the actions occur off the job.

> 75 percent of the companies said they collect information about employees beyond what workers voluntarily provide (and almost half do so without informing their employees).

Recent events have also prompted employers to take background checks more seriously. As a direct result of the terrorist attacks of September 11, 2001, many employers have conducted thorough background checks not only of job applicants, but of existing employees as well. The financial scandals at Enron, Tyco, and WorldCom have also resulted in more thorough background checks of applicants, especially for corporate executives, officers, and directors.

Finally, federal and state laws require background checks for certain jobs. Most states, for example, call for criminal background checks on applicants for certain positions, especially those dealing with children, the elderly, or people with disabilities. Many state and federal government jobs require not only background checks, but even more extensive investigations.

You know that fudging on your résumé is fraud. So it should be clear to you that doing so is not a good idea. It is not simply a legal or ethical issue; it is a practical one as well. If, in checking your references, a would-be employer discovers that you misrepresented yourself on your résumé—even if the misrepresentation is inconsequential—your credibility will be damaged and you may lose the job opportunity.

Background Checks

For many years, the city of Decatur, Georgia, had a policy of conducting highly intrusive background checks on anyone wishing to work in bars or restaurants where alcohol was served. A job applicant was required to disclose, and then permit the city to inquire into, "any and all aspects of [his or her] life." The city obtained highly personal information, including the applicant's shopping habits at drugstores and pharmacies, his or her mental and physical condition, and past tax records. Prospective candidates were also required to sign an agreement that released the city from liability for misuse of any of this information.

Decatur's policy was extreme, and the policies were later terminated in response to pressure applied by the American Civil Liberties Union (ACLU). But think about your own job-hunting experiences. Have you ever been required to take a drug test, submit to a handwriting analysis or a psychological test, sign off on releasing your credit report, or even supply your twenty-five-year-old SAT scores?

As you think about these scenarios, you should realize that your employer has great leeway to collect extensive information about you when conducting background checks. For you, the danger of an intrusive background check is that it could reveal incorrect or irrelevant personal information that bears no relationship to the job for which you are applying.

The information collected in a background check includes, but is not limited to:

- ▶ Driving records
- ▶ Criminal records
- ▶ Character references
- ▶ Court records
- ▶ Property ownership
- ▶ State licensing records
- ▶ Vehicle registration
- ▶ Social security number

- ▶ Workers' compensation claims and records
- ▶ Neighbor interviews
- ▶ Employment verification
- ▶ Education records
- ▶ Credit records
- ▶ Bankruptcy records
- ▶ Medical records
- ▶ Military service records
- ▶ Drug test records
- ▶ Sex offender lists

Be aware that some of this information may not *legally* be considered in the hiring process or can be used only with limitations (see section below for details). But once your employer receives incriminating information about you, even if it is illegal to consider, human nature makes it difficult to remember that the information is off-limits.

The records that *cannot* legally be used in the pre-offer hiring decision are:

- ▶ **Polygraph tests.** The Employee Polygraph Protection Act forbids most private employers from using polygraph tests as a screening tool on applicants or existing employees. Exceptions exist, however, in cases where the applicant or employee may be involved with a business that provides armored-car personnel, security alarm personnel, or other security personnel.
- ▶ **Workers' compensation claims.** Under the Americans with Disability Act (ADA), your prospective employer cannot use the fact that you filed a workers' compensation claim to discriminate against your application. In some states, however, your employer may access your record *after* making you an employment offer and may use the information only if the injury in question might interfere with your ability to perform the duties of the job you have been offered.
- ▶ **Medical tests.** Under the ADA, your prospective employer cannot require or conduct a medical examination (including an HIV test) *before* making you an employment offer. *After* you have received the

offer and before you begin work, you may be required to take a medical exam if:

▸ All entering employees are subject to such a medical exam;

▸ Medical information revealed by the exam is collected and maintained on separate, confidential forms and is kept in confidential files that are separated from other personnel files.

If your employer withdraws an employment offer because the medical exam reveals that you do not meet certain employment criteria, it must show either that the criteria do not tend to screen out individuals with disabilities, or that the criteria are job-related and consistent with business necessity and there is no reasonable accommodation that would enable the individual to perform the job without undue hardship on the employer.

▸ **Bankruptcies.** Your employer may not discriminate against you because you have previously filed for bankruptcy.

Your employer may need to obtain your *permission* before using the following:

▸ **School records.** Your educational records, including transcripts, recommendations, and financial information, are to be kept confidential under federal law. As a result, your alma mater will not likely release your records without your consent. However, your school may release directory information, which includes name, address, dates of attendance, degrees earned, and activities, unless you have provided written notice asking the school to do otherwise. See chapter 11, "Your Everyday Life," which discusses access to college and university records.

▸ **Military records.** For members and former members of the armed forces, your service records may be released only if you consent and only under limited circumstances. The military may disclose name, rank, salary, duty assignments, awards, and duty status without your consent. See chapter 2, "Your Personal Information and the Public Record," for more information on access to military records.

▸ **References.** When you apply for a job, you will most likely be asked for references as well as permission to contact these references.

Prospective employers rely heavily on reference checking in the hiring process, but past employers are likely to verify only your salary, job title, and dates of employment to avoid a possible defamation lawsuit. Even if your prospective employer may not obtain much revealing information in a reference check, it most likely will still try to conduct one to protect itself.

▶ **Credit information.** To check your credit, your prospective employer will provide you with a document granting it written authorization to do so (see section below). See chapter 4, "Your Credit," for more information on credit reports.

▶ **Criminal records.** A prospective employer's access to criminal records and the extent to which it can consider them as part of a hiring decision varies according to state (see section below). See chapter 2, "Your Personal Information and the Public Record," for information related to arrest records.

▶ **Drug testing, psychological testing, and genetic testing.** Laws against drug, psychological, and genetic tests as part of a background check are not consistent from state to state and depend upon the type of job, especially if you are applying for a job in a private company (see section below).

If your prospective employer violates any of the above rules, you should either move on and hope for a more scrupulous boss, or consult an attorney to discuss your legal options.

Credit Information

John recently went on a big interview with one of the top banks in the country. Halfway through the testing process, someone came into the room and asked him to leave. Apparently, the company reviewed his credit report and discovered that he had a history of late payments on his Visa card. Based on that information, the bank concluded that it would not hire John and that it was not worth continuing the interview process. Seem far-fetched? Not according to the Washington Post.

As discussed in chapter 4, "Your Credit," your credit report reveals a great deal about you. It discloses how many loans, credit cards, and mortgages you hold; your payment history for each account; whether your bank accounts are overdrawn; and what debts you owe. Your report also lists your employment history and any liens, bankruptcies, or civil legal judgments against you.

More and more companies are turning to credit reports to supplement their assessments of you during the application process. About 50 percent of employers rely on credit reports in hiring for the management level or below, and 70 percent do so for executive-level staffing, according to one national employment agency. Not only do employers consider your credit record to be a reflection of your character, but they also want to ensure that your financial situation will not adversely affect your ability to do the job. In some jobs, such as those in the financial sector, employers use your credit report to determine how you might handle other people's money.

> About 50 percent of employers rely on credit reports in hiring for the management level or below, and 70 percent do so for executive-level staffing.

Whether you think your credit report is a fair assessment of you is irrelevant. Some employers even go beyond the credit report to use Investigative Consumer Reports, which are even more intrusive. Investigative Consumer Reports contain not only your credit report, but also information on your character, general reputation, personal characteristics, and mode of living. This information is gleaned from interviews with neighbors, friends, and associates, as well as from certain public and court records.

Before obtaining either type of credit report from a consumer reporting agency, an employer must provide you with a separate document (it can't be part of a larger job application) that (1) informs you that a report may be requested, and (2) requires your prior written authorization. If your prospective employer requests an Investigative Consumer Report, the stand-alone notice and authorization must also inform you that you have a right to know the scope of the investigation requested, and that you have a right to receive a written summary of your rights under the Fair Credit Reporting Act (FCRA). Under the FCRA, if you make less than $75,000 a year, the credit search can only provide information from within the last seven years; if your income is more than $75,000, there is no limit.

When an employer accesses credit or investigative reports, you risk being rejected for a job because of damaging information that may be uncovered by the investigation. Under the FCRA, however, if an employer relied, even in part, on information contained in such reports, the employer is required to inform you of this and give you a copy of the report. Of course, an employer who learns something damaging can reject you using any number of other excuses. This means that you may never know what information ultimately sunk your chances, and you may never have an opportunity to correct erroneous information.

Apply some of these practical tips (as well as those listed in chapter 4, "Your Credit") relating to your credit report before you apply for a job:

* **Make sure the information in your credit report is current and accurate.** Order your credit report well in advance of applying for a job.

* **Correct your bad credit.** If you know you have a bad credit report, take proactive steps rather than waiting for it to be discovered by a prospective employer. In addition to correcting the report before you apply for a job, you might consider addressing the issue up front with the prospective employer so you can explain the situation. Your candor may be viewed favorably.

* **Check your other records, such as DMV and court records, to ensure their accuracy before you apply for a job.** For information on how to do this, see chapter 2, "Your Personal Information and the Public Record."

Criminal History

In 2002, phamaceutical company Eli Lilly & Co. dismissed Kimberly Kelly, a forty-six-year-old single mother who bounced a $60 check while she was going through a rough divorce. She was moving to a new town, and she closed her bank account without realizing the check had not cleared. The company to whom she had written the check pressed charges when it could not collect, and a judge found Kelly guilty of a misdemeanor check deception charge. Eli Lilly had *been conducting criminal background checks as a post–September 11 security measure.*

When employers obtain criminal records as part of a background check, the legal issue centers on balancing fairness to the employer with your privacy as an applicant. Imagine if you are a pharmaceutical employer and you have recently hired an impressive candidate who holds master's and doctoral degrees in chemistry and a law degree. What if the most basic background search would have revealed that this stellar employee had spent six years in prison for attempting to murder his wife, his medical degree had been revoked, and that he earned his law degree through a correspondence course in prison?

Negligent-hire cases are on the rise, so employers feel obligated to screen for criminal or dangerous tendencies in the hiring process. At the same time, as an applicant, you might feel violated if your prospective employer is digging around and investigating an old misdemeanor or a mistaken arrest.

For these reasons, many states have passed laws governing whether, and to what extent, an employer may consider your criminal history in making hiring decisions. Unfortunately, neither state nor federal law is completely clear. Indeed, laws vary drastically among the states. For example, some

CRIMINAL CHECKS ON CONTRACT WORKERS AND VENDORS

Some companies require extensive background searches even on people they do not directly employ, such as contract workers and vendors working on their premises. For instance, the pharmaceutical company Eli Lilly instituted a policy requiring background checks on more than seven thousand contract workers, mostly construction and food-service workers. The policy was implemented immediately after the September 11 attacks. Lilly, of course, could not directly fire the workers whose background checks did not pass muster, but, according to newspaper reports, most of the workers banned from working at Lilly promptly received pink slips from their own employers.

states outright ban a review of your criminal history; some states allow employers to consider criminal history, but only for people working in certain professions, such as child care, elder care, nursing, and law enforcement; some states do not allow consideration of arrests; and some states allow employers to consider convictions, but only if the crimes are relevant to the job. For information on criminal records and employment in your state, see www.casanet.org/program-management/volunteer-manage/criminal-bkg-check.htm. Under federal law, employers may not categorically deny employment based on the existence of a criminal history. Instead, employers must consider various factors that indicate a connection between the crime committed and the nature of the job you seek.

> ◆ ◆ ◆ ◆ ◆ ◆ ◆ ◆ ◆ ◆ ◆ ◆
>
> **Drug testing is on the rise; approximately two-thirds of employers have drug-testing policies.**

Drug Testing

How would you feel if your company required you to take a routine drug test but used that test to evaluate other health issues? In 1988, the Washington, D.C., police department admitted it used the drug test samples to screen female employees for pregnancy, without the employees' knowledge or consent.

If you have ever been required to submit to a drug test, you understand how invasive testing can be to your privacy. If you have never taken a drug test, imagine being required to urinate into a receptacle, perhaps unclothed, perhaps under direct observation by those administering the test, perhaps in a bathroom where the water supply has been shut off and the toilet water dyed blue to prevent sample tampering, and perhaps where the temperature of the sample is measured to assure that it is not too cool to be recent.

Drug testing is one of the most contentious issues in the workplace. In addition to its inherent invasiveness, several troubling issues surround drug testing. In many cases, the results are simply wrong. Many over-the-counter medicines, such as ibuprofen, Midol, Sudafed, and Vicks Nasal Spray, may cause false-positives in a drug test. Finally, companies do not always limit access to the results.

But drug testing is on the rise; approximately two-thirds of employers have drug-testing policies, according to the American Management Association. Indeed, some of the nation's most well-known corporations, including the *The New York Times,* IBM, Exxon, Federal Express, AT&T, Lockheed Martin, and about one-quarter of the Fortune 500 corporations require drug testing after making a conditional offer.

The law with respect to drug testing is not completely settled. If you work in the public sector, the Supreme Court has recognized the constitutionality of testing you if you work in a position critical to public safety or the protection of life, property, or national security. For example, if you work in aviation, the military, motor vehicle operations, law enforcement, or if you handle hazardous materials, you can reasonably expect to be tested for drugs.

> When your employer can conduct drug testing, it does not need a warrant, or probable cause, or even a suspicion that you are a drug user. Indeed, your employer may conduct drug tests as a routine part of its hiring process, or it may require you and other existing employees to be tested on a random, suspicion-less basis.

If you work in the private sector, you have even fewer rights to refuse to take a drug test. Federal law is not wholly applicable to the private sector, and state law varies considerably. Some states allow drug testing for jobs involving public safety; some states allow it for any occupation; some states do not allow it at all. For information on workplace-related drug testing in your state, visit said.dol.gov/StateLawList.asp. When your employer can conduct drug testing, it does not need a warrant, or probable cause, or even a suspicion that you are a drug user. Indeed, your employer may conduct drug tests as a routine part of its hiring process, or it may require you and other existing employees to be tested on a random, suspicion-less basis.

Finally, as an applicant applying for a job, you have even less of a legal right to claim invasion of privacy than if you were already employed. Since you are often told in advance and must consent to the test as a condition of employment, you are theoretically freely choosing to subject yourself to the test. No one is forcing you to take the test, and you are free to seek employment elsewhere.

Psychological Testing

Applicants for security guard positions with Target in California were required to take intrusive personality tests as a condition for employment. The test included true-false statements about the applicants' religious and sexual practices, such as: "I feel sure there is only one true religion," "I have been in trouble one or more times because of my sex behavior," and "I am very strongly attracted to members of my own sex." The applicants sued, the court found the questions overly intrusive, and the case ultimately settled for more than $1 million.

Robert Jordan sued after being rejected for a position as a police officer with the New London, Connecticut, Police Department. Apparently, Jordan had scored too high on a cognitive test, and the Police Department worried that he was too intelligent to last at the job. Unbelievably, the court ruled in favor of the police department.

Increasingly, prospective employers are using psychological or personality tests as an additional hiring tool, particularly in light of recent reports of workplace violence and the events of September 11. Employers use these tests not only to screen for violent or dishonest behavior, but also to determine whether or not you would fit into the company's culture and whether your traits are consistent with the job's requirements.

Whether your prospective employer can perform a psychological test as an additional means to assess you for a job is, however, of questionable legality. First, these types of tests—and there are hundreds—may run afoul of federal antidiscrimination laws, like Title VII, if the tests are not specifically job-related or if they adversely impact any minority or protected group. Second, they may violate the Americans with Disabilities Act (ADA) if the tests are construed as medical tests or include questions that are of a medical nature, such as whether you have frequent headaches, or whether you have ever sought mental health counseling. Finally, the tests may violate your privacy rights if they are not job-related or if they delve into intrusive subjects, such as sexual, religious, marital, or moral matters, as in the above case. Consult a lawyer if you believe you have been unfairly subjected to a psychological test.

Genetic Testing

Workers at a laboratory at Lawrence Berkeley Laboratory in California sued after discovering that for decades they were tested without their knowledge for syphilis, pregnancy, and the genetic trait for sickle-cell anemia. The case was settled before the court had a chance to rule.

> More than 10 percent of employers test employees for genetic predispositions to diseases.

The Burlington Northern Santa Fe Railway had been covertly testing certain employees for genetic predispositions to carpal tunnel syndrome. The railroad tested employees who submitted claims for the wrist ailment, in hopes of showing that the workers were predisposed to getting the ailment and therefore the company should not have to pay. The testing was discovered after one employee's wife, a nurse, noticed that the seven vials of blood the company was requesting was excessive for a routine medical exam. The employee refused to take the exam and was threatened with discharge. The employee went to the Equal Employment Opportunity Commission (EEOC), which filed suit. The railroad agreed to settle the case, pay $2.2 million, and halt genetic testing.

Today, companies are increasingly making use of genetic testing in the workplace. According to a 1998 survey of the American Management Association, more than 10 percent of employers test employees for genetic predispositions to diseases.

An executive order, signed in 2000 by President Clinton, bans genetic discrimination against federal employees. But no federal law exists to prevent private employers from refusing to hire you or firing you based on genetic information they discover. State law varies, with some states prohibiting genetic screening as a condition of employment; others prohibiting discrimination against individuals with certain genetic traits, like sickle cell anemia,

Tay-Sachs disease, and so forth; and others permitting testing in certain circumstances. To see whether your state has genetic nondiscrimination in employment laws, go to www.ncsl.org/programs/health/genetics/ndiscrim. htm and scroll down to view the chart.

> No federal law exists to prevent private employers from refusing to hire you or firing you based on genetic information they discover.

As an employee, you should be concerned about genetic testing. Beyond the invasiveness, such testing can have real consequences for your employment. As in the example above, such tests can be used to target and fire you or other employees who cause increased company health insurance costs or file workers' compensation claims. In addition, your test may not be kept entirely confidential, and it can be given to a future employer, thus following you from job to another.

Online Career Sites

In 2003, the popular career site monster.com posted a warning on its site that read, in part, "Regrettably, from time to time, false job listings are listed online and used to illegally collect personal information from unsuspecting job seekers."

If you are searching for a job, you have probably used one of the many popular online career sites such as Monster.com, Yahoo!, Hotjobs, or CareerBuilder.com. According to the Society for Human Resource Management, 96 percent of job seekers look at online job postings. Approximately 50 million résumés are posted on these sites.

Online job sites are convenient and helpful. At the same time, you should be aware that as career sites look to generate additional revenue, they are increasingly sharing and selling your personal information to marketers and employers hoping to target certain audiences. For example, according to a study authored by Pam Dixon, the director of the World Privacy Forum, many online career sites maintain inadequate privacy policies, fail to remove deleted résumés, and sell private data to marketers. In addition, some sites, such as USAJOBS and Studentjobs.com, have required users to key in their social security numbers to post résumés. According to the same survey, these sites have failed to disclose that their job boards are outsourced to monster.com.

CAREER SITE SCAMS

Job seekers who abandon skepticism in the desperate search for employment are prime targets for identity thieves. If you post your résumé on an online career site, you may increase your chances of being victimized. False job postings are listed on the sites and are used to illegally elicit personal information—including your social security number, credit card numbers and bank account information—from unsuspecting job seekers.

An unsuspecting user of the online career site Monster.com received a letter inviting him to apply for a managerial position at the insurance brokerage Arthur Gallagher. The job seeker wrote back and received an e-mail excerpted here:

Thank you for applying for the Marketing Manager position with Arthur Gallagher. I just had a chance to review your résumé and am going to send your application through for hiring . . . The position will require a background check because of the nature of the high level of security that we have with several of our clients. I am attaching the form in this e-mail. Just open it up, fill it out, and fax it back to 775-923-7229.

The job seeker filled out the form that asked for his age, height, weight, social security number, bank account numbers, even his mother's maiden name. When no one replied, he called Arthur Gallagher headquarters to find out what was happening with this application. During the phone call he learned that the person who contacted him didn't work there and the job posting was a fraud.

Follow these tips when using an online career site:

✳ **Never divulge personal information.** Unless and until you're hired, never give out your bank account, social security, or credit card numbers.

✳ **Carefully review the career site's privacy policy.** Make sure it does not share or sell personal information.

✳ **Consider using only sites that more fully respect your privacy.** For example, craigslist.org, nationjobs.com, and medzilla.com have been recommended for their privacy policies.

✳ **Check out recruiters and employers before you hand over any personal information.**

✳ **Use sites that have job search agents.** Don't post your résumé. Instead, have a search agent send employer information to you. The site will e-mail you when it posts jobs that fit with your criteria. You need to give out only minimal information, such as keywords (like *marketing* or *business development*), desired location, and of course, your e-mail address.

✳ **Be on the alert for scams.** (See page 273.)

On the Job

A manager in the technology department of a large corporation wrote to a newspaper columnist for advice. His job was to monitor his company's computer systems, and in doing so he had become aware of some of the most personal things about his fellow colleagues: their savings account balances, their bids on eBay, the websites they visited, and certain highly personal e-mails, with subjects ranging from the mundane to the entertaining to the graphic, including, in one case, the dimensions of the sender's intimate body parts. The poor IT manager was experiencing a sort of systems overload himself; he complained that he would never look at certain employees the same way again.

Whether you realize it or not, and whether you like it or not, your employer is constantly and increasingly snooping on you during the workday. Indeed, according to the American Management Association (AMA), an estimated 80 percent of companies in the United States electronically monitor their employees in some way. This percentage represents a dramatic increase from 1997, when only 35 percent of companies monitored their employees. What specifically does your employer monitor? Consider the following:

> **An estimated 80 percent of companies in the United States electronically monitor their employees in some way.**

- ▶ 63 percent of employers monitor employees' Internet use
- ▶ 52 percent of employers review and store employees' e-mail messages
- ▶ 30 percent of employers review and store employees' computer files
- ▶ 15 percent of employers use video surveillance to track their employees
- ▶ 12 percent of employers review and record employees' telephone calls
- ▶ 8 percent of employers review and store employees' voice mail messages

Much of this monitoring is on a spot-check basis, rather than continuous, but the reality is that, more and more, your employer is engaging in some form of monitoring.

Why are employers expending so much time and effort monitoring their employees? They do it to protect themselves. Consider how employees at Morgan Stanley brought a $70 million lawsuit against the company, claiming that racist jokes on the company's e-mail system created a hostile work environment. Likewise, female employees at Chevron brought a case against the oil company for sexual harassment. The central evidence in the case was an e-mail circulated among co-workers and listing the reasons "Why beer is better than women."

In short, your employer monitors you for the following reasons:

- ▶ To prevent and remedy sexual harassment
- ▶ To prevent workers from divulging—either intentionally or unintentionally—company trade secrets and other confidential information

- ▸ To prevent employees from engaging in illegal computer-related activities, such as downloading child pornography or copyright-protected music, videos, and software
- ▸ To prevent possible defamation or discrimination liability
- ▸ To prevent the company's system from being exposed to viruses
- ▸ To maintain employee productivity
- ▸ To maintain the company's reputation

Notwithstanding the legitimacy of these business interests, fear of litigation is the principal driver behind the rise in monitoring. According to a 2001 survey conducted by the ePolicy Institute, in conjunction with the American Management Association and *US News & World Report,* 68 percent of the companies that engaged in employee monitoring said they did so to prevent legal liability. Litigation involving misuse of e-mail, in particular, has become increasingly prevalent and costly. According to a 2003 AMA study, 14 percent of companies have been ordered by a court to produce employee e-mail, and 5 percent have fought workplace lawsuits stemming from e-mail.

As an employee, you should be aware that employers are using the information they gather from snooping to punish transgressions. For instance, more than 25 percent of the companies surveyed by the AMA fired employees for misusing office e-mail or the Internet, and 65 percent disciplined workers for such conduct. Such companies, including the *The New York Times,* Dow Chemical, and Xerox, have fired employees for e-mail or Internet misuse.

What Gives Employers the Right to Monitor?

How far can your employer go in monitoring your actions at work? The simple answer is, quite far. The Electronic Communications Privacy Act of 1986 (ECPA), which governs the monitoring of telephones, the Internet, instant messaging, voice mail and e-mail, prohibits employers from intentionally intercepting or accessing wire, oral, or electronic communications. However, this act provides you with little protection from your employer's prying eyes and ears because it contains three powerful exceptions. These exceptions grant your employer great latitude in monitoring your communications:

▶ **The service provider exception** allows the owner of a communications system to monitor communications in the normal course of business to maintain and protect the system. Under this exception alone, your employer is likely permitted to monitor employee e-mails if it provides an e-mail service through a company-owned system.

> More than 25 percent of the companies surveyed by the AMA fired employees for misusing office e-mail or the Internet, and 65 percent disciplined workers for such conduct.

▶ **The ordinary course of business exception** is similar to the provider exception, but this exception applies to interception of telephone calls and possibly e-mails in the normal course of business. Your business calls may be monitored, but not your personal calls. Once your employer realizes it is listening in on a personal call, it is required to hang up, unless you have consented to having all your calls monitored.

▶ **The consent exception** allows your employer to monitor communications if you have granted either actual, or sometimes only implied, consent. Actual consent is obtained when your employer distributes a policy stating that your communications may be monitored and you sign it (or sign an employment agreement containing similar language). Consent is sometimes implied when your employer has a monitoring policy, and even though you do not sign it, you still decide to use your company's system.

Are you starting to sense what this means for you? In the aggregate, these exceptions mean that if your employer has provided an e-mail, Internet, IM, phone, or voice mail service, and there is no policy stating that workplace communications will never be monitored, and the level of monitoring can be justified as a business need, your employer has virtually *complete license to snoop on you at the workplace.*

Further, as a result of the Enron-type scandals, Congress passed another federal law that imposes new record-keeping and investigative requirements on publicly traded companies. Under this new law, the Sarbanes-Oxley Act of

2002, if your employer is a publicly traded company, and you look at sensitive documents, your employer is *required* to monitor you to ensure the accuracy of financial reporting. Failure to do so can result in the personal liability of officers and directors at your company. Indeed, 92 percent of firms in the financial sector monitor their employees in some way, according to the AMA.

Lastly, some states require that information technology workers be legally responsible for reporting child pornography found on company computers. Illinois and South Carolina are two states with such laws. Child pornography is a disturbing and heinous crime for which there is no possible justification, but the implementation of this law creates a number of thorny issues. If you are an IT worker, you are not trained in law enforcement. So what would you do if you found a picture of your colleague's six-year-old daughter in the bathtub? Are you required to report it? If you save the picture on a disk as proof, are you then violating state law? Unfortunately, because these laws are so new, the answers to these and a host of other questions are not yet settled by the courts.

Types of Surveillance at Your Workplace

You may not like being watched, but perhaps you understand why your employer is watching you. What steps can you take to prevent your employer from monitoring *everything* you do? Here is what you need to know about the surveillance of your specific communications and activities during the workday:

E-mail

You are sitting at your desk one morning, typing out your status report and thinking about what you should order for lunch, when out of the blue you get the call. It's the head of the human resources department asking you to come to your boss's office. When you arrive in the office, the solemn faces that greet you do not bode well. You discover that you are being terminated for violation of the company's e-mail policy. You have ten minutes to clear out your desk and vacate the premises. Seized by nausea and disbelief, you know

278

only one thing. Those dirty Michael Jackson jokes you circulated last week suddenly do not seem so funny after all.

It should be very clear by now that as an employee your e-mail is rarely private. If your employer has an e-mail system, your employer is deemed to own the system and is therefore entitled to review all its contents, including your e-mails. This is true of any messages sent within the company, sent out of the company, or sent to any recipient within the company, including all attachments. This means that if your buddy sends you some off-base e-mail, attaching the Paris Hilton porn video, your boss could be viewing it at the same time you do. Embarrassment may not be all you suffer. According to a study by the Pew Internet Project, 22 percent of employers have terminated employees for e-mail infractions.

> **22 percent of employers have terminated employees for e-mail infractions.**

E-mail is not private even when you're told it is.

In the case of Smyth v. Pillsbury, *an employee was fired after his employer read e-mails the employee had sent from his home computer to his supervisor at work. The e-mails contained comments concerning the sales management staff, including a threat to "kill the back-stabbing bastards." The district court said that the employee had "no reasonable expectation of privacy" on his employer's system, despite the fact that Pillsbury had repeatedly assured employees that their e-mails were completely confidential and that they would not be used as a basis for discipline or discharge. The company's interest in preventing "inappropriate and unprofessional" conduct outweighed the employee's right to privacy.*

You should not expect your e-mail to be private even when you are told your e-mail is private. In a court of law, your employer will be able to use your e-mail against you.

E-mail is not private even when it is protected with a password and saved in a special folder.

> *Nissan in California randomly selected an e-mail from its system as part of an employee training session. The message, sent by a system analyst named Bonita Bourke, was a personal e-mail that described her boss as a "numb-nuts." Based on this discovery, Nissan reviewed all the messages sent by employees in Bourke's work group, and the company's search turned up other personal e-mails. Bourke was subsequently fired. She and her co-workers sued Nissan for invasion of privacy, claiming that because the system allowed employees to protect their e-mail access with passwords, they had a legitimate expectation that their e-mail privacy would be respected. The court in California rejected this claim.*

Even if you are given a password to access your company's computer system, or if you store your e-mails in a password-protected computer folder, the courts have ruled in favor of your employer's right to read your e-mails. In these cases, the courts have ruled that, as an employee, you have no reasonable expectation of privacy when e-mails are transmitted over your employer's system.

E-mail is not private when transmitted through a Web-based e-mail account

> *If your supervisor monitors your computer activity and finds sexually suggestive messages, he or she can fire you. You do not have to be the author of the messages; you merely have to receive them from your Web-based e-mail account.*

If you think your e-mail is private because you have been using a Web-based e-mail account in the workplace, think again. You may be using such e-mail providers as Yahoo! or Hotmail, among others, because you think e-mails on these systems are protected from your employer. In reality, however, it is almost as simple for your employer to monitor these e-mails as it is to track those that pass through the main company e-mail system. Current spy software, such as eBlaster and sniffer programs, easily captures these e-mails.

(For more on spyware, see chapter 7, "Your Computer and the Internet.") In any event, your employer is legally justified in monitoring these e-mails.

E-mail accounts are not private even after you delete e-mails

A woman sued her former boss for age discrimination after she was terminated. The employer's case looked airtight until a consultant involved in the case was able to undelete an e-mail from the company president to the HR department instructing it to "get rid of the uptight dinosaur."

If you think you are safe from your employer's e-mail snooping because you deleted certain e-mail, then you should also think again. In reality, deleted e-mail is rarely ever truly deleted.

As detailed in chapter 7, "Your Computer and the Internet," when you delete an e-mail from your mailbox, it moves into a deleted message file folder where the message continues to exist. When you delete the contents of this file folder, the message still survives on your computer or in the server until another file is saved over it. The e-mail probably still exists on backup tapes made of the system. In addition, a copy of the e-mail probably also exists on the computer of the author, and anyone copied or forwarded. There are also specialists in computer forensics who can retrieve deleted messages and even restore an e-mail from magnetic tapes that have been overwritten several times.

Whether or not an e-mail is truly deleted can have a serious effect on litigation. You probably remember the e-mail trail that confronted Bill Gates in the Microsoft antitrust trial, including the infamous "Do we have a clear plan on what we want Apple to do to undermine Sun?" e-mail.

Instant Messaging

The use of Instant Messaging (IM) is a growing trend at work. Companies like AOL have released IM platforms for the workplace. According to research by ComScore Media Metrix, the use of IM in American companies grew from 2.3 billion minutes in September 2000 to 4.9 billion minutes in September 2001. As IM becomes more popular in the workplace, more employers are beginning to monitor its usage.

Employers, especially financial companies that worry about record-keeping, want to monitor IM, and products such as Raytheon Co.'s Silent Runner and Cyber Sentinel 3.0 by Security Software Systems are the answer. These products keep an electronic record of every instant message sent, some of which may be kept without your knowledge. The courts have yet to consider a privacy challenge to IM monitoring, but it is only a matter of time. Chances are that the courts will view IM as akin to e-mail, which, as you now know, enjoys little protection.

> Employers can use monitoring software that takes surreptitious screen shots of your computer at selected intervals; they can monitor what is stored in your computer terminals and hard disks; they can track your Internet use, including the amount of time you spend visiting a particular site; and they can track every keystroke you enter into your computer.

Cybertracking

After an unpleasant tiff with your boss, you type an e-mail you plan to send to a sympathetic co-worker: "Our boss is such a $#^&*%* idiot." Before you fire off the message, you think better of it and backspace. You congratulate yourself on an admirable display of self-control, but what you fail to realize is that your company has installed spy software that recorded your every keystroke. It works by recognizing keywords (like "boss"), or phrases (like "$#^&*%* boss"), and chances are you will have some explaining to do later on in the day.

From your employer's perspective, monitoring computer and Internet use is warranted by concerns about potential liability for sexual harassment and discrimination, and possible exposure for other employee misbehavior online. Employers are also concerned that their employees are *cyberslacking,* thereby reducing their productivity. According to Websense, an Internet employee management company, U.S. businesses lose $63 billion a year from employees surfing the Internet on company time.

The surge in employer snooping has spawned an interest in both the development of and demand for monitoring products. A detailed discussion of the various monitoring tools available is beyond the scope of this book. However, you should be aware that there is a product out there for spying on everything you do on your computer. Employers can use monitoring software that takes surreptitious screen shots of your computer at selected intervals; they can monitor what is stored in your computer terminals and hard disks; they can track your Internet use, including the amount of time you spend visiting a particular site; and they can track every keystroke you enter into your computer. For instance, WinWhatWhere Investigator is software that captures keystrokes, e-mails information about your activities when key phrases are identified, and even renames itself and changes location so it will remain undetected to you as an employee. SpectorSoft's Spector Pro is another spying tool that captures screen shots, records e-mail and chat sessions, and logs keystrokes. Pornsweeper examines e-mail attachments, looking for any images remotely resembling flesh.

Unless you yourself are an IT professional, or maybe a NASA engineer, or constantly sweep your computer with the latest technology, you have little way of knowing that monitoring of your Internet use, e-mail use, or voice mail is happening.

Phone Conversations

Employers may listen in on employee telephone conversations with clients or customers for quality control purposes. According to the American Civil Liber-

---

WHO ACTUALLY DOES THE SNOOPING?

Which company employee is responsible for snooping on co-workers' e-mail and Internet use? According to a 2003 study conducted by the Center for Business Ethics at Bentley College, in the overwhelming majority of companies, the task falls to the IT department. Less often, the job is the responsibility of the human resources department. Considering how critical it is that the monitoring process is carried out in a responsible manner and that the information on fellow employees does not fall into the wrong hands, you probably want to know: Who monitors the monitors? Surprisingly, 25 percent of companies surveyed in the same study do not have procedures in place to ensure that the monitoring process is not subject to abuse, and only 57 percent had any written guidelines whatsoever regarding the monitoring process.

ties Union, employers eavesdrop on 400 million telephone calls per year at workplaces across the United States. Some states, like California, require your employer to alert the parties to the call (by either an announcement or beeping signal) that the call is being monitored. Federal law, however, allows employers to monitor such work calls without any such warning.

Although the Federal Wiretapping Act of 1968 forbids eavesdropping unless one of the parties to the call consents, the Electronic Communications Privacy Act (ECPA) amended the wiretap law in 1986 by allowing employers to listen to your "job-related" conversations. However, as soon your employer determines your call is personal, your employer is supposed to hang up. It is another matter what your employer actually does, or whether your employer may justify a little eavesdropping by saying it takes several minutes to determine whether your conversation is private or job-related. Employers also have the right to monitor the phone numbers dialed by your extension and the length of each of your calls.

Voice Mail

A male McDonald's employee had an extramarital affair with a female McDonald's employee working in a neighboring town. The male employee's supervisor retrieved incriminating messages from the company's voice mail system. (The male employee was given a password and assured his voice mail was private.) The supervisor then played the steamy messages back to the male employee's wife and boss. The male employee was fired.

Employers have a right to listen to your work voice mail messages if there is some work-related rationale for doing so. What little case law there is on this subject has been overly accommodating to the employer. If, however, your employer told you that your voice mail was private, issued you a password, and had no office policy prohibiting voice mail eavesdropping, you *may* as an employee have a privacy claim.

Tip Lines

Employers have added another surveillance tool to their arsenal: *you*. One of the most effective measures employers can take to prevent and report improper employee conduct is the employee tip line. A tip line is a telephone hot line that allows you and other employees to report suspicious activity anonymously, without fear of reprisal. Call it what you will—the truth of the matter is that bosses are using you and your fellow employees to do their dirty work, although they may view it as a legitimate means of preventing theft, or a laudable way of protecting you and your rights in the workplace. Employee tip lines are an increasingly popular trend.

You may be afraid to call from work, so tip lines are usually available twenty-four hours a day. Or you may be reluctant to use an internal tip line for fear that information leaks might reveal your identity, so your employer may have outsourced the tip line, getting an outside operation to manage it.

Video Surveillance

Security officers for Johnson County Community College were provided with a locker area in which to store their rain gear, radios, and other personal items. The security officers also used this area as a dressing and changing room. The college installed video surveillance equipment in response to reports of theft from the lockers and a suspicion that the security officers were bringing weapons on campus. The court held that the employees did not have a reasonable expectation of privacy in the locker area because it was not enclosed (the lockers were located along the wall of a storage room), and because the area was not reserved for their exclusive use.

Applicable law does not generally limit your employer's use of video surveillance as long as your employer does not record sound (as proscribed by the Federal Wiretapping Act) and as long as cameras focus on publicly accessible areas. State laws vary. You are likely to have greater legal protection from videotaping in rest rooms, locker rooms, or other places where you as an employee would have a reasonable expectation of privacy. Even then, in certain circumstances, your employer may be allowed to videotape if your company has a strong enough reason for doing so.

Audio Surveillance

In the case of audio surveillance, you have a greater expectation of privacy. Taping oral conversations by any device is usually illegal under the Federal Wiretapping Act and most state laws. Courts have found employers liable for wiretapping violations when they have attempted to record in-person live conversations. But the rulings are not applicable to employee telephone conversations. In one case, several nightshift employees successfully sued their employer when on several different days their conversations were taped by hidden, voice-activated recording devices. Accordingly, though your employer may choose to videotape you at work, your live conversations will probably not be recorded on the tape.

Searches of Persons or Property

An employee of the Philadelphia Housing Authority left in his desk a computer disk containing work-related legal documents as well as personal files. His supervisor found the disk and accessed the files on it. When the employee tried to sue for unreasonable search and seizure, the court ruled that the supervisor acted within her authority in removing the disk from the desk and accessing the files.

Long before the Internet, computers, or e-mail, employers checked up on employees by conducting physical searches. There is no doubt that modern-day employers continue to conduct searches of offices, desks, personal belongings, file cabinets, lockers, and so on.

If you work in the public sector, you may be afforded greater privacy protections by virtue of the Fourth Amendment's ban of unreasonable searches and seizures. For instance, the Supreme Court has held that federal public employers may conduct searches when they have reasonable grounds to believe the searches will reveal evidence of work-related misconduct, and when employees have no reasonable expectation that their work areas are private.

The situation is quite different if you work for a private company. In general, private employers enjoy great latitude in conducting searches for work-related reasons. Unless your employer conducts a search in such a way as to reveal information unrelated to the workplace, you should not expect any privacy from workplace searches. Your desk, bookshelf, and office are often deemed employer property and are thus searchable. For example, a search of a desk full of items, including incriminating bank statements inadvertently left after termination, is not unreasonable; nor is a search of a desk and credenza, neither of which is locked but both of which contain information needed by other employees.

> **Your desk, bookshelf, and office are often deemed employer property and are thus searchable.**

Extreme Surveillance

How would you feel if your manager kept a spreadsheet monitoring your use of the bathroom, and you were disciplined for heeding nature's call outside the approved break times?

In addition to cases that involve monitoring bathroom use or hygiene performance, here are a few other extreme surveillance methods that may be used by your employer:

- ▶ Use technology to track the attendance, amount of time spent, and performance of its executives at company gyms. Companies such as Adidas, Goldman Sachs, and GlaxoSmithKline use these technologies.
- ▶ Introduce actors as new hires and have them keep tabs on workers.
- ▶ Hire private investigators, as further discussed in chapter 12, "I Spy, You Spy," to catch workers' compensation fraud or other objectionable behavior.
- ▶ Use new, advanced, and intrusive attendance-tracking tools to monitor workers' attendance, such as biometrics, the science of measuring an individual's physical properties, for purposes of authenticating and monitoring employees. For example, instead of punching time clocks, you would punch in by placing a finger or hand on a sensor. These

practices are used on both hourly wage-earners and white-collar, salaried employees.

► Use locator technologies to keep track of employee whereabouts at all times. Many companies require employees to carry badges to get into the building and access different areas of the building. These badges can track when you've arrived at work, how many cigarette breaks you take, how long you've been at lunch, and where in the office you spend your time. Some locator technologies are more sophisticated than others. For instance, nurses in more than two hundred hospitals wear badges connected to infrared sensors to track their every move.

► Keep tabs on you using Global Positioning Systems (GPS). For instance, local news stations place GPS devices in their news trucks.

Off-Duty Conduct

A former UPS manager claimed invasion of privacy after UPS insisted he disclose information about an incident that occurred after business hours at his home. The incident allegedly involved alcohol and emotionally volatile behavior. UPS contacted the manager's mental-health providers without his consent.

A teacher who joined a swingers club was observed by an undercover police officer committing acts of oral sex with three different men at a party. She was later terminated, and her termination was upheld in court. The teacher's conduct was deemed immoral and unprofessional, evidencing unfitness to teach.

Employers have latitude to monitor your behavior off the job as well as in the office. Courts have stated that it is legitimate for your employer to know about off-duty conduct if the personal information reasonably bears upon your fitness for or discharge of your employment responsibilities. As in earlier cases, fear of litigation motivates employers to snoop beyond the physical dimensions of the workplace.

Office Romance

Your supervisor discovers that you are dating a co-worker and, cit-ing the company's antifraternization (no-dating) policy, instructs you to end your relationship with your co-worker. You refuse, telling the supervisor that you did not socialize with your co-worker on the job and that you that will continue to see your co-worker during your own time. Your company fires you under its antifraternization policy. The court supports your company, finding that the antifraternization policy did not violate public policy, and that dismissing you did not constitute outrageous conduct on the part of your employer.

Is there no limit to invasions into your privacy in the workplace? It may now occur to you that your boss can monitor everything you do, or fail to do, at work. Can your boss also tell you whom you can and cannot date? Can your boss police your dating?

With employees spending more and more time in the workplace, office romance has been on the rise. Employers are ever more apprehensive about the potential liability of these office romances. For example, a relationship between a manager and subordinate may result in allegations of favoritism from co-workers claiming that the subordinate received preferential treat-ment. Or, if the office relationship ends badly, the outcome may also be a sex-ual harassment claim brought by the spurned party.

In an effort to address such concerns, employers have adopted policies specifically addressing workplace dating. Policies range from outright prohibi-tions on dating co-workers, to policies discouraging, but ultimately allowing, office relationships. Other policies may require employees to notify manage-ment when co-workers become involved. Still others require that one party to the relationship quit and seek employment elsewhere. Whether such policies ultimately and completely insulate employers is questionable. Nevertheless, an antifraternization (no-dating) policy is usually enforceable if the policy *and* its implementation are reasonable, and it can be fairly and consistently enforced.

Protect Your Privacy in the Workplace

The bottom line is that you don't have much privacy in the workplace, but that doesn't mean you can't protect yourself. In the workplace, the best protection is educating yourself about your workplace's (or prospective workplace's) policies and limiting the information you reveal. Here are the key tips to follow:

✳ **Recognize that you have little privacy at work.** Basically, the law as it pertains to monitoring is not on your side. As they say, forewarned is forearmed. Knowing that your every move may be monitored may make you think twice before acting in inappropriate ways in the workplace.

✳ **Understand your employer's privacy policy.** Before you begin work, take time to read and understand your employer's privacy policy (if it exists) and then act accordingly. Has your employer established a clear and comprehensive communications policy? How does the policy deal with your expectation of privacy at your workplace? If your employer has a clear and comprehensive policy, has it been distributed to you *before any monitoring begins*—for instance, on the first day of employment? Did you sign to acknowledge consent to the policy?

✳ **Separate your personal life from your work activities.** Try to separate your personal life from your work activities. For example, whether or not your company maintains an antifraternization policy, consider the possible ramifications before you date someone at work. Always use separate credit cards for work expenses and personal expenditures. Finally, refrain from excessive personal use of e-mail, the Internet, the telephone, and so forth, and certainly never use company systems to engage in any inappropriate or illegal activity.

✳ **Be particularly careful with e-mail communications.** Sending out an e-mail from your company's system is akin to writing the same message on company letterhead. As a practical matter, it is generally a good idea to keep your personal e-mails separate from your work e-mails. Even if your employer has the capability to monitor Web-based e-mail accounts, you should still use such e-mail both for practical purposes and potentially legal purposes (it may be a factor in your favor to demonstrate a "reasonable expectation of privacy"). For maximum protection, use only Web-based e-mail accounts that are truly private and offer encryption. For information on encryption, see chapter 7, "Your Computer and the Internet."

✳ **Be cautious with telephone communications.** Employers have the right to monitor employee telephone conversations. The best way to protect yourself if you must make truly personal or sensitive phone calls from work is to use your digital cell phone or a pay phone.

✳ **Work for companies that respect the privacy of their employees.** When you apply for a job, you might consider an employer's stance on employee privacy as further evidence of how the company will treat you. For instance, an overly invasive hiring process or zero-tolerance communications policy may well signal an unpleasant work environment. Another indication of discord may be whether the company has hired an internal privacy officer whose job is essentially to define and protect what privacy means for business partners, consumers, and employees. *Wired* magazine ranked the best and the worst public companies with respect to their commitment to employee privacy. The top-ranked company was IBM, particularly since the appointment of Harriet Pearson as IBM's first privacy officer.

✳ **Consider your right to sue if your privacy is violated.** If you believe your employer has violated your privacy, you can attempt to sue your employer. Employees have been successful in cases where an employer used hidden recording devices to tape employees' private conversations, or where an employer used its own employees to collect urine specimens for drug testing, or where an employer searched a trucking employee's motel room. Realize, however, that courts have overwhelmingly sided with employers in invasion-of-privacy cases. Nevertheless, if you decide to sue, your success will depend on whether you sue under federal or state law, and whether you can show a reasonable expectation of privacy in the communication (or the location, in search and video surveillance cases) at issue.

THE BOTTOM LINE

▸ To an employer, a job applicant's life is like an archaeological dig. If a prospective employer runs a background check, that check will unearth more personal information about the applicant than he or she ever thought would see the light of day.

▸ The hiring process can be a good predictor of corporate culture. If a prospective employer asks for things that seem overreaching—like twenty-five-year-old SAT scores or DNA samples—it might be a sign that this might not be an ideal situation and you should look elsewhere.

▸ Check the Constitution at the door. When you are at work, using your boss's property, you have virtually no right to privacy.

▸ You have mail . . . and your boss has seen every word. Your boss has complete license to read your e-mail, even if you've been told it's private, even if you use a password, and even if you think it's deleted.

▸ Your boss can legally monitor your every move at work. This includes but is not limited to what websites you are visiting, any Instant Messages you send, what's in your voice mail messages, how often you take bathroom breaks, and how photogenic you are on the office surveillance system. Under some circumstances your boss can monitor your behavior when you are not at work.

Your Health

"I already know he's gone—it's been on the Internet."

During a routine exam you tell your doctor that you smoked a little pot years and years ago. You also mention that you smoked cigarettes when you were going through some hard times in your mid-twenties. You believe this is ancient history until you are denied health or life insurance coverage because that information was included in your file.

You ask your insurer to disclose to your employer details from your medical records that are relevant to a work-related wrist injury. Instead, the insurance company discloses to your employer not just details about your wrist, but also your comprehensive medical *records. The records include sensitive information, like specifics about your fertility treatments and a miscarriage you suffered.*

You are separating from your husband. You call your local pharmacist to ask him to maintain the confidentiality of your prescription information. The next day, your husband contacts the same pharmacy and requests your prescription records, citing tax purposes. After he receives the records, he shares the information with family and friends, as well as the Department of Motor Vehicles, to sully your reputation and damage your chances of being awarded custody of your children.

You receive a call from a hospital worker who informs you that you are HIV-positive. Two days later, after much agony and soul searching, you find out that the hospital worker was actually your doctor's teenaged daughter, who somehow accessed and collected names and contact details for a number of your doctor's patients. Your doctor's daughter thought it was a fun practical joke to call her father's patients to tell them that they were HIV-positive.

How would you feel if you were HIV-positive and a health-care worker disclosed your condition to a reporter who then disclosed your condition in a newspaper without your permission? This is exactly how the world discovered that tennis great Arthur Ashe suffered from AIDS.

Once upon a time, people developed personal relationships with family doctors and expected those relationships to be completely confidential. In a safe context, patients could discuss intimate issues such as substance use, family issues, or medical history. Most people did not worry about disclosure of their personal medical records because they believed such dossiers were protected, not only because of the confidentiality of their family doctors, but also because these files existed only on paper and were locked in the filing cabinets of local doctors' offices.

As in many areas of modern life, privacy in medicine has changed dramatically, even though the basic expectations of those involved have not. Both patient and doctor still want to protect sensitive information, but technologies that allow complete medical files to be shared electronically have compromised patient privacy for the benefits of convenience and efficiency. If you live in Rhode Island and you are receiving medical treatment in New York City, your physician in Providence can easily transmit your entire medical history to the surgeons, the anesthesiologist, and the hematologist in New York. If the benefits of this aren't obvious enough, then imagine getting in a car accident en route to New York. Wouldn't you want the emergency room physicians to know about your liver condition and your severe allergies to certain drugs? Nevertheless, the electronic med-

> Many privacy advocates believe that HIPAA forces patients to choose between access to medical care and control of their medical information.

ical file that may save your life may also allow dozens of people to access your medical history. Misuse of medical information has caused job loss, other negative employment effects, loss or compromise of child custody, social alienation, loss of dignity, and many other crises born of leaked information about people's physical or mental health, or that of members of their families.

In addition to compromises resulting from electronic medical records, your medical privacy has also been compromised by electronic billing practices, managed health care, and improved public health tracking. These new methods enable greater ease, accuracy, and advancement for the health industry. The digital records created from so many available medical sources allow new viruses to be tracked and prevented, a new drug's side effects to be studied, and large-scale patterns that unlock medical mysteries and crises to be discovered.

In response to the evolving nature of the health industry and violations of medical privacy, Congress passed the Health Insurance Portability and Accountability Act (HIPAA) in 1996 to protect the medical-privacy rights of Americans. The act finally came into effect on April 14, 2003. Intended to set a national standard for medical privacy, and touted as a protection of your rights, HIPAA is believed by federal officials to carefully balance patients' privacy and the health-care industry's responsibility to provide you and other Americans with efficient and effective high-quality care.

The response to HIPAA from privacy advocates, however, hasn't been positive. The act has been denounced as favoring Big Business (including the government, medical establishments, and health insurance companies). Many privacy advocates believe that HIPAA forces patients to choose between access to medical care and control of their medical information.

But you do have some choices concerning your health care, and you must educate yourself about your privacy rights and understand how the health-care industry works. Read on to learn how to navigate HIPAA and adopt easy, proactive steps to protect your private life to the extent possible without having to sacrifice good health care.

The Contents of Your Medical Records

In 2002, a Wisconsin emergency medical technician (EMT), who was involved in the care of a woman who had overdosed in a suicide attempt, was found guilty of sharing that information with one of the woman's professional colleagues. The co-worker later told a number of other co-workers about the woman's suicide attempt. The EMT claimed she shared the information in an attempt to help the suicidal woman, but the jury believed that the EMT violated the woman's privacy.

You might believe your medical records only include basic details such as vaccinations, allergies, and operations. And, of course, they do include this information. But getting the best possible health care and treatment often depends on the extensive and sensitive personal information that you reveal to a spectrum of health-care workers, from school counselors to personal doctors to surgeons.

Candor can be lifesaving. For example, if you have certain allergies, you may need to disclose them before undergoing anesthesia. If you have heart problems, you may need to come clean about bad eating habits for your doctor to prescribe effective treatment. If you have a depressed child in psychiatric care, your child may disclose information about sexual abuse, including the identity of the perpetrator, in the course of treatment. As you interact with your various medical providers and doctors you reveal a great deal about yourself and your family—and you can assume all the information is included in your medical record.

On a basic level, your medical records include data such as your name, address, contact numbers, insurance, date of birth, social security number, and credit card or checking/banking information. Your record also includes information related to your physical health such as height, weight, blood pressure, cholesterol levels, and lab test results. Even this basic information is revealing.

The details of your medical history, however, are more revealing. For example, your files will include any diseases you have had (such as sexually transmitted diseases), medical conditions you have (such as asthma or diabetes), and medications you take. Surgeries or procedures you have undergone are also a part of your medical records. You can also expect your report to include your family medical history, including your genetic disposition to certain illnesses. In addition, your complete medical records will include any prescriptions you take, lifestyle issues (such as smoking, alcohol consumption, sexual behavior or orientation, any substance abuses, and even participation in high-risk activities), disabilities or behavioral disorders, and mental-health conditions (like depression or agoraphobia). Finally, your communications to and notes made by a therapist in your sessions may also be contained in your medical records.

Other Sources of Your Medical Information

Researchers at the University of Minnesota mailed a survey to twelve hundred transplant recipients who were participating in its long-term research study. The university's mailing inadvertently disclosed the names of the people who had donated their kidneys to their respective recipients. Though the university blamed the breach on a software upgrade, it did admit that there was no reason to store the donors' names in that particular database.

Your doctors and health-care providers aren't the only people who collect medical information about you—and the medical records in your doctors' offices aren't the only ones that exist. Your information is also collected by various entities in other, less obvious ways, and these entities may, in turn, share your information in different situations. Consider these scenarios:

> You make a medical claim, which may have to be investigated

> You pay for a specific medical treatment by check or credit card, and a record of your treatment is contained in your banking or credit card statements

> You are covered through your employer's plan, which can make details of your health and medical history a part of your employment record

> You participate in a research study, which may or may not have committed to keeping the results private

> You file a lawsuit that involves details of your health or medical history, which then might become a matter of public record

> You undergo a free health screening offered in a mall, which may not be kept private

> Your or your child's school record might reflect interactions with nurses or counselors, vaccinations, and physical exams

> You use your own name and e-mail address in a health-related online chat room

> You owe money to a hospital, dentist, or other health service, and the debt shows up on your credit report

> You fill out sensitive personal and family health information on consumer surveys that come to your house. Some surveys are accompanied by sweepstakes offers or a chance to win free coupons

> You have your prescriptions filled by a pharmacy whose privacy notice does not satisfactorily limit disclosure of your information

> Privacy experts say that patients themselves may be the biggest source of medical information to marketers.

Your Protections Under HIPAA and Their Limits

A couple was expecting a baby in a few months, and they were making regular visits to their doctor. They developed the necessary relationship with the hospital so when delivery time came, the hospital would be ready for them. Sadly, the woman miscarried. Soon after the date when the baby would have been born, the couple started to receive mail at home that advertised great products for their new baby.

THE MEDICAL PROFILERS

For the past year you have been clinically depressed and have had episodes of migraines and outbreaks of cold sores. Suddenly, you start receiving in the mail information and advertisements for products and prescriptions that could alleviate your symptoms. This embarrasses you because whenever you go on a business trip you ask your neighbor to pick up your mail. Because of this mail, you do everything you can to avoid making eye contact with your mailman. Moreover, you're troubled by the fact that some big pharmaceutical company seems to know more about you than your mother does. How did they find out?

●●●

Who might be a bigger threat to your privacy than your doctor? You. Privacy experts say that patients themselves may be the biggest source of medical information to marketers.

Data aggregators, such as Illinois-based Medical Marketing Service, Inc., collect all the medical information they can find about you—and they get most of the information from you. How do they do this? They get it from:

▶ Surveys mailed to you, many with offers of coupons, sweepstakes, or free samples. These surveys ask questions or have you check boxes next to ailments that afflict you and your family. In addition to providing this information, you also reveal your name, address, and telephone number.

▶ Health screenings at malls and other public places

▶ Loyalty cards at the supermarket if you use the store's pharmacy

> ▶ Health-related websites and chat rooms (including online tests and quizzes)
> ▶ Newsletter subscriptions and other ailment-specific mailings that you request or buy
> ▶ Calls made to an 800 number for information about a product
>
> Medical Marketing Service, the most prominent medical data profiler, collects information from millions of surveys and the other sources listed above and sells the compiled data to pharmaceutical companies. Their data includes lists of people who are afflicted with everything from chronic chapped lips to diabetes to menopause to prostate cancer. Not only might your name be connected to a particular ailment, but the data profiler also cross-references this information with data it has collected about your age, educational level, family dwelling size, gender, income, lifestyle, marital status, hobbies, and whether or not you have children (and any information about them), whether or not you have an American Express or Visa card, and whether you plan to travel or buy certain things within the next six months. A pharmaceutical company can buy a list from Medical Marketing Service for less than $200 per one thousand names.

A dead infant was discovered in a Dumpster. The local police force subpoenaed from the local Planned Parenthood a list of women who had received positive pregnancy test results in the nine months prior to the incident, as well as contact details for each of these women. Only one woman on that list refused to answer any questions. She stated that she would rather go to jail than answer the subpoena with the records it requested.

The Health Insurance Portability and Accountability Act controls the disclosure of your personal medical information by placing limitations on certain entities that access medical information. The act creates the first national standard for accessing medical information. Prior to its introduction in April

2003, access to your records varied by state. For example, if you lived in Alabama, you would not have been able to see your own medical records. Now, states must comply with HIPAA's minimum national standard, which includes not only the right to access your own records, but also places limits on the use of your medical information in medical marketing. The act also provides an option for increased confidentiality and gives you a right to an accounting of people who have accessed your medical records. However, HIPAA does not apply to everyone who sees or accesses your health information, as detailed later in this chapter.

> In general, covered entities under HIPAA are health-care providers, health plans, and health-care clearinghouses.

The Health Insurance Portability and Accountability Act provides you with certain important privacy rights that you previously lacked. First, HIPAA establishes a national floor for your privacy protections; it is also possible that the state in which you reside provides you even greater protections. Below are the minimum privacy rights you have with respect to those entities covered by HIPAA. In general, covered entities under HIPAA are health-care providers, health plans, and health-care clearinghouses. In addition, HIPAA addresses the examples above, such as the extent to which a hospital may send you marketing materials and whether your medical records may be used to solve crimes. Unfortunately, in some cases HIPAA plays no role.

Your federal privacy rights under HIPAA include:

Access to Medical Records. Under HIPAA, you can approach any of the covered entities and request not only to see, but also to obtain copies of your medical records. In addition, you may request corrections if you identify any mistakes within your records. Although any of the covered entities may charge you for the cost of copying and sending your records, they must typically provide access to your records within thirty days of your request.

Your health-care provider as well as any other covered entity must indicate in its privacy notices how you can obtain a copy of your record. If you seek such a copy, it is wise to make the request in writing. If you are turned down, you should promptly contact the Office of Civil Rights (OCR) at the Department of Health and Human Services (HHS):

U.S. Department of Health and Human Services
Office of Civil Rights
200 Independence Avenue, SW
Washington, DC 20201
866/627-7748
www.hhs.gov

Notice of Privacy Practices. The covered entities must provide you with a notice about how they intend to use your personal medical information as well as an overview of your privacy rights with the health plan, doctor, or other covered entity. In practice, you were probably provided with the notice on your first patient visit after HIPAA's compliance date of April 14, 2003. You will also likely need to sign or otherwise acknowledge receipt of this privacy notice before your doctor will treat you. If you refuse to sign the form, your doctor may try to refuse to treat you and your insurance company may try to deny you coverage—even though HIPAA does not give your doctor or health-care provider the right to refuse to treat you if you don't sign the form.

Your health plan will mail a notice to you when you enroll in the plan and again if substantial changes are made to your policy. You are free to ask any covered entity to expand your privacy under the policy, thereby further restricting disclosure of your medical information, but the covered entity is free to deny your request.

Limits on Use of Personal Medical Information. HIPAA limits how health plans and covered providers may use health information that individually identifies you as a patient or a consumer of medical services. In particular, doctors and other covered entities must determine the minimal necessary information to provide to, for example, billing companies or to secure laboratory test results. Some commonsense exceptions exist, such as allowing doctors, nurses, and other providers to share information when it is needed to treat you as a patient. If you are in an emergency room, you want your health-care providers to be able to give you the best-quality care possible. In addition, you must sign a specific authorization before a covered entity can release your medical information to a life insurer, a bank, a marketing firm, or another out-side business for purposes not related to your health care.

Limits on Marketing. HIPAA places certain limits on the use of your information for marketing pur-poses. Unfortunately, the precise marketing areas and communications that are limited under HIPAA are open to interpretation. In theory, pharmacies, health plans, and other covered entities must first obtain your written authorization before disclosing your patient information for marketing purposes.

> Unfortunately, the precise marketing areas and communications that are limited under HIPAA are open to interpretation.

Thus, your authorization must be granted for a covered entity to sell or share details of your medical condition or lifestyle with a third party.

In practice, however, HIPAA makes exemptions, allowing certain entities to communicate with you about their own services or products, including dis-ease-management programs, many of which can aid your treatment. These kinds of exemptions potentially leave room for unacceptable practices, including:

- ▸ A company that manufactures drugs can pay a pharmacy or doctor to send refill alerts to patients
- ▸ Because of a clause regarding marketing that allows a hospital or other care facility to notify a patient of services relevant to his or her care or treatment, a patient with a sensitive medical condition may still receive mail that indicates that condition. For example, a person who is HIV-positive or who has cancer might get updates about related services.
- ▸ A mailing can be made from a hospital, for example, that specifically targets patients nearing Medicare-qualified age with information about Medicare

Explain to your health-care providers exactly how you want the use of your personal health information restricted, as HIPAA might not cover all the instances you might want to restrict. Understand that your requests will not always be guaranteed because of the exceptions made for marketing purposes. Available marketing channels are open to debate; it is likely that some of the provisions in HIPAA will be disputed in the courts.

Confidential Communications. Under HIPAA, you can request that your doctor, health plan, and other covered entities take reasonable steps to ensure that their communications with you are confidential. For example, you can ask a doctor to call you at your office rather than at your home, and your doctor must comply with any request that can be reasonably accommodated.

> A patient with a sensitive medical condition may still receive mail that indicates that condition. For example, a person who is HIV-positive or who has cancer might get updates about related services.

Accounting. HIPAA stipulates your right to an accounting of people, companies, or organizations that have accessed your medical record in the previous six years. This right may be important if you need to find a paper trail for an insurance company's rejection of your application, or for a dubious action made by your employer. However, HIPAA does not require this accounting to include any individuals who touch your records as a result of treatment, payment, or health-care operations (or TPO—treatment, payment, or operations). Given the many individuals who will see your medical records during TPO, some privacy advocates believe that an accounting of your records will invariably be incomplete.

Complaints and Penalties. Your medical privacy may be violated in many unforeseen ways. For example, your records may be vulnerable when they are transferred to a third party; enterprising health-care workers may seek to profit from your records by selling them to ambulance-chasing lawyers or other opportunists; snoops in the workplace may rummage through your file; or, in some instances, staff members in health-care facilities may even have a conversation about your medical records in a public place.

If you believe that your medical privacy has been infringed upon under HIPAA, then you can file a formal complaint with the Health and Human Services' Office for Civil Rights. The OCR is charged with investigating complaints and enforcing the privacy regulation. Before filing your complaint, you should first gather more information about filing complaints by going to the website of Health and Human Services at www.hhs.gov/ocr/hipaa or by calling 866/627-7748.

If you plan to file a complaint, the OCR requires that you do so within 180 days of a violation. After you file your complaint, the OCR will conduct an investigation and try to resolve the matter. In the case of privacy infractions, the government can impose both criminal and civil penalties. The civil penalties are cited at $100 per infraction, not to exceed $25,000 a year for one person committing identical infractions. For prohibited disclosure of personal identifying medical information, criminal penalties can be up to $250,000, and sometimes up to ten years of imprisonment—when the purpose of the disclosure can be traced to an intent to use your information for commercial or personal gain, or malicious damage.

> Given the many individuals who will see your medical records during TPO, some privacy advocates believe that an accounting of your records will invariably be incomplete.

Control Over Use of Information. HIPAA outlines cases where your information can be used without your consent; cases where your authorization is not needed; cases where your authorization is needed; and, finally, a few cases where you have an opportunity to either consent or opt out. These cases apply only to how your information is handled and do not pertain to treatment. Consent is still required for treatment. With respect to information, however, the complexities of HIPAA make it impossible to make generalizations. Here are some examples:

▶ Your medical information can be used for treatment, payment, or health-care operations *without your consent*

▶ Your medical information can be used, *without your authorization,* in situations or in connection with situations involving a requirement to disclose under federal or state law; victims of abuse or domestic violence; court or administrative proceedings; funeral directors or organ procurement; medical researchers; law enforcement agents; and threats to public safety or health

▶ You *must authorize* disclosure of your medical information when it relates to any psychotherapy notes or when it involves marketing. Certain exceptions exist in both cases. For example, a court may compel your psychotherapy notes to be disclosed in certain matters

▶ You have the opportunity to consent to or opt out of disclosure of a hospital's directory information when you are admitted to a hospital

Access to Your Personal Medical Records

In 2003, as part of a criminal investigation involving alleged doctor-shopping, Florida law enforcement officers seized the medical records of conservative talk show host Rush Limbaugh. The seizure came in the wake of a statement by Limbaugh's former employee, who claimed she had sold him thousands of painkillers known as "baby blues" (OxyContin pills) over the course of several years. The American Civil Liberties Union of Florida subsequently filed a motion stating that seizure of the records violated Limbaugh's privacy rights.

Medical records from one of the medical centers at the University of California were handled by a woman in Pakistan who was working for an overseas data-transcription service. It is not uncommon for a hospital to contract with an offshore agency to perform such services to reduce medical costs, even though U.S. medical-privacy laws are difficult to enforce overseas. The woman in this case tried to use blackmail to gain more pay: she threatened to post the medical records of many American patients online if she did not receive what she demanded. In the end she retracted her demands, but the threat lingers.

The law under HIPAA retains kinks that have yet to be fully resolved. As a result, which entities HIPAA covers and to what extent they can access your medical records is still not consistently and clearly defined. Some confusion exists about the relationship between the state medical-privacy laws and the minimum federal standards put forth under HIPAA. State law is supposed to control when state law is deemed more stringent than HIPAA. The problem, however, is that it may take a court to decide whether a state law is more or less stringent than HIPAA, given the limited time since HIPAA's enactment and the difficulty in interpreting the act's provisions. The State of Texas, for example, recently took the position that its state public-information law takes precedence over HIPAA, enabling Texas media outlets and individuals to access public information that some hospitals and authorities declined to release under HIPAA.

Even under HIPAA, medical-privacy laws can still be widely interpreted, and a comprehensive, reliable comparison study of state laws and new federal laws has yet to be published. One report, the Georgetown Health Privacy Report, offers synopses on the medical-privacy laws, as they are distinguished from HIPAA, of individual states. The report can be accessed at www.healthprivacy.org/info-url_nocat2304/info-url_nocat_search.htm.

To add to the confusion, not all entities are governed by HIPAA in the same way—and some aren't covered at all. This list details the agencies and people who have varying degrees of access to your medical records. Some are covered by HIPAA and others are not, and some are covered only to an extent:

> As long as the facility in question uses any electronic means to transmit information, as almost all health-care providers must in this modern age, that facility is bound to the regulations stated in HIPAA.

Medical Institutions and Doctors. This category includes almost anyone who supplies health care to the public. As long as the facility in question uses any electronic means to transmit information, as almost all health-care providers must in this modern age, that facility is bound to the regulations stated in HIPAA. (HIPAA refers to these entities as *health-care providers*.) This group includes a host of different people working in the hospital or in your doctor's office, any of whom might see your medical records, including nurses, consulting physicians, medical transcribers, typists, and others. During the evaluation process that determines the medical service you are to receive, still more people might review your medical records. Finally, a diverse range of other medical services and institutions, such as laboratories, pharmacies, nursing homes, and other health-care centers, are also subject to HIPAA regulations.

Health Plans. This group (referred to as *health plans* under HIPAA) encompasses entities that pay for health care, including HMOs (health maintenance organizations), group health plans, employee welfare-benefit plans, Medicare and Medicaid, dental insurers, and a good number of long-term-care insurers. Before they will pay your doctor's bill, insurance companies require you to release your medical records. Once your insurance company obtains your medical information, it may share your information with other companies, such as marketing or payment companies. If you are part of a health maintenance organization, your medical records may be shared among the network's professionals and hospitals to provide efficient medical service to you, but only to the minimum extent necessary to perform the intended purpose. Nevertheless, both health insurance companies and HMOs must comply with the HIPAA rules that govern their access to and use of your medical information.

The Medical Insurance Bureau. The Medical Insurance Bureau (MIB) is an association of U.S. and Canadian insurance companies that provides information and database management services to insurance companies. It is run as a consumer-reporting agency that maintains a database of medical profiles for about 15 million Americans and Canadians. These profiles are not comprehensive—like the records in your doctor's office—but rather are synopses of conditions and lifestyles, like a thyroid condition or a smoking habit, which are relevant to insurance practices. The hundreds of insurance companies that are part of this association research insurance policy applicants through the MIB's database, although the MIB's information is not supposed to be the sole determinant of the acceptance or rejection of an application. The Fair Credit Reporting Act (discussed in chapter 4, "Your Credit") regulates the MIB, but patients do not enjoy any extra protection under HIPAA.

Your Employer. Your employer may gain access to your medical information in different ways. In many cases, after you begin work, your employer will ask for your consent to reveal your medical information. For example, your company may be self-insured, which means that your company has set up a health insurance plan in which it pays your health-care expenses as well as those of your fellow employees. To do so, your company must maintain its own database of employee medical records; the department of your company that processes your medical claim is then subject to HIPAA. Alternatively, if your employer pays for your medical insurance, it may request from its insurance company either basic information, such as enrollment information, or more detailed information, such as copies of your medical records, to confirm payments. If your employer seeks more than the basic information regarding your health records, it will likely need to comply with HIPAA procedures. Although the Americans with Disabilities Act prevents employers from seeking medical information from you or requesting a medical exam of you prior to employment, your employer may legally seek both after you have been offered employment, if your employer demands the same of others in similarly situated positions. See chapter 9, "Your Workplace," for information on how medical data may be used in the hiring process.

> Government agencies are typically not subject to HIPAA.

Government Agencies. When you file claims for Medicare, Workers' Compensation, or Social Security Disability, the respective government agency will review copies of your medical records. In addition, public-health agencies may access your medical information for statistical data; certain federal agencies may require your records for national security and intelligence; and state agencies may need your records for the registries they maintain on births, deaths, and people with serious illnesses. Government agencies are typically not subject to HIPAA.

Courts. Your medical records can be subpoenaed under HIPAA if your medical condition is an issue in litigation, an administrative hearing, or a workers' compensation hearing. In these cases, the information in your medical records—including handwritten doctor's notes—that pertains to the case may be introduced in court.

Law Enforcement Agencies. Law enforcement agencies may, under HIPAA, use your medical records to help them solve crimes, investigate fraud, and resolve cases involving fugitives and missing persons.

Marketers. Direct marketers may use your medical records when you participate in information health screenings, including tests for high blood pressure or cholesterol levels. Different rules under HIPAA apply to marketers.

Others. A host of other people may access different parts of your medical records or medical history, including coroners, medical examiners, funeral directors, organ procurement services, and various Internet sites. The majority of these individuals or organizations are not subject to HIPAA. On the other

How to Request Your MIB Medical Records

A woman cannot get health, liability, or disability insurance. She is very healthy and leads a healthy lifestyle, so she cannot understand the difficulty. She decides to request a copy of her coded medical record from the Medical Information Bureau. When she receives her profile, she is floored to see that she has been inaccurately noted as having Alzheimer's disease as well as a heart condition, neither of which she suffers from.

●●●

Have you applied for medical insurance and been turned down? Are you even thinking of applying for it? In either case, it's a good idea to see what's in your file. The Medical Insurance Bureau allows you to access your medical records in their file. The MIB also gives you the opportunity to correct any inaccurate or incomplete information that is contained in your medical file. It is in your best interest to ensure that the information that insurance companies use to evaluate you is both accurate and complete.

To obtain a copy of your medical record, complete a Request for Disclosure Form. Send the form and $9 to the following address:

The Medical Information Bureau
Box 105
Essex Station
Boston, MA 02112
Telephone: 617/426-3660
Fax: 781/461-2453
www.mib.com
e-mail: disclosure@mib.com

Keep in mind that only 20 percent of consumers have files with the MIB. You can download the Request for Disclosure Form at the MIB website at www.mib.com or request a copy by writing to the MIB at the address above.

hand, businesses that serve as intermediaries between health providers and health plans (referred to as *health-care clearinghouses*) are subject to HIPAA. Included are any companies or organizations that receive and process health information; reformat or standardize medical data; deal with electronic storage; provide billing and pricing services; or establish health management and information systems.

In the course of business, lawyers, accountants, software vendors, and many other similar entities must work with or see your medical records in some form. In such cases, although HIPAA does not regulate their activities, your doctor or health-care provider must have an arrangement with these vendors that assures that they will adopt appropriate safeguards to protect your medical records. In addition, other companies, such as life or automobile insurance companies, Internet health sites, researchers and law enforcement agencies, among others, are not subject to HIPAA, even though they receive medical information from entities that are subject to HIPAA.

> Lawyers, accountants, software vendors, and many other similar entities must work with or see your medical records in some form. In such cases, although HIPAA does not regulate their activities, your doctor or health-care provider must have an arrangement with these vendors that assures that they will adopt appropriate safeguards to protect your medical records.

It is precisely because so many entities can access your information outside of the limits of HIPAA that privacy advocates argue that the act falls short in protecting your medical privacy.

Medical Privacy In Practice: Separating Fact from Fiction

In 1996, William Calvert, a state health worker in Florida's Health and Rehabilitation Services Department, downloaded a list of four thousand HIV-positive people to screen dates for himself. He shared the information with his friends at a local bar. Two newspapers were tipped off to Calvert's activities by an anonymous letter sent by someone who had been in the bar.

In 2002, the pharmaceutical company Eli Lilly settled charges with the Federal Trade Commission relating to the unauthorized disclosure of customers' personal information. The company had inadvertently sent a mass e-mail to customers who had registered to receive e-mail reminders about taking Prozac. The mass e-mail revealed the names and e-mail addresses of all recipients.

Are you still confused about how HIPAA applies to you and your everyday life? Myths abound regarding HIPAA, but the following should set the record straight.

Doctor Visits, Communications, and Transfer of Medical Records

A mother gets home from work and finds her daughter crying in bed, the sheets drawn over her head. Distraught, the daughter simply points to the phone answering machine. The mother plays the saved message, which says, "Hi, May. This is Karen from Dr. Falker's office. I'm calling about your mammogram. The doctor wanted to tell you to call radiology and make an appointment to take another test right away. Call at your earliest convenience at 883-3444 to schedule your appointment." May was not aware of her right to tell the doctor's staff to call her only at work.

Imagine the alarm experienced by the woman who discovered that her medical record of her difficult pregnancy had been accessed 215 times in a short period of time. As reported in 2000 in the Boston Globe, the woman was being treated at a hospital for a very uncommon reproductive disorder. The disorder was so unusual that many hospital staffers consulted the woman's records to find out the intimate details.

You may notice a few changes the next time you visit your doctor. For starters, you need to sign a privacy notice, and signs may be posted about the new HIPAA rules and regulations. You might also notice more protections to prevent patients from seeing other patients' medical information, such as screens placed around the edges of computer monitors. Your doctor or his or her assistant may still call your name in a waiting room, although sign-in sheets may no longer seek the reason for your visit.

Do you want to make sure your kids at home don't accidentally hear the results of your latest blood test? You can now dictate how communications between you and your doctor—which must be confidential—are to be handled. You can specify when and where you want your doctor to call you, and the address to which bills or any medical correspondence should be sent. Further, your doctor can still send you e-mails. The only difference required by the act is that your doctor or provider must use reasonable and appropriate safeguards to ensure the e-mail's confidentiality. Accordingly, you might now expect your doctor to send you encrypted e-mails via a secure computer network.

> Do you want to make sure your kids at home don't accidentally hear the results of your latest blood test? You can now dictate how communications between you and your doctor—which must be confidential— are to be handled.

Your doctor does not need your consent to transfer your medical records to another doctor or health-care provider if it is for treatment purposes. Under HIPAA, treatment includes "consultation between health-care providers regarding a patient and referral of a patient by one provider to another." To assist in your treatment, your doctor can send your medical records to another doctor "by fax or other means."

Hospitals

A great deal of misinformation exists regarding HIPAA regulation of hospitals. First, hospitals may still provide patient information to family members. Medical information is withheld from family only if the patient has so requested. Under HIPAA, a health-care provider may "disclose to a family member, other relative, or a close personal friend of the individual, or any other person identified by the individual" the medical information directly relevant to such person's involvement with the patient's care or payment related to the patient's care. If the patient is unable to agree or object to disclosure because of incapacity or an emergency circumstance, the covered entity may determine whether the disclosure is in the best interests of the patient. The professional judgment of the health-care provider should guide any decision regarding disclosure of protected health information to a family member or friend who is involved in the patient's care, as these disclosures are permitted, but not mandatory.

> Hospitals can continue their practice of providing directory information. However, during the admissions process, you now have the choice to prevent your name from being added to the directory.

Hospitals can continue their practice of providing directory information. However, during the admissions process, you now have the choice to prevent your name from being added to the directory. If you do not choose to do so, be aware that a hospital directory not only includes your name, location in the facility, and condition, but also discloses such information to people who only ask for the patient by name. The hospital may even disclose directory information to the media and members of the clergy. However, under no circumstances will the hospital reveal more than directory information without a patient's authorization.

Any more restricted uses of directory information, such as requiring patients to ask to be listed in, or opt into, the directory, are either the hospital's own policy or indicate confusion about this aspect of HIPAA.

Whether a hospital can notify your family if you are a patient at its facility depends on the circumstances. If you are present and conscious, you can object to the hospital's calling your family. If you are otherwise unable to object, then the hospital may disclose your presence at the hospital based upon the professional judgment of the people treating you. For example, a doctor may call your wife if you were in a car accident and are being treated in the emergency room for minor injuries; a doctor may contact your husband to let him know that you have arrived at the hospital in labor and are about to give birth; a nurse may contact your roommate to let him know that you broke your leg falling down the stairs, had surgery, and are in recovery; and a doctor may, using such professional judgment, call your adult daughter if you are incapacitated to inform her that you have suffered a stroke and are in the intensive-care unit of a hospital

Lastly, don't think that HIPAA has ended the days of patients sharing a room in a hospital. Hospitals are not required to eliminate semiprivate rooms, but doctors will likely exercise greater discretion when talking to a patient who shares a room with another.

Your Children's Medical Records

In 2001, the website of the University of Montana inadvertently posted the psychological test results and records of more than sixty children and teenagers who had visited and were diagnosed by the university.

> Any medical information contained at your child's school is not subject to HIPAA.

As a parent, you can still generally access your children's medical records. If, however, you are not the minor's legal guardian, then you do not have this right. In certain cases, even as a parent or legal guardian, you still cannot access your child's file. These cases include: (1) when the minor is the one who consents to care and the consent of the parent is not required under state or other applicable law; (2) when the minor obtains care at the direction of a court or a person appointed by the court; and (3) when, and to the extent that, the parent agrees that the minor and the health-care provider may have a confidential relationship. For example, as is the case with respect to all personal representatives under HIPAA, a provider may choose not to treat a parent as a personal representative when the provider reasonably believes, in his or her professional judgment, that the child has been or may be subjected to domestic violence, abuse, or neglect, or that treating the parent as the child's personal representative could endanger the child.

Generally, a parent would no longer be the personal representative of his or her child once the child reaches the age of eighteen or becomes emancipated, and therefore would no longer control the health information of his or her child. Of course, any individual can have a personal representative—which may include a parent—who can exercise rights on his or her behalf.

Some of your child's medical information is maintained at your child's school. If you have a child enrolled in any grade from kindergarten to twelfth grade, the school may have records detailing the results of physical examinations for sports, counselor notes, or the nature of miscellaneous visits to the school nurse. Any medical information contained at your child's school is not subject to HIPAA. Instead, the Family Educational Rights and Privacy Act (or FERPA) governs the privacy of all school records. Chapter 11, "Your Everyday Life," further explains the privacy of educational records.

Prescriptions and Pharmacies

You are sick and cannot make it to the pharmacy to pick up your prescriptions. Does this mean you cannot get your prescription filled? HIPAA allows a family member or other individual acting on your behalf to pick up your prescription. In fact, you can also ask a family member or friend to retrieve medical supplies or even X-rays. Nevertheless, your pharmacy may have its own policy that requires your individual presence to get your prescription.

Financial Records

HIPAA provides no protection when it comes to your medical bills. When you pay for treatment or doctor visits, your financial records may very well include sensitive health information. If you pay by check or credit card, your records will, at the very least, indicate the place at which you received your treatments and possibly the treatment itself. A 2003 study by the Federal Reserve showed that 50 percent of all collections showing up on credit reports are for unpaid medical bills. Anyone knowledgeable about the health-care industry may be able to surmise the nature of your treatments from your financial records.

It is nearly impossible to avoid having a financial trail for your medical treatments. As detailed in chapter 5, "Your Money," the Gramm-Leach-Bliley Act (GLB) governs access to and disclosure of your financial information. Under GLB, you may prevent your financial institution from sharing your financial information with nonaffiliated third parties. However, a financial institution may share your financial records, including any medical information contained therein, with its affiliates. In some cases, financial institutions may provide an enhanced sense of privacy for your medical information. If you are particularly concerned about sensitive medical information, you should carefully read your bank's privacy notice or ask a customer representative.

Credit Information

If you do not pay your medical bills, you can expect your unpaid bills to eventually appear on your credit report as unpaid items. HIPAA does not prevent disclosure of your medical information to either a collection agency or a consumer or credit-reporting agency (CRA) such as Equifax, TransUnion, or Experian. See chapter 4, "Your Credit," for more information.

Workplace

At one point in his life, a truck driver consulted a treatment program because he wanted help with his drinking problem. His insurance company disclosed that request to his employer, and the driver was promptly fired.

> **HIPAA provides no protection when it comes to your medical bills.**

Ben Walker, a thirty-year FBI agent, was forced to retire after the FBI randomly obtained Walker's therapy records during a fraud investigation of Walker's therapist. Upon seeing Walker's records, the FBI sought to brand Walker as unfit and took away many of Walker's responsibilities, even though he was later determined to be perfectly capable of handling his work.

Depending on the situation, HIPAA may or may not affect your medical records in the workplace. Indeed, your employment records and medical information may be combined in ways not covered by HIPAA. Understand the situation at your own place of employment, because a number of factors contribute to the overall privacy of your personal medical information in the context of your job.

If you are part of a group medical-insurance plan sponsored by your employer, HIPPA governs the plan's use of your medical information, but not your employer's activities. In this case, HIPPA restricts the information the employer may request about you from the plan itself. However, if your employer is self-insured—meaning that your employer assumes the costs of your health care as opposed to relying on an outside company—then HIPAA regulates your employer's use of your information only *in part*. That means that your employer's use of your health-care data and the claims-processing procedures that your employer establishes are restricted in the same way they are for covered entities. Therefore, regarding its employee insurance program, your employer should issue you a privacy notice, restrict the use and disclosure of your medical information, and undertake other safeguards to protect your medical information. For example, a self-insured employer is required to build a firewall between the health claims operations and normal operations of its company.

> Prospective employers may not make employment decisions based on your medical information without your authorization.

In any event, as discussed in chapter 9, "Your Workplace," prospective employers may not make employment decisions based on your medical information without your authorization. Incidents of employers making job-related decisions based on medical information may violate HIPAA or the federal Americans with Disabilities Act. Nevertheless, your employer may obtain your medical information in ways that are not covered by HIPAA. Possible sources of this information include drug testing, workers' compensation programs, credit reports obtained in background checks prior to employment, or other employee-benefit programs like life or long-term-care insurance.

Health Information and the Internet

As discussed in chapter 7, "Your Computer and The Internet," any time you enter personal information online, you are essentially making the information public. Indeed, HIPAA does not apply to the Internet. Nevertheless, the Internet is a great resource for health information, including interactive forums like chat rooms and Usenet news groups where information about conditions, treatments, and the ensuing outcomes can be found. As always, check each website's privacy notice to see if the information you are providing is used for any other purposes. If you plan to use an Internet site to purchase over-the-counter or prescription drugs, you should carefully review the site's privacy policy. For example, drugstore.com considers your customer information a business asset and will transfer your information to any company that acquires drugstore.com. Even if a privacy notice promises absolute privacy, you should be skeptical about the amount of control you retain once you have posted sensitive data online.

HIPAA and the USA Patriot Act

Your medical records are subject to the same provisions of the USA Patriot Act that require libraries to give federal law enforcement agents your computer usage and book-borrowing information upon request and without telling you. As explained in chapter 11, "Your Everyday Life," Section 215 of the USA Patriot Act applies not only to libraries, but also to any records kept by a third party, including medical records. To obtain your medical records, an agent need not even have probable cause that you are involved in any potential terrorist activity. If an agent certifies that your medical records are required for a foreign intelligence investigation, a judge will rubber-stamp the request. Your doctor would also be obliged to provide your medical records to the agent, and you would not be aware or informed that your information has been shared with the government. In this case, HIPAA provides scant protection for your privacy.

> If an agent certifies that your medical records are required for a foreign intelligence investigation, a judge will rubber-stamp the request. Your doctor would also be obliged to provide your medical records to the agent, and you would not be aware or informed that your information has been shared with the government.

Protect Your Medical Privacy

"The best patients are the worst patients. Nudge, nudge, nudge. Don't sit back and accept anything that fails to satisfy you. Speak up, protect your interests."—Claire Fagin, Dean Emerita, University of Pennsylvania School of Nursing

Here is a detailed list of tips to safeguard your medical privacy without sacrificing great health care:

✱ **Know your HIPAA rights.** As explained in this chapter, HIPAA provides you with certain rights to protect your privacy. Make sure not only that you are familiar with these rights, but also that you exercise them at appropriate times. For example, be certain you receive and read a privacy notice from any covered entities in the health-care industry with which you come into contact. Further, you have the right to access your own private medical information with these companies and providers. If you find inaccurate data in your record, you can request that the provider make alterations and amendments to the file. You may also request a list of disclosures of your medical information (with the exception of those relating to treatment, payment, or operations). In cases of particularly sensitive information, you can ask a provider or other covered entity to restrict how your medical information is used and handled, even if it is not obligated to comply with your request. Finally, you can always file a complaint with Health and Human Services.

✳ **Be proactive with your doctor or other health-care provider.** It is crucial that you investigate the privacy practices of your doctor's office, since this is where much of your medical care occurs. Your doctor's files are also the source from which much of your private medical information originates. You can accomplish this by reading your doctor's privacy notice and other communications and by talking to your doctor about your particular concerns. If need be, compare your doctor's practices to the practices of other doctors. In addition, keep these tips in mind when you visit your doctor:

  ▶ Disclose only information that is relevant to your health. Do not provide extraneous information about your medical history or lifestyle if you believe it would serve no purpose.

  ▶ If you are asked to sign an authorization for use of your medical information, read the form carefully. Try to limit how your information will be used by altering the waiver to your specifications, although your health-care provider is not required to comply with your requests.

  ▶ Ask to see your records. Make any necessary changes to correct inaccurate information.

  ▶ Make sure your doctor's office communicates with you in a manner that you want and in a way that makes you comfortable. If you do not want your doctor or your doctor's staff to leave messages on your home answering machine, provide them with your cellular or business phone number. If you do not want test results to be mailed to your home, give the doctor's staff an alternate address.

▶ Tell your doctor about your particular concerns regarding your private medical information. Perhaps your doctor can devise an appropriate solution to ease your concerns. Perhaps your doctor will delete irrelevant information in your records when those records are photocopied or otherwise sent to third parties, especially your insurance company.

✳ **Access and review your records.** Review your records periodically. In particular, determine if the Medical Insurance Bureau maintains a record on you, and if so, request a copy of the record to check its accuracy. The contact information is listed in the MIB section earlier in this chapter.

✳ **Know your other rights.** Remember that certain records and certain areas of medical treatment are covered by additional legislation. For example, medical information contained within your financial records may be governed by Gramm-Leach-Bliley (GLB), as discussed in chapter 5, "Your Money." Treatments involving substance abuse or chemical dependency, which are obviously sensitive, are regulated, beyond HIPAA, by the Public Health Service Act, which requires signed authorization by the patient for the disclosure of any personal medical information related to relevant conditions or treatment. Genetic testing is covered by HIPAA, but is additionally covered by the Genetic Nondiscrimination Act of 2003.

✳ **Pay your medical bills on time.** Once your medical records appear on your credit report, many companies and institutions are able to see part of your medical information. Accordingly, act before the information appears on your credit report. In many cases bills are sent to collection agencies because of misunderstandings. Perhaps your insurer was supposed to pay the bill. If a bill ends up in the hands of a collection agency because of a misunderstanding, you should dispute the medical bill in writing. Also consider paying the bill yourself while you try to resolve the dispute. If the dispute is resolved in your favor, your insurance company should reimburse you. For more information on your consumer rights in this regard, consult www.ftc.gov.

✳ **Be careful with your own records.** File your copies of your medical records in a secure place that others cannot access. If you need to make photo-copies for an insurance company, make sure you do not need leave additional copies at the copier. If you need to submit any records to your insurance company, submit only what is necessary.

✳ **Read any authorizations to release your information carefully.** Look for language that indicates that your information may be used for marketing purposes, such as when you complete privacy forms in your doctor's office. If you have authorized disclosure of your information and you change your mind, revoke the authorization to prevent any further disclosure by that conduit.

✳ **Limit your exposure in court.** If you ever need to submit medical records in court, limit the portion of the file to what is absolutely necessary, because whatever information is submitted can become public record. Ask to be notified by covered entities if your records are subpoenaed.

✳ **Write your employer.** If you are insured through your employer, state in writing to the administrator of health operations at your company your urgent desire to limit any wrongful disclosure of your medical information.

✳ **Avoid public health screenings.** Do not engage in health screenings offered in public places like malls and parking lots, as they are often intended to harvest your medical information for marketing purposes, or to compile medical profiles that are saleable. However, if your employer has an on-site health clinic—and that clinic transmits medical information electronically, as it is likely to do—then your visit to your employer's clinic would be subject to HIPAA regulations.

✳ **Be careful online.** Be cautious about revealing your medical information on the Internet; consider not using your real name or e-mail address in health-related chat rooms or Usenet news groups.

✳ **Avoid consumer surveys.** Do not include your own or your family's sensitive medical information on consumer reports that arrive in your mail. These mailings are often packaged as sweepstakes invitations or opportunities to win free coupons.

✳ **Be careful when ordering medical products.** When you order products from a medical-supply company, be explicit in requesting it not share your information with any other entity.

✳ **Take your name off the hospital directory.** If you are admitted to a hospital or other facility for a procedure or treatment, remember that you are to be given the choice, as part of the admissions process, of whether or not to be listed in the facility's directory.

✳ **Pay the bill yourself with cash.** In extreme cases, if you want to be certain your condition is not disclosed, visit a different doctor, do not provide the doctor's staff with insurance information, and pay the bill yourself with cash for maximum privacy protection.

✳ **Ask your insurance company questions.** Contact your insurance company, and inquire about how and if it shares your personal information with any other parties. State in writing your desire to restrict any wrongful disclosure of your information.

THE BOTTOM LINE

▸ Open up anyway. Your personal medical information and history can be revealing, extensive, and sensitive, but you still want to fully disclose your medical conditions to ensure the best possible treatment.

▸ Hip HIPAA hurray! The federal medical-privacy law referred to as HIPAA creates minimum federal standards but applies only to three types of entities: health-care providers who transmit information electronically, health-care and insurance plans, and health-care clearinghouses such as health-care billing services.

▸ HIPAA limitations. Beyond the three entities mentioned above, many other companies and institutions can access your medical information. HIPAA does not apply to many entities and therefore reinforces why you still need to be cautious with your personal medical information.

▸ HIPAA everyday. You will encounter the effects of HIPAA when you visit your doctor, go to the hospital, get prescriptions from pharmacies, pay your bills, or seek treatment for your family members. Make sure you fully understand your rights under HIPAA.

▶ Don't rely solely on HIPAA. Beyond the rights you get under HIPAA, you can protect your medical privacy in many other ways, such as being careful with your medical records, being cautious when using the Internet for medical information or medical purchases, avoiding public health screenings, staying away from medical surveys, and much more.

Your Everyday Life

I'm a little bit worried about the privacy of these new video phones

You are grocery shopping and feeling somewhat distracted. You stop to read the back of a cookie box when a man stooping behind you positions his cell phone underneath your skirt and snaps a photo. You are totally unaware of what has happened and also unaware that the photo will be seen by millions when it is published on the photographer's website.

Your family signs up for a location-tracking system that turns your cell phone into a technological tattletale. Every time you leave your house, your wife is sent an automatic e-mail alert: "John has left the house at 9:32 P.M."

Your local car rental agency has a new policy that requires renters to supply a thumbprint as identification. You learn that the company does not destroy the prints after you return the car, but keeps the prints on file for seven years with no promise of safeguarding them. Moreover, the company used a GPS device to track your entire trip in its car and plans to keep those records in your file, too.

Every time you look in your rearview mirror you see your freaky ex-boyfriend, following you to work, to the mall, and anywhere else you go. You don't know it, but he placed a GPS device under the hood of your car and the device is giving him the information he needs to stalk you.

Someone posts your personal information with an online dating service. The posting includes your picture, your real name and address, and your alleged desire to have casual sex.

As you go about your everyday life you are likely to encounter invasions of your privacy, many of which are a result of the terrorist attacks of September 11, 2001. No event in recent history has had such a profound effect on national security, law enforcement, individual civil liberties, and privacy. As a direct response to the attacks, Congress enacted the vastly complex and ominously titled Uniting and Strengthening America by Providing Appropriate Tools Required to Intercept and Obstruct Terrorism Act, commonly known as the Patriot Act. The Patriot Act greatly expanded the government's powers to access your personal records, search your home, and monitor your Internet, e-mail, and phone usage—and more.

The hijackings on September 11 changed air travel forever. New measures to strengthen security in airports and in the sky have been, or will be, implemented. Some are highly invasive, including background investigations and body-scanning at security checkpoints. A new system that would score each passenger prior to departure is still in the works.

The technologies you use every day compromise your privacy in subtle ways. These include the cell phone that keeps you connected to your family and office; your car's OnStar system, which offers directions when you are lost; the E-ZPass that speeds you through highway tollbooths; and the subway card that eliminates the need for tokens.

Your leisure time may also be hazardous to your privacy. Online dating may be a superhighway to identity theft or worse. Borrowing a book from a library, renting videos or DVDs, or getting tickets to your favorite sporting event or concert may reveal more about you than you'd ever expect.

The risks vary depending upon the technology. Use of cellular phones may allow government officials, nosy hackers, and criminals to eavesdrop on your conversations. The phones may also make you a target of cell phone fraud. Hidden surveillance cameras tape you throughout your day—at the ATM, at the convenience store, in the elevator, at a busy intersection—and they compromise your personal privacy. A photo snapped without your knowledge or consent on a stranger's cell phone camera is a privacy invasion, particularly if you happen to be dripping wet from the shower in your health club locker room. Global-positioning chips, planted in a myriad of devices, sometimes without your knowledge, allow others to track you everywhere you go.

Do you have any education or criminal records that you'd like to keep private? Depending upon the circumstances, these also might be exposed.

Who wants to know where you've been, what you buy, or what you do with your spare time? The answer is anyone, to varying degrees and by various means: the government and your neighbor, your ex-wife and your new girlfriend, the company that rented you a car, and the business that wants to sell you a car.

Privacy and the Patriot Act

Think twice before you search the Internet and send an e-mail. A Web search for information on crop dusters, for instance, may not be such a great idea even if you are a farmer. Likewise, you might reconsider sending any e-mail joke entitled "Top Ten Reasons to Blow Up Washington Monuments." Between the government's new surveillance power and the use of its old favorite, the Internet-tapping Carnivore, an eavesdropping system developed by the FBI, you may just find you have some explaining to do.

Massachusetts state representative Kay Kahn was shocked to discover that her bank blocked a $300 wire transfer because she is married to a naturalized U.S. citizen named Nasir Khan. Apparently someone may have been using her husband's name as an alias, which resulted in the Kahns being put on a watch list.

> **Nearly 250 cities, towns, and counties— encompassing more than 19 million Americans—have passed resolutions condemning the Patriot Act.**

When President Bush signed the Patriot Act into law on October 26, 2001, your expectations of privacy were dramatically reduced in one fell swoop. As a response to September 11, the 342-page law was passed hastily and with little debate or study. The act is designed to expand the resources available to law enforcement officials to investigate and prevent both international and domestic terrorism. Proponents say that the Patriot Act merely filled the holes in existing laws to fight terrorism, and that, without the act, you would not be secure. Moreover, even if your civil liberties are affected, proponents say that the United States has a history of expanding such rights in peacetime and contracting them during times of national crisis or emergencies.

Critics denounce the Patriot Act as trampling on civil liberties, privacy, and the Constitution. They feel the act's provisions are too broad, and the act enables the government to spy on law-abiding citizens. They fear that the act has been and will continue to be misused for purposes for which it was never intended. Indeed, nearly 250 cities, towns, and counties—encompassing more than 19 million Americans—have passed resolutions condemning the Patriot Act, and numerous lawsuits have been filed to challenge the act. Ordinary citizens, both liberal and conservative groups, and pundits—from the American Civil Liberties Union on the left to William Safire on the right—have been vocal in their opposition to the act.

A comprehensive analysis of the Patriot Act—with provisions on everything from immigration to money laundering—is beyond the scope of this book. Further, a number of different aspects of the Patriot Act are currently subject to judicial review at all levels from the U.S. Supreme Court to the district courts. As a result, this section will limit discussion to some of the surveillance provisions of the act, and how they threaten your privacy. These provisions apply broadly to visitors, permanent residents, *and* U.S. citizens, and you can be a target of these surveillance tools even if you are not a terrorist suspect.

This is what the Patriot Act has enabled government to do:

Access to Consumer Records. Before the Patriot Act, the government had to show probable cause (a strong reason) to obtain a search warrant before accessing your private records from third parties, such as banks, telecommunication providers, hospitals, churches, libraries, bookstores, hotels, airlines, credit card companies, and so forth. This is no longer the case. Under the act, the government need only obtain an *ex parte* court order, which does not require the government to notify you and therefore does not give you the opportunity to contest the order's validity. This court order is akin to a rubber stamp, since judges have virtually no authority to deny it. Furthermore, to obtain the court order the government does not have to offer any evidence of wrongdoing, but only has to certify that the information is relevant to an investigation. (This is equivalent to the government having a belief that the information is relevant, and it is a considerably lower standard than probable cause.) Finally, the party made to turn over your records is gagged, and thus prohibited from notifying you or anyone else about the search. For example, if a government official asks your librarian to turn over a list of all the books you've taken out and a record of your Internet usage at the library, the librarian would be required by law to immediately comply and not tell you what happened.

> If a government official asks your librarian to turn over a list of all the books you've taken out and a record of your Internet usage at the library, the librarian would be required by law to immediately comply and not tell you what happened.

Bottom line: Without a warrant and with only minimal judicial oversight, the government can conduct records searches on you and virtually anyone.

Sneak-and-Peek Searches. When investigating ordinary criminal cases, the government must obtain a warrant and give you notice before presenting it to search your home. This principle of *knock and announce* is part of the Fourth Amendment. An exception was made under the Foreign Intelligence Surveillance Act of 1978 (FISA) to make it easier to investigate foreign agents suspected of terrorism. In FISA cases, a variety of warrants called *sneak-and-peek* are obtained from a secret court. A sneak-and-peak warrant allows the government to search your home when you are not there, rummage through your personal belongings, and seize physical property including your hard drive, but not tell you about it until some point in the future. The Patriot Act expands the use of FISA sneak-and-peak warrants from terrorism cases to all criminal investigations. The act requires only that notice be given to you after a search within a reasonable amount of time, but the time may be extended for good cause. The problem is that without notice or your presence, you have no opportunity to object if the scope of the warrant is exceeded, or if the police are searching the wrong house.

Bottom line: The Patriot Act broadens what was once a limited exception to the standard probable cause and notice requirements of a legal search. Police will be reluctant to return to the previous knock-and-announce standard.

Expansion of Wiretap Laws. As in the case of sneak-and-peak searches, the act allows the government to use a lower standard than before when obtaining a wiretap order. The Foreign Intelligence Surveillance Act previously allowed wiretaps when foreign intelligence gathering was the primary purpose. The Patriot Act allows wiretaps in criminal cases and justifies them by saying that foreign intelligence gathering is a significant purpose for the tap. In addition, the act expands the government's surveillance powers by authorizing the roving wiretap. Wiretaps are no longer limited to one phone or one computer within one jurisdiction, but instead apply to any phone or computer you may use nationwide, whether or not it belongs to you. For instance, the government can order a tap on library, university, or Internet café computers and monitor not only you, but also every other user of that computer. The facility, such as the library, is not allowed to tell you or anyone else that the monitoring is taking place.

Bottom line: The wiretap provisions not only dispense with the probable cause standard of the Fourth Amendment, but they also weaken the judicial oversight that guards against government fishing expeditions.

Internet Monitoring. Pen register/trap and trace (PR/TT) searches allow law enforcement to monitor telephone numbers dialed from or received by a suspect's telephone. Monitoring addressing information alone is allowed, but the actual content of the call is off-limits. PR/TT search orders have always been available to law enforcement under a low standard; they need only show that the information is relevant to an investigation. The act expands PR/TT laws to enable the government to wiretap Internet use, e-mail, and other forms of electronic communication under the same low standard as telephone PR/TT searches. However, what constitutes content monitoring in electronic communications is not as clearly defined or limited as in the telephone context. For instance, in the case of e-mail, the addressing information and the content move together in packets. To execute a PR/TT order, the government obtains an entire e-mail message but then must separate the e-mail address from the content of the message. With no external authority monitoring the government's actions, how confident are you that the government is doing what it says it is?

CARNIVORE

Carnivore is an astonishingly invasive computer system developed by the FBI. When connected to an ISP network, Carnivore can intercept millions of e-mail messages per second. Carnivore enables the FBI to monitor not only the e-mails of its target, but also millions of unrelated e-mails of innocent people who just happen to use the same ISP as the target. Many people think the Patriot Act introduced Carnivore, when in fact Carnivore was in use for a year before the act. The deployment of Carnivore initially required a court order to monitor criminal activity, according to FBI and Department of Justice Officials.

The Patriot Act does not specifically mention Carnivore by name. Nonetheless, under the act the government has used Carnivore in PR/TT mode to gather addressing information. This means that the government does not have to obtain a full wiretap order, but instead a much lower standard court order, and can potentially see a lot more than just addressing information.

Bottom line: The government can review significantly more information than merely the website URL or the To and From lines of e-mails if it is supposed to decide for itself what constitutes content.

Combined, the categories above underscore the privacy concerns that have been voiced about the Patriot Act:

- **Centralizes power in one branch of government.** Our system of government is based on the three branches, the executive, legislative, and judicial, exerting checks and balances on each other's power. The act creates one locus of power—the executive branch—to the exclusion of all the others.
- **Secrecy.** The Department of Justice has refused to reveal anything about how the provisions of the act have been used. The department's response to any query has been that the information is classified, if it responds at all. The fact that most warrants are approved in closed courts has also contributed to the aura of secrecy surrounding the act. In the words of one staff attorney at the ACLU, "It's this wonderful union of Orwell and Kafka."
- **Ordinary U.S. citizens will be swept into the act's net.** By eroding the long-standing distinction between domestic law enforcement and foreign intelligence gathering, the act sidesteps Fourth Amendment protections. This means that U.S. citizens, legal residents, and visitors are at risk of being spied upon by the government.

Airline Travel

A mother and her baby passed through screening before boarding a flight at JFK. Security guards at the checkpoint insisted the mother drink the three bottles of breast milk in her carry-on to prove the bottles did not contain explosives.

An 80-year-old Grand Rapids great-grandmother was strip-searched at the airport after her knee-replacement set off metal detectors.

To add insult to injury, a man walked into the room where the search was being conducted because the door was not locked.

NASA, in cooperation with a commercial firm, is developing brain-monitoring devices to identify terrorists. Using noninvasive neuro-electric sensors to collect passengers' brain-wave and heartbeat patterns, the device will apparently determine if you are having any suspicious thoughts. Critics wonder if the fear of flying—or of the device itself—will trigger the sensor.

> Even if you are willing to give up *all* your privacy rights within an airport setting, are there adequate safeguards in place to ensure that the personal information you will need to reveal to fly stays confined to the airport setting?

More than 100 million Americans fly each year, and the hijackings of September 11 changed the experience for every one of us. The events demonstrated that lax security at the nation's airports could no longer be tolerated. In response, the Transportation Security Administration (TSA) implemented new security measures such as better training for screeners, machines capable of checking bags for explosives, fortified cockpit doors, and an increased number of air marshals on flights. All these measures make good safety sense.

From a privacy perspective, travelers have indicated a willingness to relinquish a certain amount of privacy for better security. But how much is too much? Some measures already in effect and others only in the planning stage may cross the line of what you think is acceptable. Even if you are willing to give up *all* your privacy rights within an airport setting, are there adequate safeguards in place to ensure that the personal information you will need to reveal to fly stays confined to the airport setting? Here are some of the surveillance technologies already in use:

▸ **Body scanners.** New technology scans some passengers through their clothing to detect plastic weapons and explosives that can slip through metal detectors. These electronic strip searches may one day be used on a large-scale basis, x-raying people as they pass unsuspecting on people conveyor belts. For the time being, the concern is that the images remain private, as you would not likely want to see your X-rays appearing on the Internet.

▶ **Biometrics.** Biometrics is technology that uses biological traits to identify individuals. The most common biometrics use fingerprint, retinal or iris scanning, or face recognition. Although scanning faces in a crowd and comparing those faces to a database of suspects (as was done at the Tampa Super Bowl) has not proven ready for prime time, other uses of biometrics, such as fingerprint scanning, are gaining popularity. Authorities began scanning fingerprints and photographing foreigners from certain countries arriving at airports as part of the Homeland Security Department's US-VISIT program. Fingerprint scanning cannot, however, weed out criminals who have yet to make it into the terrorist database. Concerns about this practice relate to how the database is stored and who has access to it. Do you want your fingerprint to be like your social security number, possibly available for sale on the Internet?

> **Do you want your fingerprint to be like your social security number, possibly available for sale on the Internet?**

▶ **Cabin videocams.** Southeast Airlines says it plans to install digital video cameras throughout the cabins of its planes to record the faces and activities of passengers. The airline plans to store the videos for up to ten years. Privacy advocates are worried that the videos would capture personal information: every business or pleasure trip taken, private conversations, and every book title a passenger reads. They also worry about improper access to the videos' content.

▶ **Smart cards.** These are ID cards equipped with memory chips that store personal data, and they can be used to track your movements. The cards would speed up airport check-in, but critics warn that they would amount to a national ID system that would facilitate government surveillance. Detractors also say that Smart Cards will not deter terrorism; terrorists, like those involved in September 11, or identity thieves would simply obtain cards that appear to be legitimate.

CAPPS II

Have you been a passenger on a Jet Blue airplane? In 2002, Jet Blue provided the records of 5 million of its passengers to a Pentagon contractor, which then used other databases from a data-mining company to augment almost half of those records with other personal information, such as income, occupation, and social security numbers. The contractor used the information to categorize the passengers based on their perceived threat levels. Jet Blue released the information in violation of its own privacy policy, and without passengers' consent. In fairness, Jet Blue apparently did not know that the contractor was conducting a data-mining program that looked like a blueprint for CAPPS II. This incident does, however, make you think twice about the sensitive data you provide when you travel.

Despite concerns from airlines and privacy advocates, the U.S. government plans to implement an upgraded and expanded profiling system known as the Computer Assisted Passenger Prescreening System, or CAPPS II. Airlines are fearful, as in the Jet Blue incident, of alienating their customers when they hand over passenger records. Privacy advocates and even Congress have grave concerns that the Transportation Security Administration (TSA) has yet to allay.

The actual date for the implementation of CAPPS II has not yet been finalized. In its current design, the CAPPS II program conducts a two-step background check on every airline traveler. First, the system verifies your identity by comparing information provided in the reservation system against an enormous commercial database, using credit reports and other information that data aggregators compile. Second, the system uses some sort of algorithm to assign you a risk score using unknown sources and secret intelligence information to evaluate whether you pose a risk to security. If you are assigned a Green rating, you will pass through security as normal; if you are assigned a Yellow rating, you will require additional screening; and if you are assigned a Red rating, you will not be allowed to fly and potentially can be detained or arrested.

The disturbing features of this profiling behemoth have been extensively discussed and critiqued by numerous groups, including the American Civil Liberties Union. The criticism has focused on four aspects of the profiling system:

▶ **What data is used?** The TSA has not indicated what data is used to probe into your identity and assess your threat risk. However, new systems may link your airline reservation to the commercial databases of data-mining companies such as Acxiom and information companies such as LexisNexis. These links may reveal certain personal and consumer information about you, such as information relating to your purchasing habits, your magazine subscriptions, or your family life. Moreover, the TSA is not legally required to indicate the types of data it will use.

> **Won't mistakes be made?** Given that 100 million Americans fly annually, and even assuming an impossibly unrealistic accuracy rate of 99.9 percent, mistakes will be made. This means that an estimated one hundred thousand individuals will be affected annually. Not only will mistakes make life miserable for a lot of innocent people, but they will also increase the difficulty of finding the real terrorists among all the false positives.

> **Is it fair?** The profiling systems will likely discriminate against certain groups, such as poor people and minorities who typically score lower on credit reports or have no credit at all, or people of certain religions or ethnic backgrounds.

> **Will it really make travel safer?** The effectiveness of the system is suspect because terrorists may bypass the system by committing identity theft and assuming an innocent person's identity.

> New systems may link your airline reservation to the commercial databases of data-mining companies such as Acxiom and information companies such as LexisNexis. These links may reveal certain personal and consumer information about you, such as information relating to your purchasing habits, your magazine subscriptions, or your family life.

Your Travel Data

CAPPS II and Jet Blue reveal the dangers of conjoining your travel data with other personal information. But travel data on its own is extremely sensitive by nature. Computerized records, such as those stored by the Galileo reservation system, one of the world's largest, can reveal myriad details on your travel history: everywhere you have ever traveled, when you traveled, your travel companions, whether you asked for one bed or two in your hotel room, your children's names, your dietary restrictions, and so on.

Unlike medical, financial, or even video records, your travel records are unregulated and open to unrestricted access.

Frequent-traveler records pose a similar privacy risk. Databases containing these records constitute one of the airlines' biggest assets. Although there are no reports of such data being sold, if an airline were ever to go out of business, the data could wind up being sold or transferred. Your information could wind up in the hands of . . . well, who knows? In and of itself, the fact that you've traveled to Florida last April might not be interesting to marketers, but if it were entered into a database and coupled with other information they have about where you stayed and who you were with and where you shopped, you might be concerned.

> Unlike medical, financial, or even video records, your travel records are unregulated and open to unrestricted access.

THE NEW MATRIX

CAPPS II is not the only massive profiling project in development; there's also Matrix. Matrix is an ominous example of a huge profiling project developed not by the government, but by a private company. Florida-based Seisint developed Matrix, and the company claims that it is the largest database on the planet, with more than 20 billion records. To date, Seisint has received $12 million in federal funding. The company combines driver's license, vehicle registration, and criminal records with other government and commercially available data to produce detailed dossiers on its targets. The profiles include names, social security numbers, photographs, birth dates, current and old addresses, financial information, driving records, criminal histories, information on family and friends, and so on. At least fourteen states have considered using Matrix, but as of the end of 2003, only Florida was using Matrix at full capacity. Nine states, including New York, California, and Texas have left the program since its inception. Worries about privacy abound. As Barry Steinhardt of the ACLU articulated, "Programs like Matrix are a quantum leap backward in the protection of our privacy."

There is little you can do to prevent programs such as CAPPS from collecting information about you, but there are a few ways to make your flying experience easier under the circumstances.

> If an airline were ever to go out of business, your frequent flyer records could wind up being sold or transferred. Your information could wind up in the hands of . . . well, who knows?

✳ **Don't joke.** Don't try to spice up your life or that of other passengers by telling inappropriate jokes about bombs, guns, or lethal tweezers. These jokes will not amuse security personnel, and they will likely result in you being delayed or possibly even arrested.

✳ **Be aware that certain ticket information might cause you to be flagged as a suspicious traveler.** Triggers include one-way tickets, tickets paid for with cash, and tickets purchased at the last minute.

✳ **Check your credit report for inaccuracies.** If possible, find out if you have an unwarranted criminal record (case of mistaken identity, case dismissed, acquittal, and so forth).

Cell Phones

Imagine if, as you passed a popular fast-food restaurant, you got the following text message on your cell phone: "We notice your visits to us have dropped off by 75 percent this month; if you are concerned about your love handles, here's a coupon for one of our new super salads."

Reports indicate that the National Security Agency may have eavesdropped on U.N. Security Council members in New York to determine how they intended to vote on a proposed resolution about Iraq. When asked about the rumors, one European diplomat was blasé when responding, "I assume every phone conversation I have either on the cell phone or at the office is listened to by several people."

Do you use a cell phone? If so, you are in good company. In 2003, approximately 90 million cell phones were sold in North America, according to Strategy Analytics, a Boston-based consulting firm, and about 500 million units were sold worldwide, according to the Gartner Group.

Are you worried that someone can listen in on your cell phone calls? It is a frightening thought, especially given the above examples. However, unless you are using an older, analog phone or are in a security-sensitive business, you shouldn't worry too much. For analog cell phone users, eavesdropping is a genuine problem. Analog cell phones transmit radio signals that can be easily overheard by anyone with a scanner.

> Digital phones still rely on analog towers during peak calling times if the digital system is overloaded, or when the user has entered a roaming area, so even digital phones are not entirely secure.

Most newer cell phones are digital. Digital transmissions are scrambled for better protection and thus are less vulnerable to eavesdropping. Digital networks carry an estimated 85 percent of wireless conversations. Unfortunately, digital phones still rely on analog towers during peak calling times (usually weekdays from 7 A.M. to 6 or 7 P.M.) if the digital system is overloaded, under maintenance, or when you enter a roaming area, so even digital phones are not entirely secure. Additionally, some Bluetooth-enabled cell phones are vulnerable to attackers who exploit a security flaw to download stored numbers and other information—a practice known as "snarfing."

It is generally illegal to purposefully eavesdrop on someone else's cell phone call, although exceptions exist for monitoring by law enforcement agencies. Under the Communications Assistance for Law Enforcement Act of 1994 (CALEA), telephone companies are required to ensure that their systems can be accessed by law enforcement. The Patriot Act has made it easier for law enforcement to eavesdrop on your cell phone calls by eliminating the need for the probable cause standard.

To protect your cell phone privacy:

✳ **Use a digital cell phone, and pay attention if your phone switches to analog mode.** When in digital mode, your phone screen may show the letter *D* on the phone's display screen. You may not be able to tell if your digital cell phone switches to analog mode.

✳ **Never divulge sensitive or personal information while talking on a cell phone.** Take this precaution even if the phone is digital, especially during peak times.

✳ **Switch off Bluetooth functionality.** If you have a Bluetooth-enabled handset, take this precaution if you're concerned about "snarfing."

✳ **Contact your wireless provider.** Ask about phones that use encryption for added security.

Recording Conversations

Can you tape your own cell phone calls? The rules vary by state. In general, the rule is similar to the rule that governs recording conversations on a landline. Some states require that both parties to the conversation consent to the recording, but the majority of states require that only one party consents. In states covered by the latter rule, you can record virtually all your conversations. A chart of all states' electronic surveillance laws is available at www.ncsl.org/programs/lis/cip/surveillance.htm.

Cell phone makers seeking to differentiate their products are adding recording features to their models, and as they do, legal and privacy issues will become a hornet's nest in the near future. Several companies, including Nokia and Japan's NTT DoCoMo, have already begun experimenting with recording features.

Cell Phone Fraud

A Florida man was charged with 139 counts of cell phone subscription fraud for illegally obtaining victims' identification information and activating cell phone accounts in their names. The fraud cost the cell phone carrier around $80,000 in lost charges.

A Florida judge sentenced a different Florida man to more than eleven years behind bars and ordered him to pay almost $1 million in restitution for running a cell phone scam while he was in prison. The scammer, pretending to be a Sony Pictures executive, used an

authentic Sony account and tax ID number he had stolen to order
more than one thousand phones for "an upcoming film shoot."

There are two types of cell phone fraud: subscriber fraud and cell phone cloning fraud. Subscriber fraud occurs when an identity thief obtains your personal information and uses it to set up a cell phone account in your name. The thief racks up charges under your name, fails to pay, and the phone company looks to you to settle the matter. The bills for the fraudulent cell phone account are not sent to you, so you have no way of knowing this is occurring until it has already happened. The Federal Trade Commission reports that phone/utility fraud is the second most common form of identity theft (after credit card fraud), and half of this fraud is wireless-subscription fraud. Tips presented in chapter 3, "Your Identity," will prevent identity theft from happening to you.

Each cell phone is equipped with an Electronic Serial Number and Mobile Identification Number (ESN/MIN). Cloning fraud occurs when a thief intercepts a cell phone signal and clones your phone's ID numbers. The ESN/MIN are then reprogrammed into the computer chip of another cell phone. After cloning, both the legitimate and the fraudulent cell phones have the same ESN/MIN combination. You, the legitimate phone user, are billed for the cloned phone's calls.

Cloning fraud is far less common for a variety of reasons, including the use of more secure, digital phones, new technological defenses implemented by the wireless companies, and the Wireless Telephone Protection Act of 1998, which criminalizes the use or sale of cloning hardware or software.

To avoid cell phone fraud, take the following steps:

✳ **Use a digital cell phone and pay attention if your phone switches to analog mode.**

✳ **Review your bills.** Look for calls that you did not make and report them to your service provider.

✳ **Never leave your phone out in public.** If you're at a coffeehouse, bring your phone with you while you run to the bathroom. If you leave the phone unattended, someone can either steal the phone or remove the phone's battery and get instant access to the ESN/MIN.

Your Image

The privacy of your image is compromised in many ways. Surveillance cameras and cell phone cameras pose particular risks.

Surveillance Cameras

> In Tuscaloosa, Alabama, a traffic-monitoring camera that usually remained stationary was panning and zooming in on pedestrians walking down the street. An officer in the state troopers' office had taken control of the camera. How was he discovered? The footage, which consisted mostly of young women's breasts and buttocks, was accidentally aired during the traffic segment of a local cable TV show.

Do you know how many times a day your privacy is compromised by unseen video cameras? Imagine a typical day in your life. You leave your house and are videotaped by your neighbor's private security camera. You buy your coffee at a local convenience store and are taped by the store's security system. You buy a fare card to ride the subway and are taped by the transit authority. You cross a busy intersection and are taped by a traffic camera installed by the city. You withdraw money from an ATM and are taped by the bank. It's only 9 A.M. and you have already had more video exposure than Paris Hilton.

Video surveillance is increasing in cities such as Washington, D.C., and New York. For instance, in the relatively small midtown area of New York, there were 284 surveillance cameras in May 2003. As surveillance cameras proliferate, people are just beginning to question whether the loss of privacy they encounter in fact results in increased security. In Great Britain, which is years ahead of the United States in surveillance, there are 1.5 million video cameras in public places, and the typical Londoner is photographed on average three hundred times per day. The cameras have not deterred street crime and there is no known instance, according to the ACLU, of a video camera thwarting a terrorist attack. There have, however, been instances of London surveillance footage making it onto Internet porn sites, and even an indecent shot of the late Princess of Wales.

In the United States, a backlash is beginning to form against surveillance cameras (called red-light cameras) used at busy intersections to catch drivers who are running red lights. Hundreds of thousands of people receive tickets every year because of photos taken by red-light cameras in use in about sixty cities and counties in the United States. Critics, many of whom object to the intrusiveness of the cameras, say that the primary motivation for installing them is profit rather than safety. In San

> As surveillance cameras proliferate, people are just beginning to question whether the loss of privacy they encounter in fact results in increased security.

Diego, the first court case was decided against the use of red-light cameras to issue tickets to speeding motorists. The court did not go so far as to ban the cameras entirely, but it did decide that the way the San Diego program operated was illegal. San Diego's program created a conflict of interest by allowing the same private company that installed and operated the cameras to collect a sizable cut from each ticket issued. San Diego has since switched to a different camera system.

Camera Phones

Imagine you are naked in your health club's locker room when you notice that the man changing next to you is holding his cell phone at an unusual angle. Did he just snap a quick photo of your genitals? Perhaps this explains why health clubs around the country are banning cell phones in their locker rooms.

Singer Britney Spears, aware of the dangers of unflattering candid camera shots, demanded that all camera cell phones be confiscated before she appeared at a Rolling Stone party in Los Angeles.

Camera-equipped cell phones are the latest fad in a world obsessed with personal communication devices. An estimated 80 million camera phones are in use today across the globe, albeit mostly in Asia and Europe. There is little doubt these devices will become ubiquitous in the United States. New phones that record videotape are already being produced.

As these camera phones proliferate, privacy has become the paramount concern worldwide. Hungary has made it an offense to photograph people without their consent; and South Korea requires that new phones emit a loud beep when taking photos. In the United States, where the phones are newer, the backlash is just beginning. Stories are cropping up in the press about camera cell phone bans at certain celebrity parties, health club locker rooms, certain federal courthouses, schools, public rest rooms, Air Force bases, and so on. Concerns

> An estimated 80 million camera phones are in use today across the globe, albeit mostly in Asia and Europe. There is little doubt these devices will become ubiquitous in the United States.

about camera phones have also caused companies such as Volkswagen and Samsung to ban the phones from their research and development departments out of fear of corporate espionage.

Portable cameras have been in use for a long time. Why the sudden outcry over camera phones? Part of the problem is that on first glance, these phones are virtually indistinguishable from regular cell phones. There is, therefore, a certain stealthiness to the camera phone, with its small size and discreet lens. Finally, the bigger problem is the ability to immediately disseminate the photos, either to other camera phones or straight to the Internet.

To their credit, camera phones do bring certain benefits that, in certain cases, outweigh their privacy risks. Indeed, camera phones have many legitimate uses, aside from taking pictures of your friends and family. For example, they have been a boon to law enforcement efforts. In one case, a New Jersey boy thwarted a kidnapping attempt by taking photos of the man who tried to lure him into a car as well as the car's license plate. Cell phone cameras have also been handy for documenting events, real estate, accident scenes, and more.

LAWS GOVERNING CAMERA OR VIDEO VOYEURISM

Technology has developed at the speed of light, but the legal system has not kept pace. As is the case with other new technologies, the law has not adequately addressed the new privacy threats posed by surveillance and cellular cameras.

Courts traditionally have held that there is no expectation of privacy in public places. As discussed in past chapters, courts only find there has been a breach of privacy when one has a reasonable expectation of privacy. As such, courts have held in the past that in places such as locker rooms, bathrooms, and dressing rooms people do have a reasonable expectation of privacy.

The first cellular camera cases to reach the courts will probably involve the use of cellular cameras in private settings, and the courts will have to balance your right to carry a phone with others' right to privacy. But the courts will also have to decide whether, just because you are in public, it is any less of a violation when someone shoots a picture up your skirt or down your blouse. A similar problem exists in the lack of a federal law to cover the clandestine use of a video camera in public, or video voyeurism as it is called. Some experts believe that, at some point, courts will find a limit to the concept of waiving your privacy rights merely because you are in public.

Some states are beginning to respond to these problems with legislation, but the coverage is usually quite specific. Missouri, for instance, bans only nonconsensual camera or video use when there is nudity involved and the filming occurs in a place where an individual would have a reasonable expectation of privacy. Only a few states, including California or Louisiana, abolish the distinction between private and public spaces. Louisiana, for instance, outlaws the use of any camera or video where the subject has not consented and the filming or photographing is done for a "lewd and lascivious purpose." Furthermore, the state also prohibits the dissemination of the images by phone, e-mail, or the Internet.

A list of states that have passed laws addressing camera or video voyeurism is available at www.ncsl.org/programs/lis/cip/surveillance.htm.

Tracking Technologies

A family that rented a car from Payless Car Rental in San Francisco was horrified to learn that it had incurred an extra $3,000 in fees by taking the vehicle beyond state lines. The family was unaware that its rental car was equipped with a device that allowed the company to track its exact route.

New technologies make it possible for your precise location to be pinpointed. Naturally, privacy concerns arise with respect to these tracking devices which include your cell phone and other Global Positioning System–enabled (GPS) technologies. According to analysts, about 42 million Americans will be using some sort of location-based technology by 2005.

Cell Phone Tracking

You are standing in front of your local upscale coffee emporium when you get an unsolicited text message on your phone from StarCoffee: "We notice you are standing in front of Hoity-Toity Coffee. Did you know that StarCoffee's lattes are cheaper than Hoity-Toity's?"

Your daughter is an hour late returning home from school. No worry, she has a cell phone that monitors her location. To see if she's at the library or at Jason's house again, all you have to do is check a map on your computer.

The FCC mandated that by 2005, wireless carriers must be able to automatically locate callers who dial 911 in emergencies. Millions of phones already are E911-capable, which means that your cell phone company can keep tabs on you by means of a Global Positioning System (GPS) chip in your cell phone. The chip calculates your geographical coordinates by receiving signals from satellites. In the United States, cell phone users already make over one hundred thousand E911 calls every day.

Your cell phone may also track you through a process called triangulation.

Triangulating phones broadcast your identification number to the nearest antennas, which enable your carrier to know where you are at any given moment. Your carrier can track you as you pass from one antenna to the next, calculating your location by the time it takes for the signal to reach the antennas around it.

Cell phone tracking systems are beneficial in case of emergency. Do you remember the horrific story of the four teenagers who drowned after dialing 911 from their boat on Long Island Sound when no one could locate them? Such technology might have saved their lives.

> What is to prevent your cell phone carrier from selling or sharing your personal location information with direct marketers?

Real privacy issues with these phones exist, and there is no legal framework established to offer guidance. What is to prevent your cell phone carrier from selling or sharing your personal location information with direct marketers, as in the StarCoffee scenario cited above? "Marketers are foaming at the mouth about the prospect of sending e-coupons," according to Jason Catlett, the founder and president of Junkbusters Corp. Location-based services (LBS)—including targeted marketing and location tracking of friends and family—offer a potentially enormous revenue stream for wireless carriers, and one that would prove hard to resist. In fact, one estimate expects that LBS could be a $15 billion market by 2007.

The Wireless Communications and Public Safety Act of 1999 requires that your location information be used for non-emergency purposes only with your express consent. The problem is that no one really understands what consent means in this context. Privacy advocates are worried that wireless carriers may bury the consent in a contract's fine print, or that they may offer no information at all. Motorola's user's manual and Verizon's website are both devoid of any information regarding the privacy of your location information. The FCC has remained silent on the topic, and in 2002 the agency actually turned down a request from privacy groups and the cellular phone industry's association to draw up location data privacy rules.

Police and government access to your location information also presents a troubling privacy problem. Police do not explicitly need warrants to access location data, and they have been using this information for years to verify alibis.

With the government's recent focus on profiling—and corporations' long-standing interest in targeted marketing—location data is sure to become a much sought-after commodity. Combined with data on your buying habits, travel plans, income, credit, and other personal data, information about your whereabouts will create a detailed picture of who you are and what you do.

GPS Gadgets

Wherify's GPS-enabled bracelet, available in Galactic Blue or Cosmic Purple, locks onto kids' wrists and pinpoints their exact locations. If someone tries to forcibly remove the bracelet, an alarm message is sent to the parents.

Scott Peterson, a California resident charged with killing his pregnant wife, Laci, and their unborn son, was tracked after his wife's disappearance. Investigators covertly mounted a Global Positioning System to his car, which pinpointed his location wherever he went. Shortly after her death, Peterson drove the car to San Francisco Bay, where the bodies would wash up many months later. The judge presiding over the case ruled that GPS data is scientifically sound enough to be admitted as evidence in his upcoming double-murder trial.

Your cell phone and your car's navigation system use GPS technology to monitor location, but so do other products. These devices are still relatively costly, but this may soon change. In the very near future, you are likely to see inexpensive tracking devices disguised as watches, belts, or backpack inserts for your kids. Although few would dispute the merit of this technology if you were trying, for instance, to recover an abducted child or locate a missing Alzheimer's patient, a very real potential for privacy abuses can occur if stringent security measures are not in place. See chapter 12, "I Spy, You Spy," for a discussion of GPS-enabled devices that are available to consumers right now.

Car Tracking

James Turner rented a van from Acme Rental Car to drive from New Haven to Virginia. The rental agency determined that during his trip Turner drove over the speed limit three times, and the company fined him $150 for each occurrence, even though he was never stopped by the police. Acme's cars were fitted with a GPS system that allowed the company to track renters' driving habits and levy fines for excessive speed.

> With the government's recent obsession with profiling—and corporations' long-standing interest in targeted marketing—location data is sure to become a much sought-after commodity.

Think your conversations are private in your own car? Think again. A recent court case revealed that the FBI had been using an OnStar-type system to eavesdrop on passengers inside a car. The court ruled against the FBI, but not on privacy grounds or on any other constitutional basis. Rather, the court based its decision on the fact that the FBI wiretap interfered with the car's emergency services. The FBI's tech teams are clearly capable of overcoming the technical problem with the wiretap. So under the ruling of this case, the agency is free to wiretap in this invasive manner as soon as it comes up with a way to do so that will not disable the emergency signal in the car.

Telematics in automobiles consists of a computer, a wireless connection, and a GPS system. Although the telematic industry is still relatively small, analysts forecast tremendous growth. Marketing consultants Frost & Sullivan estimate there will be 5.5 million telematic-equipped vehicles by 2009, up from only seventy-five thousand in 2001. Today, the OnStar system from General Motors is the most widely used telematic system. Other telematic systems can be found in high-end car brands like BMW, Mercedes, Jaguar, and Lexus.

OnStar's features include emergency assistance, stolen-vehicle tracking, driving directions, and integrated wireless phone service, all of which offer safety and convenience to drivers. But with the convenience come real privacy concerns. Even if the FBI isn't eavesdropping while you fight with your husband over who has carpool duty, the mere capability for eavesdropping should give you pause. Is it hard to extrapolate new, insidious eavesdropping incidents at the hands of experienced hackers, government officials, corporate spies, organized criminals, or the like? At the very least, this is just one more location-based service that enables someone to know where you are at all times. Do you really need Big Brother riding shotgun in your new Suburban?

> **Do you really need Big Brother riding shotgun in your new Suburban?**

Devices such as Spy-Track enable cars without telematic systems to be tracked. Spy-Track, like other such devices, is a small black box that is installed under a car bumper or car hood and tracks where you go, at what time, and at what speeds. The device, and many like it, is marketed to parents who are eager to keep tabs on their teens, employers who want to check up on their employees, and husbands and wives worried about their spouses' possible infidelities. You can purchase such devices for less than $1,000.

If you're about to lease or buy a car, follow this tip:

❋ **Ask first.** If you are concerned about the privacy issues coupled with telematic devices, ask if your rental or leasing company uses OnStar. Consider not buying or leasing a car that is equipped with the system.

Electronic Toll Collection Systems

New York and San Francisco use small electronic antennas positioned under freeway overpasses and on signs to calculate motorists' speeds by tracking drivers that pass by quickly at electronic tollbooths with E-ZPass or FastTrack devices. To date, with the exception of searches of individuals by law enforcement officials, the information provided by these systems has been used only to provide motorists with information about freeway travel times, but privacy experts worry that this information may one day be used to track individuals or to automatically issue speeding tickets. Imagine how anxious insurance companies would be to get their hands on that information.

New York City officials transferred thirty detectives out of the city's narcotics bureau for allegedly claiming false overtime. The detec-

tives were discovered passing through E-ZPass lanes miles from where they were supposed to be working.

Electronic toll systems enable drivers to avoid long lines at the tollbooth and the nuisance of grappling for change, but they also raise privacy issues. The transponder, or box that sticks on the inside of your windshield, continuously transmits location, time, date, serial number, and identification information via radio frequency to a receiver positioned at tollbooths or alongside highways. Information picked up by the receiver is encrypted, but information can be intercepted directly from the transponder by anyone with the right equipment.

> **Information picked up by the receiver is encrypted, but information can be intercepted directly from the transponder by anyone with the right equipment.**

Systems such as E-ZPass, Smart Tag, and I-Pass, to name a few, that bill travelers for using electronic toll payment, must by nature store personal information. The agencies running these programs assure their customers that the data is not shared with businesses, but privacy experts worry that this may not always be the case.

Government and law enforcement's access to electronic toll collection records is also a concern. Law enforcement is already accessing E-ZPass records to track individuals. In 2003, when the police were investigating the disappearance of a prominent U.S. attorney, they pulled the records of his E-ZPass account, which led them to Pennsylvania where his body was found. E-ZPass records have also been used in civil cases, such as child custody battles. The location data may be available without a warrant depending on where you live, because according to the New York State Supreme Court, "a reasonable person holds no expectation of confidentiality" when using E-ZPass on a public highway.

Follow these tips when you're traveling on toll roads:

✳ **Use cash.** If you're concerned about privacy issues at the tollbooth, do not use an electronic toll collection device.

✳ **Cover your transponder.** If you want to use electronic toll devices, Mylar bags or boxes will protect your transponder when it is not in use. These bags and boxes prevent your personal information from being transmitted from the transponder. Mylar bags are available for free with FastTrak, but you must remove the transponder from your windshield to store it. EZ Shield, the storage container available for E-ZPass, is a box that shields your transponder while it is still affixed to your windshield. It is available for $9.95 at www.ezshield.com.

Metrocard

> *Christopher Stewart, a subway employee, was convicted of second-degree murder and criminal possession of a weapon for murdering his girlfriend in 2001. Stewart's alibi fell apart when his Metrocard, still in his possession, revealed that he was near the crime scene just before the murder. His card revealed that about an hour before the murder he was on a southbound S54 bus, which passes near the scene of the crime. Ten minutes after the slaying he was on a northbound S54 bus.*

Metrocards are credit card-size transportation passes sold in New York. These cards are the preferred way to pay fares on New York City subways and buses. What you may not know is that the Metrocard is essentially a floppy disk with a serial number printed on it. Every time you swipe the card through a turnstile, the data contained on it is relayed back to the Metropolitan Transportation Authority's central computers.

You may also not know that if you use a credit card to buy your Metrocard, your individual location may be tracked on subways and buses. Using the number of a Metrocard paid for with a credit card or a card in a suspect's possession, police have been given access to this location information, for instance, to confirm or contest alibis.

Follow this tip when you use your Metrocard:

✳ **Use cash.** Buy a Metrocard with cash if you are concerned about the privacy of your whereabouts.

Event Data Recorders

> *The South Dakota police sought information from the black box contained in former U.S. Representative Bill Janklow's 1995 Cadillac after an accident in which he killed a motorcyclist. Janklow was*

found guilty of manslaughter. The black box in this case was of limited use because it was an older model, but the case raised the public's awareness about the use of black boxes. Since 1999, for example, all General Motors cars have contained such black boxes.

An estimated 25 million cars in the United States are fitted with event data recorders, or black boxes that record information that can be important in determining responsibility for an accident, such as the speed the car was traveling, whether the brake was pressed, whether the driver was wearing

> **An estimated 25 million cars in the United States are fitted with event data recorders**

a seat belt, and steering and airbag performance. Although these devices do not currently act as location trackers, it is not hard to imagine this monitoring feature being incorporated at a future date.

The data collected from these black boxes has public-safety value in the aftermath of car accidents. If, for instance, you claim to be going only thirty miles per hour when you strike and kill a pedestrian, the information contained in the black box may contradict your story by revealing that you were in fact going eighty miles per hour in a thirty-mile-per-hour zone.

But black boxes raise a host of privacy concerns. You may be unaware that your car is equipped with a black box. California passed the first law to protect the privacy of drivers whose cars are equipped with black boxes. The California law requires automobile manufacturers and dealers to disclose in the owner's manual or lease agreement if the car is equipped with a black box. Other privacy issues concern access to the black-box data. Should your insurance company be able to access the information to determine if you are the type of driver who obeys speed limits? Should this information be available when the company sets your policy rates? Should police be able to access the black box and its data without a warrant? The California law requires the car owner's consent before an agency can access the black box's data, except in certain cases such as when a court orders the release.

Follow this tip when you're buying a car:

☀ **If you do not want a black box in your car, do not purchase automobiles that contain them.** Most of the black boxes are in GM cars, but some Fords also have them. Ask your dealer before buying.

School Software

One mother in San Jose, California, discovered her daughter was cutting classes at Los Gatos High School. To the daughter's chagrin, the mother had logged into the school's database and accessed her daughter's attendance records.

Just as some parents use nanny cams to keep their eyes on activity at home, they can now use Web-based software to track their kids at school. At least 6,500 schools in the U.S. have installed software that enables parents to log on from their home or work computers to find out just what little Johnny and Jane are up to in school that day. Some parents monitor their kids the way that investors monitor their portfolios.

The software keeps not only a daily record of their children's homework assignments and grades, but also information about unexcused absences, detentions, missed assignments, and so forth. For more information on school software, see chapter 12, "I Spy, You Spy."

Human Biochips

Pets and livestock are sometimes implanted with tiny microchips that are used to identify them. Could microchips implanted in human beings be far off?

A Palm Beach company developed a Tic-Tac-size chip that can be injected into humans. Currently, a handheld scanner up to four feet away can read the personal information contained on the chip. Although the chip's intended use is to contain personal data, and perhaps medical information, one could easily envision this technology being used in the future to keep tabs on someone.

Your Leisure Time

You encounter situations that compromise your privacy even during your leisure time. Whether you are trying to find a date online, visiting libraries and bookstores, renting videos, or going to concerts and shows, your personal information may be revealed.

Privacy and Online Dating

Janet Brice, a fifty-five-year-old divorced woman, was excited about her new relationship and she and her boyfriend moved in together. Ten months later, while they were still living together, Janet's boyfriend decided to post a personal ad on www.jdate.com. Although Janet did not see the ad, many of Janet's friends did.

Bob was a regular browser on a large, reputable online dating site. He found a woman he thought was the perfect match; she shared his love of square dancing, Fig Newtons, and Weimaraners. After exchanging several e-mails and meaningful phone calls, they agreed to meet in person. The woman turned out to be a prostitute. She harassed Bob and attempted to shake him down for money. She was so persistent, he eventually had to move and get an unlisted number.

If online dating was at one time stigmatized as a loser-land, populated by perverts, stalkers, and weirdos, this is certainly no longer the case. Online dating has become wildly popular. Improved technology, including broadband and digital cameras, has made online dating easier. Moreover, many people are now accustomed to turning to the Internet to find what they need, and they view dating as no different. In August 2003, 40 million Americans visited an online site in search of a date. Online personals are now one of the most lucrative forms of paid online content; revenue was up 76 percent to $228 million in 2002 from 2001, according to Jupiter Research. The online dating field is crowded, with sites ranging from the large and established such as Match.com and Yahoo.Personals.com, to targeted niche sites that cater to vegetarians, pet lovers, and admirers of plus-size women.

Despite its popularity, online dating poses risks, and not just because an estimated 30 percent of those who use these sites are married men or because people often post photos that bear absolutely no resemblance to their older, pudgier selves. Online dating can be fraught with real dangers, including misrepresentation of identity, threats to personal security, and invasion of privacy and identity theft. A potential for abuse exists even if you have never visited a dating site. Recently, someone posted a profile of a real movie actress on Matchmaker.com, and the listing included the actress's real home address, telephone number, and e-mail address. The actress sued for invasion of privacy, among other things, but the court ruled in favor of the website.

New sites potentially offer more security. The wildly popular Friendster.com, for instance, is predicated on meeting and dating people through mutual friends. Meeting people through mutual friends presumably reduces the number of, in the words of one site member, "axe murderers" you will encounter. Another new site, Truebeginnings.com, is the first to conduct background checks to eliminate convicted felons from its database.

> Some unscrupulous online dating sites may sell the wealth of personal and demographic information in their databases to third parties; others share it with affiliates and may sell it as part of a company sale or bankruptcy.

Newer forms of wireless dating raise even more concerns. Location-based cell phone dating, which is popular in Japan and some parts of Europe, is starting to be introduced in the United States. To use this type of service, you use your phone to find people matching your interests who happen to be within a few blocks. You send them a quick text message and set up a date. The idea appeals to those looking for a more casual, spontaneous approach to dating, but it gives other people the creeps.

Finally, the amount of personal information that these dating websites maintain raises privacy concerns. The privacy risks are similar to those raised in chapter 9, "Your Workplace," with respect to online job search sites. Some unscrupulous online dating sites may sell the wealth of personal and demographic information in their databases to third parties; others share it with affiliates and may sell it as part of a company sale or bankruptcy.

Use these tips to protect yourself when using online dating sites, or even when dating in person:

☀ **Don't use your real name.** Don't reveal your real name or other personal information in your posting. Be cautious about revealing your personal information until you know the person you are e-mailing. Make sure the dating site strips your e-mail of your name and personal e-mail address. (Most sites should do this.)

* **Conduct your own background check.** Before going out on a date, learn about the person by executing a search of the person's name on Google, or by checking public records such as marriage certificates, felon convictions, real estate records, and so forth, to verify the person's identity. For more information, see chapter 12, "I Spy, You Spy."

* **Guard your anonymity.** When you are ready to communicate outside the security of the online dating service (which should use anonymous e-mail), set up your own anonymous e-mail account with an ISP. If you are ready to move to phone conversations with your prospective date, do not give out your work number or home number, both of which can be placed in a reverse directory to reveal your home address. Use your cell phone to make the call or, if you make the call from a landline, sign up with your phone company for blocking beforehand so your number won't appear.

* **Understand how the site operates.** Every dating site operates differently, so get a feel for how much of your personal information is stored and how that information is tracked. For example, on some dating sites, such as JDate.com, profiled subscribers can see the names of other subscribers who have read their profiles.

* **Meet in a public place.** When agreeing to meet in person, arrange to meet in a public place. Do not agree to be picked up at your home, not even in front of it, and never get in the person's car.

* **Tell a friend.** Always tell a friend or relative whom and where you are meeting, and provide them with your date's telephone number when possible.

* **Remove personal or sensitive information.** When you do feel comfortable enough to invite your date to your home, be sure to put away any bills, bank statements, or other sensitive documents that could be used by an identity thief posing as a date.

Libraries and Bookstores

Remember when Kenneth Starr outraged the nation by trying to subpoena Monica Lewinsky's book purchases from two DC book-

stores? Starr supposedly was seeking confirmation that Lewinsky bought books as gifts for the president. Rumor had it that the president was particularly interested in Nicholson Baker's Vox, a novel about phone sex, which Lewinsky purportedly bought for him. The two Washington bookstores took Starr to court, and the matter was settled only after Lewinsky herself agreed to turn over her purchase records.

> **Under the Patriot Act, searches and seizures can occur *without* notice to the target, *without* a warrant, *without* a criminal subpoena, and *without* any showing of probable cause that a crime has been committed.**

When asked by a newspaper reporter if the government had tried to use the Patriot Act to obtain book records from him, the owner of the Harvard Book Store in Cambridge, Massachusetts, said that if it had, he would not be able to tell anyone. In fact, he felt that under the law he wouldn't even be allowed to tell his lawyer. The store's owner then joked that he felt, to be prudent, he should call his lawyer every morning to report that he hadn't been approached by the FBI. That way, if one morning he didn't place that call, his lawyer could assume the worst.

Libraries and bookstores traditionally have enjoyed a high level of legal protection out of concern for your privacy and your First Amendment rights. Indeed, most states have enacted legislation to protect your records of borrowing or buying books. The Patriot Act, however, eradicated this protection. As mentioned above, under the Patriot Act, searches and seizures can occur *without* notice to the target, *without* a warrant, *without* a criminal subpoena, and *without* any showing of probable cause that a crime has been committed.

The government views libraries and bookstores as logical targets for surveillance. First, the government had evidence that the September 11 terrorists used library computers to communicate with one another. In addition, books and library computers are important sources for potential terrorists to learn about possible sites to attack or ways to devise bombs or other hazardous materials.

Critics believe that the act's provisions concerning bookstores and libraries are unconstitutional. Librarians and bookstore owners in particular have been vocal in their opposition, to the point of posting warning signs to customers and patrons regarding the effects of the Patriot Act. Librarians also have been taking other proactive steps to reduce any information that the government might access by undertaking the following:

▸ Keeping only minimal information in their records pertaining to borrowing cards
▸ Shredding borrowing records as soon as books are returned
▸ Shredding computer sign-up sheets
▸ Erasing the caches on computer hard drives

When you go to the library:

✳ **Ask first.** If you are concerned about the privacy of your library records, ask your librarian how long the library keeps book-borrowing and computer records. If it keeps them for long periods of time, you might be more comfortable trying another library.

Video Rentals

In 1988 Judge Robert Bork was a nominee for the Supreme Court. His nomination failed. During the proceedings the press obtained the judge's video rental history and printed it in the newspaper. It turned out that Judge Bork's viewing habits were mostly G-rated and relatively uninteresting, but the ability of the press to access this information scared enough members of Congress to prompt them to enact legislation. Makes you wonder what videos some congressional members are renting . . .

Worried that your eclectic video-renting habits, including rental of the occasional porn video, will be revealed and ruin your chance of success in your child custody battle? The Video Privacy Protection Act (VPPA), which passed in 1988 as a direct response to the Judge Bork incident, prohibits video providers from disclosing your customer rental records without your informed, written consent, excepting a police warrant or court order. The VPPA also requires video purveyors to destroy personally identifiable customer information within a year of the date a rental account is terminated.

Although the VPPA does not specifically cover DVDs and video games, which are also rented in video stores, the spirit of the VPPA would appear to include them. To date, no legal cases have put this issue to the test. However, a more unsettling question is whether the Patriot Act will have an adverse impact on the VPPA. It seems likely that under the act's provisions video records can be accessed in the same way as bookstore and library records.

> If you buy a ticket for Wrestlemania XX, you might just find your inbox flooded with spam.

Tickets to Sporting Events, Shows, and Concerts

Many fans order tickets to sporting events, shows, concerts, and movies through ticketing services, such as Ticketmaster or Telecharge. These ticketing services collect certain information about you, such as your name, the name and date of the event, your credit card number, your e-mail address, and your home address, to fulfill your order. The ticketing agency may need to share your information with third-party vendors or the venue in which the event is taking place. The nature of the information that is needed and the manner in which it is shared with or used by third parties varies by service. Accordingly, you need to read the service's privacy policy prior to ordering tickets.

Suppose you buy tickets through Ticketmaster, which sells 95 million event and sports tickets a year through telephone and online channels. Ticketmaster not only collects your information, but also shares your information with various event providers. These event providers may include venues, promoters, bands, teams, leagues, and others. These providers are unrestricted if they need to share your information with other parties. Moreover, Ticketmaster reserves the right to share your information with its subsidiaries, parents, and affiliates. In Ticketmaster's case, this information can be shared between and among a diverse number of affiliated companies such as Expedia, Hotels.com, Match.com, CitySearch, the Home Shopping Network (HSN), and LendingTree, all of which are owned by Interactive Corp, Ticketmaster's parent company. That means that if you buy a ticket for Wrestlemania XX, you might just find your inbox flooded with spam: Hotels.com asking if you'd like to book the Smackdown Suite at a nearby hotel; HSN hawking Wrestlemania T-shirts and trading cards; and Match.com offering to hook you up with a fellow fan to try out your moves.

Interactive's chief of business operation acknowledges that cross-marketing scenarios make sense, but he also says that the company is still coordinating the activities of its various properties so it isn't yet taking full advantage of these marketing opportunities.

College and University Education

George O'Leary, a Notre Dame football coach, resigned five days after being hired. O'Leary misrepresented his academic and athletic background, claiming to have received a master's degree when he hadn't and claiming to have lettered three years in college football when in fact he had never played in a game. The news came to light not because his alma mater released his confidential school records, but because a reporter interviewed former players and coaches of the college football team.

Your student educational records are generally confidential under the Family Educational Rights and Privacy Act (FERPA), also known as the Buckley Amendment. Under FERPA, schools may not disclose your student records without your written consent (or your parents', if you are a minor), except in certain cases. Student records include your grades, test scores, progress reports, evaluations, family information, social security number, medical records, parking records, the organizations to which you belonged, and any other information that your alma mater collects about you.

But schools may release your records *without your consent* in these limited situations:

> ▶ To teachers and school officials who have a "legitimate educational interest" (to a teacher who is concerned about a student's performance and may have a legitimate educational interest in looking at the student's standardized test scores, for instance)

▸ To concerned parties in connection with financial aid
▸ To other schools to which you are applying
▸ To comply with a judicial order or lawfully issued subpoena
▸ In the case of health and safety emergencies

In addition, schools may release student information for directories, including name, address, telephone number, major, and so forth, but they must provide you (or your parents, if you are a minor) the chance to opt out.

FERPA provides you and your parents (if you're under eighteen) the right to view your student records. FERPA also permits you and your parents to request corrections of anything contained in your records that you deem inaccurate or unfair. If the correction is not made, you and your parents have the right to place a statement in the record to indicate that the entry is inaccurate or unfair.

The Patriot Act and Student Records

The Patriot Act creates an exception to FERPA's general protection that school records remain confidential. Under the Patriot Act, schools must disclose your records without your consent to government agents who request them in connection with an investigation or prosecution of an act of domestic or international terrorism. As with library and bookstore records, the government does not need a warrant or probable cause; it only has to certify that the information is relevant to an investigation. You are not even notified if your records are requested.

To date, an estimated two hundred colleges and universities have handed over sensitive information about suspected students to the FBI, INS, or other governmental agencies, according to the American Association of Collegiate Registrars and Admissions Officers. In addition to obtaining student records, the FBI has enlisted campus police in its war on terrorism. According to the government, these steps monitor potential terrorist activity and keep tabs on the more than two hundred thousand foreign nationals studying in the United States. The government justifies its activities by the fact that several of the September 11 hijackers were trained at U.S. flight schools and one was in the country on a student visa.

Civil libertarians and privacy advocates worry that the government will abuse its broad power if left to its own devices, as it has so many times in the past. The Patriot Act allows the government to investigate any students it decides are suspicious or fit a certain profile, based, for instance, on ethnicity, on affiliations with political groups critical of government policies, or on enrollment in certain majors, such as Islamic studies or aviation.

> The Patriot Act allows the government to investigate any students it decides are suspicious or fit a certain profile, based, for instance, on ethnicity, or on affiliations with political groups critical of government policies.

Other Privacy Issues on Campus

In 2004, New York University apologized to 1,800 students whose names, social security numbers, and some of whose phone numbers were posted on the university's Web site. The information was supposed to be on a protected page of the site, but a school official had failed to activate the appropriate security mechanisms.

In addition to student records, there are other issues compromising students' privacy:

▸ **Identity theft.** According to a 2002 American Association of Collegiate Registrars and Admissions Officers survey, nearly half of U.S. colleges use social security numbers as the primary means to track students in academic databases, and almost 80 percent display social security numbers on official transcripts. In addition, some colleges print the social security number on each student's ID card; use the social security number as the log-in for the computer system; or post grades with the social security number as the identifier. Moreover, students are unusually vulnerable to identity theft because many have their bills and mail sent home, and thus are not vigilant about unusual credit activity. Few students ever review their credit reports.

▸ **Marketing alliances.** Many schools enter into marketing alliances where they sell student, alumni, and employee data to credit card marketers. The University of Tennessee, for instance, has such a deal with First USA. The deal is worth about $16.5 million.

▶ **Profiling.** Unscrupulous marketers illegally use surveys purporting to be educational in nature as a front for collecting marketing data from high-school students.

Criminal Law Records

Just days before the 2000 presidential election, a TV reporter revealed that George W. Bush had an arrest and misdemeanor conviction record for drunk driving near his family's compound in Maine.

As you know from chapter 2, "Your Personal Information and the Public Record," criminal records are public and have long been available to anyone who traveled to the courthouse. However, as people have become accustomed to accessing more and more information online, the demand for remote access to court records has increased. Ordinary citizens can perform criminal-record checks on their dates, prospective nannies, or tenants. Journalists and watchdog groups believe that online access increases the accountability of judges and lawyers. But concerns about privacy, identity theft, and potential threats to witnesses and victims must be balanced with the convenience of online records. Victims' rights advocates—particularly rape and domestic-violence groups—generally oppose making criminal records available over the Internet. These groups don't want victims' addresses revealed for fear the victims would be subject to yet more violence or other unwanted attention as victims.

In response to these concerns, federal courts (which in the past have had more experience than state courts in putting their criminal records online) must follow rules enacted in 2003 by the U.S. Judicial Conference. The rules require that personal information, such as names, social security numbers, home addresses, birth dates, names of minor children, and financial information be edited from any court documents before the records are placed online. Lawyers are scrambling to comply with the policy, which is neither well-defined nor specific about its implementation date. Some lawyers complain that requiring them to comb through thousands of pages of transcripts to edit out all personal information is too burdensome. Others are worried that failing to remove information might lead to liability; if, for instance, someone is injured or killed as a result of a lawyer not omitting some piece of personal information from court filings.

State and local courts are moving slower than federal courts in putting records online, and what they choose to post varies greatly. Certain counties in Florida, for instance, post all case documents online (with information including names and addresses); while other places, like Kentucky and New York, are conservative about what, if any, criminal records belong online. Most courts fall somewhere in between, posting dockets and final rulings, but not motions, forms, or exhibits. Other states like California have followed the Judicial-Conference policy of blocking access to personal information contained in court records.

For a list of online court sites, see: www.ncsconline.org/D_KIS/info_court_web_sites.html#State.

Expunging Errors

A Baltimore man who had spent ten years imprisoned for a crime he did not commit suffered further when the state failed to erase the erroneous robbery conviction from his criminal record. The state ignored orders by two judges and left the record open to the general public and private employers for twelve years.

Having a criminal record, even if the case was dismissed or you were found innocent, does more than harm your reputation; it hampers your ability to obtain credit, employment, and housing. When or if CAPPS II is implemented, a criminal record may also hamper your ability to travel. Many criminal records are easily accessible online these days, so more and more people are seeking to have their records expunged.

Expunging a criminal record means that your slate is wiped clean. Generally, first-time offenders of certain types of crimes can have their records expunged, as of course may people who were found innocent. Expunging a record is slightly different than having a record sealed, which means the file remains intact but can be released only to law enforcement agencies. If your record is expunged, you can honestly answer any question about prior arrests or convictions (assuming no others exist) by saying there are none.

Laws governing who is eligible to expunge records and the procedure that must be followed to do so vary greatly from state to state. You must apply to have records expunged; in most cases your record is not automatically expunged even if your case is dismissed or your arrest was deemed a case of mistaken identity. Not all convictions can be expunged. Many states do not allow felony convictions or violent crimes to be expunged. The types of offenses most likely to be expunged are juvenile and some misdemeanor charges. If you are successful in having a conviction expunged, the information may still be considered in any future sentencing should you commit another offense.

Records that result from federal criminal cases cannot be expunged, except in exceptional circumstances, such as proof of government misconduct.

THE BOTTOM LINE:

▶ Just because you're paranoid doesn't mean they're not out to get you. The Patriot Act makes it all too easy for the government to place you under surveillance, obtain your private records, and prevent you from knowing about its searches, all the while eliminating the judicial oversight that prevents potential abuse of power.

▶ Trying to escape for the weekend? With long lines, intrusive screening and surveillance methods, and future threat of color-coded profiling, the days of escaping peacefully and anonymously to a deserted island are over.

▶ Smile! You're on countless cameras. Whether you are crossing a busy intersection, pumping gas, or riding an elevator, surveillance cameras are recording your every move. If being photographed by the government and business isn't enough, now you have the average Joe with his cell phone camera to worry about as well.

▶ Modern day hide-and-seek. Your cell phone, the OnStar system in your car, your E-ZPass and even your Metrocard are all capable of revealing your whereabouts at any given time.

▶ Leisure activities, such as borrowing or buying books, getting tickets to your favorite events, and looking for companionship online, may be hazardous to your privacy.

I Spy, You Spy

Voyeurs shouldn't live across from each other.

You and five of your female friends in college collectively receive more than one hundred e-mails from the same man. The e-mails include death threats, graphic sexual descriptions, and references to your daily activities. How in the world did he get your e-mail addresses and learn about what each of you does each day? You want to know what to do to get the same information about him.

A colleague tells you that she saw you on the Camera Watch Project site, an experimental site launched by researchers at Carnegie Mellon University in 2003. It offers Web surfers access to a database of video images from thousands of public Web cams. Many of the people captured are not even aware they are being watched.

You know it will break your heart, but you want to know everything your ex says to his new girlfriend. To your delight, you learn that you can tap his phone for only $100.

It's time to 'fess up. If you are like most people, you don't like being spied on. There is something disturbing and even offensive about it. It could scar you emotionally or hurt you financially. Think about a camera filming you while you are undressing in the locker room of the gym. Think about some of the sensitive e-mails you have written and a stranger reading them. Think about someone stealing your identity to commit a crime for which you do the jail time.

But what if the tables are turned and you get to do the spying on someone else? Does that change things? Have you ever felt the urge to spy? There are many reasons for turning the tables, including simple curiosity. Today, it is almost irresistibly tempting to turn to the Internet and various online search engines to dig up a little dirt or information on someone. Indeed, this type of innocent Internet check has become so commonplace that the term "to google" someone—or research the person's background on the popular search engine Google—is part of today's lexicon.

The urge to take a quick gander at something you are not supposed to see may be too much to resist. In the biblical story, Lot's wife turns into a pillar of salt when she turns to look at a sandstorm in contravention of God's wishes. And do you remember the legend of Peeping Tom and Lady Godiva? According to legend, Lady Godiva, a beautiful long-haired woman of the eleventh century, pledged her legendary ride as a means of persuading her husband, Leofric, Earl of Mercia, to lower taxes. When Lady Godiva rode naked on her horse, Tom, a tailor, was the only person who saw her. He peeped while everyone else in town kept their windows shut.

Today, the term *Peeping Tom* has become synonymous with *voyeurism*, which has negative connotations. In the words of W.H. Auden, "Peeping Toms/are never praised, like novelists or bird watchers,/for their keenness of observation." Today you hear about Peeping-Tom cameras or electronic Peeping Toms, both of which are leaps and bounds from the time of the legendary Peeping Tom.

If you are going to spy on other people, you might as well have the tools to do so. Perhaps *spy* is too strong of a term. Maybe *investigate* is preferable. After all, who has not at one point searched the Web for the name of an old classmate? Or a childhood friend? Or researched the background of a potential date by asking others about or googling the person?

Whatever the reason, people do investigate each other. There are a variety of reasons people want to know more about other people, ranging from whimsical to serious, from well-intentioned to questionable or even unethical or outright illegal:

> Anything you do can be done back to you. Life today is a vicious circle of snooping.

- ▶ Parents keep tabs on kids' online activities
- ▶ Suspicious wives keep track of their husbands
- ▶ People research potential love interests
- ▶ Businesspeople research individuals with whom they are scheduled to have business meetings
- ▶ Insurance companies investigate customers
- ▶ Law enforcement agents and private detectives seek fugitives
- ▶ Parents check nanny applicants for criminal records
- ▶ Neighbors snoop on each other, finding out property details, court records, assets, alimony arrangements, and wealth
- ▶ People who were adopted look for birth parents, and vice versa
- ▶ Stalkers track the objects of their obsessions
- ▶ People trace their ancestries and seek other relatives in their families
- ▶ Families and organizations search for missing persons
- ▶ Voyeurs video or photograph victims
- ▶ Employers keep tabs on workers' productivity
- ▶ People involved in litigation investigate the other side's witnesses
- ▶ Suspicious husbands keep track of their wives
- ▶ Kids snoop on parents' online activity

The list begins with one situation and ends with its inverse. Welcome to the nature of snooping. Anything you do can be done back to you. Life today is a vicious circle of snooping.

The strategies, services, and products described in this chapter can be used in many ways. If you decide to use any of them, do so with a degree of caution, knowing that some techniques are currently banned or under consideration for possible legislation.

In many states, an individual who is not licensed as a detective, an agent of law enforcement, or an attorney is prohibited from investigating another individual. What this means is somewhat open to interpretation, but it can mean that you are breaking the law if, for example, you look into the windows of your subject's home. Because of legislation that protects the potential victims of stalkers, actions that indicate someone is tracking another person or spying in various ways are treated more seriously than they have been in the past. If you are an employer and you intend to do a background search on a potential employee, you are often required to obtain a signed release from the applicant before accessing certain pieces of information. Do keep in mind that recent advances in computer and other technology have outpaced the legislation that would regulate their use, albeit not for a lack of effort. Many civil liberties advocates, privacy activists, businesspeople, academics, and politicians across the country have tried to get more protective legislation passed.

If you already know that you would never use any of the tools described in this chapter, you may still enjoy an interesting exercise in ethical deliberation. The information that follows will educate you about what spy tools are accessible to you . . . and to everyone else.

Using the Internet to Conduct Searches

In a well-publicized article in the January 19, 2004, issue of the New Yorker magazine, journalist Katha Pollitt discussed her escapade of stalking her ex-boyfriend online. The article was entitled "Webstalker: When It's Time to Stop Checking on Your Ex." In the article, Pollitt acknowledged that, by day, she lived a completely normal life, but she confessed to being obsessed with tracking the details of her ex-boyfriend's life at night. After she put her daughter to bed at night, Pollitt would often surf the Internet until two in the morning, searching for information about both his professional and personal lives. Using various search engines and listserv lists, she constructed a profile of his life. She discovered details about the various seminars he attended, the papers he submitted, a char-

itable donation he made, and a book he was producing with his new girlfriend. She even tried to break into his e-mail account by constructing passwords he might use. Finally she discovered that her ex and his new girlfriend were selling their apartment. She went to the listing on the real estate company's website and clicked on the apartment's floor plan and photographs that showed the inside of the apartment. She was finally inside their lives or, at least, their apartment.

Katha Pollitt and her search aside, there are plenty of legitimate reasons to research the background of people you want to know more about. Whether you are trying to find people, learn a little background information, look for a phone number or address, or hire someone to help you in your search, the Internet is the best tool at your disposal.

Search Engines

You should first turn to the search engines. You may already have a favorite search engine, but some of the more popular ones include Google, Yahoo!, Alta Vista, and Lycos. New clustering search engines, such as Vivisimo at vivisimo.com, integrate and categorize information into various folders. These search engines will discover sites on the Internet that contain relevant and useful information for your search. As you use the various search engines, keep the following tips in mind:

✳ **Try different search engines.** Each one might turn up different sites or information.

✳ **Start by typing in the name of the person you seek, enclosing the full name in quotation marks.** The quotation marks restrict the search to a full name, so you won't get results for people who have a different last name but the same first name (or vice versa) as the person you're seeking. Depending on how common the name is, you still may get hundreds of results.

✳ **Search by nicknames or shortened versions of the name.** (Use "Bill" instead of "William.") You might also want to try searching by first initial and last name (wjohnson), using the format for many e-mail addresses.

✳ **Hone your search by using the advanced preferences offered by the search engine.**

✳ **If your search returns results that are too broad, consider narrowing your search parameters.** You might want to search the name in quotes along with the person's primary interest, profession, the town where the person resides, or one of the schools the person attended.

Online Directories

In addition to the search engines, you might want to check the many directories that include lists of phone numbers, e-mail addresses, or ways to execute a "people search." Online directories provide comprehensive information for people and businesses, including phone numbers, addresses, and often e-mail addresses and fax numbers. For example, try:

- whitepages.com
- infospace.com
- anywho.com
- whowhere.com

Yahoo! and other sites such as Addresses.com also have "people search" options that allow you to look for e-mail addresses, phone numbers, and mailing addresses by typing in a name and the state where that person lives. A number of sites will help you find someone's e-mail address, including:

- whowhere.com
- bigfoot.com
- people.icq.com/whitepages (the ICQ e-mail directory)
- aol.com/netfind/emailfinder.adp (AOL e-mail finder)

Reverse Directories

Online directory assistance services function like regular telephone books: if you have a person's name, the service can provide you with that person's listed telephone number or address. A reverse directory, on the other hand, requires that you have only a phone number to access vital statistics about an individual. For example, if a stranger calls you and you get his or her number through caller ID, or the person's telephone number appears on your cell phone's display, you can use a reverse directory to find out the caller's name and address. Some reverse directories require a zip code in addition to the number before they will allow you to access the information you seek. Reverse directories have sprung her for all kinds of information. In some cases, you need only an e-mail address to access all the personal information available for a person.

Many online directories, including Infospace.com and WhitePages.com, also offer reverse-directory search capabilities. This allows their clients to find people with only a phone number or an e-mail address in hand.

Most reverse-directory sites are free, but a few may charge a small fee. If you use services that charge a fee, you may be able to get additional information, such as:

▶ Name and address for an unlisted number
▶ Name and address for a disconnected phone number
▶ Name and address for an 800 or 900 number
▶ Name and address for a cellular phone or pager
▶ Name and address for a disconnected cell phone or pager
▶ Unlisted address for a name and city and state

Another option may be to use Finger Gateway technology, which allows users to find names from e-mail addresses. Using this technology, you can determine such things as when an Internet user last logged in and checked his or her e-mail. Many sites consider finger queries a breach of security, so the technology is becoming less accessible every year. To find a site that offers this search technology, search on Google.

Search by Interests or Background

You go out on a blind date. You're confident because you know exactly what questions to ask your date. You already know all her interests, her fantasies, and her obsessions. You didn't get this information from a Web page or a profile on a dating service. You got it by accessing your date's history of chat room messages,

373

which was not difficult to do. You also discovered not only to which forums she contributed, but also exactly what she said.

You can search for a person based on information you know about his or her interests and background. In general, many of the search engines, such as Yahoo! or Google, list various directories by subject and organization, and they are useful to check.

You can also turn to any number of specialized directories. For example, if you are looking for someone with whom you went to school, you can use subscription services, such as Classmates.com. This huge database lists more than 35 million graduates from the United States and Canada. You must pay a fee to access the information, but it is often worth it because the service has reunited many old friends. A number of other alumni-related subscription sites provide similar services. If you do not have luck with these subscription sites, try finding your school's website. For privacy reasons, you usually cannot access alumni lists without having attended the school yourself. You can, however, contact the alumni office and ask the school to pass your contact information along to the person you seek, if he or she is also an alumnus or alumna of the school.

An organization in which you may have been a member, whether it be the Junior League or a charitable foundation, will perform the same service to help you find another member. You will run up against the same privacy principles, and sometimes all you can do is leave your contact information with an intermediary at the organization and ask that it be passed on.

Searching by Profession or Company

You can look up someone by profession or company. Certain professional organizations keep comprehensive directories that list all members of the profession. To research someone by occupation, you can narrow your search by finding portals that are specific for that profession. Here are some examples:

- ▶ For doctors: Try the online Doctor Finder (AMA; www.ama-assn.org) or try MedAvenue (www.medavenue.com)
- ▶ For attorneys: Try the Attorney Directory at www.lawinfo.com or the Martindale-Hubbell Lawyer Locator at www.martindale.com

▶ For experts: Find an expert in a specific field or location at www. experts.com

▶ For contractors: Try the home contractor directory at www.contractors. com

▶ For teachers: If the person you seek is a current public-school teacher and you know the name of the town in which he or she teaches, look up the school's directory online.

> Are you curious about how the value of your house compares to the value of the home owned by your friends or neighbors?

A number of directories provide information about executives in various companies. For example, the Hoovers directory at www.hoovers.com provides information about executives who work at both public and private companies. The information includes the executives' titles, their salaries, and some biographical information. Information for public companies is also available on the Securities and Exchange Commission website, www.sec.gov, which allows users to research the officers of publicly traded companies, their earnings, and the earnings of their companies. Another comprehensive site is the LexisNexis site at www.lexisnexis.com, which provides similar information but usually costs a fee (unless you access the database at a library).

Searching Real Estate Records

Perhaps you are curious about how the value of your house compares to the value of the home owned by your friends or neighbors. Or perhaps you want to find out what your colleague paid for her new house. An easy way to find this information is to look at the websites of real estate brokerage houses. These sites list houses and apartments that are on the market, including the price of the house and photographs of the interior or exterior of the place. For greater detail, you might want to access the website of the real estate research firm NETR at www.netronline.com. This site publishes the values of homes and links to the databases of many states and counties.

Searching for Political Information

You can find out if your colleague who said he donated to John Kerry is telling the truth by researching a number of sites that identify political donors to various political candidates. As indicated in chapter 2, "Your Information Documents and the Public Record," federal law requires that political donations of more than $200 must be publicly disclosed. Two useful sites are www.opensecrets.org or www.fecinfo.com, which may also reveal the name of the person's company or occupation.

Searching for Family

Tracing the family tree is a full-time occupation for many people. You can find out not only where you came from, but also discover branches of the family or long-lost relatives who are still living. Of course, you can also discover the ancestry of other people, like the man or woman you're dating.

As with any search, start by making notes of anything you know that might be useful in charting and researching your family tree. Include as many family names and geographical origins as you can. Interview anyone in your family who might know valuable details.

Many tools are available online to help your ancestry search, including subscription services that focus on genealogy; databases of historical information, maps, and names; and chat groups that provide helpful forums for your questions, tips for searching, and forms you can use to request information from different sources.

If you search for *ancestry* or *genealogy* on Google or one of the other engines, you will turn up sites like www.ancestry.com and www.genealogy.com, which provide or link you to databases to aid your research. There are also sites where people post their own family trees, and if you register, you can search through those charts. Genealogy sites can also be quite helpful if you are trying to find a living relative or seeking to learn more about someone's background.

Searching in Discussion Groups and Chat Rooms

After perusing personal profiles submitted to various online services, Mr. Smith harassed single women in his neighborhood via e-mail and Internet chat rooms. In addition, he placed surveillance software on the victims' computers and stalked them in person. His campaign of harassment ended when he deviated from his usual pattern of behavior and focused his attentions on a married woman. The woman's husband happened to be an expert in computer security and easily tracked down Mr. Smith's name, address, and place of employment. Mr. Smith, it seems, used his skills as a network administrator to facilitate his ability to stalk his victims.

Another way to learn about people is to research online discussion groups and chat rooms. In these areas on the Internet, you might discover the specific thoughts of the target of your investigation. As discussed in chapter 7, "Your Computer and the Internet," any and every posting your target has made to a chat room or discussion group is available to any other visitor to the site. Many people do not know this is possible, and it is not just possible, it is easy.

To uncover the contributions a person has previously posted online, you can go to a number of different sites, including AltaVista's usenet search option or Google Groups at groups.google.com (formerly Dejanews). To execute the search, input a name or an e-mail address and see what you learn. Many usenet search engines have compiled online libraries of the "public e-mails" posted on the Internet's bulletin boards and in its chat rooms.

If you cannot find information on an individual anywhere else online, you may be able to make a connection by typing the person's phone number into a search engine. Most chat room users do not believe that the trail of places they visit is public. By accessing bulletin boards or chat rooms, family members can check up on each other, employers can check on employees, employers can check on job applicants, and employees can check on employers.

Public Records

As you learned in chapter 2, "Your Personal Information and the Public Record," you can learn a great deal of information about people from public records. Searching public records online can be time-consuming, because many states and counties maintain their own databases. But services that compile the databases for you are available and make the searching far more efficient. One of the largest is Search Systems, at www.searchsystems.net. This site, with more than fourteen thousand public records, links to specific database websites for different areas and different kinds of records. Some information at Search Systems is free, but a number of the databases that it lists charge a fee, and they are specified.

Portals that lead you to public-records databases include:

- ▶ www.searchsystems.net. The largest public records database with hundreds of free lists.
- ▶ www.knowx.com. This pay site is a subsidiary of ChoicePoint, one of the biggest data aggregators.
- ▶ www.intellius.com. This pay site is another popular choice for public records data.
- ▶ www.brbpub.com/pubrecsites.asp. This site lists almost seventeen hundred websites that house public records and contains a great deal of free information.
- ▶ www.willyancey.com. This accountant's site supplies free links to political and legal directories that may be helpful.

Locator Services

You can retain a locator service to research the information you are seeking. This service is also available through certain websites, including PeopleFind.com. Locator services typically charge a fee, which is based on the scope of the search you ask the service to perform. People turn to these services when they do not have the time or knowledge to execute searches themselves, or if their own searches have not yielded good results. The information you are looking for may be as minor as the address for a name you provide, but it may also be something that is more difficult to secure. Locators can do most of their work if they are equipped with a name plus one of the following: previous address, date of birth, or social security number. For less than $70 or so, you can often receive all of the following as results: the person's aliases, current and past addresses, licenses, liens, associates, relatives, property information, concealed-weapons permits, neighbors, voter registration information, domain name registration information, criminal records, bankruptcies, and more. Locators also perform specialized services such as neighborhood reports, which detail the cost of living in a certain area, the quality of life there, profiles of the neighbors, essential addresses, sex offender information, and more. As with most online services, research the service before you contract to do business with them. You never know if a site is legitimate or not without investigating.

You can also download products like Net Detective, which are essentially all the tools a locator uses, for about $30. Within minutes of downloading, you can start searching online.

Spyware or Snoopware

Imagine you use a public computer at a reputable store that offers Internet access. Three days later your accounts have been wiped out and your financial information has been sold. You eventually find out that a thief had installed keylogging software on the store's computers. The scammer captured and sold the personal financial information of almost five hundred people, and used that information to direct money into her own accounts. Amazingly, the thief used spy software that is readily available to anyone online.

As you read in chapter 7, "Your Computer and the Internet," certain types of software can almost be classified as spy tools. Use of software that tracks a person's behavior and activity online or on one's computer has been growing steadily for many years. Such software, which is known as spyware or snoopware, can be used for innocuous purposes—such as protecting your children by keeping an eye on their online activities—or more intrusive purposes—such as watching over employees' productivity or tracking a spouse's online activities. The software can also be used for illicit reasons, such as keeping a log of a computer's activities to collect vital personal information entered into that computer.

The most insidious type of software is installed on a computer so activity on that computer can be monitored from afar. Typically, the person whose computer is burdened with spyware or snoopware has no idea that anyone is tracking his or her activities, as there is virtually no sign to the user that the software is there. Spyware can be sent to an unsuspecting person through an innocuous e-mail attachment, which, once opened, installs the software on the recipient's computer.

A sampling of the different software products that are available include:

▶ Software that monitors every activity performed by a computer, including chats, instant messages, e-mails sent and received, websites visited, keystrokes, programs used and files searched or swapped with peers. One software package can also make a digital surveillance tape of every task performed by a computer. In fact, corporate networked software can perform the same surveillance on a network of computers. Employers use such software to monitor their staffs.

> Typically, the person whose computer is burdened with spyware or snoopware has no idea that anyone is tracking his or her activities, as there is virtually no sign to the user that the software is there.

▶ Remote monitoring software package that performs the same recording of activities as the spyware above, but also allows the snoop to be a watchdog from thousands of miles away. As a person writes e-mails and instant messages, strikes any keys, or visits any websites, the software records the computer's operations and sends a record of the entire tracking to the snoop's computer, sometimes seconds after the activities are performed.

▶ Software that recovers information from a hard drive even if that material was deleted. Services and software are available to repair and access deleted information on everything from cassette tapes to floppy disks to operating systems like Windows. Check www.renewdata.com/data_recovery.html for details on data recovery.

Products You Can Buy

Jerry and Robin, a highly regarded defense attorney and a real estate banker, recently had a beautiful daughter they named Alison. The couple hired a nanny to help care for their child. They discussed whether to install a nanny cam in their daughter's room, and debated the pros and cons of monitoring their child and the nanny's actions to ensure the safety of their daughter. After much deliberation, they decided against it. As an attorney who had spent his life defending the constitutional rights of his clients, Jerry could not stomach the nanny cam in their apartment.

A woman lived with her sister's fiancé. They were very good friends, and he never exhibited any inappropriate behavior. But one day the woman found cameras hidden in her bedroom, bathroom, jewelry box, and hats. The cameras were broadcasting live video feed into his bedroom.

Vasile Prisca, a Romanian inventor, created a mechanism that sent a text message to his cell phone if more than one person was in his and his wife's bed when he was not home. The device made this determination by calculating the weight on the mattress. Vasile caught his wife's infidelity this way.

The spying and surveillance products available on the market allow you to play James Bond. Items that used to be Hollywood props, outrageously expensive, or simply unavailable to the average citizen are now both quite affordable and easily accessible. Surveillance equipment is part of the age of rapidly advancing technology.

The legality of many of these products is questionable or may depend on how the product is used. Some tools are illegal while others may require the consent of one or both of the parties being listened to or videotaped, or whose computer activity is being monitored. Therefore, before using any of these items, investigate the law in your own state by contacting your state's attorney general's office. One site that provides an overview for electronic surveillance law by state is www.ncsl.org/programs/lis/CIP/surveillance.htm.

First, many widely available consumer products can be used for simple spying or investigative purposes:

▶ **Cell phone cameras.** These were originally designed for personal use and fun. But these phones have already been used to document crime scenes before police arrived, implicating perpetrators who might have otherwise gotten away, as well as having been used in health club locker rooms to take nude photographs of unknowing health club members.

▶ **GPS devices.** Global positioning is a useful tracking service that pinpoints location. It is used for many different reasons, but is especially useful as a navigation tool. Many companies offer GPS services with the specific purpose of allowing you to investigate your suspicions. GPS units can be magnetically attached to a car, and they can last fifteen days or more on batteries. Using precision mapping, they track where a vehicle goes, where it stops, and how long it stays there. Many parents use GPS devices to keep track of their children.

▶ **Nanny cams (or hidden video cameras).** Many parents install these devices, with or without a caretaker's knowledge, to confirm that their kids are getting good care. Nanny cams are generally not allowed in bathrooms or changing rooms of any sort. Keep in mind that nanny cams and baby monitors have been used against homeowners: it is possible for criminals to pick up what is going on inside the house by scanning these wireless transmissions from outside the house. See chapter 8, "Your Home," for more details.

Because technology changes so rapidly, more powerful and increasingly inexpensive tools become available every day. Here is a sampling of a few of the products that have emerged in the marketplace:

▶ A DNA test kit for spouses to investigate their suspected partners' underwear for traces of semen, when none should be there. This product costs less than $50, comes with a money-back guarantee, and offers a DNA helpline in case the test turns up positive and the test user wants to further investigate the supposed infidelity.

▶ An infrared illuminator that allows users to take pictures in total darkness, without anyone knowing. You set up the black box in a pitch-black room and then snap away for less than $90.

▶ A lamp that is actually a wireless video camera that also records sound for less than $600.

▶ A monitor that you can connect to a phone. If you dial that telephone's number, you can listen in on conversation from a remote location for less than $300.

▶ A cellular phone that operates in the same way as any other cell phone, but has added features: If you call the phone from a certain number, the cell phone will connect without ringing, so you can access any sounds and conversation happening near the phone. There is no range, so if someone takes the phone to another state, you can still call and hear everything happening via the microphones in the phone—for around $1,500.

▸ A microphone that listens through walls. The device is so sensitive that it can even pick up a whisper, for less than $250.

▸ A cellular scanner that eavesdrops on other cell phone or cordless phone conversations, for less than $300. These scanners currently work only on analog lines, because digital cell phones scramble their output. However, one Canadian company recently marketed a scanner to law enforcement officials that can capture digital calls. The cost of the scanner is in the $30,000 range.

▸ A cellular phone interceptor that allows you to enter into it up to twenty mobile-phone numbers. The device allows you to eavesdrop on conversations on any of those phone numbers whenever those phones are used. You can also decode touch-tones dialed into the phones, thereby learning pass codes to answering services and more, for less than $6,000.

Special Situations

In certain specialized situations, especially those involving people you hire in your home, you might want to conduct very specific investigations. The Internet has made searching for information about people easier than ever before, although many of the tips below are tried and true methods that preceded the Internet and other tracking technologies.

Background Search for People You Hire to Work in Your Home

You want to hire a tutor or nanny for your child. This person is going to spend a significant amount of time alone with your child, so you want to verify the information in the tutor's or nanny's application.

Because much legislation has been instituted to protect individuals' privacy and to prevent discrimination, you must be careful while conducting any investigation of another person. Laws vary by state and per category of information. It may be unlawful to conduct certain kinds of queries, and it may also be unlawful to decline an application based on certain categories of information, such as age. Educate yourself by consulting books or online information, or by contacting an attorney. Also review chapter 9, "Your Workplace," to understand the privacy rights that may apply to your child's nanny or tutor.

Notwithstanding, here are a few tips to keep in mind and steps to take:

✳ **Have the applicant fill out a job application.** Application forms are available online, in stationery stores, and at libraries. These forms often provide a space for the applicant's signature and a statement verifying that the applicant gives you permission to confirm the information he or she provided.

✳ **Ask the applicant to sign a release-of-information form.** These forms are available from the same sources. A completed form is necessary if you wish to access the applicant's credit reports, medical record, or school records.

✳ **Use information on the application to search court records on all levels, from federal to local, all of which are open to the public.** You must have the applicant's current and previous addresses to execute this search. Court records are housed at the court offices; on computer databases, which a clerk can look at for you; or online. Use www.searchsystems.net as a portal to the many databases in different states that house public records. Look for bankruptcies, lawsuits, criminal convictions, and drunk-driving charges, or any other red flag.

✳ **Request a release-of-information form to look at the applicant's credit report.** As explained in chapter 4, "Your Credit," credit reports contain a great deal of basic information that should match the application. For example, you can determine any discrepancies in job history by comparing the employers listed on the application and the employers provided in the credit report. The report also provides information about any liens, lines of credit, collections, and aliases associated with the applicant, all of which can be important in your decision to hire or reject the person.

✳ **Search medical records, although these may be difficult to access.** You probably want to look at the applicant's medical records, especially in the cases of nannies, tutors, or other intimate positions, to see if the applicant has received psychiatric treatment. You must secure a release to access this information, but even then, depending on the state and the hospital or institution you have contacted, it may be difficult or impossible to see these records.

✳ **Call references; they can be telling.** As referenced in chapter 9, "Your Workplace," some states restrict previous employers from answering questions about the referenced person to the dates the person was employed by the company.

Monitoring Your Children's Activities

As technology advances, and an individual's privacy erodes, parents grapple with how far they should go to use technology to protect or monitor their children's actions. Can you go too far? Certainly, as chapter 7, "Your Computer and the Internet," discusses, you can do a number of things to protect your children's privacy online in ways that are fairly commonplace. But what if new technological developments entered the marketplace that infringed upon your children's privacy, but *you*—not the government or marketers—were the one who would be doing the infringing?

As people's concerns about their children's safety grow, the lengths to which parents are willing to go to protect their children is also shifting. Measures that were once condemned as far too intrusive are now getting a second and third look and sometimes a cautious embrace. Do these measures in fact protect, or do they do more harm by eroding trust within families? Here are some recent examples:

School Software. To date, at least 6,500 schools nationwide have installed Web-based software that enables parents to log into the school's network from their home or work computers and find out just what their children are up to in school. Parents can potentially track more than just their children's homework assignments and grades; they can see all their children's unexcused absences, detentions, missed assignments, and so forth. Privacy experts express concerns about student privacy and data security. Hackers have already penetrated the software in Washington, Colorado, and California. Others worry that cash-strapped schools might be tempted to use the information for commercial purposes.

Kiddie GPS Products. Current products equipped with Global Positioning System (GPS) technology can track your kids' every move. One company advises parents to place GPS devices under their cars so the parents know where their teenagers are driving and whether the teens are speeding. These devices are costly, but that is about to change. By 2005, inexpensive casings for your teen's cell phone will be available. The casings include GPS components that will keep you informed about your teen's whereabouts at all times. No cell phone? How about a low-cost tracking device disguised as a watch, belt, or backpack insert? And all you have to do is log on to a website to see a map pinpointing your child's location. Few people would dispute the merit of this technology in recovering an abducted child, but there is a very real potential for privacy abuses if stringent security measures are not in place.

> One company advises parents to place GPS devices under their cars so the parents know where their teenagers are driving and whether the teens are speeding.

Chipping Your Child. This idea seems implausible; can it really be that far off? Pets and livestock are often injected with tiny microchips that are used to identify the animals. Now a Palm Beach company has developed a tiny chip that can be injected into humans. Currently, a handheld scanner can read the personal information contained on the chip from up to four feet away.

Adoption

Searches resulting from an adoption are sensitive and emotional events, so there are many specific laws and guidelines, as well as support groups, to help you navigate through them. A wealth of information is available online to get you started on finding either a birth parent or a child previously given up for adoption. Here are a few of the basics:

✳ **Acquaint yourself with the legal difference between searching for an adult birth child and a minor birth child.** The specifics on adoption law in your state are available from www.law.cornell.edu/topics/Table_Adoption.htm. Under the Uniform Adoption Act of 1994, if either a birth parent and an adoptee over seventeen or an adoptive parent of an adoptee under eighteen are willing to disclose their identities via the mutual consent registry mentioned below, the identifying information must legally be disclosed. The act also allows a suit for disclosure of identifying information for good cause.

✳ **Parents searching for children must decide between an active or passive search.** For the former, all leads are pursued. For a passive search, where the parent posts information on how he or she can be reached, it is the decision of the child to contact the biological parent(s).

✳ **Register with an international mutual-consent registry.** This procedure protects the rights of birth parents, the rights of adoptees who wish to remain unidentified, and the interests of those who wish to disclose their identities. Most states have some form of mutual-consent registry. Those states that do not maintain such a registry disclose identities only by court order. The International Soundex Reunion Registry (ISRR) is the largest free mutual consent registry in the world: www.plumsite.com/isrr/.

✳ **Contact whatever institution was used in the adoption.** This may be an agency, attorney, hospital, judge, caseworker, doctor, foster-care family that preceded adoption, state adoption unit, or county court clerk.

✳ **Gather as much paperwork as possible regarding the adoption.** Include any document that might be relevant.

✳ **Interview anyone you can find that had anything to do with the adoption.**

Mutual consent is often the critical factor in adoption investigations. Most organizations set up to assist you, whether you are the child or the parent, require such mutual consent before connecting two people in such investigations.

Hiring a Private Detective or Investigator

Are you trying to find a long-lost friend? Are you missing a loved one? Or perhaps you are wondering why your spouse is spending so many late nights at the office? If you are unable to get the information you want from your online search or accessing public records, you might consider hiring a public detective or investigator. The difference between a private detective and private investigator varies by state, and the terms are often interchangeable. The most important factor is whether the detective or investigator is licensed within the state to undertake investigations. Those that are not licensed are restricted legally in their investigative activities.

A private investigator or detective answers your questions or facilitates your search. He or she can monitor someone or a situation for your personal protection, provide pre-employment verification of an applicant's background, profile an individual's background, assist in a court case, assess insurance claims and fraud, dig up information for a child custody or child protection case, screen an individual prior to marriage, and track a spouse's supposed infidelity.

A private investigator or detective is trained to uncover a great deal of information. In addition to accessing many of the public databases and other sensitive files on your subject, he or she may also use certain surveillance techniques, including video, audio, and photographs, to provide additional information. In many cases, the additional information you receive may be key to making an important decision. For example, in the workplace, a pre-employment investigation gives employers the comfort of knowing that they are hiring a person with the experience, training, and background they need. A pre-employment investigation can also reveal careless driving habits, possible criminal history, or other undesirable information about a potential employee. By discovering this information, employers reduce their chances of facing inflated insurance costs, employee pilfering, and loss of money related to training and equipment costs for the individual.

Finding a private detective or investigator is as easy as looking in the yellow pages or searching on the Internet. But the decision to hire a professional isn't one to be taken lightly, even if doing so is a matter of course for you in the normal operations of your profession. A private investigator handles sensitive information for his or her clients, whether in a personal or professional context. In some cases, such as a delicate divorce case, hiring a private investigator can harm your case if the other party's lawyer views the investigation as harassment and convinces the jury of that view.

Here are some factors to consider when hiring a private detective or investigator:

* **Location.** Hire a detective or investigator who operates in your desired search area. Hiring a local private investigator ensures that the private investigator has a better understanding of your surroundings and also avoids additional transportation expenses.

* **References.** Ask around to see if anyone has used an investigator. References from friends and associates are sometimes the best. If you are able to get references, check them to determine if the investigator's previous clients were satisfied with the results of the agent's work. Note, however, that obtaining specific references may be difficult in certain cases because of the confidential nature of the investigations.

* **Experience.** Ask about the investigator's experience and training. Get a sense of how long the investigator has worked and his or her previous experiences. Retired police officers are sometimes the best investigators.

* **Specialty.** As with other professions, even an investigator who has a great deal of experience may not be an expert in the area for which you are hiring the investigator. Broad experience may suffice unless you have a very focused assignment for the investigator.

* **Other sources.** If you are still not satisfied, you might want to check the local State Police Certification Unit, the Better Business Bureau, or even the Chamber of Commerce to see if any complaints have been filed against the investigator you are hiring.

Stalking

Edward S. Grenawalt, a former Veterans Administration law enforcement officer, meets Paula Reynolds in an America Online chat room for law enforcement officers. For years, he threatens her over

Internet chat rooms, e-mail, and through a website dedicated to fallen police officers. The two meet in person only once: in a courtroom, after seven years of harassment and a death threat.

Robert Harvey Alexander, fifty-two, a deacon in Tampa's First Baptist Church, was a highly respected member of his community. That's why it came as a great surprise that in his spare time he had been using library computers to harass women on the Internet. He would threaten to post derogatory personal remarks or photographs of the women online unless they engaged in cyber- and phone sex with him. Upon arrest, police discovered Alexander's Victims List, with one hundred e-mail addresses of female high-school and college students.

It is one thing to snoop a little, or possibly even to research someone's background. But if you cross the line to stalking, you are entering a wholly different situation. Stalking is difficult to define precisely, but it is essentially unwanted action directed at a person. The legal definition varies by state. North Dakota, for example, defines stalking as "to engage in an intentional course of conduct directed at a specific person which frightens, intimidates, or harasses that person, and that serves no legitimate purpose. The course of conduct may be directed toward that person or a member of that person's immediate family and must cause a reasonable person to experience fear, intimidation, or harassment." For a directory of state stalking statutes, go to the Stalking Resource Center at www.ncvc.org.

Stalking has been a problem in every society throughout history, but it has come under greater scrutiny and legislative attention during the past several years. The first state stalking law was enacted in 1990 in California, and since then every state in the country has since passed some type of stalking law. In addition, many states now have specific laws that cover cyberstalking. Forty-five states now explicitly include electronic forms of communication within stalking or harassment laws. As a general rule, if the stalking is strictly online, the crime is considered a misdemeanor; more severe penalties apply when the stalking occurs in person.

On a federal level, the Interstate Stalking Act makes it a crime for any person to travel across state lines with the intent to injure or harass another person and, in the course thereof, place that person or a member of that person's family in a reasonable fear of death or serious bodily injury. A number of serious stalking cases have been prosecuted under this law, but the requirement that the stalker physically travel across state lines renders the law largely inapplicable to cyberstalking cases. Certain forms of cyberstalking may be prosecuted as a federal crime under different federal laws when the stalker uses a telephone or telecommunications device to annoy, abuse, harass, or threaten any person at the called number.

> As a general rule, if the stalking is strictly online, the crime is considered a misdemeanor; more severe penalties apply when the stalking occurs in person.

The conduct that constitutes stalking varies from state to state. But stalking typically is understood to involve inappropriate approaches or confrontations, such as appearing at the victim's work or home. It may also involve placing unwanted telephone calls, sending unwanted letters, sending unwanted e-mails, or sending threatening gifts to the victim. Finally, stalking encompasses situations in which the victim, or the victim's family, is threatened, property is damaged, or the victim is physically or sexually assaulted. As was the case with the advent of cyberstalking, new ways of stalking people are constantly emerging.

Basic Sleuthing

Keep these tips in mind when you investigate others.

✳ **Know the law in your state.** This is the most important step if you intend to do more than simply enter a long-lost friend's name into an online search engine. For example, if you intend to investigate an applicant to tutor your kids, know what you are allowed to research. Pursuing the details of the applicant's race or age might make you liable for discrimination. To learn about the law in your state, contact your state's attorney general's office, and review your state's stalking statute.

✳ **Talk to friends and acquaintances.** Perhaps the easiest thing to do is to ask questions among your network of friends and acquaintances. They may be the best people to help, and you may be most comfortable asking them for answers to sensitive questions.

✳ **Keep detailed notes.** Many people believe they can remember all the details of their search as they uncover them, but a paper trail of what you have looked into is essential. Often, small, seemingly irrelevant details can become the doorways to discovery. For example, if you are searching for a long-lost relative, and you uncover his or her marriage certificate, make a note of everything on the document. The witness may be an old friend of the relative and accessible to you. He or she might be able to inform you of the last whereabouts of the person you seek. When you begin your search, make a list of everything you know about what you are looking for. Just making that list can spark connections.

✳ **Decide if your search is worth a budget.** You will most likely run into fees or expenses if you perform any kind of in-depth sleuthing. This could run anywhere from a few dollars for an online locator service, to thousands of dollars for high-tech surveillance products. There are many ways to do free research, especially online, but sometimes spending a few dollars on certain databases, for example, can save you days of scrolling through websites.

✳ **Beware of human error.** Public records and databases of all kinds are notoriously full of errors, including the misspelling of someone's name, the attachment of a name to the wrong social security number, and the merging of two people's records into one. Try to match details like date of birth and addresses, as well as names and social security numbers, when comparing the information you have to the record you have found. If something doesn't match, try to pinpoint the error. Understand that records are not the ultimate truth. For instance, say you find a record of a landlord suing the potential renter you are researching. You may want to decline the renter's application. But the previous landlord might have been frivolously litigious, bringing a lawsuit against the renter to disguise the fact that the landlord had not made required repairs and was attempting to preempt a lawsuit by the renter. This kind of thing is not uncommon, and even if the situation is resolved in the renter's favor, the paper trail sometimes still favors the landlord. Inquire with your applicant if you have doubts about a finding.

THE BOTTOM LINE

▶ Are you a Peeping Tom? You might think it is fun to investigate others, but make sure you know your state's law before you violate any laws.

▶ What comes around goes around. Don't think you are outsmarting or outspying someone. You may be spying on someone, but they also may be spying on you.

▶ Search for love in all the right places. It is common to Google a prospective date before you go out for an evening together. The Internet can be a powerful tool to learn a great deal about others.

▶ James Bond stars in the movies only. You may be able to purchase sophisticated surveillance and software products, but you are not a secret agent. You live in the real world where federal and state laws apply to you.

▶ Proceed with caution. In special situations, such as if you hire a private investigator or if you realize you have gone too far in terms of following someone around (aka stalking), stop what you are doing. Proceed carefully and ask yourself if this is what you really want to be doing.

The Future of Privacy

NOW THAT YOU'VE READ *PRYING EYES*, you may wonder whether you have traveled in time into the future or back to 1984, that is, to George Orwell's *1984*. Written in 1948, Orwell's famous novel predicted a world without privacy and rife with paranoia. Presiding over the fictitious country of Oceania is a totalitarian power known simply as Big Brother. Big Brother and his minions employ a system of total surveillance that includes telescreens, hidden microphones, and spies. Whether Big Brother and the party actually monitor everyone's activities at all times is unknown, and is really beside the point. Orwell describes the experience of the average citizen: "You had to live—did live, from habit that became instinct—in the assumption that every sound you made was overheard, and except in darkness, every movement scrutinized."

It is not difficult to draw parallels between *1984* and today. You also live in a place and time in which your entire life can be tracked and monitored, and the technologies that perform these tasks are becoming more sophisticated by the day. The price of computers, database technologies, cameras, chips, and spyware or snoopware has decreased while the demand for detailed personal information has increased. Businesses believe they need your information to be competitive in the marketplace. Government believes it needs your information to be effective at homeland security.

> **Americans will not allow their privacy rights to erode much longer without a popular backlash.**

After reading this book you may have questions about what the loss of privacy means in the big picture. Does it mean that privacy is something of the past, and that once you lose it you can never get it back? What are the long-term consequences of the loss of privacy for our democratic system? Is a system democratic if government and business can collect information about you that you can't ever see (or correct if it's inaccurate)? Are the security measures the government has taken worth the risks to your privacy? The only honest answer to these questions is that it's still too soon to tell.

If the past is any indication of the future, Americans will not allow their privacy rights to erode much longer without a popular backlash. After all, when you live in the world's greatest democracy, you come to expect personal privacy, even if you do not enjoy a legal right to it in all situations. When telemarketing calls started to interrupt too many family dinners, Americans rallied for a Do-Not-Call Registry. When identity thieves started to steal money and peace of mind from millions of people, the public started to push for legislation against identity theft. When citizens understood how the USA Patriot Act threatened the privacy of innocent citizens and tipped the balance toward a too-powerful law enforcement, they passed resolutions against it in nearly 250 cities, towns, and municipalities throughout the country. Most Americans erroneously assume—even take for granted—that personal privacy is a pillar of this country's foundation, as are the individualistic values of life, liberty, and the pursuit of happiness.

For the love of our country and its national security, many of us are willing to temporarily defer our individual rights. But if government or business overextends itself, we as a people tend to react strongly—and it is likely that

American citizens will demand the return of our personal privacy. Again, the U.S. Constitution does not make privacy our right, but many of us see it that way. The struggle for privacy in the United States is constant and universal and will, in many ways, define the twenty-first century.

How might your privacy be spared in the long term? A responsive federal and state government may eventually limit the power of the USA Patriot Act and enact new legislation to protect your privacy. Moreover (and perhaps more likely), smart businesses may change their approach and actually protect individual personal privacy. Why? Because you and millions of others demand it, and if you demand it, then it may make good business sense. Take Citibank. Since 2003, this financial conglomerate has actively marketed its new credit card that promotes identity theft protection. The company issued the card as a response to consumer anxiety about what has become the fastest-growing crime in the country. The Internet service provider Earthlink has devoted significant resources to positioning itself as a strong protector of consumers worried about their online privacy by offering such features as parental controls and spam, pop-up, and virus blockers. On a smaller scale, consider the actions of local bookstores such as Bear Pond Books in Montpelier, Vermont. Bear Pond decided to purge its records in response to the USA Patriot Act, which required bookstore owners to divulge customer files at the request of the FBI: "When the CIA comes and asks what you've read because they're suspicious of you, we can't tell them because we don't have it," store co-owner Michael Katzenberg said. "That's just a basic right, to be able to read what you want without fear that somebody is looking over your shoulder to see what you're reading."

Retailers understand that a consumer's decision to shop in a certain place is dictated by many variables, including price, convenience, and customer service. Smart retailers know that privacy protection will become an increasingly important factor in a consumer's decision to shop at a certain place. Indeed, consumers appear to have developed their own privacy rules when companies fail to stem privacy breaches. According to a 2003 Customer Information Protection Survey, 92 percent of those surveyed said they would cease doing business with a company that reported three or fewer privacy violations. Fifty percent said they would move their business to another company if they did not have confidence in a company's ability to protect their personal data. Smart businesses cater to their customers, and as customers seek to protect their privacy by using their wallets, companies will respond in kind.

The financial area may also discover that privacy pays. As competition intensifies, financial institutions may decide to extend enticements beyond free checking and better interest rates. If financial institutions suffer from consumer backlash regarding information sharing and the extensive dossiers that are maintained, these institutions will no doubt start to change their policies. In a privacy-conscious marketplace, some financial institutions

> Consumer pressure may even force marketers and data aggregators to stop being privacy pariahs.

might differentiate themselves by becoming more attuned to privacy concerns, following in the footsteps of Citibank's identity theft credit card. New York Life, by design, exceeds the financial privacy requirements of mailing privacy notices to its customers by holding focus groups to assess customer privacy concerns and providing a special toll-free number for its customers to seek answers to their privacy-related questions. Other companies may need to commit to not sharing your customer data with either affiliates or third parties, or give you the choice to take yourself out of marketing programs altogether. You may soon discover that to win your business your financial institution wants to give you more protection than the law requires.

Consumer pressure may even force marketers and data aggregators to stop being privacy pariahs. Indeed, some direct marketers are already beginning to consider a different way of reaching their customers. Historically, marketers have distributed their marketing packages to a wide and untested audience. Sophisticated marketers are now acknowledging the efficiency of sending marketing pieces only to consumers who have previously agreed to receive information from the company. The result: higher acceptance rates and lower marketing costs, not to mention better public relations. As for data aggregators, a few sophisticated ones, including Acxiom and Equifax, have begun to actively promote their privacy policies and data security as a step toward appealing to customers, differentiating themselves from their competitors, and limiting the public-relations fallout in the event that any industry player violates customer privacy.

Businesses, too, may realize that by respecting privacy they get better results from their employees as well as their customers. These businesses may ask themselves, "Even if we have the technology and the ability to track every-body all the time, do we really want to do so? Even if it is legal, is it justifiable to infringe upon our employees' privacy? Should employees be forced to give up nearly all their privacy rights when they come to work here?" A perceptive business might conclude that excessive monitoring is demeaning and erodes the trust that should exist in the workplace. Overzealous surveillance may, in fact, be counterproductive, leading to a workforce that is less happy and cre-ative, and therefore less productive and effective.

In the past, businesses realized that they could attract top talent if they made some concessions. After all, dollars do not always dictate one's decision to accept a job. For example, companies with strong maternity policies have attracted top female talent, because women review a company's policy before accepting a job. The same is true for candidates who want to work in environ-ments that respect personal privacy. No doubt, Harriet Pearson, IBM's chief privacy officer, is pleased that IBM ranked first among the country's largest public company in terms of protecting employee privacy. The most-talented people have choices, and they are likely to choose companies that maintain the least intrusive policies over those with Big Brother-like surveillance.

●●●

Those of us who value our privacy hope that we will get it back simply because better privacy from the intrusions of big business and overbearing government is better for America. Constant monitoring is inconsistent with the values that have made America the greatest democracy in the history of the world. The United States is a land of opportunity, entrepreneurialism, and rugged individuality—characteristics that come from the freedom to create, to think differently, and to know that you can challenge the old way. In life as in business, the most creative ideas come from brainstorming ses-sions where individuals suggest ideas without fear that they will be judged or punished for those raw ideas. For a democracy to survive and flourish, cit-izens need to know that they can be free to be themselves and to express themselves without risk of repercussion. Without those freedoms, American society degenerates into the communist society of the old Soviet Union or the dystopia of Orwell's *1984*. Most of us imagine a better future for our families and ourselves.

As W.C. Fields once said, "The future ain't what it used to be." Until America turns around and values the privacy of its people, you must take action to protect your sensitive communications and important personal information. As a citizen, you need to know the ways in which your government may be tracking you and what you can do about it. You must push those you elect to office to respect your legal and constitutional rights to privacy and to adopt new and better standards. As a consumer and employee, you need to understand how companies collect your personal information, what they do with it, and how to decrease your exposure. You must force businesses to adopt policies that lead to increased protection and limitations on your personal information by seeking out stores with better privacy protections and working at companies with a greater respect for employee privacy policies. As a bearer of a social security card, a driver's license, and credit cards, you must learn the ways in which thieves can access your personal information and how to reduce your chances of identity theft.

> Until America turns around and values the privacy of its people, you must take action to protect your sensitive communications and important personal information.

In sum, you must be in a position in which you have as much control as possible over your personal information. In a world bursting with exciting and dangerous new technologies and laws that cannot possibly keep pace, you must do everything you can to empower yourself. The best empowerment comes in the form of awareness and self-protection. Scott McNealy, CEO of Sun Microsystems, raised eyebrows when he said, "You have zero privacy—get over it." He may have been at least half right when he said you have zero privacy today, but that doesn't mean you have zero control.

Notes

Chapter 1: What Privacy Means to You

p. 4 . . . *than what can be inflicted by mere bodily injury* . . . Louis Brandeis and Samuel Warren, "The Right to Privacy," *Harvard Law Review* IV, no. 5 (1890).

p. 5 . . . *the 1928 case of Olmstead* v. *United States* . . . *Olmstead* v. *U.S.*, 277 U.S. 438, (1928).

p. 5 . . . *the right most valued by civilized men* . . . *Olmstead, 277 U.S. 438.*

p. 5 . . . In *Griswold* v. *Connecticut, a landmark case concerning the privacy of a married couple's decision to use contraceptives* . . . *Griswold* v. *Connecticut,* 381 U.S. 479 (1965).

p. 5 . . . *various guarantees that create zones of privacy* . . . *Griswold,* 381 U.S. 479

p. 6 . . . *whether or not to terminate her pregnancy* . . . *Roe* v. *Wade,* 410 U.S. 113 (1973).

p. 6 . . . *Bowers* v. *Hardwick, which involved the arrest of Michael Hardwick for violating the Georgia criminal anti-sodomy statute* . . . *Bowers* v. *Hardwick,* 478 U.S. 186 (1986).

p. 6 . . . *Lawrence and Garner* v. *Texas, the Supreme Court overruled Bowers by extending the right to privacy and declaring state antisodomy laws unconstitutional* . . . *Lawrence and Garner* v. *Texas,* 539 U.S. ___ (2003).

p. 8 . . . *how often she used room deodorizers, sleeping aids, and hemorrhoid remedies* . . . Privacy Rights Clearinghouse, see http://www.privacyrights.org/ar/ftc-info_mktpl.htm

p. 9 . . . *who might have access to our personal and business e-mails, our medical and financial records, or our cordless and cellular telephone conversations* . . . See http://www.newsmax.com/archives/articles/2001/5/21/202254.shtml

p. 10 . . . *In a national survey conducted in September 2000 by the Privacy Council and Privista* . . . The author of the book was previously chief executive officer of Privista; see http://www.privista.com.

p. 10 . . . *offline database it had secured when it acquired the company Abacus* . . . Stephanie Olsen, "DoubleClick turns away from ad profiles," *CNET News.com,* 8 January 2002, see http://news.com.com/2100-1023-803593.html?legacy=cnet.

p. 10 . . . *for sharing customer information in a manner inconsistent with its privacy policy* . . . Janet Kornblum, "FTC, Geocities settle on privacy," *CNET News.com,* 13 August 1998, see http://news.com.com/2100-1023-214423.html?legacy=cnet.

p. 14 . . . *noncompliance could lead to fines or the loss of U.S. landing rights* . . . "Europe and U.S. at Odds on Airlines and Privacy," *New York Times,* 2 November 2003.

p. 14 . . . *the jurisdiction of these privacy laws will expand* . . . "Europe's New High-Tech Role: Playing Privacy Cop to the World," *Wall Street Journal,* 10 October 2003.

Chapter 2: Your Personal Information and the Public Record

p. 19 . . . *among the most restrictive states* . . . See http://www.injersey.com/access/story/1,2331,190918,00.html and http://www.dlncoalition.org/dln_issues/gaglaw.htm.

p. 19 . . . *Florida and Indiana are among the most open* . . . See http://starbulletin.com/96/09/02/news/story1.html.

p. 20 . . . *commercial use of social security numbers and public records* . . . See http://www.law.com/jsp/article.jsp?id=1046833530025.

p. 22 . . . *written permission from the student to release any information in a student's education record* . . . See http://studentsforacademicfreedom.org/archive/december/MerantoFerpa122903.htm.

p. 23 . . . *the FBI which operates secretly and is unresponsive to public criticism* . . . "The Campus Files: A Chronicle Special Report," *SFGate.com,* see http://sfgate.com/news/special/pages/2002/campusfiles/documents/3-1.shtml.

p. 24 . . . *to check if these individuals underreported their incomes* . . . Privacy Rights Clearinghouse, see http://www.privacyrights.org.

p. 26 . . . *purchased the social security numbers and home addresses of these top political appointees for $26 each* . . . "Group Found Social Security Numbers of Attorney General, CIA Director for $26," *American Morning*, CNN, 2 September 2003; for transcript, see http://www.consumerwatchdog.org/corporate/nw/nw003599.php3.

p. 31 . . . *to protect private information contained in driver's licenses* . . . Kim Zetter, "Great Taste, Less Privacy," *Wired.com*, 6 February 2004, see http://www.wired.com/news/privacy/0,1848,62182-2,00.html?tw=wn_story_page_next1.

p. 36 . . . *an identity thief can get a driver's license, a duplicate social security number, and much more* . . . See http://news.mpr.org/features/199911/15_newsroom_privacy/idtheft.html.

p. 37 . . . *and divorced her once he obtained French citizenship* . . . See http://www.gadens.com.au/docushare/dscgi/ admin.py/Get/File-317/767106.pdf.

p. 38 . . . *I am very much alive* . . . See http://www.inq7.net/opi/2003/jun/28/text/letter_4-1-p.htm.

p. 39 . . . *bank and corporate credit in the officers' names* . . . Dennis Blank, "Data from federal records used to commit identity theft," *Government Computer News*, Vol. 19, No. 29, 2 October 2000.

p. 40 . . . *veterans who had filed their DD 214s with their county courthouse* . . . Marcia Triggs, "Scams Target Veterans for Identity Theft," *Army News Service*, 22 January 2002.

p. 43 . . . *and that this information is a matter of public record* . . . "Rush fans irate at newspaper," *ABC Action News, Sound Bites*, see http://www.abcactionnews.com/entertainment/soundbites.shtml.

p. 43 . . . *Socorro was fired, and it took him seven months to find a new job* . . . "The Fight For Digital Privacy," *CBSNews.com*, 22 December 2003, see http://www.cbsnews.com/stories/2003/12/18/2003/main589352.shtml.

p. 45 . . . *the State of California has lost track of more than one-fifth of its approximately one hundred thousand registered sex offenders* . . . Sean Webby, "Police arrest sex offender," *Mercury News*, 20 February 2004.

Chapter 3: Your Identity

p. 53 . . . *Buick car company was among the golfer's many multimillion-dollar endorsements* . . . Kimberly Kindy, "DMV can't catch

tiger by his ID," *Orange County Register*, 20 December 2000.

p. 54 . . . *taken out in their names in 2002* . . . See http://www.google.com/search?q=cache:edXlq81vddEJ:mysite.verizon.net/res6uo8x/identitythievespreyingonseniors.doc+%22identity+theft%22+%22buy+a+house%22&hl=en&ie=UTF-8

p. 60 . . . *it's no surprise that identity thieves are so successful* . . . See http://www.debt-info.org.

p. 61 . . . *average American household has seven to ten credit cards* . . . See http://www.debt-info.org.

p. 61 . . . *The total loss to fraud was more than $437 million, about $228 per victim* . . . David McGuire, "FTC Identity Theft Remains Top Complaint," *Washington Post*, 22 January 2004.

p. 62 . . . *Internet-related fraud complaints, accounting for 48 percent of the total* . . . David McGuire. "FTC Identity Theft Remains Top Complaint," *Washington Post*, 22 January 2004.

p. 64 . . . *during which he had to pay restitution of $78,672.67* . . . See http://www.usdoj.gov/usao/md/press_releases/press01/lawrencesen.htm

p. 66 . . . *But I still have to prove I am me* . . . Bob Sullivan, "Identity theft tops consumer woes . . . again," *MSNBC News*, see http://www.msnbc.msn.com/id/4029541/.

p. 67 . . . *a certain cap for lost wages from taking time off from work* . . . 2003 Identity Theft Resource Center study, see www.idtheftcenter.org

p. 74 . . . *but could not start work until she cleared her name* . . . Kaja Whitehouse, "GETTING PERSONAL; ID Theft Hurts Job Seekers, Bad Drivers," *Wall Street Journal*, 30 September 2003.

Chapter 4: Your Credit

p. 78 . . . *shocked to discover a $500 lien he couldn't account for on his credit report* . . . See http://www.pbs.org/moneymoves/hot_topics/ht_105/creditscore.html.

p. 78 . . . *a fraudulent criminal record that did not bode well for Kelly's future in sales* . . . See http://www.cbc.ca/consumers/market/files/scams/idtheft/cases.html.

p. 86 . . . *transferred to his relative who was supposed to have paid the bills* . . . See http://www.worldlii.org/ca/cases/CAPrivCmr/2003/12.html

p. 88 . . . *used to access the reporter's balance, direct deposits from work, withdrawals, ATM visits, check numbers with dates and amounts, and the name of his broker* . . . Adam L. Penenberg, "The End of Privacy," *Forbes Magazine*, 29 November 1999.

p 95 . . . *took their identities, stole their money and swiped their security* . . . See http://www. cybercrime.gov/cummingsIndict.htm

Chapter 5: Your Money

p. 101 . . . *spend more on goods with cards than with cash* . . . "Just One Word: Plastic," *Fortune*, 23 February 2004.

p. 101 . . . *and checks to cards* . . . "Just One Word: Plastic," *Fortune*, 23 February 2004.

p. 103 . . . *Fleet settled the charges in 2001* . . . See http://www.ag.state.mn.us/consumer/privacy/privacy%5Flaw.htm.

p. 105 . . . *in a misleading manner to the CD holders* . . . See http://www.bankofamericasettlement.com/class-notice.html or Privacy Rights Clearinghouse, see http://www.privacyrightsnow.com/glb_act.htm

p. 105 . . . *subscribing to X-rated Internet porn sites and calling 900-number sex chat lines* . . . See http://www.consumerfedofca.org/edufund_horror.html.

p. 108 . . . *MemberWorks paid the bank $4 million plus commissions of 22 percent of net revenue on sales of club memberships* . . . Jane Hadley, "Bank One agrees to protect credit card holders from telemarketers," *Seattle Post-Intelligencer*, 1 January 2003.

p. 116 . . . *twenty thousand people were using the Diners Club credit card* . . . See http://history1900s.about.com/library/weekly/aa081601a.htm.

p. 116 . . . *a total of 7.6 cards per cardholder* . . . See http://www.cardweb.com.

p. 117 . . . *all their card information and passwords were sent to the criminals to use at will* . . . See http://www.efc.ca/pages/media/globe.10dec99.html.

p. 123 . . . *merchants lose more than $13 billion to bad checks* . . . See 2000 Report by Towers Group

p. 126 . . . *and 10 percent on checking accounts on its website* . . . "Netware Savings principals indicted," *Charlotte Business Journal*, 21 September 1998.

p. 127 . . . *reduces the risk of identity theft significantly—up to 18 percent according to one*

account . . . See http://www.technewsworld.com/perl/story/32622.html.

p. 127 . . . *to convert to online bill payment by the end of 2006* . . . "Paying Bills Online, *The Early Show*, 8 November 2003, see http://www.cbsnews.com/stories/2003/11/07/earlyshow/contributors/reginalewis/main582486.shtml.

Chapter 6: Your Shopping

p. 138 . . . *and was on trial at that time for the crime* . . . "Largest database marketing firm sends phone numbers, addresses of 5,000 families with kids to TV reporter using name of child killer," *Business Wire*, 13 May 1996.

p. 138 . . . *based on that household's specific consumer and demographic characteristics* . . . Pamela Paul, "Sell it to the Psyche," *TIME.com*, 8 September 2003, see http://www.time.com/time/insidebiz/article/0,9171,1101030915-483313-1,00.html.

p. 139 . . . *which can include real-time information on you* . . . Richard Behar, "Never Heard of Acxiom? Chances Are It's Heard of You," *Fortune*, 9 February 2004.

p. 141 . . . *whether certain individuals were purchasing an inordinate number of plastic bags* . . . "Privacy and Consumer Profiling," Electronic Privacy Information Center, see http://www.epic.org/privacy/profiling.

p. 141 . . . *it's time to mine it for marketing purposes* . . . See http://www.bicycle-forum.com/general/Retail_Performance_Stores_asking_for_customer_name_266101.html.

p. 142 . . . *TO NOT RETURN THIS CARD MAY AFFECT YOUR WARRANTY* . . . Jim Hightower, "Playground Prozac," Texas Observer, 14 April 2000.

p. 143 . . . *because of the quantities of alcohol he purchased, all recorded on his Von's Frequent Shopper card* . . . James Glave, "The Safeway to Shop," *Wired*, 8 October 1999, see also http://www.wired.com/news/print/0,1294,31791,00.html.

p. 145 . . . *eventually forced the companies to shut down the program* . . . See http://www.nocards.org/savings/archive/Waco_Tribune.htm.

p. 145 . . . *in order to track citizens' possible terrorist proclivities* . . . Erik Baard, "Buying Trouble," *Village Voice*, 24-30 July 2002.

p. 146 . . . *they did not know who put it there* . . . See http://www.accessnorthga.com/news/ap_newfullstory.asp?ID=12469.

p. 146 . . . *recommend to its client that the OJ should be positioned near the medicine* . . . "Retail Intelligence," *Primetime Thursday*, ABC News, 12 December 2002, see http://abcnews. go.com/sections/primetime/DailyNews/ retail_lab_021212.html.

p. 149 . . . *it was not testing RFID chips* . . . "Chipping away at your privacy," *Chicago Sun-Times*, 9 November 2003.

p. 154 . . . *a letter from eBay telling her that the request was not legitimate* . . . Andrew Brandt and Anne Kandra, "The Great American Privacy Makeover," *PC World*, November 2003.

p. 155 . . . *to see whether his exploits as a hacker were mentioned* . . . See http://news. findlaw.com/hdocs/docs/cyberlaw/ uslamo803cmp.pdf.

p. 158 . . . *disclose your name, city, state, telephone number, e-mail address, user ID history, fraud complaints, and bidding and listing history without a subpoena* . . . EBay Privacy Policy, see http://pages.ebay.com/help/ community/png-priv.html.

p. 164 . . . *and even a person who had died* . . . Grant Gross, "Chicago ID thieves barred from internet auctions," *ComputerWeekly.com*, see http://www.computerweekly.com/ Article127461.htm.

Chapter 7: Your Computer and the Internet

p. 178 . . . *had broken into computers at the Pentagon and commercial and educational institutions* . . . James Glave, "Pentagon Hacker Exposed by Justice Department," *Wired*, 18 March 1998, see also http://www.wired. com/news/technology/0,1282,11030,00.html.

p. 178 . . . *the city's fire department and security system* . . . "Airport Chaos Puts Boy Hacker on Spot," *Hobart Mercury*, 26 March 1998.

p. 179 . . . *software for a computer company in Germany* . . . See http://www.shk-dplc.com/cfo/ articles/hack.htm.

p. 179 . . . *some examples of what hackers can do* . . . See http://www.btinternet.com/ ~shawweb/george/hacks/info.html#damage

p. 180 . . . *crime ring set up by the FBI* . . . "Testimony to the Commerce and Economic Development Subcommittee on Electronic Commerce," House of Representatives: Commonwealth of Pennsylvania, 30 September 1999.

p. 180 . . . *slowed all traffic on the World Wide Web* . . . "New Virus Can Turn You Into a Spammer," *Wall Street Journal*, D1, 29 January 2004.

p. 181 . . . *searched for fresh computers to infect* . . . "Home users suffer web worm woe," *BBC News.com*, 13 August 2003, see http:// news.bbc.co.uk/1/hi/technology/3147147.stm.

p. 181 . . . *to periodically scan your files* . . . SecureAgent Secure eNewsletter, vol. 115, 2 September 2002, see http://www.securenotes. com/enewsletter/Volume115.htm.

p. 184 . . . *website not connected to the organization* . . . Linda Rosencrance, "Red Cross warns of Trojan Horse that steals credit card data," *Computerworld.com*, 19 October 2001.

p. 186 . . . *Turn on your virus filter* . . . Michelle Delio, "What They Know Could Hurt You," *Wired*, 3 January 2002, see also http://www. wired.com/news/privacy/0,1848,49430,00. html.

p. 187 . . . *go back and enable your programs* . . . CERT Coordinating Center, see http://www. cert.org/tech_tips/home_networks.html#II-A.

p. 186 . . . *were using encryption technology* . . . Sean Captain, "Empowering the Wi-Fi User to Foil the Snoop," *New York Times*, 11 March 2004.

p. 188 . . . *marketing companies such as DoubleClick and LinkExchange as well as Web giants Yahoo! and America Online* . . . Stephanie Olsen, "Privacy group shines light on Web bugs, " *CNET News.com*, 7 June 2001, see http://news.com.com/2100-1023-268055. html?legacy=cnet.

p. 188 . . . *to monitor the document and know who's accessing or reading it* . . . Cecily Barnes and Paul Festa, "Word documents susceptible to 'Web bug' infestation," *CNET News.com*, see http://news.com.com/2100-1023-245160.html? legacy=cnet.

p. 188 . . . *any other virus would, inflicting similar damages* . . . Cecily Barnes and Paul Festa, "Word documents susceptible to 'Web bug' infestation," *CNET News.com*, see http://news. com.com/2100-1023-245160.html?legacy=cnet.

p. 190 . . . *97 percent of the spam it received was sent to addresses harvested from the Web* . . . "Why Am I Getting All This Spam? Unsolicited Commercial E-mail Research Six Month Report," Center for Democracy & Technology, March 2003, see http://www.cdt.org/ speech/spam/030319spamreport.shtml.

p. 190 . . . *Yahoo!, Hotbot, Internet Archive, and others* . . . "Research depot: Using Search Engines," Rutgers University Writing Program, see http://wp.rutgers.edu/courses/201/ research_depot/search_engines.html.

p. 191 . . . *searching for computers with shared disks* . . . Simson L. Garfinkel, "5 biggest threats to your privacy online," *MSN Money*, see http://moneycentral.msn.com/articles/banking/online/5485.asp.

p. 191 . . . *by simply sending an e-greeting* . . . Jon Shwartz, "Spying Software Gains Power and Stirs Concern," *New York Times,* 10 October 2003.

p. 191 . . . *and he used them to access and open bank accounts on-line* . . . "Kinko's spy case highlights risk of public Internet terminals," *USA Today.com,* 22 July 2003, see http://www.usatoday.com/tech/news/techpolicy/2003-07-22-terminal-fear_x.htm.

p. 192 . . . *his children's software contained heavily encrypted spyware* . . . Dana Hawkins, "Privacy Worries Arise Over Spyware in Kids' Software," *U.S. News & World Report,* 3 July 2000.

p. 193 . . . *personal information to marketing and advertising companies* . . . See http://www.downloadatoz.com/guardie/faqs.html.

p. 196 . . . *to search and remove such software from your computer* . . . Andrew Brandt, "Privacy Watch: Don't Let Anyone Secretly Track Your Keystrokes," *PC World,* June 2002.

p. 197 . . . *not included in the Windows End Task (Ctrl-Alt-Del) dialog box* . . . See http://cexx.org/problem.htm.

p. 198 . . . *for users to report suspected spoofing* . . . Dominic Timms, "Amazon moves to tackle alleged email fraudsters," *Guardian Limited Online,* 27 August 2003, see http://www.guardian.co.uk/online/spam/story/0,13427,1030107,00.html.

p. 199 . . . *compared to only 7 percent in 2001* . . . "E-Mail Spam: How To Stop It From Stalking You," *Consumer Reports,* August 2003, p. 12.

p. 199 . . . *billion spam e-mails, in the aggregate, in a single day* . . . "E-Mail Spam: How To Stop It From Stalking You," *Consumer Reports,* August 2003, p. 12.

p. 199 . . . *as little as $500 to send 1 million e-mails* . . . "E-Mail Spam: How To Stop It From Stalking You," *Consumer Reports,* August 2003, p. 12.

p. 201 . . . *anti-spam law went into effect July 1, 2003* . . . Brad Wright, "Virginia indicts two on spam felony charges," *CNN.com,* 12 December 2003, see http://www.cnn.com/2003/TECH/internet/12/12/spam.charges/index.html.

p. 201 . . . *legal action against more than 100 spammers since 1997* . . . Grant Gross, "AOL, Earthlink sue alleged spammers," *InfoWorld.com,* 18 February 2004, see

http://reviews.infoworld.com/article/04/02/18/HNaolspam_1.html?INTERNET%20STANDARDS.

p. 206 . . . *Lee's penalty of home detention was a warning to others* . . . John Leyden, "Email snooping custody battle woman escapes jail," *Register Newsletter,* 22 October 2003, see http://www.theregister.co.uk/content/6/33535.html.

p. 210 . . . *simultaneously installed adware to track user activity* . . . "When Instant Messages Come Bearing Malice," *New York Times,* 25 March 2004.

p. 212 . . . *program that allows someone to take over the computer* . . . "Computer worm lures with alleged Zeta-Jones photos," *USAToday.com,* 14 February 2003, see http://www.usatoday.com/tech/news/2003-02-14-worm-jones_x.htm.

p. 215 . . . *take the following precautions* . . . "Ten Internet Tips for Travellers," First Step Communications, Pty. Ltd., see http://www.firststep.com.au/articles/travellers.html.

Chapter 8: Your Home

p. 219 . . . *may also reveal whether you have filed for bankruptcy* . . . See http://www.nolo.com/lawstore/products/product.cfm/objectID/567125E8-997E-4F70-82336ED531EDAE25/sampleChapter/6.

p. 220 . . . *claims to screen about fifty thousand prospective tenants each month* . . . Dennis Hevesi, "When the Credit Check is Only the Start," *New York Times,* 12 October 2003.

p. 220 . . . *or whether you made chronic late payments* . . . Dennis Hevesi, "When the Credit Check is Only the Start," *New York Times,* 12 October 2003.

p. 221 . . . *despite her persistent efforts to clean up her credit report* . . . Kenneth R. Gosselin and Matthew Kauffman, "Credit Laws Ignite a New Battle," *Hartford Courant,* 12 May 2003.

p. 223 . . . *this becomes more likely every day* . . . "Comments Of The Electronic Privacy Information Center, The Privacy Rights Clearinghouse, Us Pirg, And Consumers Union," 1 May 2002, see http://www.epic.org/privacy/financial/glb_comments.pdf.

p. 223 . . . *The co-op board felt that the buyer didn't have the right image for their building* . . . Collin Levey, "Butting In: A co-op board bans smoking—and strikes a blow for freedom," *Wall Street Journal,* 2 May 2002.

p. 232 ... *but to "reflect the lifestyle" of the target buyer* ... Deborah Schoeneman, "Talk to the Hand," *New York*, 19-26 January 2003.

p. 232 ... *stored templates (as in the case in many large-scale systems)* ... Declan McCullagh, "Scanning the Future of Privacy," *CNet News.com*, 25 March 2003, see http://news.com.com/2100-1029-994080.html.

p. 233 ... *"service providers" for "legitimate business activities."* ... Jeffrey Kosseff, "Comcast Will Redo Privacy Policy," *The Oregonian*, 23 September 2003.

p. 233 ... *"one of the great privacy issues of our time"* ... Lisa Friedman, "But Who's Watching TiVo? Congressman Concerned About Makers Selling Private Information," *Los Angeles Daily News*, 1 December 2003.

p. 234 ... *the original understanding of the Constitution into the technological age* ... Jeffrey Rosen, "A Victory for Privacy," *Wall Street Journal*, 18 June 2001.

p. 234 ... *technology-assisted searches in a variety of places, not just the home* ... Jeffrey Benner, "Kyllo: Taking the 5th on the 4th," *Wired*, 3 July 2001, see also http://www.wired.com/news/privacy/0,1848,44785,00.html.

p. 235 ... *private sexual conduct among consenting adults in their homes* ... "Supreme Court Strikes Down Texas Sodomy Law," *CNN.com*, 18 November 2003, see http://www.cnn.com/2003/LAW/06/26/scotus.sodomy/index.html.

p. 236 ... *To date, at least six states* ... California, Hawaii, New Hampshire, New Jersey, Vermont, and Washington.

p. 237 ... *receive about 4 million tons of junk mail each year* ... Clean Air Council, see http://www.cleanair.org/Waste/wasteFacts.html.

p. 238 ... *sales will surpass $1.7 trillion in 2003* ... See http://www.the-dma.org.

p. 238 ... *projections estimating almost $2.5 trillion by 2008* ... See http://www.the-dma.org/cgi/dispnewsstand?article=1569

p. 239 ... *Acxiom, Donnelley Marketing, Equifax, Experian, and TransUnion* ... Privacy Rights Clearinghouse, see http://www.privacyrights.org/fs/fs4-junk.htm.

p. 240 ... *companies with which you have a relationship* ... See http://www.dmaconsumers.org and http://www.epicenternews.org.

p. 241 ... *you can expect to receive twenty-five offers this year* ... See http://www.cardweb.com/cardlearn/faqs/2002/jun/13.amp.

p. 242 ... *Remove name from mailing list* ... See http://www.obviously.com/junkmail.

p. 242 ... *you have to communicate directly with the sender* ... Electronic Privacy Information Center, see http://www.epicenternews.org/no.more.junk.mail.htm.

p. 242 ... *entered into the National Change of Address database* ... See http://www.obviously.com/junkmail.

p. 244 ... *will not in any way affect a consumer's warranty rights* ... Privacy Rights Clearinghouse, see http://www.privacyrights.org/fs/fs4-junk.htm.

p. 244 ... *this information is not to be sold, traded, or shared* ... Privacy Rights Clearinghouse, see http://www.privacyrights.org/fs/fs4-junk.htm.

p. 245 ... *and then send them back to direct marketers* ... See http://www.smartmoney.com/10things/index.cfm?story=20031111.

p. 247 ... *for those wanting to learn more about stopping junk faxes* ... Steve Kirsch, "How Steve Kirsch discovered fax.com," *Junkfax.org*, see http://www.junkfax.org/fax/stories/Kirsch.html.

p. 247 ... *FCC has in the past levied fines in the million-dollar range* ... See http://www.fcc.gov/eb/News_Releases/nr21cen1.html.

p. 248 ... *statistics from the Federal Communications Commission* ... Yochi J. Dreazen, "Do Not Call Roster Debuts Today," *Wall Street Journal*, 27 June 2003.

p. 248 ... *preserving the Do Not Call rules and upholding their constitutionality* ... "Do Not Call rules survive recent Constitutional Attack," *USA Today*, 25 February, 2004.

p. 251 ... *increase accountability, and help in enforcement efforts* ... See http://www.ftc.gov/bcp/conline/pubs/tmarkg/donotcall.htm.

p. 254 ... *and the affiliate should provide a similar service* ... For more information about affiliate sharing of financial information, see Fact Sheet 24 at Privacy Rights Clearinghouse, see http://www.privacyrights.org/financial.htm.

Chapter 9: Your Workplace

p. 259 ... *over 40 percent of job applicants lie on their résumés* ... Fifth Annual Hiring Index Study (2002) by ADP Screening and Selection Services, Society for Human Resource Management Forum at http://www.shrm.org/ema/library_published/nonIC/CMS_006087.asp.

p. 259 . . . *both of whom included "inaccuracies" on their résumés* . . . Kris Frieswick, "Liar, liar." *CFO, Magazine for Senior Financial Executives,* December 2002.

p. 259 . . . *the U.S. Olympic Committee who lied about having earned a doctorate* . . . Charles J. Sykes, "Big Brother in the Workplace," *Hoover Digest,* 2003, No. 3, see http://www-hoover. stanford.edu/publications/digest/003/sykes. html

p. 259 . . . *beyond what workers voluntarily provide* . . . Charles J. Sykes, "Big Brother in the Workplace," *Hoover Digest,* 2000, No. 3, see http://www-hoover.stanford.edu/ publications/digest/003/sykes.html.

p. 260 . . . *half of new hires do not work out* . . . "So You're a Player. Do You Need a Coach?" *Fortune,* 7 February 2000.

p. 260 . . . *$40,000 to replace a senior executive* . . . This statistic, attributed to *Recruiting Times,* and other interesting hiring statistics, are quoted at http://www.Backgroundprofiles. com/stas.html.

p. 261 . . . *liability for misuse of any of this information* . . . "City of Decatur Modifies Employee Background Checks in Response to ACLU," ACLU, 26 February 2001, see http:// www.aclu.org/Privacy/Privacy.cfm?ID=7144& c=132.

p. 263 . . . *separated from other personnel files* . . . Martha Lester, Julie Werner, and Michele Contreras Sadati, "The Legal Nuts and Bolts of Hiring Employees." *New Jersey Law Journal,* 26 March 2001.

p. 264 . . . *not according to the* Washington Post . . . "On the Job," *Washington Post,* p. H3, 9 March 2003.

p. 265 . . . *according to one national employment agency* . . . According to Victoria Lowe, president of Alert Staffing, a national employment agency, as cited by Carolyn M. Brown in "Ways and Means: Bad Credit Blues?" at http://www.africana.com/columns/brown/ ls20031125.credit.asp.

p. 267 . . . *background checks as a post–September 11 security measure* . . . Tom Zucco, "Background check kits worry some," *St. Petersburg Times,* 22 March 2004.

p. 267 . . . *promptly received pink slips from their own employers* . . . Ann Davis, "Zero Tolerance: Employers Dig Deep into Worker's Pasts, Citing Terrorism Fears," *Wall Street Journal,* 12 March 2002.

p. 268 . . . *without the employees' knowledge or consent* . . . Melinda Hawkins, "Drug tests violate basic rights," *Alestle* (Southern Illinois University, Edwardsville), 24 January 2002, see http://www.thealestle.com/news/2002/ 01/24/Editorial/Drug-Tests.Violate.Basic. Rights-168313.shtml.

p. 270 . . . *the case ultimately settled for more than $1 million* . . . Tori Minton, "Don't get psyched out: More companies considering pre-employment tests," *San Francisco Chronicle,* 21 October 2001.

p. 270 . . . *Unbelievably, the court ruled in favor of the police department* . . . Thalia Assuras, "Connecticut Man Rejected from Police Department Because of IQ," transcript from *CBS This Morning,* 10 September 1999.

p. 271 . . . *The case was settled before the court had a chance to rule* . . . *U.S. News & World Report,* Vol. 122, no. 24, 23 June 1997.

p. 271 . . . *The railroad agreed to settle the case, pay $2.2 million, and halt genetic testing* . . . Sarah Schafer, "Railroad Agrees to Stop Gene-Testing Workers," *Washington Post,* 19 April 2001.

p. 272 . . . *50 million résumés are posted on these sites* . . . Kendra Mayfield, "The Perils of Online Job Sites," *Wired,* 6 March 2003, see also http://www.wired.com/news/print/ 0,1294,57923,00.html.

p. 274 . . . *recommended for their privacy policies* . . . Andrea Coombes, "Privacy Rare for Online Job Seekers," *Daily News,* 27 November 2003.

p. 275 . . . *52 percent of employers review and store employees' e-mail messages* . . . This figure up from 47 percent in 2001.

p. 276 . . . *65 percent disciplined workers for such conduct* . . . Romy Riblitzky, "Corporate Snooping on the Rise," *ABCNews.com,* see http://abcnews.go.com/sections/business/ DailyNews/snooping_010418.html.

p. 277 . . . *still decide to use your company's system* . . . See http://www.npelra.org/legal/ monitoring.asp.

p. 278 . . . *monitor their employees in some way, according to the AMA* . . . Mari Alboher Nusbaum, "New Kind of Snooping Arrives at the Office," *New York Times,* 13 July 2003.

p. 278 . . . *are you then violating state law?* . . . Perry Aftab and Jim Durkin, "Should IT Have to Report Child Porn?" *Optimize,* 1 May 2002.

p. 279 . . . *preventing "inappropriate and unprofessional" conduct outweighed the employee's right to privacy* . . . James Glave, "An E-mail Bill for Employees," *Wired,* 16 September 1999, see also http://www.wired.com/ news/politics/0,1283,21792,00.html.

p. 280 ... *The court in California rejected this claim* ... Bourke *v.* Nissan Motor Corp. B068705 (Cal. Ct. App. 1993); and *McLaren* v. *Microsoft Corp.* WL339015 (Tex. Ct. App. 1999).

p. 280 ... *easily captures these e-mails* ... Sam Ames and Rachel Konrad, "Web-based E-mail Services Offer Employees Little Privacy," *CNET News.com*, 3 October 2000, see http://news.com.com/2100-1017-246543.html

p. 281 ... *tapes that have been overwritten several times* ... David Bennahum, "Old Email Never Dies," *Wired*, May 1999, see also http://www.wired.com/wired/archive/7.05/email.html.

p. 282 ... *may be kept without your knowledge* ... Ryan Teague Beckwith, "Plugged In," *Newsday*, 6 August 2002; Sandra Swanson, "Employers Take a Closer Look," *Informationweek.com*, 15 July 2002.

p. 283 ... *records e-mails and chat sessions, and logs keystrokes* ... Brett Glass, "Are You Being Watched?," *PC Magazine*, 23 April 2002.

p. 284 ... *The male employee was fired* ... *Huffcut* v. *McDonald's Corp.* 94CV6589 (N.Y. 1995).

p. 285 ... *the area was not reserved for their exclusive use* ... Thompson v. *Johnson County Community College*, 930 F. Supp. 501 (D. Kan. 1996).

p. 286 ... *voice-activated recording devices* ... Desilets v.*Wal-Mart Stores*, 171 F. 3d. 711 (1st Cir. 1999).

p. 286 ... *removing the disk from the desk and accessing the files* ... Williams v. *Philadelphia Housing Authority*, WL267108 (E.D. Pa. 1993).

p. 286 ... *no reasonable expectation that their work areas are private* ... O'Connor v. *Ortega*, 480 U.S., 709 (1987).

p. 287 ... *left after termination is not unreasonable* ... State v. *Lambright*, 138 Ariz. 63, 75, 673 P.2d 1, 13 (1983).

p. 287 ... *both of which contain information needed by other employees* ... O'Bryan v. *KTIV Television*, 64 F.3d 1188, 1193 (8th Cir. 1995).

p. 287 ... *Companies such as Adidas, Goldman Sachs, and GlaxoSmithKline use these technologies* ... Andrew Brown, "Big Brother Is Watching You Sweat," *CNN.com*, 30 July 2002, see http://www.cnn.com/2002/WORLD/asiapcf/east/07/30/hongkong.fitness.first/.

p. 287 ... *have them keep tabs on workers* ... Stephanie Armour, "More Workplaces Keep Eye, and Ear, on Employees," *USA Today*, 27 February 2003.

p. 287 ... *compensation fraud or other objectionable behavior* ... Stephanie Armour, "More Workplaces Keep Eye, and Ear, on Employees," *USA Today*, 27 February 2003.

p. 288 ... *wage-earners and white-collar, salaried employees* ... Kris Maher, "Big Employer Is Watching," *Wall Street Journal*, 4 November 2003.

p. 288 ... *infrared sensors to track their every move* ... Dana Hawkins, "Who's Watching Now? Hassled by Lawsuits, Firms Probe Workers' Privacy," *U.S. News & World Report*, 15 September 1997.

p. 288 ... *GPS devices in their news trucks* ... Chris Baker, "Channel 7 Uses GPS to Dispatch its Crews; Some Workers See Privacy Invasion," *Washington Times*, 23 January 2003.

p. 288 ... *contacted the manager's mental-health providers without his consent* ... Jonathan Canter, "Drawing the Line on Privacy at Work," *CareerJournal.com*, see http://www.careerjournal.com/myc/legal/19990209-canter.html.

p. 288 ... *immoral and unprofessional evidencing unfitness to teach* ... Pettit v. *State Bd. of Education*, 10 Cal.3d 29 (1973).

p. 289 ... *outrageous conduct on the part of your employer* ... Patton v. *J.C. Penney Co.*, 301 Or. 117, 719 P.2d 854 (1986).

p. 289 ... *sexual harassment claim brought on by the spurned party* ... Alex Fennel, Christine Filosa, and Rebecca Wilson, "Romantic Relationships at Work: Does Privacy Trump the Dating Police?" *The Privacy Project*, Volume 70, Issue No. 1, January 2003, see http://www.iadclaw.org/StaticContent/pdfs/RomanticRelationships.pdf

p. 291 ... *with respect to their commitment to employee privacy* ... "Ranking Privacy At Work," *Wired*, October 2003; Best Companies: IBM, HP, Ford, Baxter Healthcare, and Sears; Worst Companies: Eli Lilly, Wal-Mart, The New York Times Company, Burlington Northern Santa Fe, and Hilton Hotels.

p. 291 ... *IBM's first privacy officer* ... As more and more companies have been criticized or sued for privacy-related practices, they have begun to hire newly created "privacy officers." Their job is essentially to define and protect what privacy is to their business partners, their consumers, and their own employees.

p. 291 . . . *hidden recording devices to tape employees' private conversations* . . . *Desilets* v. *Wal-Mart Stores,* 171 F. 3d. 711 (1st Cir. 1999).

p. 291 . . . *to collect urine specimens for drug testing* . . . *Mission Petroleum Carriers, Inc.* v. *Solomon,* 37 SW.3d 482 (Tex. App.-Beaumont 2001).

p. 291 . . . *searched a trucking employee's motel room* . . . *Sowards* v. *Norbar,* 78 Ohio App. 3d 545, (1992).

Chapter 10: Your Health

p. 294 . . . *how the world discovered that tennis great Arthur Ashe suffered from AIDS* . . . "Medican Privacy Stories: Individuals Exposed," *Health Privacy Project Newsletter,* November 2003, see http://www. healthprivacy.org/usr_doc/Storiesupd.pdf.

p. 296 . . . *the EMT violated the woman's privacy* . . . Lisa Sink "Ruling upholds patient's privacy," *Milwaukee Journal Sentinel,* 28 May 2003.

p. 297 . . . *no reason to store the donors' names in that particular database* . . . J. Marcotty, "Names of Donors Are Accidentally Included in Letter to Kidney Patients," *Minneapolis Star Tribune,* A1, 15 January 2002; See http://lists.essential.org/pipermail/med-privacy/2002q1/000310.html.

p. 301 . . . *entities under HIPPA refer to health-care providers* . . . Technically, HIPAA regulates health-care providers who transmit medical information electronically but in today's digital environment this applies to almost all heath-care providers.

p. 301 . . . *health plans, and health-care clearinghouses* . . . Health-care clearinghouses refer to such entities as health-care billing services.

p. 306 . . . *seizure of the records violated Limbaugh's privacy rights* . . . "Limbaugh admits addiction to pain medication," *CNN.com,* 10 October 2003, see http://www.cnn.com/2003/SHOWBIZ/10/10/rush.limbaugh/index.html.

p. 306 . . . *but the threat lingers* . . . Kim Zetter, "Outsourcing: Danger to Privacy," *Wired,* 20 February 2004, see http://www.wired.com/news/business/0,1367,62356,00.html.

p. 306 . . . *authorities declined to release under HIPAA* . . . Texas News, *Star-Telegram,* 2 March 2004.

p. 311 . . . *sent by someone who had been in the bar* . . . "Aids Confidentiality," *USA Today,* 10 October 1996.

p. 312 . . . *names and e-mail addresses of all recipients* . . . "Lilly Privacy Violation Charges Are Settled," *New York Times,* 19 January 2002.

p. 312 . . . *the woman's records to find out the intimate details* . . . Anne Barnard, "Doctors brace for changes on patient privacy," *Boston Globe,* 1 November 2003.

p. 315 . . . *of more than sixty children and teenagers who had visited and were diagnosed by the university* . . . "Poor Security," *Health Privacy Project Newsletter,* November 2003, see http://www.healthprivacy.org/usr_doc/Storiesupd.pdf.

p. 317 . . . *perfectly capable of handling his work* . . . Alissa J. Rubin, "Records No Longer for Doctors' Eyes Only," *Los Angeles Times,* 1 September 1998.

Chapter 11: Your Everyday Life

p. 326 . . . *prior to departure is still in the works* . . . Matthew Wald, "Privacy Issue Delays Change In Airport Screening System," *New York Times,* p. A27, 13 February 2004.

p. 328 . . . *which resulted in the Kahns being put on a watch list* . . . "Patriot Act LAW!!! George W Is Watching You Change!" *Black and White Reader,* see http://blackandwhitereader.tripod.com/.

p. 328 . . . *contracting them during times of national crisis or emergencies* . . . Eric Posner and John Yoo, "The Patriot Act Under Fire," *Wall Street Journal,* 10 December 2003.

p. 328 . . . *passed resolutions condemning the Patriot Act* . . . Dan Kennedy, "State of Surveillance: Let's Just Throw Away the Bill of Rights and the Constitution," *Boston Phoenix,* 19-25 September 2003.

p. 329 . . . *prohibited from notifying you or anyone else about the search* . . . Section 215 applies to third-party records. School records are controlled by Section 507. Both sections are discussed under "College & University Education" of the USA Patriot Act of 2001.

p. 329 . . . *can conduct records searches on you and virtually anyone* . . . Dahlia Lithwick and Julia Turner, "A Guide to the Patriot Act, Part I," *Slate,* 8 September 2003, see http://slate.msn.com/id/2087984/.

p. 330 . . . *time may be extended for good cause* . . . Dahlia Lithwick and Julia Turner, "A Guide to the Patriot Act, Part I," *Slate,* 8 September 2003, see http://slate.msn.com/id/2087984/.

p. 330 . . . *or if the police are searching the wrong house* . . . "Surveillance Under the USA PATRIOT Act," ACLU, see http://www.aclu.org/SafeandFree/SafeandFree.cfm?ID=12263&c=206.

p. 330 . . . *to tell you or anyone else that the monitoring is taking place* . . . "The USA Patriot Act," Electronic Privacy Information Center, see http://www.epic.org/privacy/terrorism/usapatriot/.

p. 331 . . . *according to FBI and Department of Justice officials* . . . Michael Meehan, "Is Carnivore Dangerous? Controversy Continues," *Computerworld.com*, see http://www.computerworld.com/securitytopics/security/privacy/story/0,10801,54998,00.html.

p. 331 . . . *does not specifically mention Carnivore by name* . . . Dahlia Lithwick and Julia Turner, "A Guide to the Patriot Act, Part III." *Slate*, 10 September 2003, see http://slate.msn.com/id/2088161/.

p. 331 . . . *a lot more than just addressing information* . . . Rachel S. Martin, "Watch What You Type: As the FBI Records Your Keystrokes, the Fourth Amendment Develops Carpal Tunnel Syndrome," *American Criminal Law Review*, 22 June 2003.

p. 332 . . . *wonderful union of Orwell and Kafka* . . . "Internet Surveillance Up Since Sept. 11th." *USA Today*, 28 May 2002, see http://www.usatoday.com/tech/news/2002/05/28/net-surveillance.htm.

p. 332 . . . *are at risk of being spied upon by the government* . . . "Surveillance Under the USA PATRIOT Act", ACLU, see http://www.aclu.org/SafeandFree/SafeandFree.cfm?ID=12263&c=206.

p. 333 . . . *will trigger the sensor* . . . Frank J. Murray, "NASA plans to read terrorist's minds at airports," *Washington Times*, 17 August 2002.

p. 334 . . . *see your X-rays appearing on the Internet* . . . Dana Hawkins and David LaGesse, "Tech vs. Terror," *U.S. News & World Report*, 8 October 2001.

p. 334 . . . *and every book title a passenger reads* . . . Elisa Batista, "Videocams Record Airline Flights," *Wired*, 18 July 2003, see also http://www.wired.com/news/print/0.1294,59652,00.html.

p. 334 . . . *ID system that would facilitate government surveillance* . . . Dana Hawkins and David LaGesse, "Tech vs. Terror," *U.S. News & World Report*, 8 October 2001.

p. 335 ... *used the information to categorize the passengers on their perceived threat level* ... Frances Fiorino, "Big Brother, Let's Talk Privately," *Aviation Week*, 29 September 2003.

p. 335 . . . *data-mining program that looked like a blueprint for CAPPS II* . . . Max Blumen-

thal, "Data Debase," *American Prospect*, 19 December 2003, see http://www.prospect.org/webfeatures/2003/12/blumenthal-m-12-19.html.

p. 335 . . . *the implementation of CAPPS II has not yet been finalized* . . . Matthew Wald, "Privacy Issue Delays Change In Airport Screening System," *New York Times*, p. A27, 13 February 2004.

p. 335 . . . *criticism has focused on four aspects of the profiling system* . . . "The Five Problems with CAPPS II: Why the Airline Passenger Profiling Proposal Should be Abandoned," ACLU, 25 August 2003, see http://www.aclu.org/SafeandFree/SafeandFree.cfm?ID=13356&c=206.

p. 335 . . . *information on family and friends, and so on* . . . Don Campbell, "High-tech Microscopes Expose Americans' Private Lives," *USA Today*, 11 November 2003.

p. 337 . . . *travel records are unregulated and open to unrestricted access* . . . Edward Hasbrouk, "Covering the Traveler's Electronic Trail," *BusinessWeek*, 22 July 2003.

p. 337 . . . *data could wind up being sold or transferred* . . . Ryan Singel, "Frequent Fliers Fear Privacy Loss," *Wired*, 18 April 2003, see also http://www.wired.com/news/print/0,1294,58470,00.html.

p. 337 . . . *only Florida was using Matrix at full capacity* . . . Madeleine Baran, "Fear Real-Life Matrix Will Be Monitoring You," *New York Daily News*, 23 November 2003.

p. 337 . . . *New York, California, and Texas have left the program since its inception* . . . "New York State Quits Terror Database," *New York Post*, p. 6, 12 March 2004.

p. 337 . . . *a quantum leap backward in the protection of our privacy* . . . Madeleine Baran, "Fear Real-Life Matrix Will Be Monitoring You" *New York Daily News*, 23 November 2003.

p. 338 . . . *or at the office is listened to by several people* . . . Colum Lynch, "Spying Report No Shock to U.N.," *Washington Post*, 4 March 2003.

p. 339 . . . *500 million units were sold worldwide, according to the Gartner Group* . . . Tom Krazit, "Cell Phones Sales Skyrocket," *PCWorld.com*, 8 December, 2003, see http://www.pcworld.com/news/article/0,aid,113788,00.asp.

p. 339 . . . *an estimated 85 percent of wireless conversations* . . . Martin J. Moylan, "Snooping on Cell-Phone Calls Is No Longer for Amateurs," *Philadelphia Enquirer*, 3 June 2002, see http://www.philly.com/mld/philly/business/3389603.htm.

p. 340 . . . *have already begun experimenting with recording features* . . . Ben Charney, "Cell Phone Recording May Breach Privacy." *CNET News.com*, 3 September 2003, see http://news.com.com/2100-1039-5070618.html.

p. 341 . . . *and tax ID he had stolen to order more than one thousand phones for "an upcoming film shoot* . . . Timothy O'Connor, "Fla. Man heads to prison for cell phone scam," *Journal News*, 18 November 2003.

p. 341 . . . *half of this fraud is wireless-subscription fraud* . . . "National and State Trends in Fraud & Identity Theft, January-December 2003," Federal Trade Commission, 22 January 2004, see http://www.consumer.gov/sentinel/pubs/Top10Fraud2003.pdf.

p. 341 . . . *the legitimate user, are billed for the cloned phone's calls* . . . "FCC Consumer Advisory: Cell Phone Fraud," Federal Communications Commission, see http://www.fcc.gov/cgb/consumerfacts/cellphonefraud.html.

p. 342 . . . *your privacy is compromised by unseen video cameras* . . . Terri Sanginiti, "Lots of cameras watch you—and catch criminals," *NewsJournal*, 23 February 2004; Currently, surveillance video captures your image 12 times each day.

p. 342 . . . *284 surveillance cameras in May 2003* . . . "Maps of Publicly Installed Surveillance Cameras in New York City," *NotBored.org*, see http://www.notbored.org/scp-maps.html.

p. 343 . . . *even an indecent shot of the late Princess of Wales* . . . Radley Balko, "Americans Need Not Trade Privacy for Security," *FoxNews.com*, 13 March 2002 see http://www.foxnews.com/story/0,2933,47823,00.html.

p. 343 . . . *red-light cameras in use in about sixty cities and counties in the United States* . . . Valerie Alvord, "Calif. Judge Says 'Stop' to Red Light Cameras," *USA Today*, 15 September 2001.

p. 343 . . . *to collect a sizable cut from each ticked issued* . . . Valerie Alvord, "Calif. judge says 'stop' to red light cameras," *USA Today*, 5 September 2001.

p. 343 . . . *camera cell phones be confiscated before she appeared at a* Rolling Stone *party in Los Angeles* . . . Charisse Jones, "Phones make your bad side visible to the world," *USA Today*, 19 October 2003.

p. 345 . . . *waiving your privacy rights merely because you are in public* . . . Amy Harmon, "Smile, You're on Candid Cell Phone," *New York Times,* 8 December 2003.

p. 345 . . . *would have a reasonable expectation of privacy* . . . *Missouri's Wiretapping and Eavesdropping Statute,* Mo. Rev. Stat. § 565.253.

p. 345 . . . *the dissemination of the images by phone, e-mail, or Internet* . . . *Louisiana Video Voyeurism Statute,* LA. Rev. Stat. § 14:283.

p. 346 . . . *car was equipped with a device that allowed the company to track their exact route* . . . Christopher Elliott, "On the Move: Keeping tabs on drivers of rental cars," *New York Times,* 20 January 2004.

p. 346 . . . *some sort of location-based technology by 2005* . . . Amy Harmon, "Lost? Hiding? Your Cellphone is Keeping Tabs," *New York Times,* 21 December 2003.

p. 347 . . . *LBS could be a $15 billion market by 2007* . . . Brendan Koerner, "Your Cellphone Is a Homing Device." 1 July 2003, see http://www.legalaffairs.org/issues/July-August-2003/feature_koerner_julaug03.html.

p. 347 . . . *regarding the privacy of your location information* . . . Brendan Koerner, "Your Cellphone is a Homing Device," 1 July 2003, see http://www.legalaffairs.org/issues/July-August-2003/feature_koerner_julaug03.html.

p. 347 . . . *the agency actually turned down a request from privacy groups* . . . Amy Harmon, "Lost? Hiding? Your Cellphone is Keeping Tabs," *New York Times,* 21 December 2003.

p. 348 . . . *GPS data is scientifically sound enough to be admitted as evidence in his upcoming double-murder trial* . . . Jason Dearen, "Judge rules to allow GPS data," *Oakland Tribune,* 18 February 2004.

p. 348 . . . *watches, belts, or backseat inserts for your kids* . . . Elisa Batista, "A Kiddie GPS for the Masses?" *Wired,* 12 October 2002, see http://wired.com/news/business/0,1367,55731,00.html.

p. 349 . . . *renters' driving habits and levy fines for excessive speed* . . . Richard Stenger, "Rental Driver Finds Big Brother Over Shoulder." 22 June 2001, CBC/Radio Canada, see http://www.cbc.ca/consumers/market/files/cars/gps/.

p. 349 . . . *will not disable the emergency signal in the car* . . . Charles R. Smith, "Big Brother on Board," *FreeRepublic.com,* 12 December 2003, see http://209.157.64.200/focus/f-news/1039373/posts.

p. 349 . . . *up from only seventy-five thousand in 2001* . . . Brad Smith, "Driving Telematics Beyond Safety, Security," *Wireless Week*, 1 January 2003.

p. 351 . . . *intercepted directly from the transponder by anyone with the right equipment* . . . Solomon Friedman, "An Envelope of Privacy for Your Car," *New York Times*, 29 September 2002.

p. 351 . . . *records have also been used in civil cases, such as child custody battles* . . . John Schwartz, "This Car Can Talk, What it Says May Cause Concern," *New York Times*, 29 December 2003.

p. 351 . . . *when using E-ZPass on a public highway* . . . Brendan Koerner, "Your Cellphone Is a Homing Device," *Legal Affairs*, 1 July 2003.

p. 352 . . . *Ten minutes after the slaying he was on a northbound S54 bus* . . . Adam L. Penenberg, "The Surveillance Society," *Wired*, December 2001, see also http://www.wired.com/wired/archive/9.12/surveillance.html?pg=1&topic=&topic_set=.

p. 352 . . . *to confirm or contest alibis* . . . Brendan Koerner, "Your Cellphone Is a Homing Device," *Legal Affairs*, 1 July 2003.

p. 353 . . . *all General Motors cars contain such black boxes* . . . Becky Worley, "Is There a Black Box in Your Car?" *Tech Live*, aired 15 July 2002.

p. 353 . . . *25 million cars in the Unites States are fitted with event data recorders* . . . Ralph Vartabedian, "Your Wheels; Black Boxes Prompt Big Brother Objections," *Los Angeles Times*, 5 November 2003.

p. 353 . . . *privacy of drivers whose cars are equipped with black boxes* . . . Matthew Wald, "Motorists' Black-Box Data Protected by Privacy Law," *Contra Costa Times*, 29 September 2003.

p. 354 . . . *unexcused absences, detentions, missed assignments, and so forth* . . . Maya Suryaraman, "School Software Helps Parents Keep Tabs on Teens," *San Jose Mercury News*, 27 October 2003.

p. 354 . . . *can read the personal information contained on the chip* . . . Robert Trigaux, "In Riskier World, Personal Security Trumps Personal Privacy," *St. Petersburg Times*, 24 February 2002.

p. 355 . . . *revenue was up 76 percent to $228 million in 2002 from 2001, according to Jupiter Research* . . . Jennifer Saranow, "Funding Potential Unleashes an Explosion of Dating Sites," *Chicago Tribune*, 24 December 2003.

p. 356 . . . *the listing included the actress' real home address, telephone number, and e-mail address* . . . *Entertainment Industry Litigation Reporter*, Vol. 15, Issue 8, 8 October 2003.

p. 356 . . . *looking for a more casual, spontaneous approach to dating* . . . Jennifer Davies, "Romancing the Phone: Cell Phones Become Latest High-Tech Means of Meeting," *San Diego Union-Tribune*, 9 December 2002.

p. 358 . . . *settled only after Lewinsky herself agreed to turn over her purchase records* . . . "Bookstores Buck Patriot Act," *CBS News.com*, 21 February 2003, see http://www.cbsnews.com/stories/2003/02/21/national/main541464.shtml.

p. 358 . . . *his lawyer could assume the worst* . . . Dan Kennedy, "State of Surveillance: Let's Just Throw Away the Bill of Rights and the Constitution," *Boston Phoenix*, 19-25 September 2003.

p. 358 . . . *probable cause that at crime has been committed* . . . Anita Ramasastry, "Why the ACLU Is Right to Challenge the FBI's Access to Library, Bookstore, and Business Records under the USA Patriot Act," *Modern Practice*, Issue 23, September 2003.

p. 359 . . . *wonder what videos some congressional members are renting* . . . "The Video Privacy Protection Act (VPPA)," Electronic Privacy Information Center, see http://www.epic.org/privacy/vppa.

p. 360 . . . *no legal cases have put this issue to the test* . . . "The Video Privacy Protection Act," Electronic Privacy Information Center, see http://www.epic.org/privacy/vppa.

p. 361 . . . *taking full advantage of these marketing opportunities* . . . David Lazarus, "A Ticket Full of Fine Print," *San Francisco Chronicle*, 18 July 2003.

p. 361 . . . *but because a reporter interviewed former players and coaches of the college football team* . . . "Academic, athletic irregularities force resignation," *ESPN.com*, 14 December 2001, see http://espn.go.com/ncf/news/2001/1214/1295624.html.

p. 362 . . . *the right to view your student records if you are over eighteen* . . . However, certain information—such as psychiatric reports and other noneducational records held by a counselor, doctor, and so forth— is off limits, even to students who are over eighteen.

p. 362 . . . *according to the American Association of Collegiate Registrars and Admission Officers* . . . Ron Southwick, "Investigators Seek, and Colleges Provide, Information on

Students," *Chronicle of Higher Education*, 12 October 2001.

p. 362 . . . *one was in the country on a student visa* . . . Dan Egan, "FBI Taps Campus Police in Anti-Terror Operations; Students, Faculty Groups Fear a Return of Spying Abuses Against Activists, Foreign Nationals," *Washington Post*, 25 January 2003.

p. 363 . . . *enrollment in certain majors, such as Islamic studies or aviation* . . . Tina Valkanoff, "McCarthyism on Campus?" The Campaign to Stop SEVIS, see http://www.stopsevis.org/content.php?aID=6.

p. 363 . . . *but a school official had failed to activate the appropriate security mechanisms* . . . Kate Meyer, "1,000s hit by 2nd recent ID flap," *Washington Square News*, 2 February 2004.

p. 363 . . . *80 percent display social security numbers on official transcripts* . . . Andrea Foster, "ID Theft Turns Students Into Privacy Activists, Colleges Respond by Reducing Reliance on Social Security Numbers in Databases," *Chronicle of Higher Education*, 2 August 2002.

p. 363 . . . *or post grades with the social security number as the identifier* . . . Chris Jay Hoofnagle, "Recommendations to Create a More Privacy-Sensitive College or University," Electronic Privacy Information Center, 20 October 2002, see http://www.epic.org/epic/staff/hoofnagle/studentprivacy.html.

p. 364 . . . *the deal is worth about $16.5 million* . . . Taylor Loyal, "Don't Leave College Without It," *MotherJones*, March/April 2002.

p. 364 . . . *a front for collecting marketing data from high-school students* . . . "The Family Educational Rights and Privacy Act (FERPA) and Student Privacy," Electronic Privacy Information Center, August 2003, see http://www.epic.org/privacy/student.

p. 364 . . . *misdemeanor conviction record for drunk driving near his family's compound in Maine* . . . "Bush confirms arrest for DUI in 1976," *USA Today.com*, 3 November 2000, see http://www.usatoday.com/news/opinion/dui.htm.

p. 365 . . . *not omitting some piece of personal information from court filings* . . . Dan Christensen, "Judicial Conference Oks Plan for Redacted Criminal Filings," *Legal Times*, 10 November 2003.

p. 365 . . . *but not motions, forms, or exhibits* . . . "Other Courts' Experiences Show Benefits, Pitfalls of Online Records," *Associated Press Newswires*, 2 December 2003.

p. 366 . . . *convictions (assuming no others exist) by saying there are none* . . . "Cleaning Up a Criminal Record," *Nolo.com*, see http://www.nolo.com.

p. 366 . . . *except in exceptional circumstances, such as proof of government misconduct* . . . See http://www.expungemynjrecord.com/faq.htm.

Chapter 12: I Spy, You Spy

p. 368 . . . *you learn that you can tap his phone for $100* . . . "Did You Know?" Digital Fortress, see www.danbrown.com/secrets/digital_fortress/didyouknow.html.

p. 371 . . . *She was finally inside their lives or, at least, their apartment* . . . Katha Pollitt, "Webstalker: When it's time to stop checking on your ex," *New Yorker*, 19 January 2004.

p. 377 . . . *used his skills as a network administrator to facilitate his ability to stalk his victims* . . . Paul Bocij: "Corporate Cyberstalking, An Invitation to Build Theory," *First Monday*, vol. 7, no. 11, November 2002, see http://www.firstmonday.dk/issues/issue7_11/bocij/.

p. 381 . . . *broadcasting live video feed into his bedroom* . . . HongDao Nguyen, "Man gets six months in jail for spying on housemates by using hidden cameras," *Mercury News*, 13 December 2003.

p. 381 . . . *Vasile caught his wife's infidelity this way* . . . Marie Szaniszlo, "Spyware finds out who's naughty or nice," *Boston Herald*, 14 December 2003.

p. 385 . . . *unexcused absences, detentions, missed assignments, and so forth* . . . Maya Suryaraman, "School Software Helps Parents Keep Tabs on Teens," *Mercury News*, 27 October 2003.

p. 385 . . . *might be tempted to use the information for commercial purposes* . . . Robert Tomsho, "How's Your Kid Doing in School? Check Online," *Wall Street Journal*, 4 June 2002.

p. 386 . . . *see a man pinpointing your child's location* . . . Elisa Batista, "A Kiddie GPS for the Masses?" *Wired*, 12 October 2002, see also http://wired.com/news/business/0,1367,55731,00.html.

p. 386 . . . *contained on the chip from up to four feet away* . . . Robert Trigaux, "In Riskier World, Personal Security Trumps Personal Privacy," *St. Petersburg Times*, 24 February 2002, see also http://pqasb.pqarchiver.com/sptimes/index.html?ts=1070318730.

p. 387 . . . *disclosure of identifying information for good cause* . . . For more information on the Uniform Adoption Act, see http://www.webcom.com/kmc/adoption/law/uaa/.

p. 390 . . . *seven years of harassment and a death threat* . . . "N.Y. Man Admits Net Death Threat," *Rapid City Journal*, 3 November 2003.

p. 390 . . . *e-mail addresses of female high school and college students* . . . "Cyber-Extortion Results in Prison Sentence," *Net4TV.com*, 8 October 2000, see http://www.net4tv.com/voice/story.cfm?storyid=2931.

Chapter 13: The Future of Privacy

p. 396 . . . *somebody is looking over your shoulder to see what you're reading* . . . David Gram, "Vt. Bookseller purges files to avoid potential 'Patriot Act' searches," *AP* 20 February 2003, see http://www.becomethemedia.com/news/2003/Bear_Pond_Books_purges_files.htm.

p. 396 . . . *a company's ability to protect their personal data* . . . . "Theft concerns have some consumers saying 'Bah Humbug' this holiday season," *vontu.com*, see http://www.vontu.com/newsevents/press_release_111903.html.

p. 397 . . . *to seek answers for its privacy-related questions* . . . "Get Ready for the Privacy Backlash," *Darwin Magazine*, 1 August 2001.

p. 398 . . . *largest public company in terms of protecting employee privacy* . . . "Report: IBM Ranks Best in Employee Privacy," *Business and Legal Reports*, October 2003.

Resources

Business and Consumer Groups

Better Business Bureau
4200 Wilson Blvd., Suite 800
Arlington, VA 22203-1838
Phone: 703-276-0100
Fax: 703-525-8277
www.bbb.org

Consumer Action
www.consumer-action.org

Consumer Federation of America
1424 16th Street NW,
Suite 604
Washington, DC 20036
www.consumerfed.org

Direct Marketing Association Mail Preference Service
To remove your name from junk mail lists:
P.O. Box 632
Carmel, NY 10512
www.dmaconsumers.org/
consumerassistance.html
www.dmaconsumers.org/
privacy.html

Direct Marketing Association Telephone Preference Service
To remove your name from telemarketing phone lists:
P.O. Box 1559
Carmel, NY 10512
www.dmaconsumers.org/
consumerassistance.html
www.dmaconsumers.org/
privacy.html

SafeShopping.org
www.safeshopping.org

ShopTheNet.org
www.shopthenet.org

Credit Bureaus

Equifax
P.O. Box 740241
Atlanta, GA 30374
Phone: 1-800-685-1111
www.equifax.com

Experian
P.O. Box 2002
Allen, TX 75013
Phone: 888-397-3742
www.experian.com

Trans Union
P.O. Box 1000
Chester, PA 19022
Phone: 1-800-888-4213
www.transunion.com

Government Agencies

Department of Motor Vehicles Online
www.dmv.org

Federal Communications Commission (FCC)
445 12th Street SW
Washington, DC 20554
Phone: 1-888-CALL-FCC
(1-888-225-5322)
Fax: 1-866-418-0232
E-mail: fccinfo@fcc.gov
www.fcc.gov

Federal Election Commission
999 E Street, NW
Washington, DC 20463
Phone: 1-800-424-9530
www.fec.gov

Federal Trade Commission
600 Pennsylvania Avenue,
NW
Washington, DC 20580
www.ftc.gov

Food and Drug Administration
www.fda.gov/oc/buyonline

Internet Fraud Complaint Center (IFCC)
www.ifccfbi.gov

National Personal Records Center
Civilian Personal Records
111 Winnebago Street
St. Louis, MO 63118

National Personal Records Center
Military Personal Records
9700 Page Avenue
St. Louis, MO 63132-5100
www.archives.gov/
facilities/mo/st_louis.html

Office of Foreign Assets Control (OFAC)
U.S. Department of the Treasury
Treasury Annex
1500 Pennsylvania Avenue,
NW
Washington, DC 20220
Compliance hotline: (202)
622-2490
www.ustreas.gov/offices/
eotffc/ofac/

Social Security Administration (SSA)
Office of Public Inquiries
Windsor Park Building
6401 Security Blvd.
Baltimore, MD 21235
www.ssa.gov

Transportation Security Administration (TSA)
U.S. Department of Transportation
Office of Civil Rights
Mail Stop: TSA-6
400 7th Street, SW
Washington, D.C. 20590
For security concerns, phone:
866-289-9673
E-mail: TSA-ContactCenter@
dhs.gov
www.tsa.gov/public/index.jsp

United States Citizenship and Immigration Services (USCIS)
425 I Street, NW
Washington, DC 20536
www.uscis.gov

United States Department for Health and Human Services
Office for Civil Rights
200 Independence Avenue, SW
Washington, DC 20201
Phone: 202-619-0257
www.hhs.gov/ocr/hipaa/

United States Department of Passport Service
111 19th Street, NW,
Suite 500
Washington, DC 20036
www.travel.state.gov/passport_services.htm

United States Government Printing Office
732 N. Capitol Street, NW
Washington, DC 20401
www.gpoaccess.gov

United States Postal Service
Privacy Office
475 Lenfant Plaza, SW, Room 10407
Washington, DC 20260-2200
Phone: 1-800-ASK-USPS
www.usps.com

Health And Medical

Medical Information Bureau
P.O. Box 105
Essex Station
Boston, MA 02112
Phone: 617-426-3660
Fax: 781-461-2453
E-mail: disclosure@mib.com
www.mib.com

Health Privacy Project
1120 19th Street, NW, 8th Floor
Washington, DC 20036
Phone: 202-721-5632
Fax: 202-530-0128
E-mail: info@healthprivacy.org
www.healthprivacy.org

Privacy Advocacy Groups— General

American Civil Liberties Union (ACLU)
125 Broad Street, 18th Floor
New York, NY 10004
www.aclu.org

Identity Theft Resource Center
P.O. Box 26833
San Diego, CA 92196
Phone: 858-693-7935
E-mail: itrc@idtheftcenter.org
www.idtheftcenter.org

Privacilla
E-mail: comments@privacilla.org
www.privacilla.org

Privacy International
1718 Connecticut Ave, NW
Suite 200
Washington, DC 20009 USA
Phone: 202-483-1217
Fax: 202-483-1248
www.privacyinternational.org

Privacy Rights Clearinghouse
3100 - 5th Ave., Suite B
San Diego, CA 92103
Phone: (619) 298-3396
Fax: (619) 298-5681
www.privacyrights.org

PrivacyRightsNow.com
www.privacyrightsnow.com

Privacy Advocacy Groups— Computers And The Internet

Americans for Computer Privacy (ACP)
E-mail: webmaster@computerprivacy.org
www.computerprivacy.org

Center for Democracy and Technology (CDT)
1634 I Street NW, Suite 1100
Washington, DC 20006
Phone: 202-637-9800
Fax: 202-637-0968
E-mail: feedback@cdt.org
www.cdt.org

ConsumerPrivacyGuide.org
www.consumerprivacyguide.org

Electronic Frontier Foundation (EFF)
454 Shotwell Street
San Francisco, CA 94110
Phone: 415-436-9333
Fax: 415-436-9993
E-mail: eff@eff.org
www.eff.org

Electronic Privacy Information Center
1718 Connecticut Ave. NW
Suite 200
Washington, DC 20009
E-mail: info@epic.org
www.epic.org

GetNetWise
E-mail: webmaster@getnetwise.org
www.privacy.getnetwise.org

Online Privacy Alliance
Hogan and Hartson
555 13th Street NW
Washington, DC 20004
Phone: 202-637-5600
E-mail: webmaster@privacyalliance.org
www.privacyalliance.org

Privacy.net
E-mail: web@consumer.net
www.privacy.net

TRUSTe
685 Market Street, Suite 560
San Francisco, CA 94105
Phone: 415-618-3400
Fax: 415-618-3420
www.truste.org

Workplace And Management Groups

American Management Association
1601 Broadway
New York, NY 10019
Phone 212-586-8100
Fax: 212-903-8168
E-mail: customerservice@amanet.org
www.amanet.org

ePolicy Institute
2300 Walhaven Ct., Suite 200A
Columbus, OH 43220
Phone: 1-800-292-7332
Fax: 614-451-8726
E-mail: experts@epolicyinstitute.com
www.epolicyinstitute.com

Society for Human Resource Management
1800 Duke Street
Alexandria, VA 22314
Phone: 1-800-283-SHRM(7476)
Fax: 703-535-6490
www.shrm.org

Index